UN PEACEKEEPING IN
SOMALIA AND KOSOVO

The concept of UN peacekeeping has had to evolve and change to meet the challenges of contemporary sources of conflict; consequently, peacekeeping operations have grown rapidly in number and complexity. This book examines a number of issues associated with contemporary multinational peace operations, and seeks to provide insights into the problems that arise in establishing and deploying such forces to meet the challenges of current conflicts.

The focus of the book is three case studies (Lebanon, Somalia and Kosovo), involving a comparative analysis of the traditional peacekeeping in Lebanon, the more robust peace enforcement mission in Somalia, and the international administration undertaken on behalf of the international community in Kosovo. The book analyses the lessons that may be learned from these operations in terms of mandates, command and control, use of force and the relevance of international humanitarian and human rights law to such operations.

RAY MURPHY is a Senior Lecturer in Law at the Irish Centre for Human Rights, National University of Ireland, Galway.

This publication was grant-aided by the Publications Fund of National University of Ireland, Galway.

UN PEACEKEEPING IN LEBANON, SOMALIA AND KOSOVO

Operational and Legal Issues in Practice

RAY MURPHY

CAMBRIDGE
UNIVERSITY PRESS

CAMBRIDGE UNIVERSITY PRESS
Cambridge, New York, Melbourne, Madrid, Cape Town, Singapore, São Paulo, Delhi

Cambridge University Press
The Edinburgh Building, Cambridge CB2 8RU, UK

Published in the United States of America by Cambridge University Press, New York

www.cambridge.org
Information on this title: www.cambridge.org/9780521114448

© Ray Murphy 2007

First published 2007
Reprinted 2008
This digitally printed version 2009

A catalogue record for this publication is available from the British Library

ISBN 978-0-521-84305-8 hardback
ISBN 978-0-521-11444-8 paperback

To my parents, Renee and Frank Murphy

CONTENTS

PREFACE AND ACKNOWLEDGMENTS

Peacekeeping was pioneered and developed by the United Nations (UN) as a means by which it could fulfil its role under the UN Charter in the maintenance of international peace and security. The concept of UN peacekeeping has had to evolve and change to meet the challenges of contemporary sources of conflict; consequently, peacekeeping and related operations have grown rapidly in number and complexity. This book is an interdisciplinary study that examines a number of operational and legal issues associated with contemporary multi-national peace operations, and seeks to provide insights into the problems that arise in establishing and deploying such forces to meet the challenges of current conflicts. The primary focus is on three case studies, Lebanon, Somalia and Kosovo, and these are used to conduct a comparative analysis of traditional or first-generation peacekeeping, and that of second-generation multi-dimensional peace operations. Each operation examined highlights serious difficulties that arise in the command and control of UN missions, although the larger, more complex UNOSOM II (Somalia) and Kosovo missions present significantly more serious dilemmas in this regard. These problems are often exacerbated by deficiencies in the municipal laws and domestic political concerns of contributing states.

An important distinguishing feature between traditional peacekeeping operations and that of more robust peace enforcement operations is the policy regarding the use of force. Devising appropriate rules of engagement (ROE) remains a key issue in the planning and deployment of any multi-national force and a number of recommendations are made on how to deal with this problem.

The matter of the applicability of international humanitarian and human rights law to multi-national forces is also relevant in a review of all three operations. Human rights issues have been highlighted in recent times by the revelations regarding abuses that occurred in the course of peace operations. The privileges and immunities enjoyed by UN personnel, although intended to protect the interests of the UN and not individuals, may have been one factor in the numbers of personnel involved in such activities. Other problems can be attributed to a lack of civilian control and lack of real accountability. Ensuring compliance with international humanitarian law norms on peace support operations also remains problematic.

The United Nations Interim Administration in Kosovo (UNMIK) was established in 1999. Working closely with the NATO-led KFOR, UNMIK performs the whole spectrum of essential administrative functions and services in the province of Kosovo. It is a unique operation in one of the most politically volatile areas of Europe. There is no obvious solution to the status of Kosovo and at the time of writing the parties at the most recent summit on the issue are reported to be deadlocked. The underlying dilemma in Kosovo is that, once force is used to protect human rights, it inevitably impinges upon sovereignty and may even alter borders.

UNOSOM II was the first real test in the post-Cold War era of UN-mandated nation-building. Events in Somalia had a significant impact on United States foreign policy and they have also cast a shadow over UN and United States involvement in similar operations from Kosovo to Afghanistan. The book analyses the lessons to be learned from the experiences of UNIFIL, UNOSOM and UNMIK in regard to these and related issues.

As I complete the final draft, violence has once more broken out between Israel and the Islamic resistance movement Hizbollah in Lebanon. At the same time, Islamic militants are consolidating their control of Somalia. The leaders of the G-8 industrial nations and UN Secretary General Kofi Annan have called for the swift deployment of international troops to end the escalating violence in south Lebanon. Reference has been made to the need for an 'aggressive' or 'robust mandate' for the proposed force, but it is difficult not to conclude that many of the lessons from previous operations are not being considered. An unfortunate consequence of the current crisis and focus on the Middle East is that attention is being deflected from equally serious humanitarian catastrophes taking place in Darfur and elsewhere.

I would like to thank my colleagues at the Irish Centre for Human Rights for providing a warm and stimulating work environment. Many people helped me in many ways over the years and it is not possible to thank everyone. I acknowledge the early advice of Professor Nigel White and the proofreading completed by Dr Megan Fairlie and Jen Smith. I want to thank Finola O'Sullivan of Cambridge University Press for her professional and supportive advice at all stages. Last, but not least, I would like to thank all my family.

MAPS

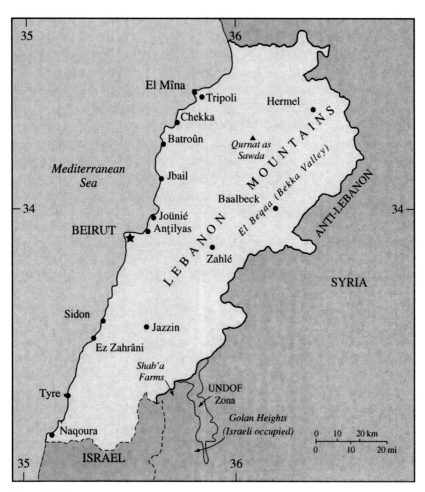

Map 1. Lebanon

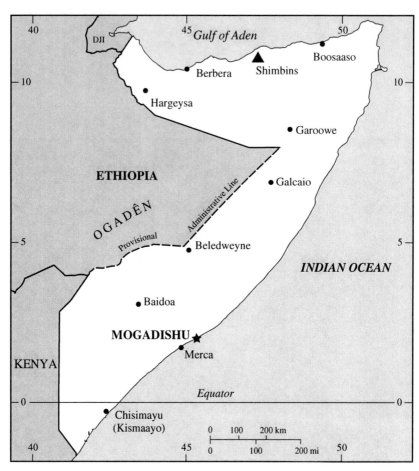

Map 2. Somalia

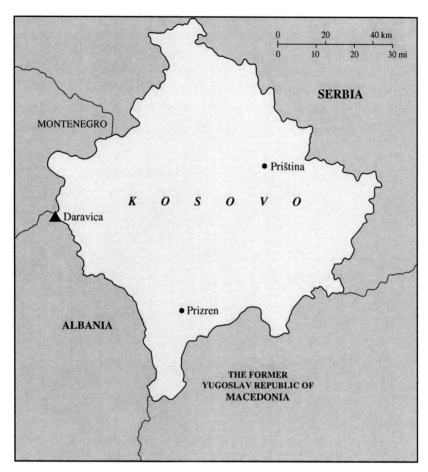

Map 3. Kosovo

1

Introduction

The UN and peacekeeping operations

The concept of peacekeeping is neither defined nor specifically provided for in the United Nations Charter.[1] Historically, it is by no means a concept associated exclusively with the United Nations (UN).[2] Consequently, it does not lend itself to precise definition. In these circumstances, it is not surprising that there is some confusion regarding what exactly constitutes peacekeeping. Indeed, it is sometimes easier to say that a particular mission or force does not possess the generally recognised characteristics of a peacekeeping operation, than it is to confirm that it fulfils the necessary criteria.[3] Part of the reason for this is the looseness with which states adopt such terms. It has a distinctly positive resonance, and those charged with the government of states are usually more concerned with public relations and opinion polls than with legal criteria or political reality. For this reason, the term is often applied to controversial situations where states intervene militarily and then seek to justify or portray their actions as some kind of benign peacekeeping operation.

---

[1] See B. Simma (ed.), *The Charter of the United Nations: A Commentary* (2nd edn, Oxford: Oxford University Press, 2002), pp. 648–700; N. White, *Keeping the Peace* (2nd edn, Manchester: Manchester University Press, 1997), pp. 207–84; United Nations, *The Blue Helmets – A Review of United Nations Peacekeeping* (3rd edn, New York, United Nations, 1996), pp. 3–9.

[2] H. McCoubrey and N. White, *International Organizations and Civil Wars* (Aldershot: Dartmouth, 1995), p. 183.

[3] The UN Emergency Force (UNEF), which was established and deployed after the British and French military intervention in Suez in 1956, is generally regarded as the first true UN peacekeeping operation; *Summary Study of the Experience Derived from the Establishment and Operation of the Force: Report of the Secretary-General*, 9 October 1958, General Assembly Official Records, 13 Session, Annex 1: Doc. A/3943. See also Docs. A/3289 and A/3302; the latter was approved by General Assembly Resolution 1001 (ES-I) of 7 November 1956. D.W. Bowett, *United Nations Forces* (London: Stevens, 1964), pp. 90–152.

The Cold War era (1945–89) between the United States and the Soviet Union was marked at the UN by continual wrangling over the correct interpretation of the Charter provisions.[4] The Charter's own ambiguity and failure to provide for specific problems contributed to these disputes. In order to survive, the Organization had to be capable of adapting to the changed political circumstances and this meant adopting roles not specifically provided for in the Charter.[5] When the required consensus among the major powers did not materialise, it seemed the UN would be unable to fulfil a significant role in the maintenance of peace; the growth of regional self-defence systems was just one indication of the lack of confidence in the Organization as the international guarantor of peace. In these circumstances, it is not surprising that the UN sought to circumvent the obstacles caused by Cold War rivalries. However, it should be stressed that peacekeeping is not the preserve of the UN. The concept predates the formation of the Organization and peacekeeping missions continue to be organised outside its framework. In this way, it can be argued that a peacekeeping force established and deployed by one or more states may legitimately profess to belong to some kind of internationally recognised category of peacekeeper. Peacekeeping operations were intended to end hostilities by peaceful means and create a climate in which the peacemaking process could be successfully applied.

When the divisions of the Cold War blocked effective action by the Security Council, the concept of UN peacekeeping was invented. In 1993, a former Under-Secretary-General for Peacekeeping Operations, Marrack Goulding, suggested the following definition:

> Field operations established by the UN with the consent of the parties concerned, to help control and resolve conflicts between them, under UN command and control, at the expense collectively of the member states, and with military and other personnel and equipment provided voluntarily by them, acting impartially between the parties and using force to the minimum extent necessary.[6]

---

[4] See generally Simma (ed.), *Charter of the United Nations*, pp. 13–32; and L. Goodrich, E. Hambro and A. P. Simons, *Charter of the United Nations* (3rd edn, New York: Columbia University Press, 1969), pp. 1–17; and I. Claude, *Swords into Ploughshares* (New York: Random House, 1956), chapter 12.

[5] N. D. White, 'The UN Charter and Peacekeeping Forces: Constitutional Issues' (1996) 3(4) *International Peacekeeping* 43–63.

[6] M. Goulding, 'The Evolution of UN Peacekeeping' (1993) 69(3) *International Affairs* 464.

Since 1985, there has been a significant increase in the number of peacekeeping missions established, with a corresponding increase in the complexity of the mandates. These are often referred to as 'second-generation' peacekeeping operations.[7] The traditionally passive role of peacekeepers has been replaced by a more active role of peacemaking, involving, *inter alia*, national reconstruction, facilitating transition to democracy, and providing humanitarian assistance.[8] There are a broad range of terms used to describe these and related activities. The nomenclature of 'second generation' or multi-dimensional peacekeeping often gives way to the more generic title of peace operations, adopted to cover the range of activities involved.[9] The UN Department of Peacekeeping Operations continues to use the term 'peacekeeping' to cover all such activities and describes these operations as follows:

> Most of these operations are established and implemented by the UN itself with troops serving under UN operational command. In other cases, where direct UN involvement is not considered appropriate or feasible, the [Security] Council authorizes regional organizations such as the North Atlantic Treaty Organization, the Economic Community of West African States or coalitions of willing countries to implement certain peacekeeping or peace enforcement functions.[10]

As the dynamic of conflict in the world changed, so too did the response of the UN, and other international organisations and states. Classical peacekeeping operations originally conducted during the Cold War usually involved the deployment of military personnel only between two states. The process leading to the deployment of a UN force was relatively straightforward: armed conflict, cease-fire, an invitation from the conflict parties to monitor the cease-fire, followed by deployment of military personnel, while negotiations for a political settlement continued.

---

[7] United Nations, *The Blue Helmets*, p. 5.

[8] J. Roper, M. Nishihara, O. Otunnu and E. Schoettle, *Keeping the Peace in the Post-Cold War Era: Strengthening Multilateral Peacekeeping* (New York: Trilateral Commission, 1993), p. 4.

[9] S. Ratner, *The New UN Peacekeeping* (London: Macmillan, 1995), pp. 117–36; and W. J. Durch, 'Keeping the Peace: Politics and Lessons of the 1990s', in W. J. Durch (ed.), *UN Peacekeeping, American Policy, and the Uncivil Wars of the 1990s* (London: Macmillan, 1997), pp. 3–7.

[10] UN Department of Peacekeeping Operations, available at http://www.un.org/Depts/dpko/dpko/home.shtml.

In contrast, contemporary peace operations are increasingly complex.[11] According to the Pearson Peacekeeping Centre in Canada, they are:

- deployed into both inter-state and intra-state conflicts;
- conducted in every phase of the conflict spectrum, from prevention through to post-war reconstruction;
- dependent on close cooperation among civilian, police, and military organizations from the international community, with parties to the conflict and war-affected populations;
- opening in new areas of international activity with conflict-affected countries, such as reforms to the security sector.

In this way, 'peace operations' is the umbrella term used to cover a multiplicity of UN field activities in support of peace, ranging from essentially preventive deployments to long-term state-building missions.[12] They include conflict prevention, conflict mitigation, peacemaking, peacekeeping, peace enforcement, and post-conflict peace-building.

The UN Charter, as finally adopted, contains two significant chapters in relation to the maintenance of international peace and security. Chapter VI provides for the pacific settlement of disputes by, among other things, negotiation and adjudication, and Chapter VII contains the collective security provisions which were intended as the cornerstone of its policy in the maintenance of world peace. It is Chapter VII of the Charter that provides for enforcement measures under the direction of the Security Council as the central military instrument for the maintenance of peace and security. If force is used or threatened against the territorial integrity or political independence of any state in a manner that is contrary to the Charter, there are two possible military options permitted in response: self-defence and police or enforcement action.[13] Either response is likely to lead to full-scale conflagration. The system

---

[11] Pearson Peacekeeping Centre, Canada, available at http://www.peaceoperations.org/en/peace_operations.asp.

[12] J. Cockayne and D. M. Malone, 'The Ralph Bunche Centennial: Peace Operations Then and Now' (2005) 11 *Global Governance* 331–50 at 331.

[13] Article 2(4) of the UN Charter prohibits the threat or use of force, while Article 51 provides for individual or collective self-defence. However, self-defence under Article 51 is only permitted until such time as the Security Council responds and takes the necessary measures to maintain international peace. See L. M. Goodrich, E. Hambro and A. P. Simons, *Charter of the United Nations* (3rd edn, New York: Columbia University Press, 1969), pp. 43–55 and pp. 342–53; and B. Simma (ed.), *The Charter of the United Nations* (2nd edn, Oxford: Oxford University Press, 2002), pp. 112–36 and pp. 788–806.

reflects the reality that the advent of the UN did not mean an end to conflict. In particular, the old system of wars of self-defence will remain until the system for global collective action and policing becomes a universal reality.

The lack of an express mention of peacekeeping in the Charter has not inhibited its development. In fact, this may have helped establish peace-keeping as a flexible response to international crises, while at the same time contributing to a misunderstanding regarding its true nature. Peacekeeping has evolved in a grey area between pacific settlement and military enforcement measures. Although authorities have differed on the exact legal basis for peacekeeping operations, the International Court of Justice has held that they are within the power of both the General Assembly and the Security Council.[14]

A further complication arises by virtue of the kind of operations conducted under Chapter VII and intended to be enforcement action in nature, despite the failure to conclude the requisite agreements between member states and the UN for the provision of armed forces under Article 43 of the Charter.[15] Military actions conducted during the Korean conflict, and more recently the so-called First Gulf War, belong to this category. Operations of this kind can be established under Article 42 of the Charter (which provides for measures by air, sea or land forces as may be necessary to maintain or restore international peace and security) by way of a decision of the Security Council, or they may be authorised by way of a recommendation under Article 39.[16] In

---

[14] International Court of Justice, *Certain Expenses of the United Nations* – Article 17(2), Advisory Opinion, 20 July 1962, International Court of Justice Reports, 1962, p. 176.

[15] Art. 43(1) states:

> All Members of the United Nations ... undertake to make available to the Security Council, on its call and in accordance with special agreement or agreements, armed forces, assistance and facilities ... for the purpose of maintaining international peace and security.

Goodrich, Hambro and Simons, *Charter of the United Nations*, pp. 317–26; and Simma (ed.), *Charter of the United Nations*, pp. 760–3.

[16] Art. 39 states:

> The Security Council shall determine the existence of any threat to the peace, breach of the peace, or act of aggression and shall make recommendations, or decide what measure shall be taken in accordance with Articles 41 and 42, to maintain or restore international peace or security.

The Korean action was taken on the basis of a 'recommendation' by the Security Council under Art. 39: Security Council Official Records, 5th Year; 473rd–474th Meetings; 27 and 28 June 1950.

the special circumstances of the Korean conflict, the Uniting for Peace resolution procedure then adopted by the General Assembly provides a possible further mechanism that could be availed of in the future, though it would be a mistake to exaggerate its potential. The resolution provides that, if, because of the lack of unanimity of the permanent members of the Security Council (United States, Russia, China, France and the United Kingdom), the Council cannot maintain international peace where there is a 'threat to the peace, breach of the peace or act of aggression', the General Assembly 'shall consider the matter immediately'. Nonetheless, Article 42 remains the central element in enforcement operations. A wide measure of discretion is left to the Security Council as to whether a particular situation calls for the application of military enforcement measures, and if so the determination as to its nature and extent.

In spite of the controversy and problems encountered by peacekeeping missions, the concept of peacekeeping has survived and developed. One of the primary reasons for its success is that it has combined adherence to basic principles with extraordinary flexibility. In particular, it has managed to maintain the essence of what is acceptable to the UN membership at large, while at the same time adapting individual peacekeeping operations to the needs of particular circumstances. The Secretary-General plays a pivotal role in the conduct of peacekeeping operations, but the exact nature and extent of this role has not been defined, and problems of demarcation with that of the Security Council remain unresolved.[17] In the course of the peacekeeping operation in the Congo (ONUC, 1960–4), serious difficulties arose in this regard.[18]

The legal authority for the creation of UN peacekeeping forces remains unsatisfactory and there seems little prospect of a change in their *ad hoc* nature. While it may be argued that agreement on basic principles would lessen the opportunity for conflicting interpretations of the Charter and divisive controversies, there is merit in maintaining a

---

[17] See L. Gordenker, *The United Nations Secretary General and the Maintenance of Peace* (New York and London: Columbia University Press, 1967), pp. 235–60; and D. Sarooshi, *The United Nations and the Development of Collective Security* (Oxford: Clarendon Press, 1999), pp. 50–85.

[18] See generally R. Higgins, *United Nations Operation in the Congo (ONUC) 1960–1964* (London: Royal Institute of International Affairs, 1980); Gordenker, *The United Nations Secretary General*, pp. 261–96; and B. Urquhart, *Hammarskjold* (New York: Alfred Knopf, 1972), pp. 389–456.

flexible and adaptive approach to peacekeeping operations. Traditional peacekeeping operations were sometimes said to be based on 'Chapter $VI\frac{1}{2}$' of the Charter and required, in principle, invitation or consent on behalf of the recipient state(s). The consent of the host state to the presence of a peacekeeping force confers the legitimacy required for a lawful presence in its territory and it is normally specified in an agreement concerning the rights and duties of the force.[19] In fact, the legality of a peacekeeping force on any country's territory should be guaranteed in a legal instrument known as the Status of Forces Agreement (SOFA).[20]

The issues of host state consent to a UN military presence and domestic jurisdiction raise difficult questions in the context of internal conflicts or civil wars. There were reservations about UN involvement in the Congo, Somalia, Lebanon and Kosovo for these very reasons. But the criterion of consent should be applied with some caution. Even in the case of UNIFIL, when deployed in 1978 with the consent of the Lebanese government, the authority of the government barely extended beyond west Beirut. Likewise, in the more recent case of Albania (1997), the government there consented to the deployment of a 'coalition of the willing' under a Chapter VII enforcement mandate. However, internal conflicts frequently escalate into regional conflicts and these in turn may involve breaches of international law, thereby removing the conflict from the reserved domain of domestic jurisdiction.

The resolution of internal or domestic conflict has been a dominant feature of recent peacekeeping operations and has involved the establishment of democratic governments culminating in the nation-building attempted for a time in Somalia, and currently underway in Kosovo. International administration of this kind, like peacekeeping itself, is not specifically provided for in the UN Charter. It is not subject to a clear UN doctrine, and it appears to be handled by the Department of Peacekeeping Operations more by default than by design. Operations in eastern Slavonia, Bosnia-Herzegovina, Kosovo and East Timor have been characterised by the UN and other international organisations assuming responsibilities that evoke the historically sensitive concepts

---

[19] *The Peacekeepers Handbook* (New York: International Peace Academy, 1984), p. 362.

[20] D. Fleck (ed.), 'Present and Future Challenges for the Status of Forces (Ius in Praesentia): A Commentary to Applicable Status Law Provisions', in *The Handbook of the Law of Visiting Forces* (Oxford: Oxford University Press, 2001), p. 47.

of trusteeship and protectorate.[21] Making such administrations accountable and preventing them from adopting neo-colonial roles is imperative. Any interventions by UN forces may, intentionally or otherwise,
alter the delicate balance of power between the warring parties.[22]
Maintaining impartiality can present peacekeepers with a dilemma,
especially when they confront situations in which civilians are victi-
mised, or when UN forces are themselves the subject of attack.[23] The
question of the consent of the host state or parties to a conflict to a UN
presence is particularly problematic in these situations and the blue
berets involved must be prepared to resort to force rather than be
bystanders to large-scale human rights abuses or even genocide.

Peacekeeping and enforcement operations

There is a great deal of semantic and conceptual confusion surrounding
peacekeeping and peace enforcement operations.[24] In general terms,
peacekeeping involves non-coercive intervention and is based on the
consent of the parties to a conflict and the non-use of force, except in
self-defence.[25] Many discussions are characterised by a failure to distinguish traditional peacekeeping from peace enforcement, and to understand the grey zone that lies between the two.[26] This was especially
evident in debates on Somalia, which involved a combination of operations and mandates embodying all three elements mentioned, and more
besides. Not surprisingly, the continuum from peacekeeping to peace
enforcement can be difficulty to track. Peacekeeping remains quite
distinct from the enforcement measures envisaged under the UN

---

[21] M. Berdal and R. Caplan, 'The Politics of International Administration' (2004) 10
Global Governance 1–5 at 2.

[22] J. Peck, 'The UN and the Laws of War: How Can the World's Peacekeepers Be Held
Accountable' (1995) 21 *Syracuse Journal of International Law* 283–310 at 288.

[23] United Nations, *The Blue Helmets*, p. 5.

[24] J. G. Ruggie, 'Wandering in the Void: Charting the UN's New Strategic Role' (1993)
72(5) *Foreign Affairs* 26; and A. Roberts, 'From San Francisco to Sarajevo: The UN and
the Use of Force' (1995–6) 37(4) *Survival* 26; and generally E. Schmidl, *Peace Operations
Between War and Peace* (London: Frank Cass, 2000); and I. J. Rikhye, *The Politics and
Practice of United Nations Peacekeeping: Past, Present and Future* (Clementsport, NS:
Canadian Peacekeeping Press, 2000).

[25] A. James, *Peacekeeping in International Politics* (London: Macmillan, 1990), pp. 1–13;
and White, *Keeping the Peace*, pp. 232–47.

[26] T. Weiss, 'Rekindling Hope in UN Humanitarian Intervention', in W. Clarke and
J. Herbst (eds.), *Learning From Somalia* (Boulder: Westview Press, 1997), pp. 207–228
at p. 211.

Charter. Nonetheless, both concepts are based on similar conditions, in particular, the availability of military forces and the effective co-operation of members of the Security Council. Consequently, there is considerable confusion regarding these very distinct and separate concepts. Deployments in the late 1990s in Albania (1997) and East Timor (1999–2002) could be described as hybrid operations comprised of coalitions of the willing based on consent; but the consent involved, especially in the case of East Timor, was somewhat qualified by the international pressure brought to bear on the Indonesian government at the time.

Peace enforcement must also be distinguished from enforcement action as envisioned under the collective security provisions of Chapter VII of the UN Charter. Peace enforcement does not involve identifying an aggressor, but it may involve the threat and actual use of force to 'compel or coerce' the implementation of international norms or mandates.[27] For this reason, the two most important characteristics that distinguish traditional peacekeeping from the more robust peace enforcement operations are the use of force and the issue of host state consent to the presence of the UN force. Closely linked to these issues, and also of crucial importance, is the principle of impartiality. Impartiality is easily maintained in traditional peacekeeping, but difficult in enforcement operations. Insistence that interventions in intra-state conflict adhere to the principles of host state consent and impartiality is not always practical and may prove counterproductive. It is generally accepted that the peacekeeping force in Lebanon (UNIFIL, 1978) was based on the traditional peacekeeping model, and that the UNITAF (Unified Task Force, 1992) and UNOSOM II (United Nations Operation in Somalia II, 1993–5) may be categorised as peace enforcement operations. In Kosovo (UNMIK/KFOR, 1999), the UN was authorised under Chapter VII of the Charter to undertake a mission that was unprecedented in both its scope and structural complexity. No other mission had ever been designed in such a way that other multilateral organisations were full partners under UN leadership. In this way, it may be

---

[27] D. Daniel, 'Wandering Out of the Void? Conceptualizing Practicable Peace Enforcement', in A. Morrison, D. Fraser and J. Kiras (eds.), *Peacekeeping with Muscle: The Use of Force in International Conflict Resolution* (Cornwallis: Canadian Peacekeeping Press, 1997), pp. 1–15 at p. 4. The quote is from *FM 100–23: Peace Operations* (Washington, DC: Department of the Army, 1994), p. 12.

described as the quintessential multi-dimensional peace operation with a peace enforcement mandate.

The recent UN Secretary-General's report on threats and challenges has referred to the characterisation of peacekeeping missions in terms of 'Chapter VI' or 'Chapter VII' (of the UN Charter) operations as somewhat misleading.[28] It acknowledges that there is a distinction between operations in which a robust use of force is integral to the mission, and the more 'traditional peacekeeping' where there is a reasonable expectation that force may not be used. However, in peacekeeping as much as peace enforcement cases, it is now the usual practice for a Chapter VII mandate to be given (even if it is not always welcomed by troop contributors). This practice is easily explained: an otherwise benign environment can turn hostile, and it is desirable that there is complete certainty about the mission's capacity to respond with force, if necessary.

The semantic confusion is not helped by the application of the term 'peace enforcement' to large-scale international military operations, such as the First Gulf War.[29] It undermines the credibility of genuine attempts by the UN to keep or enforce the peace, as the case may be, when operations involving enforcement measures by a group of states are erroneously portrayed in these terms. In practice, few situations can accurately be described as peace enforcement operations, for example, the NATO-led force (IFOR) in the former Yugoslavia following the Dayton Accords and the more recently deployed Kosovo Force (KFOR). The notion of host state consent also marks an important distinction between peacekeeping and related humanitarian aid missions on the one hand and humanitarian intervention on the other. Humanitarian intervention is generally understood to mean intervention by a third party in the affairs of another without that country's consent in order to prevent serious human rights violations being

---

[28] United Nations, *A More Secure World: Our Shared Responsibility, Report of the High-Level Panel on Threats, Challenges and Change*, UN Doc. A/59/565, 2 December 2004, paras. 212–14. See also S. Chesterman, 'The Use of Force in UN Peace Operations', External Study, Best Practices Unit (UN DPKO, 2004), p. 6.

[29] The term is often used by UN officials: see D. Shagra, Legal Officer, Office of Legal Affairs, and R. Zacklin, Director and Deputy to the Under-Secretary-General, Office of Legal Affairs, 'The Applicability of International Humanitarian Law to United Nations Peace-keeping Operations: Conceptual, Legal and Practical Issues', *Symposium on Humanitarian Action and Peacekeeping Operations Report* (Geneva: ICRC, 1994), p. 40.

inflicted on the local population. However, its meaning can be of much broader scope, depending on the circumstances.[30]

Collective security and the role of the Security Council

While the Security Council has 'primary' responsibility for the maintenance of international peace and security, it does not possess an exclusive competence in this area.[31] Peace was to be maintained by international co-operation, as embodied in the UN Organization itself, rather than through some kind of new world governmental system. However, the collective security provisions were seriously flawed, as the basic premise of major power consensus in international affairs did not materialise and the provisions upon which so much depended were inoperable from the beginning. In this way, the former allies became classical victims of their own propaganda.

In hindsight, it is difficult to see how the drafters of the Charter could have expected this system to work. The so-called 'big powers' or Permanent Five (P-5) had a right of veto in the Security Council rendering collective security unenforceable against them, yet it was they that posed the greatest potential threat to international peace. In spite of the fact that this created a ruling oligarchy within the Security Council that was to some extent imposed on the smaller states, the UN did not confer power where it did not in fact already exist. It merely reflected the reality of post-World War II economic and political dominance. Unfortunately, peoples and nations not part of the formal state system were not represented at all. However, in examining the collective security provisions of the Charter, it is important to bear in mind that peace depends more upon international co-operation than on the mechanisms contained in the Charter. While the threat or actual use of the veto may prevent the UN from taking action, the real problem is a

---

[30] J. L. Holzgrefe and R. O. Keohane (eds.), *Humanitarian Intervention* (Cambridge: Cambridge University Press, 2003); and International Commission on Intervention and State Sovereignty, *The Responsibility to Protect: Report of the International Commission on Intervention and State Sovereignty* (Ottawa: International Development Research Centre, 2001), pp. 8–9.

[31] Goodrich, Hambro and Simons, *Charter of the United Nations*, pp. 257–343; S. D. Bailey and S. Daws, *The Procedure of the United Nations Security Council* (3rd edn, Oxford: Clarendon Press, 1998), pp. 353–77; and H. McCoubrey, 'International Law and National Contingents in UN Forces' (1994) 12 *International Relations* 39–50.

lack of consensus among the major powers, and the veto merely reflects the reality of the international political system.[32]

Since no formal agreement exists under the Charter for the provision of troops to the UN, member states are under no legal obligation to supply the Security Council with armed forces. They do so only on a voluntary basis. In recent years stand-by arrangements and other 'offers' have been made by states, and it is on this basis, in contrast to what was intended for enforcement measures, that states usually provide the necessary troops to make up a peacekeeping force. The course of UN peacekeeping has not always run smoothly and the crisis that occurred during the operation in the Congo threatened the existence of the whole Organization for a time.[33]

Peacekeeping and contemporary issues

Since its establishment, the UN has been kept on a tight rein and prevented from developing its full potential. During the Cold War, both sides used the threat of veto in the Security Council to good effect, and both shared a common interest in hindering the General Assembly from developing its full capacity. The collapse of the Soviet Union and the end of the Cold War has given rise to a situation where there is in effect one superpower, the United States. The 'new world order' was intended to unlock the UN mechanism for the maintenance of international peace, and exploit opportunities for peacekeeping and nation-building.[34] Instead, there is a perception and fear in the countries of the global South that the UN is being exploited to police a world order based on the interests of the powerful few.[35] This fear is linked to the lack of

---

[32] For proposed reform of the Security Council, see *Report of the High-Level Panel on Threats, Challenges and Change*, paras. 244–60; B. Fassbender, *UN Security Council Reform and the Right of Veto: A Constitutional Perspective* (The Hague: Kluwer, 1998), chapters 8 and 9; and D. Malone, *Decision Making in the UN Security Council: The Case of Haiti, 1990–1997* (Oxford: Clarendon Press, 1998), pp. 7–36.

[33] E. Lefever, *Crisis in the Congo: A United Nations Force in Action* (Washington, DC: Brookings Institution, 1965); and McCoubrey and White, *International Organizations and Civil Wars*, pp. 177–8.

[34] A. Roberts, *Humanitarian Action in War* (Adelphi Paper 305, Oxford: Oxford University Press, 1996), pp. 10–31.

[35] J. Ciechanski, 'Enforcement Measures under Chapter VII of the UN Charter: UN Practice after the Cold War', in M. Pugh (ed.), *The UN, Peace and Force* (London: Frank Cass, 1996), pp. 82–104, esp. pp. 97–99; and I. Johnstone, *Aftermath of the Gulf War: An Assessment of UN Action* (International Peace Academy, Occasional Paper Series, Boulder and London: Lynne Rienner, 1994), p. 10 and pp. 43–5.

success in reforming the Security Council in order to make it more representative.[36] It was also evident in the debate surrounding the composition of the Peacebuilding Commission.[37] However, one of the biggest problems confronting the UN remains one of its most banal, i.e. lack of finance. This problem more often than not reflects political division among members, rather than financial difficulty.

In June 1992, the UN Secretary-General, Boutros Boutros-Ghali, published *An Agenda for Peace*.[38] This was an important report that stimulated a major international debate about the role of the UN, and the international community, in securing and maintaining peace in the post-Cold War era. The report expressed the optimism and confidence of the time, but these were to be very short lived. Subsequent events have highlighted the deficiencies in the UN system, in particular the controversy over UN action and policy in Somalia and Rwanda, and the failure to secure peace and protect Bosnia in the former Yugoslavia. Despite the noble aspirations of the Charter, for many millions the world is still a dangerous and miserable place in which to exist. War, famine, pestilence and disease continue to ravage the peoples of this planet, especially those subsisting in the abject poverty prevalent in most states of the global South. These exacerbate pre-existing cultural, ethnic and political tensions. The end of the Cold War has witnessed a resurgence of conflict, especially within states, as old enmities come to the fore.

The UN and the international system seemed unprepared and ill-equipped for the potential consequences of the 'new world order'. Not surprisingly, the UN has come under considerable criticism, much of which is warranted. Some have even suggested replacing the UN with another organisation or 'alliance of democracies'.[39] However, the criticism is sometimes misplaced in that it fails to identify the real problems of the

---

[36] See generally M. Reisman, 'The Constitutional Crises in the United Nations' (1993) 87(1) *American Journal of International Law* 85–6; and O. Otunnu, 'Maintaining Broad Legitimacy for United Nations Action', in Roper, Nishihara, Otunnu and Schoettle, *Keeping the Peace in the Post-Cold War Era*, pp. 67–83.

[37] The new Commission has thirty-one members: seven (including the five veto-holding members) drawn from the Security Council; seven from the fifty-four-nation Economic and Social Council; five from the ten top contributors to the UN; five from the ten top troop-contributing countries to peacekeeping operations; and another seven to ensure geographical balance by regional grouping. W. Hoge, 'UN Creates Commission to Assist Nations Recovering from Wars', *New York Times*, 21 December 2005; and E. Leopold, 'UN Creates New Body to Help States out of War', Reuters, 20 December 2005.

[38] UN Doc. A/47/277-S/24111 (June 1992).

[39] S. Charat, 'An Alliance of Democracies', *Washington Times*, 27 January 2005, p. A17.

Organization as a whole and to recognise its many achievements. In addition, there is sometimes a failure to distinguish between the UN and its separate organs, especially the Security Council. In this context, there is merit in remembering that the institution is only as strong or effective as its member states will allow. Therefore, some of the blame for the ineffectiveness of the institution can be laid at the feet of the member states that vote to take action, but then fail in subsequent resolutions to provide the means to support the very operations they had earlier deemed critical.

The end of the Cold War has also heralded a significant increase in the UN's willingness to pursue its role in the maintenance of international peace and security by the adoption of military solutions. The importance attached to the Security Council's power to order military measures did not stem from expectations that it would often be necessary to do so. It was thought that the threat of military action would be sufficient to deter aggression and to induce states to comply with measures deemed appropriate by the Security Council to maintain or restore international peace. However, the reality is that, although the military agreements envisioned under Article 43 of the Charter did not materialise, the UN has had a significant involvement in military operations of one kind or another since the first major UN-authorised operation during the Korean conflict in 1950.

The adoption by the UN of resolutions under Chapter VII of the Charter involving enforcement measures has been one of its most controversial actions in recent years. The real problem is not the legality of such activity, but the question of which states decide when it is appropriate and the criteria used to form that decision.[40] The current practice allows the permanent members of the Council to determine the agenda, thus facilitating a very selective, secretive and undemocratic response to international crises. The situation is made worse by the ambiguity surrounding the extent to which peaceful settlement procedures, including diplomatic efforts, must be exhausted before military sanctions are applied.[41] The problem has been compounded by the willingness of

---

[40] This is so despite the fact that the practice of the Security Council authorising states to use armed force does not correspond to the express text of Chapter VII of the UN Charter.

[41] This was a source of controversy and debate before the adoption of Resolution 678 (1991), which authorised collective measures against Iraq and led to Operation Desert Storm. O. Schacter, 'United Nations in the Gulf Conflict' (1991) 85 *American Journal of International Law* 452; and L. C. Green, 'Iraq, the UN and the Law' (1991) 29(3) *Alberta Law Review* 560.

states to take action outside the framework of the UN such as occurred in Iraq (2003) and Kosovo (1999), and the role of the industrialised G-8 group of nations, especially in relation to Kosovo, which has been to function as a kind of shadow Security Council, but with no real accountability.

Co-operation with regional bodies and coalitions of the willing is a characteristic of contemporary UN-approved operations, a situation which has been brought about by a number of factors, not least the lack of finance.[42] Substantial co-operation between NATO and the UN was compelled by the need to respond to the Yugoslav crisis. A similar situation arose between the UN and the African Union (formerly the Organization of African Unity) with regard to the situation in Darfur, Sudan.[43] 'Outsourcing' peace enforcement operations to coalitions of the willing is now common. The complex nature of many contemporary conflicts requires significantly larger and more heavily equipped forces and this, in turn, has led to greater participation by the permanent members of the Security Council. The distinction between peacekeeping and enforcement action remains crucial. Nonetheless, this distinction has become blurred in the grey area that exists between peacekeeping and peace enforcement, and by the number and complexity of peace-keeping operations in the post-Cold War era. Prior to 1990, the UN had authorised two enforcement missions, those against North Korea in 1950 and the Congo in 1960 (ONUC). The ONUC operation was complex in nature and amounted to at least *de facto* enforcement action against a party to the conflict as opposed to action against a state under Chapter VII of the UN Charter.[44] The Security Council has since approved a number of major operations with similar characteristics, in Kuwait, Somalia, the former Yugoslavia, Kosovo, East Timor, Albania (which had elements of traditional peacekeeping and peace enforce-ment combined in one mandate), the Central African Republic, Sierra Leone, the Democratic Republic of the Congo, Liberia, Côte d'Ivoire

---

[42] Though costs are minuscule compared to the national defence budgets: E. Schoettle, 'Financing Peacekeeping', in Roper, Nishihara, Otunnu and Schoettle, *Keeping the Peace in the Post-Cold War Era*, pp. 17–48 at p. 20.

[43] E. Leopold, 'UN Contemplates Military Operation for Darfur', Reuters, 4 December 2005.

[44] N. D. White, 'The UN Charter and Peacekeeping Forces: Constitutional Issues', in Pugh (ed.), *The UN, Peace and Force*, pp. 43–63 at p. 53. See further *Certain Expenses of the UN* – Article 17(2), Advisory Opinion, 20 July 1962, (1962) ICJ Reports 177, where the ICJ said that 'the operation did not involve "preventative or enforcement measures" against any state under Chapter VII'.

and Sudan. However, some of these are UN-mandated forces, while others are merely authorised 'coalitions of the willing'.[45]

It is difficult to find a working definition of contemporary peace-keeping operations that does justice to the multiplicity of complex tasks undertaken. It is evident that there are clear differences between governing a province like Kosovo, and keeping the peace in south Lebanon or along the border between Ethiopia and Eritrea. The International Peace Academy has defined peacekeeping as:

> the prevention, containment, moderation and termination of hostilities between or within states through the medium of third party intervention, organized and directed internationally, using multinational military, police and civilian personnel to restore or maintain peace.[46]

The broad nature of the definition is such that it is still useful today, but it does not reflect the complex developments in the field since then. In 1992, the then UN Secretary-General, Boutros Boutros-Ghali, defined peacekeeping in his *An Agenda for Peace* as:

> the deployment of a UN presence in the field, hitherto with the consent of the parties, normally involving UN military and/or police and frequently civilians as well. Peacekeeping is a technique that expands the possibilities for both the prevention of conflict and the making of peace.[47]

In general, the definitions provided in textbooks and elsewhere are so vague that it is best to understand the nature of any single mission by examining its mandate and how it sets about achieving the mission.[48]

---

[45] It is best to view the action by NATO forces in Kosovo during 1999 as *sui generis*: see B. Simma, 'NATO, the UN and the Use of Force: Legal Aspects' (1999) 10 *European Journal of International Law* 1–22; K. Ambos, 'NATO, the UN and the Use of Force: Legal Aspects: A comment on Simma and Cassese' (1999) 2 *Humanitäres Völkerrecht, Deutsches Rotes Kreuz* 114–15; A. Cassesse, 'Ex Iniuria Ius Oritur: Are We Moving Towards International Legitimation of Forcible Humanitarian Countermeasures in the World Community?' (1999) 10 *European Journal of International Law* 23–30; and C. Guicherd, 'International Law and the War in Kosovo' (1999) 41(2) *Survival* 19–34. See also 'The Kosovo Crisis and International Humanitarian Law' (2000) 837 *International Review of the Red Cross*, in which the whole issue is devoted to contributions on the topic.

[46] *The Peacekeepers Handbook* (New York: International Peace Academy, 1984), p. 22.

[47] UN Doc. A/47/277-S/24111 (June 1992), p. 11.

[48] Lett offers some good insights into finding a workable definition in his analysis on why peacekeeping fails: D. C. Lett, *Why Peacekeeping Fails* (New York: Palgrave, 2001), pp. 13–20.

According to the *Handbook on UN Multidimensional Peacekeeping Operations*, depending on its mandate and with a significant civilian component, a multidimensional peacekeeping operation (also referred to as peace operations) may be required to:

- Assist in implementing a comprehensive peace agreement;
- Monitor a ceasefire or cessation of hostilities to allow space for political negotiations and a peaceful settlement of disputes;
- Provide a secure environment encouraging a return to normal life;
- Prevent an outbreak of spillover of conflict across borders;
- Lead states or territories through a transition to stable government based on democratic principles, good governance and economic development; and
- Administer a territory for a transitional period, thereby carrying out all functions that are the normal responsibility of government.[49]

This latter task facilitated the development of the Integrated Mission concept adopted in 1999 to ensure an effective division of labour between different actors operating on distinct mandates of peace implementation in Kosovo.[50] It largely succeeded in resolving day-to-day 'technical' issues, but failed to overcome the lack of cohesion among major powers, especially relating to differing and contradictory goals that contributed to the overall incoherence of the international response mechanisms. The concept was revised and adapted to UN missions in Timor-Leste, Sierra Leone, Afghanistan, Liberia, the Democratic Republic of the Congo, Burundi, Haiti, Iraq, Côte d'Ivoire and Sudan. The UN adopts a broad approach to integrated missions according to the following interrelated principles:

- Restoration of stability, law and order;
- Protection of civilians;
- Providing the foundations for long-term recovery, development and democratic governance.[51]

In the circumstances, it should come as no surprise that military establishments are revising doctrine to reflect the changing nature of

---

[49] *Handbook on UN Multinational Peacekeeping Operations* (New York: UN, 2003), pp. 1–2.

[50] E. B. Eide, A. T. Kasperen, R. Kent and K. von Heppel, *Report on Integrated Missions*, Independent Study for the Expanded UN ECHA Core Group (May 2005), p. 12.

[51] *Ibid.*

peacekeeping operations.[52] The challenges confronting such operations in the 1990s, particularly in the Balkans, prompted a wide range of European states, including the United Kingdom, Sweden and Ireland, to re-evaluate their peacekeeping doctrine.[53] Some commentators have even gone so far as to argue that the era of Chapter VI operations is now past.[54] The United Kingdom's manual on peace support doctrine reflects the evolutionary process taking place and defines peace support operations as:

> An operation that impartially makes use of diplomatic, civil and military means, normally in pursuit of UN Charter purposes and principles, to restore or maintain peace. Such operations may include conflict prevention, peacemaking, peace enforcement, peacekeeping, peacebuilding and/or humanitarian operations.[55]

It goes on to provide that the UK government usually undertakes action of this nature as part of a UN-led operation, or as part of a multinational endeavour. Occasionally, unilateral action may be undertaken, as occurred in Sierra Leone in 2000. The NATO definition and policy is similar:

> Normally NATO will be invited to act in support of an internationally recognized organization such as the United Nations (UN) or Organization for Security and Co-operation in Europe (OSCE). In exceptional circumstances, the North Atlantic Council (NAC) may decide to take unilateral action.[56]

---

[52] S. Wills, 'Military Interventions on Behalf of Vulnerable Populations: The Legal Responsibilities of States and International Organizations Engaged in Peace Support Operations' (2004) 9 *Journal of Conflict and Security Law* 387–418 at 395.

[53] The FINABEL group (France, Italy, Netherlands, Germany, Belgium, Spain, Luxembourg – and now also Portugal and Greece) also revised peacekeeping doctrine: Lt-Col. P. Wilkinson, 'Sharpening the Weapons of Peace: The Development of a Common Military Doctrine for Peace Support Operations', International Security Information Service (ISIS), Briefing Paper No. 18 (April 1998), http://www.isis-europe.org/isiseu/english/no18.html.

[54] Gen. R. Daillaire, former UN commander in Rwanda, quoted by C. Offman, 'Everything Humanely Possible', *Financial Times Magazine*, 12 March 2005, pp. 14–15.

[55] UK Ministry of Defence, *The Military Contribution to Peace Support Operations*, Joint Warfare Publication (JWP) 3-50 (2nd edn, Shrivenham: Joint Doctrine and Concepts Centre, 2004), Glossary, para. 7.

[56] Allied Joint Publication (AJP) 3.4.1, *Peace Support Operations* (July 2001), para. [0102].

Hence, there were calls for NATO troop deployment, with UN authorisation, to support the African protection mission in Darfur.[57] The UK manual acknowledges the need to integrate doctrine with the emerging practice of humanitarian intervention, and provides that:

> There are occasions when a national government or sub-national organs of government fail to uphold international norms. They may be unable or unwilling to prevent abuse, or perhaps prove to be the sponsors of abuse; they may be unable or unwilling to prevent a faction or group being subject to or threatened with significant harm ... Consequently, a responsibility to provide protection may fall upon the international community ... [T]hose who are tasked with, or choose to assist with, upholding, renewing or restoring acceptable governance need an expansion of the concepts and doctrine that guide their actions.[58]

While acknowledging that the legality of some of these operations is controversial, it goes on to state that recent debates have struggled to balance the precepts of sovereignty with theories that support a higher imperative to protect human rights. It suggests that state and regional organisation practice, coupled with UN precedents, indicates that changes in international law, or its interpretation, are occurring. This would also seem to be the view of the recent high-level report on UN reform, commissioned by the Secretary-General, Kofi Annan, on 'threats, challenges and change', which suggests that military intervention for human rights protection may be necessary as a last resort.[59] While it was once argued that only major powers could threaten international security,[60] there is a growing consensus today that disputes between smaller states and internal conflicts may also endanger international peace.

The report declares that the most widely respected authority for a peacekeeping operation is that conferred by a UN mandate; this is qualified by the statement that regional mandates can provide for a timelier preventive or responsive action than might be possible through the UN. At the same time, it recognises that the legitimacy of unilateral action is often challenged and that this can compound the underlying causes of the conflict, especially when an operation is perceived as

---

[57] M. Albright and others, 'NATO to Darfur', *International Herald Tribune*, 26 May 2005.

[58] *The Military Contribution to Peace Support Operations*, JWP 3-50, para. [113].

[59] *Report of the High-Level Panel on Threats, Challenges and Change*, paras. 199–203.

[60] R. Thakur, *International Peacekeeping in Lebanon* (Boulder and London: Westview, 1987), p. 16.

reflecting colonialist or hegemonic pretensions and a disregard for international law. Nevertheless, it concludes that regional mandates can offer an attractive compromise between responsiveness and political legitimacy.

The NATO approach differs in some significant respects from that adopted by the majority of states in Africa and elsewhere. Africa is the region where extensive efforts have been made to formalise the relationship between the UN and the regional organisation, in this case the African Union.[61] Africa remains the primary focus of contemporary UN peacekeeping, and the current missions in the Democratic Republic of the Congo (MONUC, 1999) and Sudan (UNMIS, 2005) may well come to be viewed as pivotal missions in Africa and the ultimate test of contemporary UN peacekeeping doctrine. MONUC's adoption of a robust response to civilian protection, even if late in coming, may herald a new era that acknowledges the lessons of Srebrenica and Rwanda. But similar comments were made in relation to Somalia in the early 1990s. Militias cannot defeat any reasonably equipped and competently commanded UN force, but they can adapt tactics and embark on insurgency-style attacks against soft targets such as happened in Iraq. They may then wage a war of attrition until the next crisis deflects attention elsewhere and the UN ultimately leaves. The question may also be asked, why the Ituri region in the Congo and not Darfur?

The African manual, *Peace Support Operations: A Working Draft Manual for African Military Practitioners* (DWM 1-2000),[62] emphasises the need for an appropriate legal basis under the UN Charter, and respect for international humanitarian law (IHL). Much greater stress is placed on the non-use of force and state sovereignty. These are similar to the views of the UN's Special Committee on Peacekeeping Operations, which did not support the doctrinal shift proposed in the Brahimi report's review of peacekeeping operations.[63] This is in contrast

---

[61] See M. Vogt, 'Cooperation between the UN and the OAU in the Management of African Conflicts', in M. Malan (ed.), *Whither Peacekeeping in Africa?*, ISS Monograph 36 (Pretoria: Institute for Security Studies, April 1999).

[62] *Peace Support Operations: A Working Draft Manual for African Military Practitioners*, DWM 1-2000 (February 2000), www.iss.co.za/Pubs/Other/PeaceSupportManualMM, produced as a result of a workshop held at the SADC Regional Peacekeeping Training Centre in Harare, Zimbabwe, 24–26 August 1999.

[63] *Comprehensive Review of the Whole Question of Peacekeeping Operations in All Their Aspects*, UN Doc. A/57/767, 28 March 2003, para. 46; and *Report of the Panel on UN Peacekeeping Operations* (Brahimi Report), UN Doc. A/55/305-S/2000/809, 23 August 2000.

to the responsibility-to-protect principle outlined, *inter alia*, in the *Report of the High Level Panel on Threats, Challenges and Change*[64] and endorsed in less forthright terms at the World Summit in September 2005.[65] Given the human rights record of many of the governments in the region, the motivation may have as much to do with fear of intervention by outside states or organisations as with support for provisions relating to domestic jurisdiction and non-use of force contained in the UN Charter. Nonetheless, in July 2000, the Constitutive Act of the African Union included a right to intervene in a member state 'in respect of grave circumstances, namely: war crimes, genocide and crimes against humanity'.[66]

Reporting in 2003 on the implementation of the UN Millennium Declaration, the Secretary-General stated that serious debate among member states is required on the future of 'robust peacekeeping'.[67] Such a debate has yet to take place in earnest. He went on to state:

> There are instances where peace must first be established and the situation stabilized before a peacekeeping presence can be deployed. In such circumstances, the 'Blue Helmets' are not the appropriate instrument. For these reasons I advised against their deployment in favour of multinational forces under the operational control of lead nations in Afghanistan, Côte d'Ivoire, Bunia in the Democratic Republic of the Congo, and, more recently, Liberia.[68]

As the institutional capacity of the UN is stretched to conduct military operations under Chapter VII, regionalised peacekeeping operations offer what may seem an attractive alternative to deficiencies in the UN system. However, these are not without their inherent pitfalls. The idea of a regional approach to global security was considered and rejected in the debates that led to the establishment of the UN. Among the reasons for rejecting this approach were fears of encouraging semi-imperial spheres of influence and the inherent inequality in resources and capacity of different regions. These reservations are equally valid today. The practice of regional responses has been uneven, and the League of Arab

---

[64] *A More Secure World: Our Shared Responsibility: Report of the High-Level Panel on Threats, Challenges and Change*, UN Doc. A/59/565, 2 December 2004.

[65] A/RES/60/1, 24 October 2005, para. 139.

[66] Constitutive Act of the African Union, adopted in Lomé, 11 July 2000, Art. 4(h).

[67] *Report of the Secretary-General – Implementation of the United Nations Millennium Declaration*, UN Doc. A/58/323, 2 September 2003, para. 35.

[68] *Ibid.*

States has often complained that the Security Council does not deal with regional organisations on an equal footing.

The success of European Union (EU) peacekeeping operations in the Democratic Republic of the Congo and Macedonia reflect a significant development in the EU's Common Security and Defence Policy. However, these were relatively limited operations. EURFOR in Bosnia-Herzegovina marks an important precedent and coming of age for EU activities in the field of international peace and security. Similarly, while small units of British and French soldiers had some success in Sierra Leone in 2000 and the eastern Congo in 2003, the United States' airlift and military capacity is required for operations of a larger scale and longer duration. The will to change the reliance on NATO (i.e. American) military assets does not seem to exist in Europe. Furthermore, the EU's relationship with the UN is unclear. The UK and France have indicated that they do not regard operations under the EU's Common Security and Defence Policy to be subordinate to the Security Council. This view is not shared by other EU states. In 2003, the United States Secretary for Defense, Donald Rumsfeld, called for the creation of a multi-national peacekeeping force under United States command and outside the auspices of the UN.[69] Although in searching to expand international forces in Iraq the United States modified this position, such developments have serious implications for the UN's system of collective security, and its primary role in the maintenance of international peace and security.

The end of the Cold War has not brought the realisation of the early optimism associated with it, and the ambitions for the UN and the Security Council reflected in the Secretary-General's *An Agenda for Peace* have not materialised. The Secretary-General sought to give legitimacy to the concept of peace enforcement by formally proposing the establishment of such units. However, the concept of peace enforcement can prove to be a contradiction in terms, and it was disastrous when attempted in Somalia. Ultimately, it merely served to discredit UN activities in the maintenance of international peace and security. A more sobering and reflective sequel to this was published a short time later, in which the Secretary-General acknowledged certain limitations.[70]

---

[69] R. Thakur, 'US Considers UN Approval of Force Optional', *UNU Update*, No. 25, June 2003; and P. Slevin and V. Loeb, 'UN Troops Considered for Iraq Duty', *Washington Post*, 28 August 2003, p. A01.

[70] *Supplement to An Agenda for Peace* (New York: United Nations, 1995).

In order to respond to the problem of intra-state conflict, there is need for reform of doctrinal foundations and structures in the UN system. This will require more than the creation of a Peacebuilding Commission in order to stabilise and rebuild societies emerging from conflict. Today's international environment is more permissive of intervention, while the concept of peace and security has expanded to incorporate a broad range of issues outside the scope of the current UN organisation.[71] Military intervention in any internal conflict is fraught with uncertainty. The number and nature of armed conflicts has changed in recent times. Multilateral diplomacy through the UN may take some credit for the reduction in conflicts between states which now constitute less than 5 per cent of armed conflicts.[72] Nevertheless, there is a consensus that much greater emphasis must be placed on preventive measures, as opposed to reactive corrective strategies that are, more often than not, too little and too late. In particular, this practice suffers from the limited ability of the Security Council and the Secretary-General to deploy, direct and command enforcement operations in response to threats to the peace, breaches of the peace or acts of aggression. The consequences of this are well known, but worth restating. While the UN has had some success in preventing armed conflicts, international and internal armed conflicts have continued to erupt around the globe. With the UN's inability to respond effectively to these crises, the Security Council has left the establishment and management of international forces to individual member states, especially the United States. In some of these cases, the UN has divested itself explicitly of its competence in leading enforcement actions and has instead 'authorised' member states to undertake enforcement measures by use of force. Some have described this action by the Security Council as a form of abdication of responsibility, with little or no command and control by the UN, and no strategic direction either.[73]

---

[71] L. Fawcett, 'The Evolving Architecture of Regionalization', in M. Pugh and W. P. S. Sidhu (eds.), *The United Nations and Regional Security* (Boulder: Lynne Rienner, 2003), p. 16.

[72] *Human Security Report*, University of British Columbia, October 2005 available at www.humansecurityreport.info; and *Report of the High-Level Panel on Threats, Challenges and Change*, paras. 74–88.

[73] White, *Keeping the Peace*, pp. 115–28, esp. pp. 117–18.

The structure of the book

The primary focus of the book is on three case studies, Lebanon, Somalia and Kosovo. These are used to conduct a comparative analysis of traditional or first-generation peacekeeping, and that of second-generation multi-dimensional peacekeeping. These were chosen as representative of the types of operations undertaken by and on behalf of the UN, and as reflecting the problems that are associated with their establishment, deployment, command, use of force, and applicability of IHL and international human rights law. They also reflect operations conducted in three different geographic regions – Africa, the Middle East and Europe.

Contemporary peacekeeping operations face many of the same operational challenges as early missions. After an exhaustive analysis of a number of operations, Lett concluded:

> There are therefore many pitfalls that can contribute to the failure of peacekeeping in the pre-deployment, deployment, and post-deployment phases. Regardless of how the peacekeepers do their job, external actors, internal resources, and the parties themselves can conspire to make success impossible to achieve.[74]

This book illustrates the lessons that ought to be learned from the experiences of the selected operations, demonstrating how certain factors can have a significant impact on the outcome of a mission. The conduct of UN forces in Somalia, and the outcome of the multi-national operations there, had a profound effect on the willingness of states to support subsequent UN multi-national peacekeeping. UNOSOM II was one of the most ambitious and controversial multi-dimensional operations ever mounted by the UN. It reflected the optimism associated with the dawn of a 'new world order' and an effective Security Council.

The UN Administration in Kosovo (UNMIK) was established in 1999. Working closely with the NATO-led Kosovo Force (KFOR), UNMIK performs the whole spectrum of essential administrative functions and services in the province of Kosovo. It is a unique operation in one of the most politically volatile areas of Europe. There is no obvious solution to the status of Kosovo, and tension remains concerning the policy of the international community that minimal international standards in governance must be met before the issue of status is resolved.

---

[74] Lett, *Why Peacekeeping Fails*, p. 168.

The underlying dilemma in Kosovo is that, once force is used in this way to protect human rights, it inevitably impinges upon sovereignty and may even ultimately lead to alteration in borders. Despite denials by Western governments that humanitarian intervention is becoming the new imperialism, Kosovo does establish a precedent that states can lose their sovereignty over a portion of their territory if they oppress the majority there to such an extent that there is a revolt that enlists the support of powerful members of the international community.[75]

In contrast to Somalia and Kosovo, the UN operation in Lebanon (UNIFIL) was a less ambitious traditional peacekeeping mission. However, this did not serve to make the mission free from controversy, as the force encountered serious difficulties implementing its apparently more straight-forward mandate. Each operation shows that, whatever the nature of a peacekeeping operation, its role and effectiveness is dependent upon support from the Security Council. Without political support and adequate resources, especially at the time of its establishment, a UN force remains at the mercy of the parties to the conflict.

UNOSOM II was the first real test in the post-Cold War era of UN-mandated nation-building. Events in Somalia had a significant impact on US foreign policy, and the images of American servicemen lying among the wreckage of downed helicopters in the streets of Mogadishu later haunted planners in Washington. Somalia has also cast a shadow over UN and US involvement in similar operations from Kosovo to Afghanistan.

The UNOSOM II mission was multi-dimensional and involved the UN in a nation-building operation that is often perceived as a failure for the Organization and the international community as a whole. Yet, while the Somalia operation was an important precedent for subsequent interventions, much of the accepted 'wisdom' in regard to what happened is not based on reasoned and comprehensive analysis. One of the most frequently cited criticisms of the overall operation is that the mission changed or that it was subject to 'mission creep'. In order to test these theories, this work examines both the background to the adoption of the relevant resolution(s) of the Security Council, and the subsequent interpretation and implementation of what was often an ambiguous mandate in the first instance.

---

[75] M. Ignatieff, *Empire Lite: Nation-Building in Bosnia, Kosovo and Afghanistan* (London: Vintage, 2003), p. 70.

Adopting criteria to determine the success of an operation is problematic, as no internationally accepted criteria exist at present.[76] Despite this, most commentators still need to find some formula for evaluating the performance of peacekeeping and related operations. This quandary is usually solved by using a variety of criteria based on the extent to which the mandate or objectives of the mission were fulfilled, and/or the extent to which the operation limited armed conflict, or promoted relative peace and security in the area.[77] There is also a need to be aware of the timeframe used to determine 'success' or 'failure'. Were the short-term efforts to feed the starving successful, and what then of the long-term strategy and eventual withdrawal?

Most of the systematic studies of UN peacekeeping have been of the case study and comparative nature. Such studies often focus on particular dimensions of peacekeeping in the context of a selected mission or missions;[78] this is the model adopted in this book. Many studies have also tended to place too much emphasis on what is theoretically desirable, rather than politically and practically possible. In truth, it is probable that there are no definitive criteria to determine the ultimate success of any UN military operation absolutely, and the more complex second-generation multi-dimensional operations are even more problematic in

[76] Paul Diehl identified two criteria for evaluating a traditional peacekeeping operation, i.e. the extent to which it limited armed conflict and promoted conflict resolution: P. Diehl, *International Peacekeeping* (Baltimore and London: Johns Hopkins University Press, 1993), pp. 3 and 34. However, this theoretical framework has flaws: see the review by R. Johansen in (1994) 38 *Mershon International Studies Review* 307–10. For an excellent but somewhat dated analysis of this question with respect to the entire UN, see K. Stiles and M. MacDonald, 'After Consensus, What? Performance Criteria for the UN in the Post Cold War Era' (1992) 29 *Journal of Peace Research* 299–311. See also D. Lett, *Why Peacekeeping Fails* (London: Macmillan, 2000), esp. pp. 1–20.

[77] Brown identified three criteria for determining success: Was the mandate fulfilled, as specified by the appropriate Security Council resolution? Did the operation lead to a resolution of the underlying disputes of the conflict? Did the presence of the operation contribute to the maintenance of international peace and security by reducing or eliminating conflict in the area of operation? M. A. Brown, 'United Nations Peacekeeping: Historical Overview and Current Issues', in *Report for Congress* (Washington, DC: Congressional Research Service, 1993). See also D. Bratt, 'Assessing the Success of UN Peacekeeping Operations', in Pugh (ed.), *The UN, Peace and Force*, pp. 64–81. Rikhye emphasises the importance of the mechanics and logistical dimensions of peacekeeping, in particular the role of 'command and control' and the role of the superpowers in a peacekeeping operations success: Rikhye, *The Politics and Practice of United Nations Peacekeeping*, pp. 81–2.

[78] For example, legal questions, the organisational aspects, political and military aspects or how the operation fits into the larger security regime.

this regard than the generally straightforward traditional peacekeeping operations. In the latter case, it may be possible to evaluate the extent to which a cease-fire was maintained, but multi-dimensional operations require analysis from a number of perspectives.

Nevertheless, a useful means of providing a framework to evaluate the performance of a force is to apply factors identified as essential for its success. In his report to the Security Council on UNIFIL, the Secretary-General outlined three essential conditions that needed to be met for the force to be effective. First, it must at all times have the full confidence and backing of the Security Council. Secondly, it must operate with the full co-operation of all the parties concerned. Thirdly, it must be able to function as an integrated and efficient military unit.[79] The now retired Under-Secretary-General of the UN with special responsibility for peacekeeping operations, Brian Urquhart, elaborated upon this in 1983 when writing about the Multi-National Force in Beirut, stating that successful peacekeeping depends, *inter alia*, on a sound political base, a well-defined mandate and objectives, and the co-operation of the parties concerned.[80] The requirement of a well-defined mandate and objectives was a somewhat glaring omission from the Secretary-General's otherwise pragmatic report. Using these factors as criteria, chapter 2 focuses on the establishment and deployment of the UN forces in Lebanon, Somalia and Kosovo. The chapter explains how the background influenced the outcome of the operations, highlights the central role played by the United States throughout, and contends that the lack of support from the permanent members of the Security Council, especially the United States, undermined the political base and viability of each of the operations from the beginning.

In the case of Lebanon, the mandate adopted was controversial and was considered to be deficient in a number of respects. While UNIFIL was deployed with undue haste against the advice of many commentators at the time, its survival should not be seen as a reflection on the appropriateness of the mandate. The UN operations in Somalia were more ambitious in comparison and involved significantly more resources. Initially at least, they were also less controversial. The consensus and enthusiasm for involvement in Somalia changed quickly as 'mission creep' set in and doubts were expressed about the efficacy of UN policy there.

---

[79] UN Doc. S/12611, 19 March 1978, para. 3.
[80] B. Urquhart, 'On UN Peacekeeping', *New York Times*, 19 December 1983, p. A19.

The question of command and control of UN and other multi-national operations is a fundamental issue confronting the formation of international forces and is examined in chapter 3. Problems encountered at the international level often have their origins in the national policy of contributing states, and legal issues in relation to Ireland and Canada are discussed in this context. In theory, the command structure of such forces is straightforward, but in reality it is fraught with difficulties arising from subjective human factors and objective legal constraints. It is a fundamental issue upon which the success of the mission may largely depend. Each operation examined highlights the serious difficulties that arise in the command of UN-authorised or -approved missions, with the larger, more complex UNOSOM II and Kosovo missions presenting significant dilemmas in this regard. Perhaps the greatest challenge faced in this area relates to the establishment of a satisfactory arrangement that translates into an effective chain of command for the proper management of all components of the operation, both civil and military. This aspect of the UNOSOM II mission was problematic and controversial from the start. Unless the Security Council has specifically delegated command to a particular country, no one government should effectively control a UN operation.

The most controversial aspect of recent UN operations has been the policy employed with regard to the use of force, a fundamental determinant of the nature of any peacekeeping operation. Despite their differing natures, the operations in Lebanon, Somalia and Kosovo present remarkably similar problems in this regard. Hurdles were encountered in each mission when it came to the creation and adoption of appropriate rules of engagement (ROE) and, later still, when those rules were applied, due to inconsistent interpretations as to when, and to what degree, the use of force is warranted in a UN multi-national operation. Devising appropriate ROE remains a key issue in the planning and deployment of any multi-national force. Chapter 4 examines the use of force and the experience of UNIFIL, UNOSOM II and KFOR. The premise of the analysis is that strict adherence to the principle of self-defence is the only option available in traditional peacekeeping operations. Furthermore, the nature of the UNOSOM II mission meant that the coercive enforcement measures adopted inevitably led to its role as a third-party UN force being converted to that of factional participant. However, when there is no other option, the security component of a peace operation mandated to protect the local population will have no choice but to use minimum force to prevent ethnic cleansing and similar human rights abuses from occurring. If a force is not trained and prepared to protect the minority population in places such as Kosovo, then legitimate questions may be asked as to why it is there in the first place.

Chapter 5 examines the applicability and relevance of international humanitarian law (IHL) and international human rights law to all types of military action undertaken by or on behalf of the UN. Despite the adoption of a Convention on the Protection of UN Personnel in 1994, a Secretary-General's Bulletin on the Applicability of IHL to UN forces (1999), and a further Bulletin on Special Measures for Protection from Sexual Exploitation and Sexual Abuse (2003), the situation remains unsatisfactory. Owing to the controversy surrounding action by UNOSOM forces in Somalia, and the inaction of the UN forces at Srebrenica and Rwanda (and more recently in the Democratic Republic of the Congo in 2004), the question of respect for the principles of IHL by UN forces has been the subject of controversy and debate. Linked to this is the issue of the appropriate course of action for UN forces confronted with a situation wherein a party to the conflict perpetrates serious violations of international human rights and IHL against innocent third parties. Experiences in Rwanda and the former Yugoslavia (and more recently in Kosovo) exposed the UN as a paper tiger and saw UN troops relegated to the role of bystander while gross violations took place before their very eyes. The UN has maintained that peacekeepers should not be placed in positions where they are forced into the role of witness or bystanders to serious violations of human rights or IHL. The question, then, is whether there is a legal duty on UN forces to intervene in such circumstances, and if so when and how. Even the less controversial traditional peacekeeping missions can involve important issues of IHL, especially when the situation that UNIFIL found itself in after the Israeli invasion of Lebanon in 1982 is considered.

The UN system was designed carefully to make war illegal and unnecessary, and nowhere in Chapter VII, and Article 42 in particular, is 'war' mentioned. The obvious implication of this is that military action taken by the UN is not to be regarded as 'war', and this was the commonly accepted view of the UN action in Korea. While there appears to be no record of the UN ever claiming that IHL does not apply to operations authorised by or undertaken on behalf of the Organization, the issues raised are complex and the policy of the UN remains ambivalent.

Peacekeepers involved in post-conflict peace operations have also been accused of human rights abuses, especially with regard to trafficking in persons and sexual exploitation.[81] Trafficking in persons is a criminal activity that amounts to a modern form of slavery, and, although it can be attributed to a variety of reasons, the trafficking of women and girls for sexual exploitation is particularly sinister and pervasive. It is also contrary to the terms and spirit of Security Council Resolution 1325 (2000) which requires gender mainstreaming in UN peace initiatives and provides for a comprehensive framework to this effect.[82] Peacekeepers in Africa have been accused of rape and similar serious abuses. The privileges and immunities enjoyed by UN personnel, although intended to protect the interests of the UN and not individuals, may have contributed to the numbers of UN personnel involved at various levels in such activities.

Amnesty International has repeatedly raised concerns about instances in which individual peacekeeping forces led by NATO in Kosovo and Bosnia-Herzegovina have failed to adhere to international human rights law and standards when detaining suspects.[83] Alleged violations include incidents of illegal and arbitrary arrest, ill-treatment and failure to protect the rights of people in custody. Amnesty attributed this to a lack of accountability and civilian control. Mechanisms to address these problems must be put in place immediately.

These are important issues confronting today's peacekeepers, most especially those participating in the so-called 'robust' peacekeeping operations similar to that of UNOSOM II and Kosovo. While none of the existing conventions or protocols addresses the specific issue of UN forces, or forces acting on the authority of the UN, in situations of armed conflict, it could be said that this situation leaves military forces acting under the control of the UN in somewhat of a limbo. Human rights are a fundamental issue in guaranteeing effective peacekeeping.[84] Recent UN operations have involved authorised and mandated missions

---

[81] J. Murray, 'Who Will Police the Peace-Builders? The Failure to Establish Accountability for the Participation of United Nations Civilian Police in the Trafficking of Women in Post-Conflict Bosnia and Herzegovina' (2003) 34 *Columbia Human Rights Law Review* 475–527.

[82] Adopted 31 October 2000.

[83] Letter from Amnesty International concerning lack of accountability of KFOR and SFOR, 20 October 2003.

[84] M. Katayanagi, *Human Rights Functions of Peacekeeping Operations* (The Hague: Kluwer, 2002); D. Garcia-Sayan, 'Human Rights and Peace-Keeping Operations' (1995) 29 *University of Richmond Law Review* 41–65 at 45; D. Forsythe, 'Human Rights and International Security: United Nations Field Operations Redux', in M. Castermans, F. van Hoof and J. Smith (eds.), *The Role of the Nation State in the 21st Century* (Dordrecht: Kluwer, 1998), pp. 265–76.

being mounted in situations of conflict where clashes involving UN soldiers were inevitable. Many contemporary conflicts do not involve soldiers from regular armies but militias or groups of armed civilians with little discipline and an ill-defined command structure. Fighters of this nature do not always fit within the defined status of 'combatant' under IHL.

Despite the dangers involved, the international community and the UN have a responsibility not to shy away from complex and dangerous situations. Esoteric debates on legal principles have a value, but they should not be allowed to detract from the establishment and deployment of peacekeeping operations as facilitators of conflict resolution. Apart from deciding on an appropriate and authoritative mandate, the real issue is who will decide when these forces will be deployed and their subsequent command and control. In this regard the role of the Security Council is vital, especially for middle and small powers like Ireland. The *Report of the Panel on UN Peacekeeping Operations* (the Brahimi Report) called for more robust rules of engagement (ROE) in operations involving intra-state/transnational conflicts.[85] While the report acknowledged that this would involve 'bigger forces, better equipped and more costly', it did not seem to take full cognisance of the fact that the use of force must be accompanied by political will, a willingness to accept casualties (UN personnel, civilians and others), and a need for an effective command mechanism to ensure cohesion and uniform application. It also failed to address the issues associated with regional peacekeepers or coalitions of the willing acting under the authority of the UN. As Adam Roberts observed in relation to humanitarian intervention:

> A curious problem in much past writing about humanitarian intervention has been a lack of any systematic attention to what the intervening armed forces are actually supposed to do, and also what the eventual results of the intervention are supposed to be.[86]

---

[85] *Report of the Panel on UN Peacekeeping Operations* (Brahimi Report), UN Doc. A/55/305-S/2000/809, 23 August 2000, para. 49. In a follow-up to Brahimi, the Security Council adopted Resolution 1327 of 13 November 2000, which stated that the Council '[u]ndertakes to ensure that the mandated tasks of peace operations are appropriate to the situation on the ground, including such factors as the prospects of success, the potential need to protect civilians, and the possibility that some parties may seek to undermine peace through violence' (Annex II).

[86] A. Roberts, 'The So-Called "Right" of Humanitarian Intervention' (2000) 3 *Yearbook of International Humanitarian Law* 3 at 42.

The same may be said of peacekeeping operations, with Kosovo serving as a prime example. Often it appears that all the energy is expended on finding some form of agreement to deploy in the first instance, with too little attention paid to what the operation will achieve and how this will be accomplished in the long term. Somalia shows that robust ROE and increased size are not enough and, while it is imperative not to employ an emasculated UN force, the UN operations in Somalia, Lebanon and Kosovo demonstrate that it is essential to have a clear military and political strategy agreed at the outset.

2

The political and diplomatic background to the establishment of peace support operations in Lebanon, Somalia and Kosovo

Introduction

There are as many contrasts as there are comparisons in the forms of peacekeeping adopted to deal with the conflicts that arose in Lebanon, Somalia and Kosovo. In the case of Lebanon, UNIFIL emerged as a result of difficult negotiations that required a compromise by the parties to the conflict. Its survival in what were often difficult circumstances is testimony to the professionalism of those charged with implementing the mandate, rather than reflective of the merit of the mandate itself. By contrast, the UN operations in Somalia were bolder, more costly and, initially, less contentious. In Kosovo, the response of the international community arose from the aftermath of an eleven-week NATO air campaign against Yugoslav and Serbian security forces. Although a relatively small geographical area, this province of Serbia (formerly the Federal Republic of Yugoslavia)[1] presented a range of complex problems that exist to this day, especially in relation to the question of its future status. As in the case of Somalia, it is difficult to ascertain any national interest or motivation in intervening. The situation that arose in Kosovo during 1999 also demonstrated the powerlessness of the UN. Ensuring compliance with Security Council resolutions can be problematic at any time, but in this instance neither China nor Russia was willing to authorise the use of force against Serbia. This is the Achilles' heel in the UN system of collective security.

---

[1] In November 2002, an agreement was reached on a new Constitutional Charter, which changed the name of the country from the Federal Republic of Yugoslavia (FRY) to 'Serbia and Montenegro'. Under the new Constitutional Charter, Kosovo and Metohija officially remain a province of the state of Serbia. Montenegro declared independence in June 2006.

This chapter examines the experiences of each force, bearing in mind the prerequisites denoted by the Secretary-General in his first report on UNIFIL, namely, the need for the full support of the Security Council, the full co-operation of all the parties to the conflict and the ability to function as an integrated and efficient military unit.[2] It further considers the imperative of a well-defined mandate and objectives,[3] and the relevance of the deficiencies in the organisation and structure of the forces, especially when parties to the conflict fail to provide a requisite level of support.

Factors influencing the decision to intervene

When the Lebanese civil war was at its height during 1975 and 1976, serious efforts were made to determine the feasibility and value of establishing a UN peacekeeping force for the country. Ultimately, however, no such force was established after strong reservations were expressed regarding its practicality in what was essentially a civil war situation. Similar reservations were later raised with regard to UN intervention in Somalia, with the added dimension that Somalia was of no strategic importance to the members of the Security Council. There were also financial considerations, and substantial resistance at first from the United States and Russia to plans for a more proactive UN policy in Somalia, as both countries were in considerable arrears in peacekeeping accounts even before the operation began. In both Lebanon and Somalia, the actual decision to intervene was taken against a background of ongoing civil war and a state imploding on itself. The situation in Kosovo in 1999 was unique, and, while not a civil war as such, the political vacuum created by the Serb withdrawal and the aftermath of ethnic cleansing left a traumatised population and a devastated province. The Balkans continued to be a powder keg that could be ignited by a spark from what many observers might otherwise have deemed to be a storm in a teacup. However, a failure to deal with atrocities and their aftermath also undermined the democratic values of those that looked on and did nothing. There was also the humanitarian imperative presented by the situation in Kosovo, reference to which had already been made in a number of Security Council resolutions, notably 1160 (1998), 1199 (1998) and 1203 (1998).

---

[2] Security Council Doc. S/12611, 19 March 1978, para. 3.
[3] B. Urquhart, 'On UN Peacekeeping', *New York Times*, 19 December 1983, p. A19.

In the case of Lebanon, the decisive factor was that of third-party intervention, namely, the Israeli invasion of south Lebanon in 1978.[4] At that time, there was no real effective government in Lebanon, and the south of the country was dominated by Palestinian forces in and around the old city of Tyre, in an area often referred to as the 'Iron Triangle'.[5]

As with most problems of this nature brought before the Security Council, the parties to the conflict in Lebanon sought a solution within the framework of the UN only when the problem otherwise proved insoluble. In this context, the major player was not a direct party to the conflict, but the United States whose role in each conflict studied proves crucial, but for different reasons. In the case of Lebanon, the real agenda was the Middle East peace process, yet in Somalia it is difficult to discern any ulterior motive apart from recognising and living up to its responsibilities as a major power, and a desire to rebuild the institutions of state in a war-torn society. Though the policy of replicating Western democratic values in east Africa should not be underestimated, humanitarian disaster was the primary motivation for the UN and the United States major post-Cold War intervention in Somalia.[6] The situation there was not an unresolved international problem deriving from the Cold War. But the Cold War had helped to shape the crisis that led to UN intervention in 1992. The aftermath of the inter-clan fighting had left it without any semblance of a state, and with no one party or clan that could conveniently be treated as the legitimate government in order to provide the UN with the 'consent' required for the deployment of a traditional Chapter VI peacekeeping force. This left the Organization with a number of serious dilemmas, one of the more significant of which was with whom to negotiate.

After the attempt to deploy a peacekeeping force failed, the consequent intervention planned for Somalia had no clear precedent in UN

---

[4] Security Council Doc. S/12600, 15 May 1978. See K. Whittingham's report, *Middle East International*, No. 81 (March 1978), pp. 16–18 and 'Israel "Severs the Arm"', *Time*, 27 March 1978.

[5] E. A. Erskine, *Mission with UNIFIL* (London: Hurst, 1989), p. 117.

[6] J. Mayall (ed.), *The New Interventionism 1991–1994: United Nations Experience in Cambodia, Former Yugoslavia, and Somalia* (Cambridge: Cambridge University Press, 1996), p. 9; R. Thakur, 'From Peacekeeping to Peace Enforcement: The UN Operation in Somalia' (1994) 39(3) *Journal of Modern African Studies* 387–410 at 388; J. Hirsch and R. Oakley, *Somalia and Operation Restore Hope* (Washington, DC: US Institute of Peace, 1995), p. xviii; and A. S. Natsios, 'Humanitarian Relief Interventions in Somalia: The Economics of Chaos' (1996) 3(1) *International Peacekeeping* 68–91. For an alternative point of view, see M. D. Abdullahi, in 'Somalia: US–UN Intervention', Africa Institute of South Africa, Occasional Paper No. 61 (1995), pp. 12–15.

peacekeeping practice. The force could not be deployed at the request or with the consent of a host government or on the bases of an agreement between the parties. For these reasons, the Security Council was required to invoke the enforcement provisions of Chapter VII of the Charter in order to authorise the United States-led multinational force (UNITAF) and for UNOSOM II.[7] This marked the first occasion such action was taken in order to deal with a conflict within a state. It occurred in the slipstream of success generated by the dramatic result of Operation Desert Storm and the First Gulf War (1991), and the deployment of UN forces in Bosnia-Herzegovina and Croatia. A fundamental matter that seemingly was not appreciated at the time was the unique and complex nature of the situation in Somalia. The First Gulf War conflict had arisen from a classical act of aggression by one state against another and constituted a textbook example of the illegal use of force against the territorial integrity of a member state. It was against this backdrop of optimism and hope for the effective functioning of the UN that the decision to launch one of the most complex and challenging UN operations in the post-Cold War era was taken.

The decision to intervene, like the nature of the actual forces ultimately established, was very different in the case of Lebanon in 1978, Somalia in 1992 and Kosovo in 1999. None of these crises had developed overnight, and there had been many calls for assistance on the basis of the threat posed to the respective regions by the civil wars and the humanitarian disaster unfolding, in Somalia in particular. The crises in Lebanon and Somalia also shared a common handicap from the beginning, in that the real focus of attention was elsewhere when the decision was made to deploy UN military personnel. In the case of Lebanon, the United States administration was primarily concerned with the Egyptian–Israeli peace treaty and the Camp David Accords.[8] In the early 1990s, on the other hand, the break-up of the Soviet Union and the outbreak of fighting in the former Yugoslavia overshadowed the Somali crisis. By the time the international media brought attention to bear on the plight of the people of Somalia in 1992, the Somali state had ceased to exist and its people sought the only security they could

---

[7] *The United Nations and Somalia 1992–1996*, United Nations Blue Book Series Vol. VIII (New York: United Nations, 1996), p. 4.

[8] President Carter was later to identify this as his most significant foreign policy achievement: J. Carter, *Keeping Faith: Memoirs of a President* (London and New York: Bantam Books, 1982). See also B. Reich and R. Hollis, 'Peacekeeping in the Reagan Administration', in P. Marantz and J. G. Stein (eds.), *Peace Making in the Middle East: Problems and Prospects* (London: Croom Helm, 1985), pp. 133–55.

find from the clan system. Kosovo, too, had been a neglected long-term issue arising from the break-up of the former Yugoslavia. The failure to address the grievances of the Kosovar Albanian population in the Dayton Accords caused resentment that later found expression in support for the violent methods advocated by the Kosovo Liberation Army (KLA).

The UN is often blamed for failing to resolve an intractable problem not of its making in Lebanon and Kosovo, and for failing to fulfil its ambitious programme in Somalia. It is easy to place the blame on an international organisation that even its strongest defenders accept to have weaknesses. However, the UN can only succeed if given the support and the means to do so. When it appears to fail, the permanent members of the Security Council are quick to point the finger at the Organization itself and thereby deflect attention from themselves. But it was members of the Security Council, in particular the United States, that originally sponsored the initiative to establish UNIFIL, and then failed to give the force the support it needed to be effective. Furthermore, neither the United States nor the Soviet Union put sufficient pressure on their respective allies in the region to co-operate with UNIFIL. From the outset it was clear that the force needed certain essential conditions to be fulfilled before it could be effective, in particular, the co-operation of the parties concerned. The actual fulfilment of these conditions was largely outside either the Secretary-General's or the force's control. This was one of the primary reasons for the apparent inability of UNIFIL to carry out its mandate.

In Somalia, after initial hesitancy, the United States became one of the main backers of the operation. But the American aspirations for UN involvement were not matched by a willingness to take the necessary risks or commit additional resources to what were defined and limited objectives. In the end, the United States effectively terminated the operation, having hijacked aspects of the mission when its own unilateral actions backfired. The Clinton administration, in a classic damage limitation and deflection exercise, blamed the UN for what amounted to deficiencies in American policies.

Response to the interventions in Lebanon, Somalia and Kosovo

The case of Lebanon

Lebanon achieved independence in 1944, and a complex system for the distribution of political power was devised under the National Pact of

1943.[9] This became Lebanon's unwritten constitution, allocating power on a communal basis until 1975. The Pact was problematic from the start as it was based on outdated census figures that did not take adequate account of demographic changes to come, and the complexity of the existing political and religious tensions. In effect, it facilitated the Christian community (who looked to the former colonial power, France, for protection) ruling a majority Muslim population. In this way, 'it did not abolish sectarianism, it merely regularised and institutionalised it'.[10] This situation was exacerbated by the presence of large numbers of Palestinians, especially in the south of the country. In 1969, the PLO concluded the so-called Cairo Agreement with the Lebanese army.[11] This gave the PLO certain military rights in Lebanon, including the right to use the south of the country as a base from which to launch attacks on Israel. After fighting between Jordanian forces and the PLO in the early 1970s, large numbers of Palestinian fighters moved to south Lebanon. In time they assumed *de facto* control of parts of the south, especially around the city of Tyre.

In April 1975, civil war broke out between Christian factions and leftist Muslim Lebanese, the latter supported by the PLO,[12] which led to the collapse of the Lebanese administration and the division of the security forces. By this time the combined Muslim communities outnumbered the Christians, and, within the Muslim group, the former majority Sunnis found themselves overtaken by the Shia. The constitutional arrangements for power sharing could not accommodate the conflicting aspirations brought about by demographic changes. The civil war when it erupted was not unlike the conflict in Northern Ireland, more a struggle for power between rival communities of different faiths than a religious war. The confessional system[13] on which the

---

[9] A. James, *Peacekeeping in International Politics* (London: Macmillan, 1990), pp. 284–9 and 335–51; and R. Thakur, *International Peacekeeping in Lebanon* (Boulder and London: Westview, 1987), pp. 36–46.

[10] P. J. Vatikiotis, 'The Crisis in Lebanon: A Local Historical Perspective' (1984) 40 *World Today* 88.

[11] The text of the Agreement is given by W. Khalidi, *Conflict and Violence in the Lebanon: Confrontation in the Middle East*, Harvard Studies in International Affairs No. 39 (Cambridge, MA: Harvard University Center for International Affairs, 1980), pp. 185–7.

[12] These included, among others: Maronite Christians, who, since independence, had dominated the government; Sunni Muslims, who had prospered in business and shared political power; the Druze; and Shiite Muslims.

[13] The 1943 National Pact, which established the political foundations of modern Lebanon, allocated political power on an essentially confessional system based on the 1932 census. Seats in parliament were divided on a 6:5 ratio of Christians to Muslims,

allocation of political power was based also facilitated outside intervention. In June 1976, Syrian forces intervened to protect the Christian community. The Riyadh peace plan of October 1976 saw the deployment of an
Arab League peacekeeping force (the Arab Deterrent Force) to end hostilities and keep the peace. This was a predominantly Syrian force with token
representation from other Arab states, which, when deployed, was perceived as posing a serious security threat to Israel. The other Arab forces
soon began to withdraw, ultimately leaving some 25,000 Syrian troops in
Lebanon, the last of which were not withdrawn until April 2005.[14] Israel
threatened to take countermeasures if the Arab Deterrent Force
advanced beyond an imaginary east–west 'red line' to the south.[15]

Although the civil war officially ended in October 1976, fighting
continued in southern Lebanon, where government control was never
restored[16] and the Arab Deterrent Force could not deploy to restore
order. In addition, the planned withdrawal of PLO fighters under the
Chtaura Peace Accord of July 1977 did not take place. Fighting continued between Israeli-supported Christian militias and elements of the
Lebanese Nationalist Movement, a loose association of Muslim and
leftist groups, supported by the PLO. The civil war proved to be a crucial
event in the forging of an Israeli–Christian Lebanese alliance. This
involved support to local militias along the armistice line and a more
strategic alliance involving Israeli Defence Forces aid to the Christian
Phalange militia to the north around Beirut.[17] Palestinian camps had
existed around Beirut for some time; however, the influx of fighters meant
that the PLO became a dominant force in the south and in raids commenced
across the Lebanese–Israeli armistice line. These attacks led to retaliatory
action by Israel. On 11 March 1978, a group of Palestinian guerrillas
launched a series of armed attacks in Israel, including an attack on a civilian
bus along the Haifa–Tel Aviv highway. Thirty-seven Israelis were killed and
another seventy-six wounded. The guerrillas came from Palestinian bases in

until 1990 when the ratio changed to half and half. Positions in the government
bureaucracy are allocated on a similar basis.

[14] On 2 September 2004, the Security Council adopted Resolution 1559 calling for the
withdrawal of all foreign forces from Lebanon.

[15] United Nations, *The Blue Helmets: A Review of United Nations Peacekeeping* (3rd edn,
New York: United Nations, 1996), p. 83.

[16] During the civil war between March 1975 and November 1976, an estimated 40,000
Lebanese were killed and 100,000 wounded. Syrian troops then intervened at the request
of the Lebanese and brought large-scale fighting to a halt. In 1977, the civil war again
flared up and continued until 1990.

[17] B. Morris, *Righteous Victims: A History of the Zionist–Arab Conflict, 1881–2000* (New
York: Vintage, 2001), p. 502.

Lebanon. The Israelis responded by invading south Lebanon, a matter that was brought to the immediate attention of the Security Council, which held an urgent meeting on 17 March to consider the situation. On 19 March, the Council adopted Resolutions 425 and 426 (1978) establishing UNIFIL.[18] By this time, Israel was in effective control of all south Lebanon below the Litani river, with the important exception of the so-called Iron Triangle, a PLO stronghold concentrated around the city of Tyre.

The controversy surrounding the actual adoption of Resolution 425 (1978) provides important clues to understanding the problems confronted by UNIFIL on the ground. In contrast to the changes in the mandates and forces deployed in Somalia, the original UNIFIL mandate remained intact. It was the United States that did the work behind the scenes and then made the formal proposal to establish a peacekeeping force. The Lebanese government's strategy at this time was to internationalise and highlight the problem and thereby extricate itself from the regional conflict taking place in Lebanon between Israel, the Palestinians and Syria.[19] With this in mind, it successfully obtained UN support for the establishment of a peacekeeping force. The debate in the Security Council shows that, while there was general support for this, there was no like agreement as to what the mandate should be. Furthermore, all parties involved were critical of aspects of Resolution 425 (1978). Even at this very early stage, the lack of political consensus within the Security Council, which was to hinder the effective functioning of UNIFIL thereafter, was apparent. The mandate ultimately agreed did not reflect the problems associated with the presence of the PLO in southern Lebanon and the Israeli determination to occupy part of this by proxy.[20] Rather, Resolution 425 defined the UNIFIL mandate in the following terms:

- confirming the withdrawal of Israeli forces;
- restoring international peace and security; and
- assisting the government of Lebanon in ensuring the return of its effective authority in the area.

The fact that the debate and Resolution 425 ignored the Palestinian problem, and the need for a comprehensive settlement of the overall Middle East question, caused many members to vacillate in their express

---

[18] The full terms of Resolution 425 are set out in Appendix 1 below.

[19] G. Tueni, *Une guerre pour les autres* (Paris: Jean Claude Lattes, 1985), pp. 200–4. Mr Tueni was Lebanon's Ambassador to the UN at the time.

[20] B. Urquhart, *A Life in Peace and War* (London: Weidenfeld and Nicolson, 1987), p. 289.

support for UNIFIL. In the event, the establishment of a peacekeeping force with ambiguous and unrealistic objectives and terms of reference was agreed to hastily in order to solve the immediate crisis.[21]

The urgency of reaching some agreement on the crisis precluded consideration of a more long-term solution. It is hardly surprising, therefore, that UNIFIL encountered major difficulties in implementing its mandate. This same urgency was also the main determinant in deciding the extent to which the United States consulted with other members of the Security Council and the parties involved in the conflict. The exact extent of the consultations with Israel is not known but, as the United States' most reliable ally in the region, it was undoubtedly both informed and consulted on the initiative. It is also evident that Israel was not happy with all of its aspects but was forced to succumb to American pressure; as a result Resolution 425 was greatly resented in Israel.[22]

The Lebanese government had requested that the United States sponsor the peacekeeping initiative, as it realised that America was the only country likely to be able to bring about sufficient Israeli co-operation. This premise was certainly true; however, the Lebanese government seems to have overlooked the dilemma that this would create for the United States as guardian both of Israeli and Lebanese interests. The Lebanese appeared to have exaggerated their own importance in American foreign policy.[23] Moreover, even though relations between Israel and the United States were often turbulent, the Lebanese government may also have underestimated the influence of the Jewish community in the United States.

The early years of UNIFIL's deployment also coincided with a series of crises in American foreign policy. First, the Iranian Revolution took place. Then the seizure of the American hostages in Teheran occurred.

---

[21] In this regard, the Secretary-General had this to say: '[W]hen a peacekeeping operation is firmly based on a detailed agreement between the parties in conflict and they are prepared to abide by that agreement, it is relatively easy to maintain . . . (e.g. UNEF and UNDOF) . . . [W]hen, however, an operation is mounted in an emergency with ambiguous or controversial objectives and terms of reference, and on assumptions which are not wholly realistic, it is likely to present far greater difficulties. This is undoubtedly the case with UNIFIL.' K. Waldheim, in R. Schiffer (ed.), *Building the Future Order* (London: Collier Macmillan, 1980), p. 45.

[22] C. Cruise O'Brien, *The Siege: The Saga of Israel and Zionism* (London: Weidenfeld and Nicolson, 1986), p. 584. See also N. A. Pelcovits, *Peacekeeping on Arab-Israeli Fronts* (Boulder and London: Westview Press and Foreign Policy Institute, 1984), p. 18.

[23] E. E. Azar and K. Shnayerson, 'United States–Lebanese Relations: A Pocketful of Paradoxes', in E. E. Azar (ed.), *The Emergence of a New Lebanon: Fantasy or Reality* (New York: Praeger, 1984), pp. 219–75. See also H. Kissinger, *Years of Upheaval* (London: Weidenfeld and Nicolson, 1982), p. 792; and O'Brien, *The Siege*, pp. 400–3.

This series of related events, along with the Soviet invasion of Afghanistan, preoccupied the final fourteen months of President Carter's term in office, much to the detriment of other significant foreign policy issues.[24] In particular, it meant that little attention was paid to the peacekeeping force in Lebanon. Consultation with certain parties was also difficult. While Resolution 425 (1978) specifically mentioned Israel and Lebanon, it did not refer to the PLO which was not recognised as an official party to the conflict. However, the co-operation of the PLO was necessary to ensure the success of UNIFIL. The PLO's initial reaction was critical of the failure to tackle what it perceived as the real problem in the Middle East, namely, the question of Palestine.[25] In spite of this, the leadership did give certain assurances; yet serious problems later arose when PLO elements refused to co-operate, and clashes occurred when UNIFIL attempted to deploy in areas controlled by the PLO.[26]

When the proposal to establish UNIFIL was made, the situation was not unlike that of Somalia, in that some senior UN officials expressed strong reservations regarding the UN assuming such a role.[27] There was grave concern at some of the assumptions upon which the United States policy was based. An Israeli withdrawal from all of south Lebanon was central to the success of UNIFIL's mission, yet it was not clear that Israel would co-operate fully. How was a peacekeeping force to restore Lebanese government authority to an area where it was non-existent, when the Lebanese army was divided and the government concerned probably could not maintain control for very long anyway? There was also no clear policy as to how the peacekeeping force would deal with the various armed elements or what action it would take if the Israelis did not withdraw completely. A resolution establishing a peacekeeping force in a region of such conflicting American and Soviet interests had to be a delicate balance of political pressure and persuasion. A minor change in emphasis risked causing either superpower to exercise its right of veto. Further, a prolonged discussion could therefore have jeopardised the whole initiative.[28]

---

[24] H. Jordan, *Crisis: The Last Year of the Carter Presidency* (New York: G. P. Putnam's Sons, 1982); Reich and Hollis, 'Peacekeeping', pp. 133–4.

[25] Interview, Lt-Gen. Erskine, Dublin, July 1986.

[26] UN Doc. S/12620/Add.4, 5 May 1978.

[27] I. J. Rikhye, *The Theory and Practice of Peacekeeping* (London: Hurst and Co., 1984), p. 109.

[28] United Nations, *The Blue Helmets*, pp. 88–9.

Security Council fails to support UNIFIL

As established, the Secretary-General outlined three essential conditions which had to be met in order for UNIFIL to be effective.[29] The requirements were the full confidence and backing of the Security Council and of all the parties concerned as well as the ability to function as an integrated and efficient military unit. These could be said to be essential conditions for any peacekeeping force. The fact that the Secretary-General felt constrained to expressly state them in this manner indicated that he was concerned some of the conditions might not be fulfilled.

The most important of these conditions is that a force receives the full backing of the members of the Security Council, in particular the permanent members who propose or support its establishment. The Secretary-General is responsible for the implementation of the decisions of the Council. Once established, the overall direction of the operation is the Secretary-General's responsibility, acting on behalf of and answerable to the Security Council. The significance of proper support from the Council cannot be overstated, yet this support has not always been forthcoming and is often too ambivalent in nature. The serious problems that this can cause were evident during the UN peacekeeping operation in the Congo (ONUC, 1960–4).[30] Within three months of the establishment of ONUC, the consensus among the permanent members of the Security Council had disintegrated, and this placed the Secretary-General in an impossible position. In the case of UNIFIL, some eight years after this pivotal requirement for the success of the mission was highlighted, the Secretary-General declared that it had not been fully met.[31] This unusual step of openly criticising the organ to which he is personally responsible is indicative of the frustration felt after many years of trying to make UNIFIL work, while the reasons for failure were outside of his control.

The Secretary-General refrained from criticising any particular member of the Council; however, the Soviet Union abstained from voting on every

---

[29] UN Doc. S/12611, 19 March 1978, was approved by Security Council Resolution 426, 19 March 1978.

[30] D. W. Bowett, *United Nations Forces* (London: Stevens and Sons, 1964), p. 160. At one stage, in answer to criticism of his handling of ONUC, the Secretary-General reminded the Security Council that it was their responsibility to 'indicate what you want to be done . . . but if no advice is forthcoming . . . then I have no choice but to follow my own conviction'. GAOR, 15th Session, 871st Plenary Meeting, p. 96.

[31] UN Doc. S/17965, 9 April 1986, para. 51.

resolution concerning UNIFIL from 1978 until April 1986.[32] From the beginning, the Soviet Union maintained that it was not satisfied with the mandate. It disagreed with UNIFIL's function in assisting with the return of effective Lebanese government authority in the area as well as with the absence of a time limit on the force's stay in Lebanon. Yet, in 1986, in an attempt to regain some of its lost credibility, the Soviet Union did a U-turn and announced that the force had an important role to play in confirming the Israeli withdrawal. It saw an opportunity to play a more meaningful role, since the decline in America's fortunes in Lebanon and the Middle East. The United States' support for the Israeli Lebanon Agreement of 1983, and the debacle of its involvement in Lebanon, weakened the American position.[33] The key to US influence in the area, especially since 1973, had been the American role as mediator in the Arab–Israeli peace process. A central element in the Soviet Union's policy at the time was the reconvening of an international conference, where it could occupy a position equal to the United States, and all parties to the Middle East conflict, including the PLO, could attend.[34]

The Soviet Union's influence in the region had been receding for some time, and it declined further as a result of the 1982 Israeli invasion of Lebanon, when its credibility was undermined by its failure to respond to appeals from the PLO and Syria for aid. Its warnings to the United States not to commit its forces had been ignored and Soviet weaponry again proved qualitatively inferior to the American equivalent. In a lame response during this period, the Soviet Union attempted to exploit the propaganda value of resorting to the Security Council to bring pressure upon the Israelis to withdraw. In this way, they achieved the optimum result. They avoided the danger of direct involvement, while at the same time drawing attention to American support for Israel and United States vetoes of certain resolutions in the Security Council.

---

[32] The Soviet Union voted in favour of Resolutions 508 (1982), 509 (1982), 512 (1982), 513 (1982), 515 (1982), 516 (1982), 517 (1982), 518 (1982), 520 (1982) and 521 (1982) which condemned Israel and called for a withdrawal from Lebanon. However, it continued to abstain on the vote for a renewal of the UNIFIL mandate during this period when Resolutions 511 (1982), 519 (1982) and 523 (1982) were adopted.

[33] See K. Nakhleh and C. A. Wright, *After the Palestine Israel War: Limits to US and Israeli Policy* (Belmont, MA: Institute of Arab Studies, 1983).

[34] See R. O. Freedman, *Soviet Policy Toward the Middle East Since 1970* (3rd edn, New York: Praeger, 1982); and R. O. Freedman, 'The Soviet Union and a Middle East Peace Settlement: A Case Study of Soviet Policy During the Israeli Invasion of Lebanon and Its Aftermath', in Marantz and Stein (eds.), *Peacemaking in the Middle East*, pp. 156–68.

The situation after the Israeli redeployment in 1986 could have enabled the Soviet Union to further erode the role of the United States in the region, and thereby enhance its own influence. However, Soviet policy in the Middle East was overtaken by events in Eastern Europe and what is now Russia. It is probable that the Soviet Union's conversion to the cause of UNIFIL did not stem from a genuine interest in the plight of Lebanon. In this regard, its policy was similar to that of the United States. Lebanon was perceived by both superpowers not as an end in itself, but as a means to gaining influence and power in the region as a whole. Even if the political will existed to pressure Israel to co-operate with UNIFIL, it is doubtful that the backlash from the American Jewish community could have been endured by any United States President for a sufficient period to allow this pressure to be effective.

Lack of co-operation from the parties in Lebanon

As to the second condition identified by the Secretary-General as essential for the effective operation of UNIFIL, namely, the full co-operation of the parties concerned, many of the parties did not co-operate as anticipated or as promised. In particular, the Israelis and their allies in south Lebanon, known generally as the *de facto* forces or the 'South Lebanon Army', deliberately harassed UNIFIL and prevented it from carrying out its mandate. Some of the problems that arose in the field of party co-operation are directly related to assumptions made concerning the deployment of the force. The ill-defined reference to an area of operation was the most serious such flaw. While it was impossible for the mandate to be more specific, as contemporary discussions in the Security Council and consultations with the governments of Israel and Lebanon revealed profound disagreement, the ambiguity caused major problems when UNIFIL attempted to deploy in certain areas where the PLO maintained strongholds and from which the Israeli Defence Forces withdrew without handing over to UNIFIL.

The dangers of not defining the precise area of operation became evident when UNIFIL troops from the French contingent attempted to deploy around key PLO strongholds.[35] The PLO put up significant resistance which was combined with a diplomatic campaign on their behalf by Arab states at the UN. The PLO objected to UNIFIL's deployment in these areas because they had never been occupied by the Israeli

---

[35] UN Doc. S/12845, 13 September 1978, paras. 36–8; and United Nations, *The Blue Helmets*, pp. 88–9.

Defence Forces. As, during the invasion, this area, known as the 'Tyre pocket', was bypassed, the PLO considered that UNIFIL should not be deployed there. The matter was complicated by the 'Cairo Agreement' which legitimised the PLO's presence in Lebanon and supposedly governed its activities there.

At the time, the Force Commander and the Lebanese government were in favour of taking stronger action against the PLO. However, UNIFIL was not a combat or enforcement mission, and, tellingly, the PLO stronghold had been bypassed by the much more militarily capable Israeli Defence Forces. Furthermore, UNIFIL was a very precarious political creation and it is almost certain that the Soviet Union, and the pro-Palestinian lobby at the UN, would have strenuously objected to such action. UNIFIL was a peacekeeping mission and, as such, it relied on the co-operation of the parties concerned. Any problem of this nature had to be resolved by negotiation, however unsatisfactory a subsequent agreement turned out to be. It is no surprise that deployment in the area 'was not pressed'.[36] Later, the Secretary-General was able to report that relations with the PLO in the area had not created major problems,[37] but the agreement did have its drawbacks and propaganda value to those opposed to UNIFIL. It also provided the *de facto* forces with an ideal excuse for refusing to allow UNIFIL to deploy in the area under their control.

Initially, it appeared that Israel would withdraw fully from Lebanon and that some kind of working relationship could be established with the *de facto* forces of Major Haddad. It quickly became apparent to Irish officers serving with UNIFIL, however, that these forces were armed, trained and financed by the Israelis. There was also a suspicion that the Israelis would not co-operate with UNIFIL in their final withdrawal, despite the smooth execution of the first three phases. Unfortunately, the Lebanese government and the UN then made a major error in judgment when Major Haddad was provisionally recognised as *de facto* commander of the Lebanese forces for the purpose of facilitating UNIFIL's mission. As Haddad was essentially a renegade officer under Israeli tutelage, this put UNIFIL in a difficult position and compromised the effort to implement the mandate.

In the circumstances, the Secretary-General had no option but to reach some accommodation with the PLO. If a firm stance had been

---

[36] UN Doc. S/12845, 13 September 1978, para. 37.
[37] UN Doc. S/12929, 18 November 1978, para. 18.

taken against the PLO at this stage, it would have been equally important to take similar action against the *de facto* forces. It is probable that neither the United States, nor the Soviet Union, would have been willing to support such a policy in the Security Council. Moreover, many of the contributing countries, including Ireland, would have been unwilling to continue supplying troops to a force suffering the number of casualties that offensive action of this nature would entail. It would also have been incompatible with the respective foreign policies of some troop-contributing countries, as well as being clearly outside the terms of reference of UNIFIL that it would only act in self-defence.

As events unfolded, it became clear that the Israelis and Major Haddad's forces would not co-operate with UNIFIL. There were strong objections to the agreements concluded with the PLO.[38] If the UN did not take full control of the PLO territory, then it would not be permitted to deploy in the areas controlled by the *de facto* forces. From their perspective, UNIFIL was allowing the PLO to re-establish itself in its area. This was not true, but, having backed down from confronting the PLO, it was not unreasonable to assume it would do so again in this case.

By the time the Lebanese government decided to revoke the provisional recognition given to Major Haddad, much valuable time and ground had been lost. As far as Israel was concerned, it had fulfilled its part in the implementation of Resolutions 425 and 426 (1978), which, it was claimed, did not require control of any area to be turned over to UNIFIL.[39] This was a narrow and erroneous interpretation of the resolutions in question and failed to receive the support of even the United States. The scene was then set for further hostilities. Over the following years, the *de facto* forces not only harassed UNIFIL, but indiscriminately shelled and fired on its positions. They also attempted to seize UN positions, and were indifferent to the safety of both UN and civilian personnel.

---

[38] Letter dated 13 June 1978, from the representative of Israel to the Secretary-General, UN Doc. S/12736. For the Secretary-General's description of the 'accommodation' reached with the PLO, see UN Doc. S/12845, 13 September 1978, paras. 39–42. It was agreed, *inter alia*, that UNIFIL would only deploy in areas physically used or held by the Israeli Defence Forces, and that armed PLO elements (approximately 140 in six positions) in the UNIFIL area would be allowed to remain but these would not be used for military purposes.

[39] UN Doc. S/12840, letter dated 8 September 1978, from the representative of Israel to the Secretary-General.

The case of Somalia

Peacekeeping in Somalia, if that is the correct term, was complex and difficult. In effect it was a mixture of peacekeeping, peace-making, peace enforcement and nation-building. There were so many changes in direction and strategic goals that it is not possible to generalise. Somalia brought the terms 'mission creep' and crossing the 'Mogadishu line' into the everyday vernacular of commentators and observers. With the full backing of the United States, the Secretary-General and the Security Council embarked on an expansive and ambitious programme which many in Somalia perceived as an attempt to establish a *de facto* trusteeship. The result of these series of UN military engagements was to bequeath a legacy that would profoundly affect United States and UN policy on peacekeeping thereafter.[40]

The UN was deeply involved in Somalia, particularly in the field of humanitarian assistance, well before it ever considered deploying military observers and peacekeepers in 1992. Although there is a long history to the conflict, it was the overthrow of the regime of Said Barre in January 1991 that marked a significant stage in the deterioration of the overall situation there.[41] The withdrawal of UN relief agencies in early 1991 was a fatal decision for the people of Somalia. At that stage, although lawlessness and anarchy were rampant, famine was not widespread. The necessity for some form of non-coercive intervention by the UN to prevent the humanitarian situation from worsening was obvious.[42]

The slow response of the UN inevitably meant lost opportunities for mediation and preventive diplomacy at an earlier stage. Such approaches have a fairly good chance of success without great expense or the

---

[40] See generally, I. Daalder, 'Knowing When to Say No: The Development of US Policy for Peacekeepers', and W. Durch, 'Keeping the Peace: Politics and Lessons of the 1990s', in W. Durch (ed.), *Peacekeeping, American Policy, and the Uncivil Wars of the 1990s* (New York: Macmillan, 1997), pp. 1–34, and 35–68, respectively; and T. Farrell, 'Sliding into War: The Somalia Imbroglio and US Army Peace Operations Doctrine' (1995) 2(2) *International Peacekeeping* 194–214.

[41] Abdullahi, 'Fiasco in Somalia', pp. 1–11; United Nations, *The United Nations and Somalia*, pp. 9–13; Human Rights Watch/Africa, 'Somalia Faces the Future: Human Rights in a Fragmented Society' (1995) 7(2) *Africa Report* 13–16; and Lee V. Cassanelli, 'Somali Land Resources Issues in Historical Perspective', in W. Clarke and J. Herbst (eds.), *Learning from Somalia* (Boulder: Westview Press, 1997), pp. 67–76.

[42] See T. Deagle, 'Famine Threatens Somali Capital as Thousands of Refugees Flock in', *The Times*, 23 May 1991, p. 11. See also Abdullahi, 'Fiasco in Somalia', pp. 8–9.

need for a large military presence.[43] However, the lack of an early and effective response must be considered in the context of contemporaneous events. Despite the end of the Cold War, the UN continued to face crippling financial difficulties and its peacekeeping role was overstretched dealing with, among others, major events in the former Yugoslavia and in Cambodia. Moreover, intervention in a civil war or internal conflict situation presents special difficulties, which explains in large part the view of those at UN headquarters that its response should be limited to delivering humanitarian aid. This position was also significantly influenced by the United States and Russian reluctance to become involved. In fact, the possibility of a peacekeeping or similar initiative by the UN was not even considered at first as the issue of state sovereignty hampered efforts to decide on a plan of action. There was no government to request assistance or give its consent, and intervention was not favoured by the then Organization of African Unity.

In early 1992, in a somewhat belated attempt to respond to the crisis, the Security Council adopted Resolution 733 (1992) which imposed a mandatory arms embargo and strongly urged the various armed factions to observe a cease-fire.[44] It still amounted to a less than enthusiastic response from the Security Council, and the resolution was little more than an expanded humanitarian and diplomatic effort. In a country awash with weaponry of all kinds, such a resolution was bound to have little practical effect, although it did create the impression that the international community was responding to the crisis.

Early mediation efforts had limited success but did secure agreement on a cease-fire between the leaders of two major factions, General Aideed and Ali Mahdi, and the deployment of a UN technical team. Although any agreement on a cease-fire was welcome, the pact in question was vague in some crucial respects. In particular, it was unclear as to the warring factions included and left most of the country unaffected.[45] It also had the unintended effect of focusing on Mogadishu to the detriment of the remainder of the country and it may have even intensified the rivalry for control between Aideed and Mahdi in the city. As parties to the agreement, it allowed each to claim legitimacy through

---

[43] Mohamed Sahnoun, *Somalia: The Missed Opportunities* (Washington DC, US Institute of Peace, 1994), pp. 5–11.

[44] Resolution 733 of 23 January 1992, paras. 4 and 5.

[45] This cease-fire was signed in New York on 14 February 1992. Signatories represented the 'Interim Government of Somalia' and the Central Committee of the United Somali Congress, Security Council Doc. S/23693, 11 March 1992.

dealing with the UN. Local clan leaders and elders felt excluded from the process, and concluded that the problems of the remainder of the country were not recognised.[46] This factor complicated the UN's later task of rebuilding the state which would ideally involve all of the parties in negotiations.

Although the policy of dealing with leaders like Aideed and Mahdi was based on pragmatic considerations owing to limited options, it ignored each man's record as leader of a group responsible for serious breaches of human rights and humanitarian law during the conflict.[47] The UN's emphasis on the importance of a good working relationship with all the parties may be a barrier to confronting recalcitrant leaders effectively.[48] Worse still was the inconsistency of the policy throughout the period. Such shifts did little to inspire confidence among traditional Somali leaders and elders, and must have been somewhat bewildering for the 'warleaders' as well. There were other, less obvious factors at play in the lead up to UN intervention. Aideed was opposed to any deployment of UN personnel and to a cease-fire. He perceived these as means of freezing the *status quo* and preventing him from defeating Mahdi, which he considered he was in a position to do in a relatively short time. There was also significant historical animosity between Aideed and the new Secretary-General which went back to the time when Boutros Boutros-Ghali was the Egyptian minister responsible for foreign policy and the Egyptian government supported the Said Barre regime. This 'baggage', or personality factor, was to significantly influence events throughout the period of UN involvement.

Deployment of UNOSOM I

As the situation in Somalia during early 1992 continued to deteriorate, the need for some form of intervention to improve the security situation became even more imperative. Aid workers and the general population were being terrorised, and there were reports of crop failures in the agriculturally rich region to the south. It was against this background

---

[46] Personal interview, Ambassador Sahnoun, Dublin, November 1993. Aideed also manipulated Jonah's visit so that no contact was made with neutral clans such as the Murasade who had played a central role in resolving earlier fighting. Jonah may also have compromised UN neutrality by declaring Aideed the greatest obstacle to a cease-fire in the war: see Africa Watch, 'A Fight to the Death?' (13 February 1993), pp. 7–10.

[47] Human Rights Watch/Africa, 'Somalia Faces the Future', pp. 17–32.

[48] See S. Stedman and D. Rothchild, 'Peace Operations: From Short Term to Long Term Commitment' (1996) 3(2) *International Peacekeeping* 17–35 at 24.

that Mohamed Sahnoun was appointed the Special Representative of the Secretary-General (SRSG) in Somalia, and soon afterwards the first UNOSOM ('UNOSOM I') mission was established.[49] Resolution 751 (1992) was the legal basis for the UN's attempt to deploy a small number of cease-fire observers and a small force of security personnel for the protection of humanitarian relief operations in the capital. Though such a move was certainly warranted, it was likely to be considered threatening by Aideed and had not been endorsed by him.[50]

The deployment was based on traditional peacekeeping premises, i.e. the consent of the parties to the conflict. However, this was a failed state and the application of conventional thinking and methods was inappropriate. Not surprisingly, there was poor co-operation from some factions and outright opposition from others, leading to long delays in the deployment of these units and a consensus that it would be completely ineffective. The linking of action to the agreement of the warlords at a time when Somalis were starving damaged the credibility of the UN in the eyes of Somali people. It was also an abdication by the Security Council of its responsibility and a lost opportunity for early intervention. Agreement and consensus is preferable, but, given the humanitarian crisis, a deadline should have been set for intervention to impose a cease-fire and secure humanitarian aid.

The first Bush administration had initially opposed the deployment of 500 armed troops as it was concerned at the escalating cost of peacekeeping in an election year, despite the fact that the overall cost was small in comparison with other operations.[51] This was an untenable position to adopt and, in the circumstances, it is not surprising that the Secretary-General grew frustrated at what he saw as the West's preoccupation with 'a rich man's war' in the Balkans, while it was prepared to

---

[49] Security Council Resolution 751, 24 April 1992. It is referred to as UNOSOM I to distinguish it from the later UNOSOM II mission. Sahnoun was an experienced Algerian diplomat. See also 'Security Council New UN Operation in Somalia' (1992) 29(3) UN Chronicle 12–15 at 14.

[50] In the Secretary-General's report (S/23929, para. 23), he noted 'that under the Agreements [with Aideed] the UN is to consult the parties before determining the number of security personnel required for the protection function'.

[51] The operation was to be established for an initial period of six months, at an estimated cost of US$23.1 million (UN Doc. S/23829 and Adds. 1 and 2). See also W. Throsell, 'If Sarajevo, Why Not Somalia?', Globe and Mail, 22 July 1992, p. A18. Bush was also concerned at his perception as having more interest in foreign than domestic policy in an election year: P. Lewis, 'Reined in by US, UN Limits Mission to Somalia', New York Times, 26 April 1992, p. 15.

ignore the plight of the people of Somalia.[52] In the event, Resolution 751 (1992) approved, in principle, the Secretary-General's plan to deploy as soon as possible a 500-person armed security force to escort deliveries of humanitarian supplies to distribution centres.

In July, the Secretary-General reported that, while the cease-fire had held reasonably well, banditry and looting had become more widespread in Mogadishu, and attacks on UN and non-governmental personnel were on the increase. The maintenance of the cease-fire was largely a result of Sahnoun's considerable diplomatic effort, but the UN bureaucracy could not keep up with the pace of the humanitarian disaster. It was evident that the situation continued to be critical, and, in an effort to begin the process of rebuilding the Somali state, the SRSG had begun negotiations with traditional elders and political leaders.[53] Sahnoun's delegation pursued a strategy of putting the clan system to work for Somalia.[54] This bottom-up approach has much to recommend[55] and it was a means of restoring the political balance in favour of more traditional leadership, which had been consistently urged on UNOSOM by the Uppsala Advisory Group.[56]

The slow response of the UN may indeed have been the result of structural rigidity.[57] But the scale and complexity of the problem meant that the UN had no precedent to follow. Should the UN deal with the warlords and, if so, in what way? There were no political structures in Somalia, and physical infrastructure was almost non-existent. In Resolution 767 (1992), the Security Council approved the establishment

---

[52] B. Boutros-Ghali, *Unvanquished*, p. 55; and E. Sciolino, 'UN Chief Has to Direct Peace Efforts at US, Too', *New York Times*, 16 October 1993, p. A1.

[53] *Report of the Secretary-General on the Situation in Somalia*, UN Doc. S/24343, 22 July 1992, especially paras. 21, 22 and 63. The sheer scale of the crisis was evident from Sahnoun's report to the donors' conference convened in Geneva on 12 October 1992, quoted in M. Sahnoun, *Somalia, the Missed Opportunities* (Washington DC: United States Institute of Peace, 1994), pp. 27–9.

[54] S. Normak, 'Building Local Political Institutions: District and Regional Councils', paper to the Comprehensive Seminar on Lessons Learned from the UN Operation in Somalia, Lessons Learned Unit, Department of Peacekeeping Operations, Plainsboro, NJ, 13–15 September 1995, p. 3; and W. Clarke, 'Failed Visions and Uncertain Mandates in Somalia', in Clarke and Herbst (eds.), *Learning from Somalia*, pp. 3–19 at p. 7.

[55] Interview, International Concern worker in Somalia at the time, Galway, Ireland, January 1999. See also W. Durch, 'Introduction to Anarchy, Humanitarian Intervention and "State Building" in Somalia', in Durch (ed.), *Peacekeeping*, pp. 310–565 at p. 316.

[56] This was based in the Horn of Africa Centre of Life and Peace Institute of Uppsala. It was comprised of a number of social scientists with expertise on Somalia drawn from a number of countries.

[57] Interview, M. Sahnoun, Dublin, Ireland, 26 November 1993.

of four operational zones with the hope that UN involvement would adapt to the complexity of the situation and enhance the effectiveness of humanitarian operations.[58] This decentralised system made UNOSOM and the relief agencies less dependent on the conditions prevailing in Mogadishu and promoted the new regional leadership which was badly needed by Somalia. Another technical team was sent to assess how best to use UN security guards to protect aid workers and to convene a conference on national reconciliation. Whether it was strictly necessary to dispatch this additional team is a moot question now, but it is strange that the Secretary-General did not rely more on his own SRSG in Somalia at this time. Sahnoun had the confidence of the non-governmental organisations (NGOs) and local elders, though in doing so he was earning the ire of the UN bureaucracy.[59]

Owing to the inexcusable delay in deploying the 500 troops agreed, the security environment had worsened. The actual plan to establish a traditional peacekeeping operation with the mandate to use force, if necessary, to protect the food convoys was well conceived. The decentralised concept and the engagement of regional organisations and all Somali factions in control of territory had much merit. Had it been successful it would have cost very little in comparison with what was to follow. The truth is that UNOSOM I was never really given a chance to succeed. Several serious problems were created by incorrect and unjustified moves on behalf of the UN management, both at headquarters and by some agencies' representatives in the field.[60] These hampered Sahnoun's efforts leading to strained relations; but his primary sin in the eyes of the UN hierarchy was to make his views known publicly. After 'arduous negotiations', and with the help of local elders, Sahnoun obtained the consent of Aideed, Mahdi and other faction leaders to the deployment of the 500 armed UN 'security personnel' to protect

---

[58] Resolution 767, adopted 24 July 1992. The four zones were Bossaso, Berbera, Kismayu and Mogadishu. It also called for co-operation in the deployment of the 500-person security force agreed to in Resolution 751 (1992), paras. 4–5.

[59] Personal interview, International Concern worker in Somalia at the time, Galway, Ireland, January 1999. Sahnoun was particularly critical of the UN relief agency efforts, and he believed that not enough had been done to establish the necessary distribution networks. As a result, those who co-operated with his reconciliation efforts could see no tangible improvements in their living conditions. See W. Durch, 'Introduction to Anarchy, Humanitarian Intervention and "State Building" in Somalia', in Durch (ed.), *Peacekeeping*, pp. 310–565 at p. 316.

[60] M. Sahnoun, 'Prevention in Conflict Resolution: The Case of Somalia' (1994) 5 *Irish Studies in International Affairs* 5–13 at 10.

aid coming through Mogadishu port. This was not the victory it seemed, as Aideed and others probably realised that the aid could be hijacked as soon as it left the port anyway. However, before these individuals even touched down in Somalia, the Security Council agreed, at the request of the Secretary-General, to increase the size of the force to 3,500.[61]

Unfortunately, Sahnoun was neither consulted nor informed of the decision in advance, thus undermining his authority and causing him to appear duplicitous in the eyes of Aideed. From the point of view of the Secretary-General, it was a logical progression given the deteriorating situation in Somalia but Aideed was enraged by the lack of any consultation, and it added to his sense of insecurity at the growing UN involvement. Furthermore, the leaders of the neighbouring countries, who had been supportive to date and kept informed of events by Sahnoun, were also ignored. This was probably the most significant example of the bureaucratic approach of UN headquarters, and its tendency to ignore UNOSOM's advice in regard to sensitive matters, especially those related to security.

An additional incident was also to have a profound impact on the trust gained by UNOSOM and the UN up to that point: it became known that a Russian plane with UN markings, chartered by a UN agency, delivered currency and military equipment to Aideed's major rival in the north, Mahdi. It later transpired that the plane was doing some unauthorised 'moonlighting'. A proper investigation should have been held into the incident and appropriate action taken. It added to the difficulties of the UN personnel on the ground. The delivery of arms was also in direct contravention of Security Council Resolution 733 (1992), which imposed a 'general and complete embargo on all deliveries of weapons and military equipment to Somalia'. The incident rekindled all of the earlier fears about a partisan UN approach to the conflict, and, although false, the rumours and circumstantial evidence were not rebutted in the proper way. Unfortunately, the criticism of the UN handling of this incident and other issues by Sahnoun did not help his already troubled relationship with headquarters.[62]

At around the same time, the United States was beginning to take a more active interest in Somalia, as reflected in the Department of State's public statement in favour of dispatching armed UN security elements.

---

[61] Resolution 775, 28 August 1992, para. 3.

[62] Sahnoun resigned after losing the confidence and support of the Secretary-General: Interview with Sahnoun. See also Sahnoun, *Somalia: The Missed Opportunities*, p. 40. For a less sympathetic perspective, see Boutros-Ghali, *Unvanquished*, p. 56.

This was the first indication of American approval of a more proactive security policy since the crisis began. The Bush administration and public opinion were beginning to come around to the point of view that something radical needed to be done. The sequence of events leading to the first dramatic humanitarian intervention led by the United States in Somalia was set in motion.

Options facing the Secretary-General and the deployment of UNITAF

UN intervention in Somalia arose from the urgent need to respond to the famine and appalling suffering of the Somali people. The response was slow and deliberate; each Security Council resolution expanded and modified the role of UNOSOM. As the situation deteriorated and the operation floundered in late 1992, the Secretary-General faced up to the dilemma and outlined five options.[63] The first was to continue with a peacekeeping, i.e. consensual and non-forceful mission. This option did not seem viable, given the scale of the problems. A second option was to withdraw, but this would have been an unacceptable public admission of failure that might also have been interpreted as setting a bad precedent for ongoing operations in the Balkans. A further option was to be more assertive and forceful in the capital, in the hope that this would have an influence in the country as a whole. Alternatively, a UN enforcement mission could be launched under its own command and control. However, it is unlikely that the UN possessed either the capability or capacity to do so, then or now. Not surprisingly, when the United States indicated that it would be prepared to spearhead a UN-sanctioned forceful mission to establish a secure environment for humanitarian operations, the Security Council agreed.

Initially, the United States had been reluctant to become involved. Then Secretary-General Boutros Boutros-Ghali put pressure on the first President Bush, pointing out, among other things, the perception that the United States manipulated the UN only when it served its own interests, as in the First Gulf War. While the United States was prepared to act unilaterally, they were understandably anxious to have international support on the ground and in the Security Council. As there was to be no dilution of US command and control of the operation, the Secretary-General declined to permit the forces deployed to wear the 'blue helmets' traditionally worn by peacekeepers, and the troops that

---

[63] UN Doc. S/24868 dated 30 November 1992.

participated in the Korean war. It seems that the actual decision to intervene was taken by the President Bush. No doubt this decision was influenced by criticism from non-governmental agencies, Capitol Hill and the Clinton camp. But it was probably also a conclusion by the military that they could 'do the job' if called upon that had most influence on the President. The decision was generally popular with the American public and Congress, and endorsed by President-elect Clinton.[64] Nevertheless, even before the operation was mounted there were those who questioned its appropriateness.[65] In any event, it should have been evident that the conflict was not going to be of the short, sharp, overwhelming kind that politicians and military planners believe is vital to sustain a public consensus for involvement.

In December 1992, acting under Chapter VII, the Security Council unanimously adopted Resolution 794 which included the following preambular and operative paragraphs:

> Recognizing the unique character of the present situation in Somalia and mindful of its deteriorating, complex and extraordinary nature, requiring an immediate and exceptional response.
>
> Determining the magnitude of the human tragedy [mass starvation] caused by the conflict in Somalia, further exacerbated by the obstacles being created to the distribution of human assistance, constitutes a threat to international peace and security.
>
> . . .
>
> 7. Endorses the recommendation of the Secretary-General ... that action under Chapter VII ... should be taken in order to establish a secure environment for humanitarian relief operations in Somalia as soon as possible;
>
> 8. Welcomes the offer made by a Member State [the United States] ... concerning the establishment of an operation to create such a secure environment;
>
> 9. Welcomes also offers by other Member States to participate in that operation;

---

[64] J. L. Woods, 'US Decisionmaking During Operations in Somalia', in Clarke and Herbst (eds.), *Learning from Somalia*, p. 158.

[65] Africa Rights, *Operation Restore Hope: A Preliminary Assessment* (London, May 1993). Oxfam America, Oxfam UK and Concern Worldwide supported it, while Médecins Sans Frontiers and Save the Children opposed it: see Save the Children, 'Imposing Troops Could Destroy the Effort', Press Release, 26 November 1992; interview, Concern Worldwide worker in Somalia at the time, Dublin, Ireland, 1999.

> 10. Acting under Chapter VII of the Charter of the UN, authorizes the Secretary-General and Member States cooperating to implement the offer referred to in paragraph 8 above to use all necessary means to establish as soon as possible a secure environment for humanitarian relief operations in Somalia;
>
> 12. Authorizes the Secretary-General and the Member States concerned to make the necessary arrangements for the unified command and control of the forces involved, which will reflect the offer made in paragraph 8 above . . .

In authorising UNITAF, a large multinational force led by the United States, to use 'all necessary means to establish as soon as possible' a secure environment for humanitarian relief operations, the Security Council took an important step in redefining its role in the maintenance of international peace and security.[66] This was a familiar UN euphemism for authorising the use of force and it was in stark contrast to the UN intervention in Lebanon, which occurred along traditional peacekeeping lines and for which there were established precedents. Implicit in the resolution was a recognition that the situation was beyond that to which the normal rules of peacekeeping would apply. Its adoption reflected a new consensus on what constituted a 'threat to peace' justifying military enforcement action under Article 42 of the UN Charter (which provides for measures by air, sea or land forces as may be necessary to maintain or restore international peace and security) by way of a decision of the Security Council or recommendation under Article 39.[67] Article 39 was interpreted as including a humanitarian disaster caused by mass starvation. This was a significant precedent from the more traditional approach to the use of force under Article 42.[68]

---

[66] N. D. White and O. Ulgen, 'The Security Council and the Decentralized Military Option: Constitutionality and Function' (1997) 44(3) *Netherlands International Law Review* 378–413 at 398; see also M. R. Hutchinson, 'Restoring Hope: UN Security Council Resolutions for Somalia and an Expanded Doctrine of Humanitarian Intervention' (1993) 34 *Harvard International Law Journal* 624–40.

[67] Art. 39 states: 'The Security Council shall determine the existence of any threat to the peace, breach of the peace, or act of aggression and shall make recommendations, or decide what measure shall be taken in accordance with Articles 41 and 42, to maintain or restore international peace or security.'

[68] Although the resolution was adopted by a unanimous vote, there was not the same unanimity among the members regarding the significance of the vote. Some seemed reluctant to recognise that they were creating a precedent that could be followed in the future. They stressed the unique nature of the situation in Somalia, and special emphasis was placed on the lack of any government. See SCOR, 47th Session, 3 December 1992.

Like the enabling resolution in respect of UNIFIL, Resolution 794 (1992) was the result of both political and pragmatic considerations and, as such, it was not a perfectly crafted document. It would have been preferable if the objectives of the mandate had been precisely defined and limited in time in order to prepare the way for a return to peace-keeping and post-conflict peace-building. It was ambiguous in certain important respects, but it was clear that, like Resolution 425 (1978), it required the co-operation of the parties in Somalia in order to be effective. It was also evident, in correspondence from him to the Security Council and to President Bush, that the Secretary-General perceived one of the primary objectives of the mission to be the neu-tralisation of the heavy arms of the regular forces of the factions, and the disarmament of irregular forces.[69] In the final draft of the resolution, this objective was dropped in favour of more neutral language, which was more acceptable to all members of the Security Council. This was a significant omission that subsequently contributed to the most impor-tant difference in interpretation of the objectives of the mandate by the United States and the Secretary-General, namely, the issue of disarming the factions.

The Secretary-General had also recommended that the mandate be defined to include a country-wide intervention under UN command and control and a specific time limit within which disarmament would take place, after which the operation would be handed over to UN peacekeeping forces.[70] The Security Council instead opted to authorise a 'unified command and control system' which would reflect the offer made by the United States to manage the operation. In this regard, the Council had little option, as the United States would not accept UN command in almost any circumstances, and certainly not when leading enforcement operations under Chapter VII. For this reason, despite the fact that the UN approved the UNITAF mandate, the UN neither organised nor commanded the troops that were sent to fulfil the man-date. This was one of the most significant differences between UNITAF and the UNOSOM I and II missions. It was also a feature that distinguished

---

[69] UN Doc. S/24868, 30 November 1992; and letter from the Secretary-General to President Bush dated 8 December 1992, reproduced in United Nations, *The United Nations and Somalia*, p. 216.

[70] UN Doc. S/24868, 30 November 1992.

it from the traditional model of command and control adopted for UNIFIL and other peacekeeping operations.[71]

Although there was liaison between the existing UNOSOM force and the Secretary-General's representative on the one hand, and UNITAF on the other, it was evident that the United States was in the driving seat and would determine policy and strategy. This was not as unreasonable an arrangement as might first appear. The United States supplied the majority of the troops and the bulk of the military hardware at its own expense. Furthermore, there had been no misrepresentation by the United States of the terms under which it would command the operation. Resolution 794 (1992) placed emphasis on the establishment of a secure environment that would permit the Security Council to make the necessary decision for a prompt transition to continued peacekeeping operations. There was no mention of a plan or terms of reference as to how this could be achieved. In this regard, the long-term strategic goals of both the UNIFIL and the UNITAF operations were anything but clear from their respective enabling resolutions.

The process of implementation was bound to give rise to varying interpretations that would inevitably lead to political difficulties at the highest level and military dilemmas on the ground. The differences between the approach adopted by the United States and that proposed by the Secretary-General were all too apparent in the latter's first report on UNITAF to the Council.[72] These constituted fundamental disparities that could not be glossed over at a later stage. The United States did not seem to appreciate the nature of UN peacekeeping operations, nor the political and military constraints under which any UN-led operation must function. It further failed to recognise that a force cannot operate under a peace enforcement mandate, even if motivated by humanitarian considerations, and later revert to a traditional peacekeeping role with the consent of the parties. This was even more apparent later when United States forces carried out offensive operations as part of the UNOSOM II mission.

As part of a strategy to alleviate the fears of developing states about major power interference in the internal affairs of other states, the United States was not mentioned by name in Resolution 794 (1992). While this was indicative of the level of political compromise, it amounted to little more

---

[71] It is also noteworthy that the costs of the operation were borne by the countries supplying troops and by the countries that contributed to a voluntary trust fund set up by the Security Council.

[72] UN Doc. S/24992, 19 December 1992.

than a cosmetic exercise that could only prove counterproductive in the long term. It was also contrary to an open and transparent system of decision-making. As 'Operation Restore Hope' was getting into full swing, Boutros Boutros-Ghali promised the people of Somalia that the force would 'feed the starving, protect the defenceless and prepare the way for political economic and social reconstruction'.[73] The Security Council also authorised the United States to deputise on its behalf, and, significantly, linked human rights issues to a threat to international peace and security. Expectations of what might be achieved by American involvement were high in New York and on the ground in Somalia, but, though successful in ensuring delivery of foodstuffs to the starving, UNITAF failed to seize the opportunity to achieve much more at the time.

The dilemma of disarmament and the creation of a safe environment in Somalia

The UNITAF stage of the overall Somalia operation was generally considered successful. Despite UNITAF's Chapter VII mandate, the United States relied heavily on traditional peacekeeping principles. This would have been admirable in another context, but neutralising the clans' heavy weapons and disarmament was essential to creating a secure environment, and achieving the long-term strategy of handing over to a peacekeeping force. It is easy to portray an operation that sets itself limited goals as an unqualified success when it fulfils these narrow objectives. The reality may be somewhat different, especially if the force has the capability to achieve much more. UNITAF was such an operation and in the execution of its mandate it avoided the main obstacles to a long-term restoration of peace.[74]

The American refusal to live up to the consequences of its intervention was especially damaging to this critical issue.[75] With around 30,000 troops under a unified system of command, UNITAF certainly had the capacity to disarm the warlords.[76] But the political rhetoric did not

---

[73] UN Press Release SG/SM/4874, 8 December 1992, and *UN Chronicle*, March 1993, p. 16.

[74] Boutros-Ghali, *Unvanquished*, pp. 59–60. Boutros-Ghali believed that three critical steps were needed: disarming the warring groups, establishing a secure environment and creating a working division of labour between the US and the UN on the ground.

[75] W. Clarke and J. Herbst, 'Somalia and the Future of Humanitarian Intervention' (1996) 75(2) *Foreign Affairs* 70–85 at 75; and Clarke and Herbst (eds.), *Learning from Somalia*, pp. 239–53.

[76] It had a number of well-trained and 'elite' units from European armies such as the French Foreign Legion, Belgian paratroop commandos and Italian paratroopers.

translate into effective action on the ground. In President Bush's own words, 'Our mission is humanitarian, but we will not tolerate armed gangs ripping off their own people ... [Troops] have the authority to take whatever military action is necessary to safeguard the lives of our troops and the lives of Somalia's people.'[77] Instead, it chose to evade this difficult task by requesting that weapons be moved out of the areas 'controlled' by UNITAF to other locations. Although adopting such an approach did avoid confrontation and inevitable casualties, the policy was flawed as a concentrated effort to remove and destroy the Somalis' heavy weapons, including the infamous 'technicals', was an achievable goal at that time that would have laid the ground rules for the subsequent UN operation. It would also have been an ideal way of showing serious intent to restore order. The UN and the Somalis themselves had expected disarmament to take place. UNITAF could also have used the clan leaders' agreement to disarm in the Addis Ababa Accords of March 1993 to argue that it was an impartial force facilitating this agreement. While it is fair to argue that Mogadishu could no more be disarmed than urban areas in Western countries, in order to create a secure environment in which some degree of normality was restored, it was necessary to confiscate weapons carried openly and to seize the infamous 'technicals'. Failure to do so meant the failure to create a secure environment in which some degree of normality was restored, and it ensured that those with the most weapons continued to wield the most power.

At the time the conduct of United States military operations abroad was governed by a zero casualty policy and the decision not to disarm the factions was designed to avoid exposure to risk. The marines commanded the operation and the experience with the Multi-National Forces established to protect civilians and assist the government in Lebanon in the early 1980s had an important influence on their thinking.[78] This type of policy, however, would not have been possible if Resolution 794 (1993) had expressly addressed the crucial issue of disarmament. It may be the case that the United States considered that the planned UN force intended to succeed UNITAF could deal with this issue, but it is hard to accept that they could have been that naive.

The warlords, in particular Aideed, realised that they would not face a serious challenge from UNITAF and that, by biding their time, they would

---

[77] See G. Bush, 'Humanitarian Mission to Somalia: Address to the Nation, Washington DC, December 4, 1992', US Department of State Dispatch 3(49), 7 December 1992.

[78] On MNF I and MNF II, see Thakur, *International Peacekeeping in Lebanon*, pp. 90–103.

later encounter a militarily weaker UN force. There were no long-term strategic or political objectives that might threaten the warlords' supremacy, and it soon became apparent that adopting a wait-and-see policy was the most prudent response until UNITAF left. By the time the United States formally acknowledged that disarmament of the clans was necessary, it was too late. Of the false promises made by UNITAF, it was the claim that it had created a secure environment that really angered the aid agencies. It seemed that, despite pleas by the UN for the force to remain longer, UNITAF wanted to ensure the mission was deemed a success and that the situation was ripe for a handover to UNOSOM II in May 1993.

Although a much less militarily capable force, the mandate of UNOSOM II was both wider and sufficiently imprecise, so as to 'offer many hostages to fortune'.[79] Acting under Chapter VII, the new force was not constrained by the issues of consent or the use of force in self-defence. The 'demands' on disarmament, 'requests' for national reconciliation and the 'consolidation, expansion and maintenance of a secure environment throughout Somalia' contained in Resolution 814 (1993) were easy to make, but later proved impossible to achieve.[80] Among the main problems with disarmament were the related issues of consent and confrontation. Any task of this nature is a delicate balance between co-operation and confrontation. The risks are high, especially with the added dimension of national contingent interpretation of the rules of engagement and differing policies of contributing states. UNOSOM II showed that some national contingents were not prepared to take part in enforcement operations.[81] In addition, delay in weapons control implementations eroded the trust between UNOSOM II and the parties and led to increased boldness on behalf of the warring factions.[82] There are many potential pitfalls in the use of limited force, the most obvious being the likelihood of escalation and loss of control. The Somalia case illustrates how quickly a UN force can slide into combat when enforcing

[79] Resolution 814, 26 March 1993. The quote is from I. Lewis and J. Mayall, 'Somalia', in J. Mayall (ed.), *The New Interventionism* (Cambridge: Cambridge University Press, 1995), pp. 94–225 at p. 94.

[80] Resolution 814, 26 March 1993, Section A, para. 4, and Section B, paras. 7–14. See F. Tanner, 'Weapons Control in Semi-Permissive Environments: A Case for Compellance' (1996) 3(4) *International Peacekeeping* 126–45 at 140.

[81] G. Anderson, 'UNOSOM II: Not Failure: Not Success', in D. Daniel and F. Hayes (eds.), *Beyond Traditional Peacekeeping* (New York: St Martin's Press, 1995), p. 274.

[82] See questionnaires on Somalia, analysed by J. W. Potgieter in *Disarmament and Conflict Resolution Project: Managing Arms in Peace Processes: Somalia* (United Nations Institute for Disarmament Research, 1995), pp. 135–231.

compliance. The stricter rules regarding disarmament enforced by UNOSOM II led to tense relations with the clans. Insecurity and suspicion replaced consent and trust, and, when the organisational confusion surrounding the handover from UNITAF to UNOSOM II was added to the overall situation, the Somalia cease-fire disarmament concept declined rapidly.

Reconciliation and mediation efforts in Somalia and Lebanon

A criticism sometimes made of UN peacekeeping and military intervention is that it 'freezes' the problem but does not solve the underlying causes of conflict. Efforts at national reconciliation and mediation by the UN in Lebanon and Somalia ultimately came to naught, but the varying approaches to nation-building in each case help to explain the fundamental differences between the two operations.

In recent years, operations have tended to be multi-functional in nature and to include a nation-building and national reconciliation policy. In this regard, the mandate(s) governing the UNOSOM mission in Somalia was significantly different from that of UNIFIL. UNOSOM II was, as Boutros-Ghali pointed out, the first operation of its kind. It was not constrained by the issue of consent or by the rules governing the use of force in peacekeeping operations. The mandate for fostering national reconciliation was contained in Resolution 814 (1993), which authorised UNOSOM II, under Chapter VII, 'to assist the people of Somalia to promote and advance political reconciliation'.[83] In fact, national reconciliation was an integral part of UNOSOM's mandate from the beginning. There was no similar mandate in respect of Lebanon and, while assisting the government there in restoring its authority in the area could be interpreted broadly, it did not equate to nation-building or even the facilitation of national reconciliation.

The conflict in Lebanon also had to be seen in a regional context and it was inextricably linked to the wider security and geopolitical concerns in

---

[83] Resolution 814, 26 March 1993, para. 4(c). This was a broad mandate which included: political reconciliation; the building of political and administrative structures; disarmament and demobilisation of fighters; enforcement of the arms embargo from within Somalia; the re-establishment of the Somali police and justice system; the return of refugees and internally displaced persons; demining; and rehabilitation and reconstruction. See generally O. Halim, 'A Peacekeepers Perspective of Peacebuilding in Somalia', in Ginifer (ed.), *Beyond the Emergency*, pp. 70–86.

the Middle East. This made finding a resolution to the conflict difficult and it prevented the UN from playing a significant role in a resolution of the underlying causes of the conflict. For this reason, the UN (and Syria) were effectively excluded from the negotiations leading to the first serious attempt to resolve the conflict since the establishment of UNIFIL, i.e. the Israeli-Lebanon Agreement of 1983. The military and other concessions granted to Israel under the agreement were inconsistent with UNIFIL's mandate. Moreover, by assigning a very minor role to UNIFIL, it appeared to grant a significant victory to Israel. Israeli policy was consistent and well known, but what was surprising was the role of the United States at the time. The United States representative to the UN had supported UNIFIL's continued existence in January of that year, yet the nation then appeared to play a major part in the Agreement that effectively excluded the UN from any real role in southern Lebanon. The Agreement entailed a proposal to ensure the safety of Palestinians in refugee camps was fraught with difficulty and had the potential to involve UNIFIL in Lebanon's factional war in a way similar to that of the Multi-National Force II in Beirut during 1983–4.[84] What would UNIFIL do to gain control in the event of rival Palestinian factions fighting one another in the camps? Would UNIFIL be responsible for ensuring that no militant groups operated from the camps and who would protect those outside the camps? Any request to protect the camps would first have to be made by the Lebanese government. UNIFIL would be there at the behest of the government, but it could lead to the absurd situation where UNIFIL might well be protecting the camps from attacks by legitimate Lebanese forces or forces allied to the government. The plan and agreement in general was not properly thought out and the exclusion of Syria was bound to backfire by precipitating a Soviet veto of any change of mandate in the Security Council.

The United States believed it could convince Syria to accept the agreement, an optimism not shared by UN personnel.[85] The Agreement called for the withdrawal of all foreign forces, thus linking Israeli withdrawal with that of Palestinian and Syrian forces. Syria objected to having its forces

---

[84] Thakur, *International Peacekeeping in Lebanon*, pp. 90–103.

[85] Interview, Lt-Gen. Callaghan, Force Commander, UNIFIL, Dublin, 1998. See J. W. Jabbra and N. W. Jabbra, 'Lebanon, Gateway to Peace?' (1983) 38 *International Journal* 606; and D. Gilmore, *Lebanon: The Fractured Country* (London: Sphere Books, 1984), p. 188. It was also suggested that Syria could only be induced to leave if the US gave a commitment to persuade the Israelis to withdraw from the Golan Heights and the West Bank.

equated with those of Israel, and probably feared the Agreement would diminish in some way its chances of recovering the Golan Heights, a strategic piece of territory between Israel and Syria seized during the 1967 'Six Day War'. The Agreement came to symbolise for Syria and the Lebanese opposition the political advantages gained by the Christian Phalangists as a result of the Israeli invasion. In this way, the failure to acknowledge Syria's vital interests was naive and amounted to a rebuke to the Syrians. Many of the preconditions set for its implementation were unrealistic.[86] The minimum price Syria would have demanded for co-operation was similar concessions in the Bekaa valley to those given to Israel in the south and the withdrawal of Israel from the Golan Heights. Syria's co-operation was essential to the success of the Agreement but, unlike Israel, it was under no pressure to comply. Its lines of supply in Lebanon were relatively short, its army was not suffering casualties from hostile forces, there was no strong domestic or international pressure to withdraw, and other states such as Saudi Arabia continued to give it financial support.

The United States regarded the conclusion of the Agreement as an important aspect of its policy in Lebanon, while Syria saw its failure as an opportunity to embarrass the Americans and as a means of achieving a diplomatic victory. A combination of factors worked against the Agreement from the start and, in the course of 'national reconciliation' talks held in Geneva later that year, it was agreed to 'freeze' the Agreement. With US efforts in tatters, the UN was permitted to play a more central role in the second significant round of negotiations to secure an Israeli withdrawal which were convoked by the Secretary-General in Naqoura during late 1984 and early 1985.

The Israeli position during the 'Naqoura talks' can be summarised as an attempt to gain an advantage through negotiations that they were unable to gain militarily, a strategy that was not acceptable to other parties. The Lebanese position was unrealistic and even irresponsible, given the communal violence that would have followed a unilateral Israeli withdrawal. The outbreak of such violence would have lessened the capability of any factions to attack Israel and might even have

---

[86] Israel required the prior withdrawal of Syria, the return of prisoners held by Syria, and the return of Israeli soldiers buried in Syria. Israel was also given rights of intervention and flights over Lebanese territory while these were specifically denied to Syria. The Syrian representative at the UN stated that the 'agreement must be overturned' since it was imposed under the shadow of occupation. GAOR, A/38/PV9, 28 September 1983; and SCOR, 2496th Meeting, 11 November 1983.

reduced pressure on the state to withdraw from all of Lebanon. An influx of pro-Israeli Christians to the south could also have helped Israel's security along the frontier in the predominantly Shia south. Yet, in addition to war reparations, the Lebanese insisted on an unconditional Israeli withdrawal. There were to be no arrangements for Israel's security apart from UNIFIL and the Lebanese army. For its part, Israel accepted that UNIFIL had a role to play after the withdrawal, but this was not the same as agreeing to rely exclusively on the UN to secure Israel's northern frontier.

In the event, neither the Naqoura talks nor the 1983 Agreement produced a plan for an Israeli withdrawal acceptable to all parties. While the failure of UN efforts can be attributed in part to unrealistic demands made by the Lebanese at the behest of Syria, the fact remains that some of the Israeli conditions were inconsistent with Security Council resolutions since 1978. These conditions amounted to a demand for approval by the UN for the continued occupation of part of Lebanon and recognition of the surrogate militia there. This would have made a mockery of UNIFIL's original purpose and the intentions of the Security Council, in particular the proposal to deploy around Sidon. Such a move would also have shifted responsibility for inter-communal violence from the Israelis to the UN. It seemed that prior to the negotiations the parties had misled the Secretary-General and that from the beginning there was little hope of finding agreement.

The UN efforts at reconciliation in Somalia were more proactive than those in Lebanon, but they too failed to achieve any long-term success.[87] Among the factors militating against this was the initial controversy that such efforts generated, not least because they failed to take cognisance of the post-Barre Somalia and found support among those who no longer held power and influence in the country. Conventional analyses at the time tended to blame deficiencies in policies and personalities within the United States and the UN, and the Somali body politic.[88] These views may have underestimated the complexity of the factors adversely affecting efforts at reconciliation, but the policies of the UN exacerbated this

---

[87] The UN sponsored several major peace conferences and a number of national reconciliation meetings, but, despite two significant national accords, the Somali parties failed to honour the commitments they had made. United Nations, *The United Nations and Somalia*, pp. 6–7.

[88] K. Menkhaus, 'International Peacebuilding and the Dynamics of Local and National Reconciliation in Somalia' (1996) 3(1) *International Peacekeeping* 42–67.

situation. UNOSOM I might have succeeded if the intervention had been earlier and the strategy advocated by the SRSG, Sahnoun, pursued.

The approach of rebuilding a society from the 'bottom up' had much to recommend it. If it had been combined with an even-handed and firm policy on disarmament from an early stage, and if resources had been applied to the restoration of the police and justice system in particular, matters might have worked out quite differently. As it turned out, Sahnoun's term was short-lived and ultimately overtaken by events.

Later, the focus of what UNOSOM termed the 'bottom up' approach for political reconstruction involving local leaders and groups was the district council. While this idea was good, its implementation was not well thought out. There were criticisms that it was too neo-colonial in style. There was also criticism of the haste with which each council was established and the lack of consultation with traditional authorities in each district.[89] Part of this was due to the fact that insufficient attention was paid to demographic changes, and in some places the warlords ensured that their person was selected. A counter-argument could be made that the assessment of the crisis was so serious that it required rapid and drastic measures to immediately prevent matters worsening. The result was that the regional councils, from which it was intended to select representatives for the Transitional National Council, were seriously flawed.[90] Further, there were differences in the UNOSOM II and Somali interpretations of how to form some of the proposed political institutions, and the lack of resources to support them proved crucial. The attempt to adopt the policies of Sahnoun was ill-conceived and indicated the inconsistencies in the overall UN policy of nation-building in Somalia, in which warlords vacillated in stature from national leaders with whom the UN would work to international war criminals and terrorists deserving the odium of the international community.

An integral part of the reconciliation process was the need to rebuild the Somali police and justice system. But this was handicapped from the beginning by the requirement that resources for this programme be

---

[89] Human Rights Watch/Africa, 'Somalia Faces the Future', pp. 32–3.

[90] An example of the insensitive approach of the UN was provided at the third UN co-ordination meeting held in Addis Ababa and signed on 27 March 1993. The agreement provided for a 'transitional system of governance' that included a Transitional National Council that was to be 'the repository of Somali sovereignty'. This was offensive to the representatives of the self-proclaimed Somaliland Republic in the relatively peaceful northwest who had left the conference before the agreement was signed and who subsequently disassociated themselves from this provision.

obtained from voluntary contributions. This was almost certain to ensure its failure and showed the lack of commitment to a comprehensive strategic plan to achieve nation-building.

In recent years the international community has been actively engaged in promoting the rule of law in many countries emerging from internal conflicts through a range of international organisations, bilateral agencies and non-governmental organisations. A consequence of the involvement of so many actors is that there has been a lack of co-ordination and harmonisation between actors and programmes. In addition, there has been inadequate sensitivity to the relevant political context and a failure to recognise that a workable system must be built on indigenous traditions and involve the local population.

The problems in re-establishing the police and justice system derived primarily from the failure of the UN to treat the matter with urgency, ensure proper consultation and funding, and implement a UNOSOM Justice Division's programme. This was despite the urgent need to prioritise civil affairs and re-establish the rule of law. Because of the security situation, re-establishing a viable police force was one of the key elements to restoring normalcy. Unfortunately, even Sahnoun failed to capitalise on what every report on the police noted, i.e. that the Somali police were well trained, disciplined and non-tribal. It is also worth noting that there was no proposal for the establishment of an International Criminal Tribunal for Somalia. Somalis expected that the United States would call for a war crimes tribunal, especially given the evidence of, *inter alia*, crimes against humanity by the Barre regime. One interpretation of this is that the political will did not exist to do so, and that African lives were not equated with European ones. A less benign interpretation is that independent investigation might point to complicity on behalf of the United States and European and regional powers with the Barre regime and others in Somalia.

Resolution 814 (1993) placed the UN at the centre of reconciliation in Somalia. But Somalia was crowded for a time with those interested in peace-building, and not all camps agreed, among themselves or with each other, as to what the appropriate strategy should be. Given the lack of any central government or administration, it was predictable that local reconciliation was bound to have the greatest impact. This was also the view of NGOs working in the country.[91] The one important exception to this general finding concerned areas that had been conquered by

---

[91] Interviews with Concern Worldwide and GOAL workers, Dublin, Ireland, 1999.

clans during the conflict. In essence, all politics is local and any observer with experience of conflict situations will testify to the relevance of the local situation to the detriment of the national. It is difficult for villagers to identify with national efforts if these do not translate into meaningful gains in personal security and well-being on the ground. Although the United States special envoy, Robert Oakley, made worthwhile attempts to involve women's groups and others in the reconciliation process, these efforts were overtaken by events. Moreover, none of the UN-sponsored reconciliation conferences had any long-term impact. The Addis Ababa Conference on national reconciliation in March 1993 failed to exploit in full the apparent consensus among the major factions, and fudged on essential details that later led to disagreement among the factions, and among UN officials.[92] The commitment to disarm in the timeframe agreed was unrealistic and there was no real mechanism in place to accomplish it. The different expectations of the parties and the marginalisation of Aideed led to conflict on the ground. The process seemed artificial, and it is impossible to gauge if the initial consensus was in fact genuine. In the end, any consideration of the efforts at national reconciliation in Somalia must take cognisance of many factors, but must especially be aware of the centrifugal social, economic and political forces prevalent in Somalia that undermined the process at every level.

Intervention in Kosovo

As with most situations of internal conflict, the circumstances that gave rise to NATO intervention in Kosovo in 1999 owe their origins to the history of the province. The source of the ethnic rivalry is contentious, and Kosovo has been used as a metaphor by both Albanians and Serbs for the suffering and injustices inflicted on both nations in the course of their often-turbulent histories. The region is at the crossroads where the Western and Orthodox branches of Christianity and Islam either meet or collide, depending on the perspective of the observer. The historical animosity between Serbs and Albanians is rooted in the latter's links to the Turks. Having converted to Islam, Albanians are perceived as having conquered Serb lands on the strength of Turk expansion. Albanians, on the other hand, perceive the Serbs as having taken the land where

---

[92] J. Chopra, A. Eknes and T. Nordbo, 'Fighting for Hope in Somalia', *Peacekeeping and Multinational Operations*, No. 6 (Oslo: Norwegian Institute of International Affairs, 1995), pp. 61–5, and Hirsch and Oakley, *Somalia and Operation Restore Hope*, pp. 92–9.

Albanians had lived for centuries. According to Albanian myth, they are descendants of the ancient Illyrians that had originally inhabited the region of which Kosovo was the bigger part. The armed conflicts in that region of Europe originated from the demise of the Soviet Union and from the decision of a number of federated republics of the former Yugoslavia to secede. While there was a constitutional basis for these acts of secession, no such authority existed for Kosovo, which was an autonomous province of the Yugoslavian federation up until 1989. Yet, while there is no general international support for the use of force by ethnic groups to secede from a state, this may alter when such groups are subject to repression and persecution.

Ethnic tensions have been a source of conflict in the region for centuries, but this can be used to provide an over-simplistic explanation of events. Distorted historical perspectives have fuelled unrest. According to Pearson, '[a] mosaic of shifting stones, a patchwork quilt and a living kaleidoscope are just a sample of the metaphors resorted to by specialists finding their descriptive powers taxed to the limit by contemplation of the ethnic variety of eastern Europe'.[93] While there is a consensus that relations between the Albanians and Serbs in Kosovo were not good in the years prior to the rise to power of Slobodon Milosevic, matters deteriorated significantly after his ascent in 1987. When the autonomous status of Kosovo was revoked in 1989, this situation only worsened.

The borders drawn in the aftermath of World War I at the Treaty of Versailles (1919) were intended to be permanent. As Thornberry noted, 'while secession from Western Empires has resulted in the creation of States, these same States deny the possibility of further secession by disaffected groups which are required to accept the dogma of the territorial integrity of States'.[94] The Albanians had sought to change their situation by non-violent methods with the recognition of independence for Slovenia held out as an example for Kosovo to follow. Rather than confronting the Serb authorities about the inequalities and human rights abuses being perpetrated, the Albanian population developed parallel structures of education, welfare and taxation, which included political representation. It was ironic then that the increased

---

[93] R. Pearson, *National Minorities in Eastern Europe 1849–1945* (London: Macmillan, 1983), p. 1.

[94] P. Thornberry, *International Law and the Rights of Minorities* (Oxford: Oxford University Press, 1991), p. 14.

Serb oppression precipitated the seizure of an unprecedented degree of *de facto* control of economic and political affairs by the Albanians. Illegal parliamentary elections were held and a moderate democrat, the leader of the Democratic League of Kosovo, Ibrahim Rugova, appointed president. Many Albanians saw this as a clear demonstration of their ability to manage their own affairs after independence.

Unfortunately, the peaceful attempts to improve the situation of the Albanian population did not prove effective. Matters came to a head after the 1995 Dayton Peace Accords provided the general framework for peace in Bosnia-Herzegovina, but ignored Kosovo and left the situation of Kosavar Albanians unchanged. In the words of Richard Holbrooke, seasoned negotiator and one of the main architects of the Dayton Agreement, the 'long feared crisis in Kosovo was postponed, not avoided'.[95] This precipitated a radicalisation among young Albanians who had spent years being told that they should wait for the international community to impose a final settlement which would address the issue of the former Yugoslavia. The majority believed that independence from Serbia was the only way to guarantee their national rights. Was it unreasonable to ask why Kosovo should not have a status similar to that accorded the Republic of Srpska within post-Dayton Bosnia-Herzegovina?

In 1996, the Kosovo Liberation Army (KLA) began a campaign of resistance in earnest and commenced guerrilla attacks on Serb targets in Kosovo. Most of the funding for the KLA came from the European and North American Albanian diaspora. In addition, from the beginning the KLA was linked to criminal activities involving, among other things, prostitution and extortion networks in Europe. The target of some of its earlier attacks was the moderate Democratic League of Kosovo. The KLA was still classified as a 'terrorist organisation' by the United States State Department in 1998. It received a major boost when a political crisis occurred in Albania in the spring of 1997 after the collapse of a fraudulent pyramid-banking scheme led to serious civil unrest. Rioters broke into arms depots, and the security forces, in particular the army, lost control. Suddenly there was a plentiful supply of small arms available, with Kalashnikov rifles on sale for as little as $10 each. Almost inevitably, many of these ended up being smuggled to the KLA.

The militant tactics of the KLA caused the Serb authorities to adopt even more repressive measures. In 1998, the Serbian security forces initiated a policy of ethnic cleansing. On 4 March 1998, probably in revenge for the

---

[95] See R. Holbrooke, *To End a War* (New York: Random House, 1998), p. 357.

deaths of Serb policemen, Serb military police raided the village of Prekaz in the KLA stronghold of central Kosovo. The entire Jashari clan, fifty-eight in all, including women and children, were killed. Such events prompted the KLA to action and had the concurrent effect of mobilising Albanian-American opinion which shifted support overnight from the Democratic League of Kosovo to the more militant KLA. Flush with the success of having 'liberated' parts of Kosovo, the KLA could hardly believe its good fortune. After an initial period of indecision, the Serb authorities had little option but to go after the KLA. The KLA realised that they could not fight Serb forces along conventional lines and withdrew to the hills. In the course of the ensuing offensive, Serb security forces caused an estimated 2,000 casualties as they rampaged, raped and pillaged their way through Albanian towns and villages, creating some 400,000 displaced persons. The plight of the Albanians, especially to European audiences with the events of Srebrenica still fresh in their collective memory, prompted the 'international community' to take action.

The ultimate goal of the KLA was independence, but this was inconsistent with European Union and United States policy. The latter considered that political autonomy and guaranteed minority rights formed the only internationally acceptable solution to the status of Kosovo. Attempts to negotiate a settlement with Milosevic were undermined by his intransigence and Russian insistence that the matter be dealt with under the auspices of the UN, thereby securing the right to veto any outcome that did not favour its Serbian allies. Russia was also concerned about the precedent being set and of possible intervention in the Chechnya problem.

In October 1998, Richard Holbrooke, former US Assistant Secretary of State for European and Canadian Affairs, was called on again to try to broker a compromise with Milosevic. Milosevic agreed to pull back his forces and to allow the deployment of international monitors under a deal that recognised the issue of Kosovo as a matter of international concern. The presence of 2,000 unarmed OSCE monitors did restore some degree of stability for a time. However, the KLA were accused of kidnapping and killing Serb civilians, while the Serbs also stood accused of atrocities. The most notorious was the death of some forty-five civilians from the village of Racak in January 1999 (although the facts surrounding the deaths are contested). As the KLA used the opportunity to reoccupy territory, both parties prepared for a spring campaign.

The so-called Racak massacre prompted intense diplomatic activity. The Contact Group, including its Russian contingent, decided to summon the parties with the intention of agreeing a withdrawal of Serb forces, the introduction of an effective international military presence, and autonomy for Kosovo.[96] This led to the Rambouillet negotiations in February 1999 in which the Albanian delegation had to be persuaded to participate by a mix of coaxing and duress. Although moderate leader Rugova led the delegation, it was clear from the presence of militant leaders such as Hashim Thaqi that the KLA was now a force to be reckoned with. The proposed deal had its elements of constructive ambiguity to permit both sides to portray it in terms favourable to their respective constituencies.[97] While it did not promise a referendum on independence after a three-year interim period, it did not rule out such a prospect. In addition to the international recognition received by the KLA, it also obtained the approval of United States Secretary of State, Madeline Albright, who supported the transformation of the KLA from 'terrorist' organisation to legitimate civil defence force. This policy still has important ramifications in Kosovo today. But Rambouillet was also about imposing some internal discipline within NATO and reaffirming United States leadership in defending stability in Europe.

Although Kosovo was not 'vital' to most of the European countries in terms of conventional 'realpolitik', the resolution of the problem was important to both the United States and Europe.[98] The vision of a united and democratic Europe was seen as crucial to United States security, and this could not be achieved if the Balkans remained unstable. While Milosevic would have accepted UN peacekeepers comprised of non-NATO European states like Ireland, along with contingents from Russia, Ukraine and Belarus,[99] Rambouillet was seen by the Serbs as a recipe for facilitating the independence of Kosovo and as allowing a NATO occupation. Not surprisingly, Milosevic rejected the agreement and refused to engage in follow-up talks in Paris. This was the last throw of the dice by Milosevic and it precipitated intervention by NATO.

---

[96] The Contact Group comprised France, the United Kingdom, the United States, Germany, Italy and Russia. It is the principal group of nations that monitors and supervises international policy in Kosovo. This informal grouping first came together in response to the crisis in Bosnia. With the addition of the European Union, it now regularly consults on the situation in Kosovo.

[97] Text of agreement available at http://www.state.gov/www/regions/eur/ksvo_rambouillet_text.html.

[98] General W. Clark, 'The Strength of an Alliance', in W. Buckley (ed.), *Kosovo: Contending Voices on Balkan Intervention* (Grand Rapids, MI, and Cambridge: Eerdmans, 2000), p. 254.

[99] Arnaud de Borchgrave United Press International, 'Interview with Slobodan Milosevic', in Buckley (ed.), *Kosovo: Contending Voices*, p. 281.

The NATO intervention, when it came, did successfully end the repression of the Albanian majority, but there was criticism of its conduct. The use of air power in Iraq during 1998 and 1999 suggested to the United States and the United Kingdom that the use of force without express Security Council approval was a politically feasible option. Nevertheless, the actual air campaign created significant political and military risks for those involved. In order to reassure American domestic opinion, President Clinton undertook not to commit American troops to a ground campaign, as he could not risk having young Americans coming home in body bags. This was fine in theory, but to secure territory it is necessary to deploy infantry soldiers on the ground. It is not possible to protect a civilian population from the air. Milosevic, on the other hand, did not want to expend his already depleted military assets in a campaign against vastly superior forces that even a master of political spin could not disguise as anything other than defeat.

Serbia has been described as the sole European country ever bombed by NATO, and the only country in the world with a McDonald's franchise that was bombed by United States planes.[100] The high-altitude bombing was considered by some observers to fall short of the requirements of international humanitarian law, and an investigation was initiated into NATO's conduct of hostilities by the Office of the Prosecutor for the International Criminal Tribunal for the former Yugoslavia.[101] Although no prosecutions were initiated, mistakes were made and the bombing led to many civilian casualties. A major practical weakness in the campaign was the fact that it permitted the Serbs to continue targeting the Albanian population on the ground. In this way the NATO bombing campaign ironically facilitated the Serbian goal of 'cleansing' Kosovo of Albanians. The latter were forced to seek protection in neighbouring countries that, in turn, were destabilised by floods of refugees. It also highlighted Europe's inferior military capacity compared to that of the United States. Russia, on the other had, did not want any attention drawn to the political and military inadequacies that precluded it from protecting its traditional ally in the region. In the end, the intervention came too late and the refusal to commit ground forces, along

---

[100] D. Anastasijevic, 'Not Exactly New Hampshire: A Short Survey of Contemporary Serbian Politics', in Buckley (ed.), *Kosovo: Contending Voices*, p. 196.

[101] *Final Report to the Prosecutor by the Committee Established to Review the NATO Bombing Campaign Against the Federal Republic of Yugoslavia*, 1999, available at http://www.un.org/icty/pressreal/nato061300.htm.

with the failure to anticipate the attempt to ethnically cleanse Kosovo of all Albanians, meant that even Muslim countries gave only qualified support.

The national strategy of the Albanians was to create a Western protectorate under NATO, the OSCE and the European Union, with subsequent independence through a referendum. The KLA proved one of the most successful guerrilla organisations of recent times. Having manipulated events in such a way as to prompt NATO intervention, the objective of defeating the Serbs and creating an Albanian Kosovo was all but achieved in name.

Operation Allied Force: the NATO air campaign

Air strikes began on 14 March 1999 and ended with the Kosovo Peace Accords of 3 June 1999, some seventy-eight days later.[102] NATO claimed that it took action first and foremost to stop the humanitarian tragedy,[103] yet failure to act threatened the ideal of Europe as a common political, economic and security region. The situation also posed a threat to stability in the Balkans. Bosnia had taught NATO leaders many lessons, but chief among these was that acting promptly might well be less costly in the long term. It was claimed that all other means had failed and military intervention was necessary to break the impasse.

The bombing campaign lasted much longer than anticipated. The legality of NATO's action was challenged by, among others, Russia, China and India. The action was said to be outside the framework of the UN Charter. A number of Security Council resolutions had been adopted prior to the NATO action, three of which had referred to Chapter VII of the UN Charter. Even allowing for an expansive interpretation of the sometimes coded language of such resolutions, there was no express authorisation of military action.

---

[102] According to a North Atlantic Council statement of 12 April 1999, NATO had five goals. Air strikes would be pursued until President Milosevic: (1) ensures a verifiable stop to all military action and the immediate ending of violence and repression; (2) ensures the withdrawal from Kosovo of the military, police and paramilitary forces; (3) agrees to the stationing in Kosovo of an international military presence; (4) agrees to the unconditional and safe return of all refugees and displaced persons and unhindered access to them by humanitarian organisations; (5) provides credible assurance of his willingness to work on the basis of the Rambouillet Accords in the establishment of a political framework agreement for Kosovo in conformity with international law and the Charter of the United Nations.

[103] J. Solana, Secretary-General of NATO, 'Fresh Cause for Hope at the Opening of the New Century', in Buckley (ed.), *Kosovo: Contending Voices*, p. 218.

China had consistently opposed NATO intervention, and called for a fair and reasonable solution to the problem by negotiation. It objected to the view that state sovereignty is contingent on maintaining acceptable standards of human rights within frontiers, but accepted that action might be justified in certain circumstances. It considered the air strikes to be unjust and inhuman.[104] Later, the bombing of the Chinese embassy in Belgrade and the seventy-eight-day campaign made the Chinese even more suspicious of NATO and American intentions.

The International Commission on Kosovo considered the bombings illegal but legitimate, in that they had the effect of liberating the majority of the population from a long period of oppression.[105] The less certainty there is about the legality of international action, the greater the recourse to arguments based on morality. The British Prime Minister described the intervention as being 'fought not for territory, but for values'.[106] Likewise, echoing the views of the International Commission, the United Kingdom House of Commons Foreign Affairs Committee considered the use of force of 'dubious legality', but justified on moral grounds.[107] NATO also assumed a humanitarian image, and its website represented the Kosovo operation as combining 'humanitarianism' and 'preventive diplomacy'.[108] Such efforts did little to assuage the fears of those opposed to the bombings, and countries like Russia felt validated in their belief that NATO was a predatory, destabilising influence in the region. Nevertheless, on 26 March 1999, when asked by Russia to condemn NATO action, the Security Council rejected the proposed resolution, by twelve votes to three. This could be interpreted as an endorsement of the NATO campaign, just two days after it had commenced.

The dilemma that Kosovo presented exemplifies the old adage, 'hard cases make bad law'. This is clear from the views expressed by the UN Secretary-General, Kofi Annan, who stated that there are times when the use of force may be legitimate in the pursuit of peace, even if initiated without Security Council approval.[109] According to Annan, failure to

---

[104] 'Behind the Bombing of the Chinese Embassy' (1999) 42(21) *Beijing Review* 5.

[105] Independent International Commission on Kosovo, *Kosovo Report: Conflict – International Response – Lessons Learned* (Oxford: Oxford University Press, 2000), p. 4.

[106] Tony Blair, 'A New Generation Draws the Line', *Newsweek*, 19 April 1999.

[107] UK House of Commons Foreign Affairs Committee, Fourth Report, Session 1999–2000, para. 138.

[108] M. Pugh, 'Peacekeeping and Critical Theory' (2004) 11 *International Peacekeeping* 49.

[109] K. Annan, 'The Effectiveness of the International Rule of Law in Maintaining International Peace and Security', in Buckley (ed.), *Kosovo: Contending Voices*, p. 222.

obtain Security Council approval risks anarchy, but failure to act when confronted by gross violations of human rights may well betray the very ideals that inspired the founding of the UN. Subsequent events have since illustrated the danger of adopting this approach. The more controversial initiation of armed conflict in Iraq in 2003 was based on a similar humanitarian imperative argument, and, when the weapons of mass destruction failed to materialise, the moral imperative of regime change took on even greater weight than before.

Among the consequences of the air campaign was the creation of a humanitarian disaster, with an estimated 850,000 persons forced to take refuge in neighbouring states and an additional 600,000 internally displaced. The campaign also effectively silenced whatever opposition to Milosevic that existed in Serbia. Unfortunately, once committed, NATO had little option but to continue, as a failure to proceed could have meant even more catastrophic consequences for the Albanians remaining in Kosovo. Their fate would likely have been much worse than the Kurds in northern Iraq at the end of the First Gulf War, and might well have resembled the Bosnian Muslims at Srebrenica in 1995. The build-up of Serbian forces during the negotiations and the efficiency of the ethnic cleansing in Kosovo was evidence that this was not just a response to the NATO attack. Serbian society was said to have undergone a radicalisation over the previous fifteen years. There were no demonstrations against ethnic cleansing or similar policies, and the political landscape was dominated by strident nationalists.[110] Prior to the intervention, the KLA came close to defeat after a massive Serbian offensive. Reinforcements from abroad and the NATO bombing turned the campaign in the KLA's favour. Although depicted as a favourable outcome that preserved Alliance unity, the length of the bombing campaign revealed some serious tensions within the alliance.

The Military Technical Agreement and UN Resolution 1244[111]

The short-term political and military aims of Operation Allied Force were achieved when Serb forces withdrew (with the exception of undermining popular support for Milosevic which he had ceased to enjoy even

---

[110] M. A. Sells, 'Vuk's Knife: Kosovo, the Serbian Golgotha, and the Radicalization of Serbian Society', in Buckley (ed.), *Kosovo: Contending Voices*, p. 133.

[111] Adopted under Chapter VII of the UN Charter, 10 June 1999. There were fourteen votes in favour, and China abstained.

before the campaign began). The NATO-led Kosovo Force (KFOR) entered on 12 June 1999, in accordance with the terms of the Military Technical Agreement with the governments of the Federal Republic of Yugoslavia and the Republic of Serbia. The Agreement provided for deployment following the adoption of an appropriate Security Council resolution. The requirement for a UN mandate, and the absence of any reference to a referendum on independence after a three-year provisional period, distinguished it from the Rambouillet Agreement. Prior to Security Council involvement, the G-8 group of industrialised states effectively functioned as a kind of shadow Security Council. The adoption of Resolution 1244 put the UN centre-stage in Kosovo, and mandated a UN mission (UNMIK) supported by an international military force (KFOR). The mandate explicitly referred to Kosovo as part of the Federal Republic of Yugoslavia, albeit while reaffirming the call in previous resolutions for substantial autonomy. The resolution required the demilitarisation of the KLA and an agreement to this effect was signed on 20 June 1999. The KLA were quick to exploit the political vacuum, as almost all Serbian administrative structures collapsed. A provisional government was established under the former militant leader Hashim Thaqi, but revenge attacks against Serbs were commonplace.

The overall mandate given to UNMIK and KFOR was unprecedented in its complexity and the broad range of tasks it assigned to a UN transitional administration.[112] Resolution 1244 authorised the Secretary-General to establish an international civil presence in order to provide an interim administration for Kosovo. By combining territorial administration and peace maintenance, UNMIK comprises a functional duality that combines global and domestic governance.[113] The tasks of UNMIK include:

- promoting the establishment of substantial autonomy and self-government;
- performing basic civilian administrative functions for as long as required;
- organising and overseeing the development of provisional institutions for democratic self-government, including holding elections;

---

[112] See generally M. J. Matheson, 'United Nations Governance of Post Conflict Societies' (2001) 95 *American Journal of International Law* 76.

[113] L. von Carlowitz, 'Crossing the Boundary from the International to the Domestic Legal Realm: UNMIK Lawmaking and Property Rights in Kosovo' (2004) 10 *Global Governance* 307–33 at 308.

- transferring its administrative responsibilities, and supporting local provisional institutions;
- facilitating a political process designed to determine Kosovo's future status, taking into account the Rambouillet accords;
- supporting infrastructure and economic reconstruction;
- supporting humanitarian and disaster relief;
- maintaining civil law and order, including establishing local police forces and the deployment of international police personnel;
- protecting human rights; and
- ensuring the safe and unimpeded return of all refugees and displaced persons to their homes.[114]

The four-pillar structure of UNMIK, which is divided into administrative districts, is complex. It consists of an interim civil administration led by the UN. In 2006, the pillars were as follows:

Pillar I: Police and Justice, under the direct leadership of the UN (originally, this was humanitarian affairs led by the United Nations High Commissioner for Refugees);

Pillar II: Civil Administration, under the direct leadership of the UN;

Pillar III: Democratization and Institution Building, led by the Organization for Security and Cooperation in Europe; and

Pillar IV: Reconstruction and Economic Development, led by the European Union.[115]

The structure presents formidable co-ordination challenges. The head of UNMIK is the Special Representative of the Secretary-General for Kosovo (SRSG).[116] He or she is responsible for the overall mission and the political process intended to determine Kosovo's future status. Since UNMIK's inception, there has been a high turnover in SRSGs. This has not helped with deciding on an overall long-term strategy for UNMIK. In this way, the international administration in Kosovo may

---

[114] Security Council Resolution 1244, 10 June 1999, para. 11.

[115] January 2006. Review and restructuring for final status is ongoing.

[116] As the most senior international civilian official in Kosovo, the SRSG presides over the work of the pillars and facilitates the political process designed to determine Kosovo's future status. Each pillar is headed by a Deputy Special Representative of the Secretary-General. Dr Bernard Kouchner (France) served as head of UNMIK from July 1999 to January 2001. The second head of UNMIK was Mr Hans Haekkerup (Denmark) who served from February 2001 to December 2001. Mr Michael Steiner (Germany) served from January 2002 to July 2003. Mr Harri Holkeri (Finland) served from August 2003 to June 2004. Mr Soren Jessen-Petersen (Denmark) served from 2004 to August 2006, and was succeeded by Mr Joachim Rücker (Germany) in September 2006.

still be described as a 'work in progress'.[117] On the ground, there is insufficient operational planning and joint strategies between the pillars. UNMIK has sustained criticism for its lack of competence in governing Kosovo, and its unwillingness to address the issue of future status. Much of the blame can be attributed to the international community's lack of focus and strategy but, in addition, UNMIK has been characterised by structural inefficiency, in-fighting and a lack of direction. There have also been allegations of corruption among UNMIK officials and police.

Under Resolution 1244, KFOR is a NATO-led multi-national force responsible for the overall security environment in Kosovo. It is comprised of four Multi-National Brigade (MNB) areas and the Force is specifically tasked with:

- monitoring, and verifying when necessary, and enforcing compliance with the agreements that ended the conflict, including demilitarisation of the KLA;
- establishing and maintaining a secure environment, including public safety and order;
- providing assistance to UNMIK, including core civil functions until these were transferred to UNMIK.[118]

The overall effect of Resolution 1244 was to create an international protectorate, which left almost no role for the Yugoslav and Serbian governments. In fact it gave the legislative, executive and judicial power to the UN and the relevant international organisations. This has been described as creating 'a unique political and institutional hybrid, a UN protectorate with unlimited powers whose purpose is to prepare the province for substantial autonomy and self-government'.[119] The UN was placed centre-stage, with the OSCE and the European Union playing subordinate roles. The overall plan envisaged four stages of political evolution: (1) an interim period of governance by a designated administrator; (2) an international civil presence; (3) substantial autonomy for the people of Kosovo; (4) the development of provisional democratic self-governing institutions. The plan had some serious flaws and contradictions. Its references to the Rambouillet accords, and the principles of sovereignty and territorial integrity of the Federal Republic of Yugoslavia were inherently problematic. The Belgrade regime hailed it as a national

---

[117] A. Yannis, 'The UN Government in Kosovo' (2004) 10 *Global Governance* 67–81 at 69.
[118] Security Council Resolution 1244, 10 June 1999, para. 9.
[119] Independent International Commission on Kosovo, *Kosovo Report*, p. 259.

triumph that secured the status of Kosovo within Serbia in the future. Rambouillet provided for *de facto* occupation by NATO forces and a referendum on autonomy, but this was effectively skirted around in the turgid language and inherent ambiguity of elements of the agreement.

The major problem was that, to achieve the overall objectives of the plan, NATO forces would have to impose unpalatable terms on the Albanian population of Kovovo. There was a certain irony in this. After having intervened on the side of the Albanians, NATO would now find itself resisting or even fighting with them over the issue of independence and minority rights. The mandate referred to negotiations between the parties, but who were the parties, and was it realistic that any kind of agreement could be achieved? UNMIK found itself in a position not dissimilar to that of a colonial power denying the colonised a right of self-determination.

Creation of provisional institutions of self-government and the protection of minorities in Kosovo

In December 1999, an agreement was concluded between UNMIK and the main political parties which led to the voluntary abolition of the Albanian provisional government and other parallel structures, replacing them with a Joint Interim Administrative Council. Many of those involved in the political leadership of the KLA were rewarded with portfolios in the provisional government and the municipalities.[120] The provisional government seems to have expected to be recognised as a partner by the international community. However, despite providing some degree of stability and governance, it had no legitimacy. Its continued existence would have been incompatible with Resolution 1244 and many of its decrees and policies were at variance with UNMIK's existence. The Joint Interim Administrative Structure created in January 2000 was an attempt to share administrative powers with the local politicians and to involve them in the decision-making process. It was also a non-confrontational method of incorporating the original Albanian parallel structures into the UNMIK administration. From the beginning, the participation of the Kosovan Serbs was intended to be an integral part of the process. Yet, although the agreement was just a stepping-stone to finding some kind of constitutional framework for

---

[120] International Crisis Group, *What Happened to the KLA*, Balkans Report No. 88, 3 March 2000, p. 3.

the governance of Kosovo, it was not accepted by the Serb population. Later, the introduction of the Constitutional Framework in May 2001 provided the requisite legal basis for provisional institutions of self-government created in March 2002. In time, UNMIK began to transfer non-reserved competencies to the Kosovar Provisional Institutions of Self Government (which included the President, Prime Minister and the Kosovo Assembly, the government, the courts, and other bodies and institutions set out in the Constitutional Framework). The key determinant of the success of the process was the extent to which it engaged and protected minority communities within Kosovo.

Although minorities are not referred to in Resolution 1244, the protection and promotion of human rights is touted as one of the main responsibilities of the international civilian presence. The failure to expressly mention the need to protect minorities was a serious omission, especially as this was central to the justification for the continued international presence in Kosovo. It was also fundamental to the reconciliation process aimed at achieving a multi-ethnic Kosovo. An acknowledgment of the importance of this issue would also have facilitated UNMIK and KFOR in persuading the parties of its significance in the promotion of a multi-ethnic society.

The problems associated with the protection of minorities in Kosovo are compounded by the fact that there is no agreed international definition of what constitutes a minority. A minority has been referred to as:

> A group of citizens of a state, constituting a numerical minority in and in a non-dominant position in that state, endowed with ethnic, religious or linguistic characteristics which differ from those of the majority of the population, having a sense of solidarity with one another, motivated, if only implicitly, by a collective will to survive and whose aim is to achieve equality with the majority in fact and in law.[121]

While Kosovar Albanians could be described as a minority within Serbia, they were a clear majority within Kosovo itself. Since it was problematic to determine which ethnic groups qualified as a 'minority', UNMIK adopted the term 'communities' in its place. The Constitutional Framework of Kosovo defines a 'community' as

---

[121] J. Deschenes, quoted in P. Thornberry, *International Law and the Rights of Minorities* (Oxford: Oxford University Press, 1991), p. 7.

'inhabitants belonging to the same ethnic or religious or linguistic group'.[122] No numerical threshold is required in order to qualify, and the normal criteria applied did not seem to fit the Kosovo model. For this reason, a pragmatic policy was adopted which acknowledged that each ethnic group is a minority somewhere in the territory of Kosovo.[123]

Linked to the issue of minority protection was the matter of applicable law. The legal system in Kosovo is a complex mixture of legislation previously enacted (provided it is not discriminatory, does not contravene international human rights instruments applicable in Kosovo, and does not overlap with laws in force), UNMIK Regulations and Administrative Directions, and laws passed by the Kosovo Assembly. To prevent chaos at an early stage, the SRSG declared that: 'All legislative and executive authority with respect to Kosovo, including the administration of the judiciary, is vested in UNMIK and is exercised by the Special Representative of the Secretary-General.'[124] Owing to its sweeping terms, this regulation became known as the 'mother of all regulations'. For its part, UNMIK was authorised to issue such legislative acts in the form of Regulations as it deemed necessary. In this way, the SRSG established the supremacy of his office over any legal issues in Kosovo, and that of UNMIK Regulations over existing laws. This was to create separate problems in relation to accountability which are explored in Chapter 5. The situation remains confusing and somewhat chaotic. All laws passed by the Kosovo Assembly and all UNMIK Regulations, as a rule, supersede all previous laws on the same matter. The theory is fine, but the reality on the ground is confusion exacerbated by a lack of translation and no official legal procedure regarding the publication of laws.[125] Furthermore, not everyone shared the broad

---

[122] UNMIK Regulation No. 2001/9, On a Constitutional Framework for Provisional Self-Government in Kosovo, 15 May 2001, Chapter 4, para. 4.1. See also UNMIK Regulation 2000/45, On the Self-Government of Municipalities in Kosovo, 11 August 2000, Chapter 1, Section 2, para. 2.3.

[123] A list of recognised 'communities' can be found in the Constitutional Framework of Kosovo. In addition to the Albanians and the Kosovo Serbs, the Roma, Ashkali, Egyptian, Bosnian, Turkish and Gorani communities are recognised as eligible to participate in the Kosovo Assembly. This list omits the Croat and Cerkezi groups, most likely due to their small numbers within Kosovo. UNMIK Regulation 2001/9, On a Constitutional Framework for Provisional Self-Government in Kosovo, Chapter 9, para. 9.1.3(b).

[124] UNMIK/REG/1999/1, 25 July 1999, Section 1, para. 1, amended by UNMIK/REG/2000/54, 27 September 2000.

[125] European Commission for Democracy Through Law (Venice Commission), *Opinion on Human Rights in Kosovo: Possible Establishment of Review Mechanisms*, Opinion No. 280/2004 (Strasbourg: European Commission, 11 October 2004), p. 13.

interpretation of the mandate and the effective suspension of Yugoslavia's sovereignty over Kosovo. The powers of the international administration were considered to be far in excess of what peacekeeping operations traditionally require, and more akin to the extensive mandates of UN trusteeships and international protectorates.[126]

Constitutional Framework for Provisional Self-Government

The Constitutional Framework for Provisional Self-Government established a comprehensive legal framework for self-government in the legislative, executive and judicial fields.[127] While it gave wide competencies to these institutions, it retained ultimate authority for UNMIK alone.[128] It was also the first Regulation in which the rights of communities were addressed in some detail. As noted, the term 'community' is broadly defined as 'inhabitants belonging to the same ethnic or religious or linguistic group'.[129] Since this definition does not include numerical, geographical or any specific detail that would further differentiate between the numerous communities, it places each Community on an equal footing. This rendered it more a political statement, reinforcing the principles of equality and non-discrimination, rather than an extra legal protection for minorities.

The Constitutional Framework was an important milestone in Kosovo's legal system. However, the legislation was not without its critics. It has been described as a 'no confidence vote in Albanian leaders' who have done little or nothing to stop the violence against Serbs and other minorities in Kosovo.[130] According to Amnesty International, the Constitutional Framework is lacking because it fails to provide any judicial review mechanisms through which individuals and groups

---

[126] Yannis, 'The UN Government in Kosovo', p. 71.

[127] UNMIK/REG/2001/9, On a Constitutional Framework for Provisional Self-Government in Kosovo, 15 May 2001.

[128] M. Brand, 'Effective Human Rights Protection When the UN "Becomes the State": Lessons from UNMIK', in N. D. White and K. Klassen (eds.), *The UN, Human Rights and Post-Conflict Situations* (Manchester: Manchester University Press, 2005), pp. 347–75 at p. 354.

[129] UNMIK/REG/2001/9, On Constitutional Framework for Provisional Self-Government in Kosovo, 15 May 2001, Chapter 4, para. 4.1.

[130] T. Judah, 'A Sensible Plan for Kosovo', *New York Times*, 23 May 2001, p. 27.

could enforce their constitutional rights.[131] The failure to establish a Constitutional Court was one glaring deficiency.

From an early stage, the UN interim administration supported the participation of minorities in public life through affirmative action legislation. The governing Regulation requires that all communities be involved in the provisional administrative management and that they be fairly represented.[132] This was fine in theory, but it left the issue of protecting the Serb and other vulnerable communities unresolved. A further important step towards ensuring minority participation was taken in August 2000 when the SRSG promulgated the Regulation on Self-Government of Municipalities in Kosovo. This was intended to establish provisional institutions for democratic and autonomous self-government at the municipal level as a step in the progressive transfer of administrative responsibilities from UNMIK,[133] pending a political determination of the future status of Kosovo.

There are a number of additional UNMIK regulations that incorporate anti-discrimination clauses and references to the rights of communities.[134] In general, the UN has created a detailed and sophisticated system that is intended to protect the rights of minorities. However, there has been very little progress on the ground.

In July and September 2002, during his assessment visit, the Council of Europe's Commissioner for Human Rights observed:

> The security situation for ethnic Serbs, and to a lesser extent, for returning Roma, Egyptian and Ashkali remains difficult. Indeed, except for returns to established Serbian enclaves, returnees effectively require round the clock KFOR protection and are barely able to travel without escort.[135]

---

[131] Amnesty International Report, Serbia and Montenegro (Kosovo/Kosova), *Prisoners in Our Homes, Amnesty International's Concerns for the Human Rights of Minorities in Kosovo/Kosova*, AI Index: EUR 70/010/2003, p. 8.

[132] UNMIK Regulation 2000/1, On the Kosovo Joint Interim Administrative Structure, 14 January 2000, Section 1(d).

[133] UNMIK Regulation 2000/45, On the Self-Government of Municipalities in Kosovo, 11 August 2000, Chapter 1, Section 1.

[134] For example: UNMIK Regulation 2001/36, On the Kosovo Civil Service; UNMIK Regulation 2002/19, On the Promulgation of a Law Adopted by the Assembly of Kosovo on Primary and Secondary Education in Kosovo; and UNMIK/REG/2003/14, 12 May 2003, On the Promulgation of a Law Adopted by the Assembly of Kosovo on Higher Education in Kosovo.

[135] A. Gil-Roberts, Council of Europe Commissioner for Human Rights, *Kosovo: The Human Rights Situation and the Fate of Persons Displaced from Their Homes* (Strasbourg: Council of Europe, 16 October 2003), Introduction, para. 6.

In April 2003, Amnesty International concluded that, despite the efforts of KFOR and the UNMIK police to provide security and protection, members of minority communities continued to suffer assaults on their persons and property by the majority community.[136] The figures for those actually displaced by the violence are uncertain.[137] In December 2004, over two thousand of those that fled nearly six years earlier remained displaced. Their status may be attributed to a number of reasons. While there were problems in the rate and manner of home reconstruction, security was also a key concern.[138] A successful return involves more than the transport of people to their rebuilt former homes. In order to survive, the displaced persons need security and the means to sustain themselves. Families require access to health care, education for their children, and a means to make a living. Thus the return of displaced persons needs to be seen in the context of the broader issue creating a sense of normality among and between the ethnic groups.

The security deficit and the de facto partition of Kosovo

The rapid withdrawal of the Yugoslav military and police created a serious security vacuum. The deployment of KFOR eased this situation somewhat, but the slow deployment of the international civilian police and the poor quality of many of its officers[139] meant that there was no real trained security personnel to deal with ordinary public order and criminal activities. This situation added to the vulnerability of minorities.

The first wave of attacks against the minorities came from the KLA. The victims were civilian Serbs, Roma, Croats, Bosniaks and those Albanians suspected of collaboration. The KLA used similar tactics to those of the Yugoslav army and police. People were killed and abducted, women were raped, houses were destroyed, farms looted and cars burned. Threats and harassment became a part of everyday life. This was a clear policy of ethnic cleansing, in spite of the presence of KFOR and UNMIK. The majority of those that were in a position to do so chose to leave. UNHCR estimated

---

[136] Amnesty International Report, *Prisoners in Our Homes*, p. 2.

[137] See 'The Lausanne Principle: Multiethnicity, Territory and the Future of Kosovo's Serbs', European Stability Initiative, June 2004.

[138] Personal interview, UNMIK officials, Kosovo, December 2004. Those from places like Svinjare, Slatina, Vushtri and Obilic were especially concerned with security.

[139] W. O'Neill, *Kosovo: 'An Unfinished Peace'* (Colorado and London: Lynne Rienner Publishers, 2002), pp. 99–101; and Independent International Commission on Kosovo, *The Kosovo Report*, p. 110.

that over 230,000 ethnic Serbs, Roma and other minorities fled Kosovo[140] in the first few months after the UN and KFOR assumed control.

The security situation for those who stayed remained tense and volatile with significant numbers facing arson attacks, threats to their person and, in extreme cases, murder. Many of these were already vulnerable groups such as the elderly or the poor who could not afford to start a new life elsewhere.

A further wave of ethnic violence followed the return of hundreds of thousands of Kosovar Albanians. Many found their relatives and neighbours dead or unaccounted for, their homes looted and destroyed, and no ordinary services, such as water and electricity, functioning. Inflamed by these events and exploiting the absence of a police presence and functioning judicial system, large numbers sided with the KLA and took part in the atrocities.[141] Leading Kosovar Albanian politicians and the media failed to condemn the attacks and, in some cases, actually incited them.

UNMIK and KFOR were unprepared and unable to deal with the scale of violence which, in the initial months, was mistakenly perceived as the spontaneous (and somewhat understandable) reaction to the horrors of the past years. It was then believed that as life returned to normal the violence would subside; this proved a false expectation. By the end of September 1999, it was evident that there was an organised campaign designed to attack Serbs, Roma and other minorities simply because of their ethnicity. According to the Office of the High Commissioner for Human Rights, these communities were 'effectively disappearing from Kosovo'.[142] The Independent International Commission on Kosovo reported that:

> After the summer of 1999, Kosovo was characterized by a high level of crime and aggression, much of which was directed against the minority population, especially Serbs. The inability to stop a new wave of ethnic cleansing in Kosovo, in spite of the presence of 40,000 armed soldiers, was a major failure for the international community. More than half of the Serb population left the province ... the remaining Serb population is living in enclaves or divided cities.[143]

---

[140] Data available on the UNHCR website, http://www.unhcr.ch/cgi-bin/texis/vtx/balkans-country?country=kosovo. On 15 October 1999, the Yugoslav Red Cross and local authorities indicated that the total number of registered internally displaced persons from Kosovo in both Serbia and Montenegro stood at 230,884.

[141] Interview, senior UNMIK police officer, Pristina, Kosovo, December 2004.

[142] High Commissioner for Human Rights, *Report on the Situation of Human Rights in Kosovo, Federal Republic of Yugoslavia*, E/CN.4/2000/10, 27 September 1999, para. 130.

[143] Independent International Commission on Kosovo, *The Kosovo Report*, p. 7.

Many of the problems confronting Kosovo today can be traced to the failure to deal with the early violence and to provide a secure environment, as required under Resolution 1244.

The situation in the city of Mitrovica in northern Kosovo is a microcosm of many of the issues confronting Kosovo as a whole. It has been effectively divided between a northern portion controlled by the Serbs, and a southern portion controlled by the Albanian population. In the initial chaos that followed the withdrawal of Yugoslav forces, a *de facto* partition of the province took place. Traditionally, mostly Serbs inhabited the northern part of Kosovo that borders Serbia proper, while the Ibar river provides a geographical divide from the rest of the province. Its proximity to Serbia means that it was one of the first areas affected by ethnic cleansing in 1998. The result of allowing a *de facto* green line across the bridges of the Ibar has been to create two Mitrovicas. In the words of the International Crisis Group, '[i]f the international community cannot re-establish Mitrovica as a single city, efforts to preserve a united Kosovo will also fail'.[144] Yet KFOR's early decision to erect checkpoints on both sides of the main Ibar bridges, in order to avoid clashes between the two communities, reinforced their division. Albanians were not allowed to cross into northern Kosovo. In the south, about 8,000 internally displaced persons waited[145] for the situation to improve. It was said that the French troops sent to secure Mitrovica in June 1999 acted as if they were in Bosnia,[146] where the UNPROFOR mandate required keeping warring factions apart. By contrast, the mandate in Kosovo specifically authorised KFOR to establish UN authority throughout the province. Despite this, nothing was done to bridge the gap between the various communities. Mitrovica became something akin to Mostar in Bosnia, with a bridge at the centre of the separation of two ethnic groups. As a result, the Serbs remained in the majority in the northern part of the town and in the northern areas of Kosovo in general and their numbers grew with the addition of internally displaced persons from elsewhere in Kosovo.

In the autumn of 1999, despite the presence of KFOR troops, further population displacements took place. Attacks on the approximately

---

[144] International Crisis Group, *Kosovo's Linchpin: Overcoming Division in Mitrovica*, ICG Balkans Report, No. 96, 31 May 2000, p. iii.

[145] UNHCR/OSCE Report, *Preliminary Assessment of the Situation of Ethnic Minorities in Kosovo*, 26 July 1999, para. 13.

[146] M. Ignatieff, *Empire Lite: Nation-Building in Bosnia, Kosovo and Afghanistan* (London: Vintage, 2003), p. 67.

2,500 Albanians who lived in the north prompted around 1,700 Albanians, Muslim Slavs and Turks to flee from there in early 2000. Those who remained became effective prisoners in their own areas. Soon a self-proclaimed 'civil defence' group was established. The so-called 'Bridge Watchers' were a well-organised and armed group of Serbs. They had the capacity to mobilise up to 1,000 demonstrators at short notice and often arranged blockades in the town, limiting UN and KFOR freedom of movement, sometimes for days at a time. Since the UNMIK police were unable to establish a permanent presence in this area, the 'Bridge Watchers' grew into an alternative 'law enforcement' body that patrolled the city and kept order. This situation was exploited by the regime in Belgrade, and members of the Serbian police[147] in civilian clothes also operated in Mitrovica. They effectively sealed off the northern part of the city from the rest of Kosovo, and denied the UN control of the area.

The immediate effect of the hostile environment was that the free movement of minorities became extremely limited. In many situations, complete villages were guarded by KFOR and the inhabitants were unable to travel without escort. In urban areas, districts and houses where minorities were known to live were surrounded by barbed wire and secured by static KFOR guards. The denial of freedom of movement meant denial of access to essential services and opportunities for employment and, even if they could access the services run by the majority, they were faced with harassment and discrimination. Phone lines and electricity were cut; mail was not delivered. In the circumstances, it was almost impossible to prevent a further deterioration in ethnic relations.

The problem of parallel political structures[148]

The failure of UNMIK and KFOR to provide a secure environment impacted on every aspect of life from education, to access to health, social services and employment. Finding a job in a post-conflict environment is a difficult task for all, but the lack of security and freedom of

---

[147] The police of the Serbian Ministry of Interior Affairs (Ministarstvo Unutrasnih Poslova, or MUP).

[148] OSCE Mission in Kosovo, Rule of Law and Human Rights Office, *Parallel Structures in Kosovo*, October 2003. This describes parallel structures as bodies that have been or still are operational in Kosovo after 10 June 1999 and that are not mandated under UN Security Council Resolution 1244. In the majority of cases, these institutions operate under the *de facto* authority of the Serbian government and assume jurisdiction over Kosovo from Serbia proper, or operate in the territory of Kosovo.

movement, the inability to communicate in the majority language, and the application of discriminatory practices made it specifically difficult for minorities. In such circumstances, unemployment among the vulnerable communities increased dramatically.

It is not surprising then that members of minority groups, especially the Serbs, boycotted the UN administration and its institutions. The existence of functioning parallel structures, wherein both the UN and the government in Belgrade assumed authority over issues such as the judiciary, social services, health care and education, made such a boycott possible. The Kosovar Serbs never accepted the UN and NATO presence in their country and maintained separate courts where the Serbia-Montenegrin state laws are applied, and judges and prosecutors receive their salary from Belgrade. Schools, post offices, hospitals, factories and the public administration function according to Serb rules and their staff receive their payment from Belgrade. Social care and pensions come from the capital too. In reality, as a response to the inability of the UN to stop the hostilities and to provide a reasonable standard of living for the Serbian minority, a parallel political and social system has been established.

The situation created by the maintenance of parallel structures has caused confusion and uncertainty and has exacerbated tensions between Albanians and Serbs. Although UNMIK has never officially accepted these structures, there was little in practice that it could do about them. The minorities have few options. Even if UNMIK could manage to stop Belgrade interfering in public affairs, that would leave a large number of people not only outside the Serbian social scheme, but also without access to the most basic services.

In a recent report, the OSCE explained that the existence of the parallel structures was perceived as necessary, owing to security concerns and the mutual mistrust between both communities. However, in its recommendations the report failed to address these fundamental issues. Instead, it suggests:

> to improve the services offered by UNMIK and the PISG [Provisional Institutions of Self Government] and thus gain public confidence, to reduce supply of parallel services by negotiations with the suppliers for cutbacks and to impose certain policies/measures that can be enforced in order to ... reduce, and eventually eliminate the dependence of some communities upon parallel structures in Kosovo.[149]

---

[149] *Ibid.*, p. 8, Recommendations.

It also suggests that the impasse can only be solved by a political agreement between UNMIK and the Serbian authorities.

This analysis is flawed in that the Serbs' use of parallel structures is not a reflection on the quality of the services provided by UNMIK or on the fact that there are no enforceable policies. It is the failure to provide a secure environment and the consequent pervasive mistrust and discrimination existing on all sides that have left Serbs with little alternative. The failure to recognise and address this situation facilitates its maintenance, and many on both sides have a vested interest in maintaining the *status quo*. Kosovar Albanians want all obstacles to the creation of a mono-ethnic state removed in order to clear the way for final independence. This includes the Serb presence in most of Kosovo, and the parallel structures. The Serbs want to remain, and to retain Kosovo, or as much of it as possible, as part of Serbia. They also want to exploit the discrimination against Serbian and other minorities in order to postpone the decision about Kosovo's final status for as long as possible.

The peace agreement reached in the aftermath of the NATO bombing was concluded hastily and left many issues unresolved. The Kosovar Albanians were not happy with Resolution 1244 because it did not give them independence. The Serbs were unhappy because they were coerced into accepting it. Actually, during the years of UN rule, neither party has complied in full with the resolution. UNMIK is not a post-peace-agreement peacekeeping force based on the consent of the parties. No real progress will be made until there is some accommodation between the parties and no UN laws or regulations will change this fundamental fact. The UN has played a major role in developing the legal and administrative system. It also has a role in supporting reconciliation and confidence-building among the communities. It is the responsibility of the political leaders on all sides to persuade their constituencies that violence will not provide a long-term solution.

The situation relating to minorities and their protection remains problematic. The atrocities perpetrated against the Serbs and other vulnerable groups demonstrate that there are no 'good guys' and 'bad guys' in the complex mosaic of Balkan identities and conflicts. Despite UNMIK Regulations dictating affirmative action, there has been little real improvement in their situation. The violence directed against vulnerable minorities in the initial months resulted in an exodus of almost half of the Serb, Roma and other non-Albanian population. The UN and KFOR were unable to deal with these large-scale attacks. It became evident that the violence was part of an organised campaign with the express purpose of ethnically cleansing Kosovo. As a result, mono-ethnic enclaves and separated urban areas were spontaneously created.

The demilitarisation of the KLA and the prevention of a civil war between supporters of the KLA and Ibrahim Rugova's Democratic League of Kosovo was a significant accomplishment in the early period of UNMIK and KFOR's deployment. Resolution 1244 demanded that the KLA and other armed Kosovar Albanian groups bring an immediate end to all offensive actions and comply with the requirements for demilitarisation. The KLA was quick to realise the necessity of co-operating with NATO. It took just ten days for the Undertaking of Demilitarisation and Transformation to be signed. The first article of the agreement mandated the KLA's 'disengagement from zones of conflict, subsequent demilitarisation and reintegration into civil society'. A timetable was also agreed, as was a policy of preferential access to available places in the Kosovo Protection Corps and the Kosovo Police Service.

A practical difficulty with any guerrilla organisation is its lack of a unified command structure. It is certain that many weapons were not handed over, but this should not detract from the overall achievement in a short timeframe. The demobilisation of a somewhat disparate guerrilla group such as the KLA into a civil defence corps was a unique challenge for the UN. It also posed a potential threat to the sovereignty of the Federal Republic of Yugoslavia over Kosovo. Unfortunately, KFOR did not take the initiative and move against those elements that retained large weapons stocks and were behind much of the violence against the minority communities. These have since become major players in Kosovo's criminal underworld, seeking to subvert the fragile democratic process unfolding there[150] and contributing to the law and order problem that is so prevalent in Kosovo.

The successor to the KLA, the Kosovo Protection Corps, has not received full international acceptance. Many KFOR contingents do not trust the Corps and disapprove of the United States' unequivocal support for it. The manner in which the structure of the Corps replicates that of the KLA and the integration of KLA leaders into similar positions in the Corps poses serious questions about its role in post-conflict Kosovo. However, post-conflict nation-building requires more than

---

[150] Interview, senior UNMIK police officer, Pristina, Kosovo, December 2004.

disarmament. The Kosovo Protection Corps itself is a legal entity created by the international community. It was conceived as a compromise between the need for demilitarisation and the need to accommodate the KLA'S aspiration to become a standing army. The international community has a responsibility to reform and resource the Corps so that it can fulfil its intended function in a professional manner. This is an urgent priority. Concerns about links with organised crime or war criminals must be addressed, but before this is possible they must be spelled out in clear terms and those responsible held accountable. The Kosovo Protection Corps could be disbanded, but such an option is not realistic or advisable. It risks inflaming the Albanian population and creating a dangerous security threat.

Military effectiveness and problems of command and control

UNOSOM II

The establishment of the UNOSOM II force had many similarities with that of a traditional peacekeeping force such as UNIFIL. A Turkish General, Cevic Bir, commanded the force, and the contingents under his control hailed from a wide political spectrum. The force was established under Resolution 814 of 26 March 1993, which included a provision that the force would be supervised closely by the Secretary-General and the Security Council. More importantly, it cited Chapter VII, which expressly authorised UNOSOM II to use force. This was the first such occasion since the ONUC operation in the Congo, which prevented the attempted secession of the Katanga province, that a UN operation of this nature was authorised to use force in this way. The operative paragraphs of Resolution 814 contained the following provisions:

> Acting under Chapter VII of the Charter of the UN,
>
> 5. Decides to expand the size of the UNOSOM force and its mandate in accordance with the recommendations contained in paragraphs 56–88 of the report of the Secretary-General of 3 March 1993, and the provisions of this resolution;
>
> 6. Authorizes the mandate for the expanded UNOSOM (UNOSOM II) for an initial period through 31 October 1993, unless previously renewed by the Security Council;
>
> 7. Emphasizes the crucial importance of disarmament and the urgent need to build on the efforts of UNITAF in accordance with paragraphs 59–69 of the report of the Secretary-General of 3 March 1993;

8. Demands that all Somali parties, including movements and factions, comply fully with the commitments they have undertaken in the agreements they concluded at the Informal Preparatory Meeting on Somali Political Reconciliation in Addis Ababa, and in particular with their Agreement on Implementing the Cease-fire and on Modalities of Disarmament (S/25168, annex III); . . .

12. Requests the Secretary-General to provide security, as appropriate, to assist in the repatriation of refugees and the assisted resettlement of displaced persons, utilizing UNOSOM II force, paying particular attention to those areas where major instability continues to threaten peace and security in the region; . . .

14. Requests the Secretary-General, through his Special Representative, to direct the Force Commander of UNOSOM II to assume responsibility for the consolidation, expansion and maintenance of a secure environment throughout Somalia, taking account of the particular circumstances in each locality, on an expedited basis in accordance with the recommendations contained in his report of 3 March 1993, and in this regard to organize a prompt, smooth and phased transition from UNITAF to UNOSOM II; . . .

18. Requests the Secretary-General to keep the Security Council fully informed on action taken to implement the present resolution, in particular to submit as soon as possible a report to the Council containing recommendations for establishment of Somali police forces and thereafter to report no later than every ninety days on the progress achieved in accomplishing the objectives set out in the present resolution.

UNOSOM II took over formally from UNITAF/UNOSOM I on 4 May 1993.[151] This was not as early as had originally been planned, but there had been no major crises in the meantime and the United States could claim to be handing over the ship in good shape. A new United States administration was now at the helm, and one of the primary concerns was ensuring that President Clinton was not exposed to risk in a foreign intervention handed on from the Bush administration. But the United States had invested a lot of energy and prestige in Somalia and it could not now slip away quietly. Nor could it be seen to allow the follow-up operation to fail, and in these circumstances the United States continued to play a leading role in every facet of UNOSOM II's

---

[151] In accordance with Resolution 814, 26 March 1993. It provided for a multi-national force of 20,000 troops, 8,000 logistical and 3,000 civilian support staff. The US also agreed to provide a tactical quick reaction force.

organisation and mandate.[152] In many ways this suited the UN Secretariat and Boutros-Ghali, who realised that the operation depended on American military and political support. The United States agreed to provide logistical and tactical support under a complex command and control arrangement but this, among other things, was later to cause a serious rift between the Clinton administration and the Secretariat.[153]

While in theory the United States had handed back control of the operation to the UN, the reality was much different. A convenient mechanism to allow the US to ensure that one of its own officers retained full command of United States troops in Somalia was put in place by the appointment of General Montgomery as Deputy Force Commander. It was no coincidence either that an experienced NATO officer would command this 'strange and fragmented operation' or that retired American Admiral Howe would act as the SRSG.[154] The system put in place gave significant influence to the United States, even if it did not formally command the mission. The full implications of this set-up are explored in Chapter 4. In addition, this complex system was made even more cumbersome by the US decision to establish a Quick Reaction Force outside the UN chain of command.[155] This amounted to the establishment of a parallel United States chain of command that was intended to exist alongside, but independent of, the UN command structure. This was a recipe for confusion and potential disaster in time of crises. The continued American domination proved to be a mixed blessing for UNOSOM II, and events showed that the structures put in place proved unable to maintain cohesion under pressure and ultimately contributed to the demise of the force.

---

[152] Ultimately, this caused serious differences between the Secretary-General and the Clinton administration: Boutros-Ghali, *Unvanquished*, pp. 92–102. For an overview of the experience of the larger European armies involved in Somalia, see G. Prunier, 'The Experience of European Armies in Operation Restore Hope', in Clarke and Herbst (eds.), *Learning from Somalia*, pp. 135–47; and, for US conditions on participation, see *Message from the President of the United States – A Report on the Military Operation in Somalia, October 13, 1993* (Washington, DC: US Government Printing Office, 1993).

[153] See Boutros-Ghali, *Unvanquished*, pp. 93–4; and J. Howe, 'Relations Between the United States and the United Nations in Dealing with Somalia', and H. Johnson and T. Dagne, 'Congress and the Somalia Crisis', both in Clarke and Herbst (eds.), *Learning from Somalia*, pp. 173–190 (esp. pp. 179–84) and pp. 191–204, respectively.

[154] This was the description used by Boutros-Ghali, *Unvanquished*, p. 93.

[155] The United States also deployed a specially constituted Task Force Ranger, which remained at all times under the direct command and control of the commander-in-chief of United States special operations.

UNIFIL

The issue of command and control was closely linked to the final condition that the Secretary-General considered essential for the effective operation of UNIFIL, namely, that it function as an integrated and efficient military unit. Many officers who served with UNIFIL since 1978 consider that this condition was not met, and it is the consensus among participants and commentators that this was also true of UNOSOM II. While it would be futile to argue to the contrary in respect of UNOSOM II, the situation of UNIFIL is worthy of further comment. The Secretary-General's own choice of words were unfortunate in that they may have created the impression that the force established was to be a conventional military unit properly constituted for traditional military operations. This is not the case. The UNIFIL mission, even if unclear in certain respects, was a peacekeeping mission based on well-established principles and precedents. Even today, peacekeeping is a relatively novel military concept and the conduct of such missions is very different from conventional military operations.

KFOR

The four KFOR multi-national brigade areas, though multi-national, were dominated by France, Germany, the United States and Finland. Italy is the lead nation in the Multinational Specialized Unit, which is a police force with military status and an overall police capability. Despite the race by Russian forces in 1999 to seize Pristina airport, Russia was not granted a security zone, as this might have facilitated a *de facto* partition of Kosovo if large numbers of Serbs decided to move there.

KFOR troops come from thirty-five NATO and non-NATO member countries.[156] Although this undermines the military effectiveness of the force as a whole, it is not the biggest problem confronting KFOR. Each brigade is responsible for a specific area of operations and, under Resolution 1244, they are under the unified command and control of

---

[156] The NATO member states participating in KFOR (December 2004) are: Belgium, Bulgaria, Canada, the Czech Republic, Denmark, Estonia, France, Germany, Greece, Hungary, Italy, Lithuania, Luxembourg, Norway, Poland, Portugal, Romania, Slovakia, Slovenia, Spain, Turkey, the United Kingdom and the United States. The non-NATO participating states are: Argentina, Armenia, Austria, Azerbaijan, Finland, Georgia, Ireland, Morocco, Sweden, Switzerland, Ukraine and the United Arab Emirates.

Commander KFOR. This is a military term that involves only a limited form of transfer of power over troops. In addition, each contributing state has entered caveats in respect of the participation of its troops. In reality, the Multi-National Brigade Commanders have a significant degree of actual autonomy of command, and the overall KFOR Commander has restricted operational command and control. He or she can certainly task the Brigade Commanders, but there is no real sanction should they decide to ignore the 'orders' emanating from headquarters. This means that national governments have a decisive role in the strategy and policies adopted by KFOR. Not surprisingly, there are significant differences in the priorities and standard operating procedures adopted in each Multi-National Brigade area.

Deficiencies in the UN organisation and structures

The UN Organization does not have a military branch.[157] Despite the establishment of the Department of Peacekeeping Operations (DPKO), problems remain at Secretariat level, and the Brahimi Report recommended that a number of structural adjustments be made to address these.[158] The conduct of peacekeeping operations has been on an *ad hoc* basis to date; and, due to the inability of members to agree a comprehensive set of guidelines to govern all UN operations, this is likely to remain the *status quo*.[159]

The omission of military personnel from the Secretariat stems from the deliberate policy to maintain the strictest possible control over the military. However, the potential political ramifications of all decisions made by the Force Commander or his subordinates on the ground has also been a major factor in determining the UN's reluctance to relinquish any part of its overall control and responsibility for peacekeeping operations. Much more

---

[157] While the Secretary-General has a military adviser, he does not have sufficient military staff employed in the headquarters for the planning and organisation of operations. Article 47 of the UN Charter provides for the establishment of a military staff committee. No agreements have been concluded to place armed forces at the disposal of the Security Council under Article 43 to date. Nor has the committee been involved in peacekeeping operations.

[158] See the *Report of the Panel on UN Peacekeeping Operations* (Brahimi Report), UN Doc. A/55/305-S/2000/809, 23 August 2000, esp. the Summary of Recommendations, paras. 9–18; and M. Berdal, *Whither UN Peacekeeping*, Adelphi Paper 281, October 1993, pp. 52–61.

[159] See *Comprehensive Review of the Whole Question of Peacekeeping Operations in All Their Aspects*, UN Doc. A/31/337 (1976).

so than in conventional military operations, almost every move in peace-keeping is liable to have political consequences. A seemingly inconsequential initiative in the field may precipitate an international incident. This may cause frustration among the military involved in a peacekeeping force and may lead some to conclude that it is not functioning effectively as a military unit. The problem is often exacerbated by the political necessity of implementing a deliberately vague mandate.

In order that the force be acceptable to the Security Council, the parties involved and the international community, it is necessary to ensure that there is a wide geographic distribution and a political balance among the contributing states. This is often detrimental to the smooth operation of the force as an integrated military unit. When disparities in culture, training and experience are taken into account, it is remarkable that a multi-national force can operate at all.

There were more serious problems in respect of UNOSOM II. The command and control mechanism was complex. When this was applied to a multi-national force with a difficult mandate in a failed state like Somalia, the overall effect was a recipe for disaster. The problem of double allegiance has arisen in respect of UNIFIL, UNOSOM II and KFOR missions. However, it was much more acute in the case of UNOSOM. The commander of a peacekeeping force has both civilian and military functions, and the troops are usually considered international civil servants for the duration of their UN service. Nevertheless, they continue to remain part of the armed forces of their respective countries. It is now accepted that contingents will consult their national governments on decisions which may not conform to defence or foreign policy directives back home. In this regard, serious problems arose in the course of the operation in the Congo (ONUC, 1960–4), when contributing states disagreed with UN policy, in particular its apparent reluctance to take stronger action to resolve the situation in Katanga. In the case of UNIFIL, no similar problems can be noted. Unfortunately, one of the practical lessons from UN involvement in Somalia (and the former Yugoslavia) is that the organisation 'cannot manage complex political military operations'.[160] However, the well-publicised differences between the commander of the Italian contingent and the UNOSOM II force commander show how serious this problem was in Somalia.[161]

---

[160] C. Crocker, 'The Lessons of Somalia: Not Everything Went Wrong' (1995) 74(3) *Foreign Affairs* 5.
[161] Boutros-Ghali, *Unvanquished*, p. 96.

The Secretary-General considered that the Italians were a 'mistake' and that as a former colonial power they pursued their own agenda. They favoured a less confrontational approach and attempted to resolve any difficulties with local militias by means of negotiation. The Italians felt that this had worked well for them and they linked the high casualties of the Pakistanis to the strict enforcement policy of the UNOSOM II command.[162] The dispute between the Italian commander and the Force Commander caused serious operational difficulties on the ground and hindered the effectiveness of the force at a critical period. Other contingents had less publicised difficulties in this regard also. As contingents are usually placed under the operational control, and not under the full command, of a force commander of multi-national forces, this is a problem that will inevitably reoccur.

There were also occasions when national governments, most notably the French, interfered in the operational affairs of UNIFIL. The most serious occasion for the Irish contingent occurred in 1989 when the French government prevented members of the French contingent from assisting in the search for three Irish soldiers who had been kidnapped.[163] The French probably feared becoming embroiled in another clash with Shiite militias similar to that which occurred in 1986.[164] Whatever the reason, it indicates the problems which can arise in an international UN force. The military effectiveness of UNIFIL was also hampered by the location of its headquarters, which were situated in the enclave controlled-by the *de facto* forces.

The need for a comprehensive briefing and training for all personnel prior to commencing duty with a peacekeeping force is vital. Many regular officers, in particular those from large countries accustomed to a more aggressive, conventional military role, must be given the opportunity to adjust to restrictions on the use of force and the lack of a proper military intelligence network. Taking into account the essential nature of UNIFIL and the many constraints under which it operated, its success as an integrated and efficient military unit is remarkable. In any event, a peacekeeping mission must be judged primarily by how it fulfils its

---

[162] UN Doc. S/1994/653, *Report of the Commission of Inquiry Established Pursuant to Resolution 885 (1993) to Investigate Armed Attacks on UNOSOM II Personnel*, 1 June 1994, paras. 125–50, esp. para. 147.

[163] Interview, senior UNIFIL staff officer, Naqoura, Lebanon, October 1989.

[164] The French contingent became embroiled in serious clashes with members of the Amal militia after a French sentry shot and killed a local Amal leader and his bodyguard at a checkpoint on 11 August 1986. This incident is discussed in Chapter 4 below.

political purpose and not solely on its military efficiency. If this is applied to the Somalia operations, then the intervention in all its manifestations must be judged a failure. Although financial concerns should not be allowed to dictate the pace or scale of intervention, the reality is otherwise. For this reason it is worth keeping in mind that the Operation Restore Hope component of the mission cost six or seven times more than the total United States development assistance to Somalia for three decades, and more than the total assistance to sub-Saharan Africa in 1994–5.[165]

Critics of UNIFIL can point to its military ineffectiveness in terms of its mandate, and to the costs of maintaining the operation. However, it did provide an international presence and a restraining influence on the parties to the conflict, even if this was not at a level many critics found acceptable. When the time was ripe, there was a pre-existing UN force on the ground to facilitate the Israeli withdrawal in 2000.

Conclusion

An often overlooked factor in the criticism of the UN is that states most often resort to the Organization when it suits their purposes and the problem at hand otherwise seems insoluble. The situation created by the 1978 invasion of Lebanon was such an instance. This is not to say that organisational failures, such as those identified by the Brahimi Report, did not contribute to the difficulties, but that this was part of the problem. The UN, the European Union and the African Union have all found that responding to internal conflicts is very difficult. The establishment of UNIFIL was primarily sponsored by the United States to expedite an Israeli withdrawal and to ensure the peace negotiations between Israel and Egypt were not jeopardised. UNIFIL also went on to help prevent the outbreak of another major conflict between Syria and Israel. Israel and the United States, despite their otherwise strong links, did not always share perceptions as to what constituted a common threat in the Middle East. Co-operation from the Israelis was vital to the success of UNIFIL. When it became clear that it was not forth-coming, the United States never brought sufficient pressure to bear on the Israelis to ensure that they would succumb. The mandate agreed upon for UNIFIL was unrealistic and lent itself to different

---

[165] This item of information is cited in T. Weiss, 'Rekindling Hope in UN Humanitarian Intervention', in Clarke and Herbst (eds.), *Learning from Somalia*, pp. 207–28 at p. 216.

interpretations by opposing parties. Many elements of the overall plan for the deployment of UNIFIL had obvious deficiencies. In this way, its success has remained dependent on factors outside its control.

Recent multi-national interventions, whether under the banner of the UN or an independent coalition, have often failed to make a long-term improvement in the crisis situation. At the operational level, there has been a tendency to rely on short-term political expediency to the detriment of long-term strategic policies. In general, the military components of multi-dimensional operations have developed a doctrinal approach that largely ignores the realities of the crisis environment and instead seeks to rely on the limited version of the problem that can be resolved by military means.[166] This is a natural response from a conventional military that perceives its role as essentially limited to the provision of security, and, even then, its first priority will always be its own security.

The Somalia experience demonstrates that military establishments need to re-examine their role in complex political and humanitarian emergencies. There is considerable mistrust between civil and military components. For a multi-dimensional peacekeeping operation to be effective, humanitarian and developmental aspects must be accorded equal status. Attempts at co-ordination by the military were interpreted as attempts at control by NGOs and humanitarian agencies on the ground. The establishment of civil–military co-ordination (CIMIC) mechanisms in all current operations has helped matters, but there is still a need for the military to expand its concept of security to consider much more than 'keeping the lid' on things and to embrace the security of the local population, reconstruction and rehabilitation. The mandates of recent UN peacekeeping operations reflect this by invoking Chapter VII of the UN Charter and acknowledging a responsibility to protect civilians. The failure to disarm the clans was a serious flaw in the implementation phase of the UN operations in Somali, but even this would have been insufficient without the creation of a safe environment.

---

[166] J. MacKinlay and R. Kent, 'A New Approach to Complex Emergencies' (1997) 4(4) *International Peacekeeping* 31–49 at 45–6. See also A. de Waal and R. Omaar, 'Can Military Intervention Be "Humanitarian"?' (March/June 1994) *Middle East Report* 5–8; and T. Weiss, 'Military–Civilian Humanitarianism: The "Age" of Innocence is Over' (1995) 2(2) *International Peacekeeping* 157–74. For a military perspective, see S. L. Arnold, 'Somalia: An Operation Other Than War' (December 1993) *Military Review* 26–35; and W. D. Freeman, 'Operation Restore Hope: A US Centcom Perspective' (September 1993) *Military Review* 61–72.

The narrow focus on humanitarian and military issues meant that the underlying political problems did not receive sufficient attention. What political agenda existed was overtaken by military events and the adoption of a coercive response. Events in Somalia should not be used to discredit second-generation peacekeeping, or to deny the imperative to respond that global human crises such as those of Rwanda, East Timor or Darfur. The offensive operations launched by UN peacekeepers against militia forces in the Democratic Republic of the Congo during 2005 and 2006 indicate that the UN has learned from the mistakes of the past.

One of the consequences of the NATO intervention in Kosovo is the impact it had on how the organisation is perceived around the world. It was no longer a mere defensive security arrangement. The by-passing of the UN and the lack of a real effort to reach a negotiated solution was a clear harbinger of what was to come, especially as the United States grew ever more confident in the projection of its power and ideology. It is no coincidence that, having dithered for three years, in the second half of 1999 Russia decided to resolve the Chechnya issue by the use of force. Although influenced by the Kosovo case, Russia could still also argue that there was no violation of international law as the breakaway republic was part of Russian territory.

For both Russia and China, it would have been preferable had the Kosovo intervention been interest-driven. In such situations, there is always room for compromise. But Kosovo was norm-driven, and such norms are seldom invoked with a view to compromise.[167] To critics of NATO action, the cure greatly worsened the Milosevic disease.[168] In a world in which the challenges of Darfur and Kosovo will reoccur, we face the painful dilemma of being damned if we do and damned if we don't.[169] All sides in a conflict can manipulate events for their own purposes. The Albanians provoked a Serb response in order to precipitate NATO intervention. In this way NATO, and especially the United States, became a tool of the KLA. Once this occurred, the oppressed quickly assumed the role of oppressors.

---

[167] C. Bell, 'Force, Diplomacy, and Norms', in A. Schnabel and R. Thakur (eds.), *Kosovo and the Challenge of Humanitarian Intervention* (Toyko and New York: United Nations University Press, 2000), pp. 448–62 at p. 460.

[168] R. Falk, 'Reflections on the Kosovo War' (1999) 1(2) *Global Dialogue* 93.

[169] R. Thakur and A. Schnabel, 'Unbridled Humanitarianism: Between Justice, Power and Authority', in Schnabel and Thakur (eds.), *Kosovo and the Challenge of Humanitarian Intervention*, pp. 496–504 at p. 497.

The NATO campaign did not lead to a formal peace agreement, but rather a cessation of hostilities. This and the mandate of the UNMIK administration left political and constitutional issues unresolved. Despite official United States opposition to independence for Kosovo, there was a widespread belief in the State Department that some form of political division between Kosovo and Yugoslavia was inevitable.[170] In contrast to the proposed Rambouillet Agreement, the Military Technical Agreement indicated the retention of the *status quo*, while Resolution 1244 is seized upon by Albanians as a road-map to independence. Kosovo is effectively a partitioned and undefined political entity. Changing the facts on the ground may prove difficult to accomplish and impossible to maintain. The Kosovo situation is contrary to where other states in Europe have evolved, i.e. the voluntary relinquishment of sovereignty and the convergence of liberal democracies in a system that respects and protects minorities.

According to Henry Kissinger, the 'ultimate legacy of Kosovo will depend on whether our diplomatic endgame matches the display of power'.[171] It might have been preferable to have determined the status of Kosovo first, and then to have worked towards ensuring the protection of its minorities and any new borders agreed. Russian suspicion of NATO action in Kosovo was overtaken in time by a sense of humiliation and, despite the pre-emptive seizure of Pristina airport, Russia was ultimately denied a separate sector as part of KFOR. Likewise, Chinese opposition became more vocal and populist after the bombing of the Chinese embassy in Belgrade. Unable to discern a clear foreign or security policy objective, the concept of humanitarian intervention was perceived as a Trojan horse for imperialist desires. The failure of aerial bombardment to resolve the crises did not surprise most Europeans and added to the lack of confidence in American judgment. The high-tech military campaign was undertaken in a way that suggested the underlying premise was that the life of one NATO serviceperson was not worth risking to avoid endangering hundreds of Kosovar lives and the deportation of thousands of others.

The NATO intervention and subsequent UN administration in Kosovo have created an unprecedented legal and political situation.

---

[170] W. Buckley, 'Not Losing Sight of Justice: A Response to Halperin's Statement', in Buckley (ed.), *Kosovo: Contending Voices*, pp. 231–45 at p. 239.

[171] H. Kissinger, 'Kosovo and the Vicissitudes of American Foreign Policy', in Buckley (ed.), *Kosovo: Contending Voices*, p. 305.

According to Security Council Resolution 1244, Kosovo is not an independent state; it remains an integral part of Serbia and Montenegro. However, the same resolution authorised the Secretary-General to establish an international civil presence in Kosovo and to administer the province under UN rule. In this way, the province is *de jure* part of a state, but *de facto* Serbia does not have any influence over the matters within Kosovo. This has created an environment where the protection of human rights, especially minority rights, is problematic. Unfortunately, the riots of March 2004 were perceived by the Serb community and Belgrade as the culmination of a process intended to push the Serbs out of Kosovo, especially its larger towns, with the exception of the north. The elections at the end of 2004 did not succeed in encouraging the Serb community to participate, and this may well put their interests and protection at greater risk in the long term.

The surrogate UN administration does not have the 'legal personality' to act as a state under public international law;[172] therefore it cannot become a party to any of the international human rights treaties. People who live in the territory of Kosovo are not able to invoke the protective mechanisms of the International Covenant on Civil and Political Rights, the European Convention on Human Rights or any other treaty even though – according to the Framework Constitution – many of the treaties are directly applicable in Kosovo. What is more, the UN administration cannot be held legally responsible for human rights violations as it is not a state.

The NATO campaign did succeed in facilitating the return of one million refugees and displaced persons to their homes in Kosovo. However, NATO and the UN later presided over the ethnic cleansing of Serbs and failed to protect other vulnerable communities in Kosovo. The credibility that the initial intervention earned for NATO has since been undermined. Somalia shows that robust ROE and increased size are not enough, and, while it is imperative not to employ an emasculated UN force, it is important to have a clear military and political strategy agreed at the outset. The problem was essentially political and not a result of the phenomena associated with the end of the Cold War; moreover, lessons learned in the Congo during the ONUC operation in the 1960s and elsewhere were ignored. It was the neo-colonial attempts to mould future Somali political arrangements that led to

---

[172] See Montevideo Convention on the Rights and Duties of States, entered into force on 26 December 1934.

UNOSOM II becoming a party to the conflict. It is not true to say that the UN broadened the mandate against the wishes of the United States; in fact the United States drafted many of the resolutions and presented these to the UN for implementation, especially Resolution 814 (1993)[173] on nation-building.

UNIFIL, in contrast, had an almost exclusively military mandate. When this proved impossible to implement, the *de facto* mission became the provision of a secure environment for the local population. It took nearly twenty-three years for UNIFIL to fulfil this mandate, but its ultimate success in achieving this goal may be said to have vindicated the role of traditional peacekeeping. The same may not be said of the intervention in Somalia. Apart from the loss of life on all sides, the tragedy of Somalia is the failure to learn the right lessons from a situation where the UN was called upon to fulfil a range of impossible and confused tasks.

[173] 26 March 1993; see note 80 above.

3

Legal framework of UN peacekeeping forces and issues of command and control

Introduction

The question of command and control of UN and other multi-national operations is one of the more serious issues confronting the formation of international forces. Command of UN forces is fraught with difficulties arising from both subjective human factors and objective legal constraints. This chapter examines these and related issues with particular reference to the Lebanon (UNIFIL), Somalia (UNOSOM II) and Kosovo (UNMIK/KFOR) operations. The problems encountered at an international level often have their origins in municipal law and the national policy of contributing states. For example, under Canadian law, at no stage in any international operation is national command of Canadian Forces to be handed over to a foreign commander.[1] Yet it is axiomatic that unity of command is a necessary component for the success of any military force, including international UN forces. The submission of national contingents serving in UN forces to foreign command is unavoidable in multi-national UN forces.[2] In theory, the command structure of such forces is straightforward, but in practice this is seldom the case. A mechanism to overcome the difficulties created has been described as follows:

> The multi-national character [of UN forces] introduces difficulties that otherwise might not be encountered. Command is normally a national matter, and some countries, in recognition of this basic fact, have specific prohibitions precluding their military forces from taking orders from nationals of another country. Fortunately ... a modus vivendi [can] be

[1] M. H. MacDougall, 'UN Operations: Who Should Be in Charge?' (1994) 33 *Revue de droit militaire et de droit de la guerre/The Military Law and the Law of War Review* 21–87 at 27; D. W. Bowett, *UN Forces* (London: Stevens, 1964), esp. pp. 337–47; and *The Preparedness Gap: Making Peace Operations Work in the 21st Century*, Policy Report of the United Nations Association of the USA (2001), pp. 3 and 15.

[2] H. McCoubrey and N. White, *The Blue Helmets: Legal Regulation of UN Military Operations* (Aldershot: Dartmouth, 1996), p. 144.

found during actual operations . . . by using [national] . . . officers on the Force Commander's staff to transmit force directives.[3]

How this works in practice is evident from the command structure of German forces in Somalia. These remained under the full command authority of the German Minister for Defence, but the forces came under the 'operational control' of the United States commander of the Logistic Support Command. In a like manner, Canadian law and military custom permits operational control to be vested in a Force Commander or equivalent, but requires that operational command be retained by a member of the Canadian Forces. This system seems to operate without any serious difficulty for Canada or the international forces to which Canada contributes.

The situation with regard to Ireland is more problematic. As will be illustrated, Ireland's contribution to the peacekeeping force in Lebanon was significant, yet the Force Commander of UNIFIL does not appear to have been vested with lawful command over the Irish Defence Forces that formed part of the peacekeeping force. As will be developed later in this chapter, this matter has certain implications under Irish constitutional law which do not appear to have been considered.

One of the fundamental characteristics of a UN peacekeeping force is its international character, and, as such, it represents neither contributing states nor the host state. It logically follows that a peacekeeping force should not take the side of any party to a conflict, in particular, where there has been a breakdown in law and order to the extent that it is difficult to determine which, if any, forces represent the legitimate interests of the state concerned. The consent of the host state to the presence of a peacekeeping force is normally specified in a legal instrument known as the Status of Force Agreement (SOFA) which outlines the rights and duties of the force.[4]

Legal framework of UN operations and the SOFA

In order to understand the international legal context within which the municipal laws of contributing states apply, it is necessary to examine

---

[3] J. M. Boyd, *UN Peacekeeping Operations: A Military and Political Appraisal* (New York: Praeger, 1971), p. 150; and Lt-Col. Vogt, 'Experiences of a German Legal Adviser to the UNOSOM II Mission' (1996) 35 *Revue de droit militaire et de droit de la guerre/Military Law and Law of War Review* 219–27 at 220.

[4] *The Peacekeepers Handbook* (New York, International Peace Academy, 1984), p. 362.

the legal framework of UN peacekeeping and similar forces.[5] The main legal structure adopted for the majority of peacekeeping forces derives from the precedent of the first ever such force established in 1956, the United Nations Emergency Force in Egypt (UNEF I, 1956–67).[6] Nonetheless, individual forces possess their own distinctive legal characteristics. Before a peacekeeping force commences operations, the Force Commander must receive some guidance. For this reason, the Secretary-General issues a Directive based on the mandate which provides the Force Commander with instructions for carrying out the tasks assigned. At the same time, a SOFA must be negotiated with the host state that will enable the force to carry out its functions within the area of operations without undue interference. Based on these two documents, the Force Commander will issue instructions and standing operating procedures. Ideally, both the Directive and the SOFA are signed and ready when the force is being deployed, but this is seldom the case. Most peacekeeping forces are rushed affairs and tying up the loose administrative and legal strings is not a priority. As a result, the legal framework for UN peacekeeping forces is usually made up of the following:

- the resolution of the Security Council or the General Assembly;
- the SOFA or Status of Mission Agreement (SOMA) between the UN and the host state;
- the agreement by exchange of letters between each of the participating states and the UN; and
- the regulations for the force issued by the Secretary-General.

The need to define in advance the legal basis upon which the force relies has been accepted for some time as most advisable given the difficulties that can be encountered. In the absence of a SOFA, the status of foreign military personnel travelling to a host country is essentially that of foreign tourists.[7] Whereas the mandate establishing a force defines its purpose, a SOFA provides the more detailed principles under which a force functions and specifies its relationship with the host government and other countries party to the conflict. In this regard,

---

[5] P. Rowe, 'Maintaining Discipline in UN Peace Support Operations: The Legal Quagmire for Military Contingents' (2000) 5(1) *Journal of Conflict and Security Law* 45–62.

[6] *Secretary-General's Report to the Security Council on the Implementation of Resolutions,* UN Doc. S/12611, 19 March 1978, para. 4.

[7] D. Fleck, 'Present and Future Challenges for the Status of Forces (Ius in Praesentia): A Commentary to Applicable Status Law Provisions', in D. Fleck (ed.), *The Handbook of the Law of Visiting Forces* (Oxford: Oxford University Press, 2001), p. 47.

it provides for special freedoms, privileges and duties that are necessary to enable a peacekeeping force to carry out its mission. These include, *inter alia*, freedom of movement, freedom to carry arms, unrestricted communications in its area of operations, immunity for its members from criminal prosecution so that they are subject to the exclusive jurisdiction of their national state, landing and procurement facilities etc. The general nature of SOFAs is described by Professor Kirgis as follows:

> When peacekeeping forces are to be stationed on the territory of a state, arrangements need to be made between the UN and the state regarding such things as logistics, facilities, privileges, and immunities of persons from property, dispute settlement etc. Beginning with the First UN Emergency Force in Egypt, these arrangements have been embodied in formal arrangements between the UN and host governments. Drawing on this experience, in 1990 the Secretary-General (at the request of the General Assembly) prepared a model agreement to serve as the basis for individual agreements subject to modifications appropriate for particular cases.[8]

The obvious difficulty that arises in situations like Lebanon and Somalia is the question of who represents the legitimate interests of the state. In Somalia, all semblance of normality had disintegrated and there was no effective government with which to negotiate and agree terms for deployment. In these circumstances, even if agreed, the SOFA would be worthless on the ground.

The issue of the consent of a host government to the presence of a peacekeeping force embodies one of the fundamental principles upon which traditional peacekeeping is based. Despite this, the question was dealt with in the UNIFIL SOFA in a remarkably fudged and ambiguous manner. The actual status of the force is addressed in Article 5 of the Agreement, which states:

> UNIFIL and its members shall refrain from any action or activity incompatible with the impartial and international nature of their duties or inconsistent with the spirit of the present arrangements. The Force Commander shall take all appropriate measures to ensure the observance of those obligations.

---

[8] F. L. Kirgis, *International Organizations in Their Legal Setting* (2nd edn, Egan, MN: West Publishing Co., 1992), pp. 722–33.

For its part, the government of Lebanon undertook to respect the exclusive international nature of UNIFIL.[9] With regard to freedom of movement, Article 12 of the SOFA provides that 'UNIFIL and its members shall enjoy ... freedom of movement throughout Lebanon'. These articles are based on similar provisions in the model SOFA, with the overriding consideration that balance be attained between the sovereign rights of a host state and the peacekeeping interests of the international community. There is no specific provision governing revocation of consent and it seems that Lebanon's consent remains imperative to ensure respect for sovereign rights and that this consent may be withdrawn at any time. This is linked to the issue of the duration of the operation, of which there is no mention in the UNIFIL SOFA. The question of whether a peacekeeping force must withdraw if there is a unilateral revocation of host state consent is still a controversial matter which has become more problematic in the context of peace enforcement operations of recent years. Yet, if the experience of UNEF I is anything to go by, revoked consent may equate to the termination of the mission.[10] Much could be gained from incorporating into the SOFA, or appending thereto, a more detailed definition of the force mandate and the conditions for its execution. However, such a change is unlikely, as its omission is almost certainly deliberate: most mandates are couched in politically ambiguous terms to make them acceptable to the parties involved.

UNIFIL

In the case of UNIFIL, the force existed for nearly twenty years without a SOFA, and reliance was therefore placed on the principles of Articles 104 and 105 of the UN Charter. These articles provide that UN organs enjoy such privileges and immunities in the territories of member states as are necessary for the independent exercise of their functions.[11] The UN

---

[9] Article 6 of the UNIFIL SOFA, December 1995.

[10] UNEF I was withdrawn in controversial circumstances during May–June 1967 at the request of the Egyptian government, which informed the Secretary-General that it would no longer consent to the stationing of the force on Egyptian territory and in Gaza. See A. Di Blase, 'The Role of Host State Consent with Regard to Non-Coercive Actions by the UN', in A. Cassese (ed.), *UN Peacekeeping: Legal Essays* (Dordrecht: Sijthoff and Nordhoff, 1978), pp. 55–94, esp. pp. 67–73.

[11] Articles 104 and 105 of the UN Charter. See B. Simma (ed.), *The Charter of the United Nations: A Commentary* (2nd edn, Oxford: Oxford University Press, 2002), pp. 1302 and 1314.

Convention on Privileges and Immunities and the practice and custom of peacekeeping forces reflected in previous agreements also played a role in the initial years of the life of the force.[12] However, the Convention was inadequate in certain regards, most notably that criminal immunity only exists in respect of acts in the course of official duties.

The absence of a formal agreement at the outset of UNIFIL's mission did not create as serious a situation as might be anticipated, nor was its situation unique. Other peacekeeping forces have awaited formal signature and promulgation for over eighteen months after their establishment. Moreover, even when such agreements have been concluded almost immediately, as in the case of the peacekeeping force in Cyprus, these agreements are not perfect.[13] The absence of a formal agreement did, however, place the force in a vulnerable position insofar as its rights and status were concerned. Though, in most instances, UNIFIL functioned adequately on the basis of a 'gentleman's agreement', the reliance on such an agreement is only satisfactory for so long as the parties consider it to be to their advantage to respect its terms and to negotiate amicably any differences that may arise. As certain freedoms are integral to the nature of peacekeeping, the absence of a formal agreement may contribute to reluctance by member states to participate in peacekeeping duties.

The Secretary-General of the UN has wide powers in relation to the internal affairs of peacekeeping forces. He may be authorised to issue appropriate regulations and instructions to ensure the effective functioning of the force. The authority to issue such regulations stems from the UN's exclusive competence to direct and operate a peacekeeping force. The regulations, if issued, can also constitute an important part of the legal framework of a force. Regulations usually govern the issue of command orders and matters such as the powers and responsibilities within the structure of the force. They also govern administrative, executive and financial arrangements, and general rights and duties of members of the force. As no formal agreement was concluded with the Lebanese government until December 1995, the status of UNIFIL, and

---

[12] Interview, Mr R. Rosetti, Legal Adviser to the Force Commander, UNIFIL, Naquora, September 1989.

[13] The SOFA for UNFICYP took effect on 24 March 1964, three weeks after the Security Council approved its creation. G. I. A. D Draper, 'The United Nations Force in Cyprus' (1967) 6 *Revue de droit pénal militaire et de droit de la guerre/The Military Law and the Law of War Review* 58–62.

that of its personnel, was based upon the Security Council resolution establishing the force. This could only be interpreted by reference to the guidelines that were published for the force.[14] These provided, *inter alia*, that the force was under the command of the UN, by power vested in the Secretary-General under the authority of the Security Council. Command in the field was exercised by the Force Commander, who was responsible to the Secretary-General. As with the SOFAs concluded for the peacekeeping forces in Cyprus and the Congo, the relevant guidelines provide that the force enjoys freedom of movement and the relevant privileges and immunities provided for by the Convention on the Privileges and Immunities of the UN. The guidelines contain considerably less detail than the SOFA for other peacekeeping forces. This reflects the hasty manner in which UNIFIL was established and the fact that the authority of the government of Lebanon did not extend to the area where the force was deployed. In these circumstances, guaranteeing the exclusion of the jurisdictional competence of the host state was probably seen to have little practical value.

Certain matters not provided for in the UNIFIL guidelines laid down by the Secretary-General could have been included in Force or Staff Regulations, as these were issued for all of the peacekeeping forces instituted prior to UNIFIL. These have been created pursuant to the authority given to the Secretary-General to establish a peacekeeping force. However, no such regulations were issued for UNIFIL; instead the force relied on a series of standing operating procedures (SOPs), which set out the guidelines and defined the method by which the operation was to be conducted. Although not signed by him, these appear to have been issued on behalf of the Force Commander. Despite questionable legal standing, the SOPs have worked, due primarily to the goodwill and the co-operation of participating contingents.

KFOR

In the case of the NATO-led Kosovo force (KFOR), no SOFA as such was concluded. As Serb forces withdrew, KFOR entered in accordance with the terms of the Military Technical Agreement concluded with the governments of the Federal Republic of Yugoslavia and the Republic of Serbia on 12 June 1999. Although Appendix B of the Agreement states

---

[14] These are contained in UN Doc. S/12611, 19 March 1978, and they were approved by Security Council Resolution 426, 19 March 1978.

that the parties will agree a SOFA as soon as possible, this did not happen. A restrictive SOFA might undermine the role of KFOR and UNMIK and curtail to an unacceptable degree the authority of KFOR.[15] Hence no such agreement has been concluded to date. The extent of KFOR's authority is reflected in the terms of the Military Technical Agreement itself. Paragraph 2 of Appendix B reads:

> The international security force ('KFOR') commander shall have author-ity, without interference of permission, to do all that he judges necessary and proper, including the use of military force, to protect the interna-tional security force ('KFOR'), the international civil implementation presence, and to carry out the responsibilities inherent in this Military Technical Agreement and the Peace Settlement which it supports.

The terms of the Agreement have often been invoked to authorise action not expressly granted in the Agreement or under the terms of Resolution 1244. Both UNMIK and KFOR have acted in a manner that indicates they are not subject to the jurisdiction of Serbia and that the Security Council has authorised their respective missions in the area. This inter-pretation dispenses with the need for the rights and privileges usually associated with concluding a SOFA.

Originally, KFOR's strength was about 45,000, with five brigade-sized units in designated zones. By 2003, that number had been drastically reduced to around 18,000, in four brigade zones. Interestingly, as in the case of SFOR in the former Yugoslavia, the Russian contingent had a special command and control relationship so as not to come exclusively under the command of NATO. In a significant improvement over the situation in Bosnia, the UN and the OSCE organised their field structures to conform to those of KFOR. A major structural dis-advantage of KFOR, however, like that of SFOR before it, is NATO's long-established standing arrangements on operational control for troop-contributing member states.[16] In accordance with these, each Multi-National Brigade command has a large degree of discretion over the operational policies and standing operating procedures in its own area, which means that KFOR is not the unified NATO-led force that it might at first appear to be.

---

[15] See generally M. J. Matheson, 'United Nations Governance of Post Conflict Societies' (2001) 95 *American Journal of International Law* 76.
[16] J. G. Cockell, 'Civil–Military Responses to Security Challenges in Peace Operations: Ten Lessons from Kosovo' (2002) 8(4) *Global Governance* 483–502 at 489.

Consequences for Irish and Canadian personnel in breach of UN regulations

The force regulations issued for previous peacekeeping forces, and the standing operating procedures in respect of UNIFIL, are intended to be legally binding, although in many instances they are general in nature and open to different interpretations. These apply in spite of a subsequent SOFA and do not affect it to any appreciable extent. In the circumstances, it is not clear what the consequences are if a UN soldier or commander at any level is in breach of UN regulations, or other established procedures. Can such a breach be regarded as an offence under military law? The mere fact that a state concluded an agreement to contribute troops to UN peacekeeping does not mean it has automatically amended its municipal law, or that it has a legal obligation to do so. It may well be the case that breaches of UN regulations or procedures are also offences against military law, but, if this is so, it is not because of any UN regulation having municipal effect. In this way, the situation of an Irish or Canadian soldier or officer charged with the violation of a specific UN regulation or similar instruction is unclear. A potential defence might be that no such offence is known to Irish or Canadian municipal or military law.

On the other hand, it could be argued that a breach of UN regulations is an example of conduct to the prejudice of good order and military discipline, contrary to section 168 of the Irish Defence Act 1954 or to section 129 of the Canadian National Defence Act of 1985.[17] Military authorities often use sections 68 and 129 as a form of safety net in the event of a more specific charge being struck down or when there is uncertainty regarding the exact nature of the offence committed. A formal charge under either section in Canadian or Irish military law against a participant in a UN operation raises fundamental issues, namely, which military discipline is covered by the Act, that of the relevant armed forces, or that of the UN. It is submitted that it would not be possible to establish, beyond a reasonable doubt, that every act that violates UN regulations is *per se* prejudicial to the military discipline of either the Irish or the Canadian Forces. The matter was made all the more difficult in UNIFIL owing to the fact there were no regulations,

---

[17] Section 168 of the Defence Act 1954 (Ireland) provides, *inter alia*, that 'every person subject to military law who commits any act, conduct, disorder or neglect to the prejudice of good order and discipline is guilty of an offence against military law'. Section 129 of the National Defence Act (Canada) states that '[a]ny act, conduct, disorder, or neglect to the prejudice of good order and discipline is an offence'.

and the standing operating procedures were unsigned and of dubious authority.

The legal difficulty in relation to the binding effect of regulations is also common to other contingents and peacekeeping forces. In order to overcome these potential difficulties, an amendment to the Irish and Canadian legislation is required, to the effect that any conduct of members of their respective contingents part of a UN peacekeeping or other force which breaches UN regulations or procedures shall be considered to be conduct to the prejudice of good order and discipline for the purpose of section 168 or section 129 respectively.

Command and control

An even more serious problem than that outlined above arises in the case of command, as the command of UN missions has always been 'a somewhat delicate issue'.[18] In this context, there are three interlinked and essential features of the military system, namely, command, discipline and leadership. At the head of the system stands the commander. The term 'commander' is used generally to refer to any officer in a position of command. In the Canadian and Irish forces, the term 'commander' can be used generally to describe an officer who is appointed to a position of command of a command,[19] unit or element of the armed forces.[20] Traditionally, command is defined as the legal authority to issue orders and to compel obedience. In this way, command is the authority lawfully exercised by a commander over his or her subordinates by virtue of the rank or appointment held. Command

---

[18] H. McCoubrey, 'International Law and National Contingents in UN Forces' (1994) 12(3) *International Relations* 39–50 at 41. On the issue of command and international humanitarian law, see C. Greenwood, *Command and the Laws of Conflict* (Shrivenham: Strategic and Combat Studies Institute, 1993).

[19] Command of a command in Ireland refers to a specific territorial area, whereas in Canada it denotes a particular branch such as 'air', 'land' or 'maritime' command. For an overview of Canadian forces and command issues in peacekeeping, see S. M. Maloney, 'Insights into Canadian Peacekeeping Doctrine' (1996) 76(2) *Military Review* 12–23.

[20] In the Canadian Forces and the Irish Defence Forces, an officer commanding a command is usually a general officer appointed by the Chief of the Defence Staff (in Canada) or the Minister for Defence (in Ireland). Officers are also appointed to command units, e.g. the 65th Infantry Battalion, UNIFIL or the Canadian Airborne Regiment. The major difference between command appointments is that they all have graduated powers of punishment and other powers drawn from the National Defence Act and the Defence Acts, respectively.

provides the power and responsibility for effectively planning and executing the employment of assigned resources to accomplish a mission. Thus, command, decision and organisation are highly integrated.[21]

Control, on the other hand, is the process through which a commander, assisted by staff, organises, directs and co-ordinates the activities of the assigned forces. The command and control process establishes how the commander and staff accomplish the mission, i.e., in the case of a UN force, fulfils the mandate. Command is a human activity that involves procedures, methodologies and techniques used to understand the prevailing situation, to decide what action to take, to issue instructions and to supervise the execution of orders. As it is a process involving options and judgment, it also has an ethical dimension. Traditionally, commanders are held ethically responsible for their acts or omissions. All members of the Canadian and Irish forces are ethically responsible for observing a code that is implicit in the custom of the service and military regulations.[22]

Command and control issues are not new to the UN or to multinational forces. In 1945, a collective security system was put in place to ensure that recalcitrant states could be dealt with in accordance with the provisions of the UN Charter. An essential element in this collective security mechanism was the planned provision of national contingents that together would comprise the UN armed forces. This never materialised; whilst the signatories to the Charter agreed upon a model for the command and control of UN forces, Cold War political developments prevented its actual adoption.[23] The model retains its value, however, as to some extent it is the benchmark by which one may examine all subsequent arrangements for command of international UN forces. In effect, the Charter model was replaced by systems of command and control that evolved to meet the needs of two quite distinct UN missions. The most common of these systems evolved to cater for the unique nature of peacekeeping operations, but even this system is not as straightforward as it might first appear. The other general system to

---

[21] H. Eccles, *Military Concepts and Philosophy* (New York: Rutgers University Press, 1965), pp. 118–19.

[22] These are traditions and customs that, although unwritten, have come to be accepted aspects of military practices and behaviour. Interview, Defence Forces Legal Officer, March 2003.

[23] J. W. Houck, 'The Command and Control of UN Forces in the Era of Peace Enforcement' (1993) 4(1) *Duke Journal of Comparative and International Law* 1–69 at 11; and L. Goodrich, E. Hambro and A. Simons, *Charter of the UN* (3rd edn, New York: Columbia University Press, 1969), pp. 314–26.

emerge was designed to address the more complex and controversial multi-national enforcement operations.

Like the concept of peacekeeping, these command and control systems emerged outside the express constitutional framework of the UN Charter. They were created in response to the need to provide some workable alternative in the context of Cold War suspicion and mistrust. Nevertheless, even with the end of the Cold War, the problems surrounding this issue remain. In order to analyse the complexity of the problems involved in command and control, it is useful to outline some definitions and an historical background.

In order to understand how command and control of armed forces operates in practice, it is necessary to examine what these concepts mean in practical military terms, and the legal implications of the different categories and levels utilised in national and international armed forces. The actual operation of the system of command and control in the Canadian Forces is outlined and defined in the *Canadian Forces Joint Doctrine Manual*. Although this is a Canadian military document intended primarily for NATO, and possesses no legal status under either Canadian or international law, it does outline what is internationally accepted as constituting the three levels of military command, namely, full, operational and tactical command.[24] These are defined in the Manual as follows:

- Full command is the military authority and responsibility of a superior officer to issue orders to subordinates. It covers every aspect of military operations and administration and exists only within national services. It is sometimes referred to as national command. A UN Force Commander, or an alliance or coalition commander, does not have full command over forces assigned to him or her. Full or national command is the 'command' referred to in the Irish Constitution and legislation governing command of all Irish Defence Force personnel.
- Operational command is the authority of a commander to assign missions or tasks, redeploy forces and reassign forces. It does not include responsibility for administration or logistics.
- Tactical command is the authority of a commander to assign tasks to forces under his or her command. It is narrower in scope than operational command.

---

[24] *Joint Doctrine for the Canadian Forces Joint and Combined Operations* (Ottawa: Department of National Defence, undated), pp. 2-1 and 2-2.

The concept of control is also an integral part of the overall command of armed forces. It is the authority exercised by a commander over part of the activities of subordinate organisations or other organisations not normally under command. Control is also defined more specifically in military doctrine as operational, tactical, administrative or technical,[25] as follows:

- Operational control is the authority of a commander: to direct forces assigned so that the commander can accomplish specific missions or tasks, which are usually limited by function, time or location; to deploy units concerned; and to retain or assign tactical control of those units.
- Tactical control is the authority of a commander to give detailed direction to and to control the movement of units necessary to accomplish a mission or task.
- Administrative control is the direction or exercise of authority over subordinates regarding administrative matters.
- Technical control is control within specialised areas such as medical or legal jurisdiction, parallel to but outside the chain of command, for purely technical issues. Operational commanders can override this control if it is seen to jeopardise the mission.

Even in a military alliance such as NATO where extensive co-ordinating authority is vested in the NATO commander, full command remains under national authority.[26] In this way, the term 'command', when used in an international context, means something less than in a national context. No NATO commander has full command over the forces assigned to him or her. When assigning forces to NATO, national governments grant either operational command or operational control. It is usual in multi-national operations for each participating nation to be represented by a national commander who is responsible for ensuring that full command can be exercised and that national laws and policies are observed.

The Security Council was to be assisted in the management and 'command' of UN forces by a special committee. Article 47 of the UN Charter provides for the establishment of a Military Staff Committee to advise and assist the Security Council on all questions relating to the

---

[25] Ibid.

[26] D. Fleck, 'Multinational Units', in Fleck (ed.), The Handbook of the Law of Visiting Forces, pp. 33–44 at p. 40.

Security Council's military requirements.[27] It envisioned an important role for the Military Staff Committee, once UN forces became involved in a conflict situation. The article provides that the Committee 'advise and assist' the Security Council on the 'employment and command of forces placed at the disposal of the Security Council'. In addition, it vests the Committee with the power to provide strategic direction to the Security Council in regard to any armed forced placed at the Council's disposal.

While strategic direction is not defined in this context, its meaning can be discerned in light of the fact that the Military Staff Committee was modelled on the function and structure of the Allied Combined Chiefs of Staff during World War II. The latter operated on the basis of regular consultation regarding the broad objectives of the war and, after establishing a common position in relation to an issue, the members would consult their respective civilian leaders for approval.[28] Therein the crucial link in the chain of command emerged, as military commanders translated the political direction received from the civilian leadership into a military plan. This was then communicated to the subordinate operational commanders on the ground for execution. In this way, it appears that the strategic direction referred to in the UN Charter intended to operate as a system or process whereby the Military Staff Committee would fulfil the vital link in the chain of command from the Security Council to the operational commander of UN forces on the ground. In practice this would mean that, after considering the views of the operational commander on the ground, the Military Staff Committee would advise the Security Council of the military options available to it and the implications of any military plan of action. Likewise, the Security Council would outline to the Military Staff Committee the decision and objectives to be achieved and these would be translated into a military plan that would be communicated to the field commander(s) for action.

The Military Staff Committee was not intended to be involved in the day-to-day operational or tactical command of UN forces. It was considered preferable to vest the detailed operational and tactical decisions in a single commander. This was certainly consistent with conventional military operations and practice. Interestingly, there seemed to be a consensus about the meaning of command, and the only problems

---

[27] Simma (ed.), *The Charter of the United Nations*, pp. 769–75.
[28] W. Churchill, *The Grand Alliance* (London: Cassells, 1950), pp. 686–7.

relating to command centred on agreeing a mechanism for selecting and appointing commanders. In the event, this latter issue remained unresolved and it was agreed that the selection of individual commanders would be determined on the basis of the requirements of each case.[29]

Early on, the Military Staff Committee presented a report to the Security Council on the planned permanent UN force. While there were areas of insurmountable disagreement,[30] the question of command and control was not one of them. The report recommended that the UN force remain under exclusive national command except when operating under the Security Council. When required by the Security Council to act under the provisions of the Charter, the UN forces would then come under the control of the Security Council and the Military Staff Committee would be responsible, under the Security Council, for their strategic direction. It was also agreed that national contingents would remain under the command of national commanders. More significantly, the Security Council was to have the authority to appoint an overall supreme commander or its equivalent, although the appointment of subordinate commanders of air, sea and land forces remained an unsettled issue.

This, then, was the command and control model to be adopted for Chapter VII operations. Yet, when the two major UN enforcement operations in Korea and the Persian Gulf are examined, it is evident that the model envisioned under the Charter was not followed. In fact, Security Council involvement was marginal. After initial authorisation, the Security Council had little political control over the operations, largely due to the divisions within the Council itself and the military requirements of each operation. In the circumstances, the one military power with the capacity to act took the lead. In this way, *de facto* command and control of the operations was in the hands of the United States. Despite this, the actual command and control mechanism for each of these operations was significantly different.

The current force in Kosovo represents the reality of a Chapter VII peace enforcement operation in the post-Cold War era and an emasculated UN. While it is UN-mandated and 'deployed under UN auspices', the enabling resolution stipulates that the 'international security

[29] R. C. Hilderbrand, *Dumbarton Oaks: The Origins of the UN and the Search for Post War Security* (Chapel Hill, NC: University of North Carolina Press, 1990), pp. 157–8.

[30] Report of the Military Staff Committee, *General Principles Governing the Organization of the Armed Forces Made Available to the Security Council by Member Nations of the UN*, UN Security Council Official Reports Supplement (No. 1), UN Doc. S/336 (1947).

presence with a substantial NATO participation must be deployed under a unified command and control'.[31] In practice, this means that it is NATO-led under the North Atlantic Council with a command structure that incorporates SHAPE (Supreme Headquarters Allied Powers Europe). Within SHAPE, there is an Inter Co-ordination Centre for Non-NATO Troop Contributors. In reality, this is a NATO-led and *de facto* NATO-commanded operation with no real power in the Secretary-General or the Security Council.

Command and control of peacekeeping operations

The situation regarding the command and control of peacekeeping forces was problematic for a number of years and linked to institutional difficulties surrounding the establishment of peacekeeping operations.[32] The then Soviet Union and its allies believed that any action by the UN involving the use of force should be the primary responsibility of the Security Council, and that the Military Staff Committee should be at the disposal of the Council. The majority of member states took a different point of view. Peacekeeping operations were regarded as a special kind of UN activity involving the consent of the states concerned and, therefore, outside the scope of Chapter VII enforcement provisions. In the circumstances, it was permissible, and even necessary, that the control of peacekeeping operations vest in the Secretary-General. Many of the early difficulties have been resolved since the establishment of UNEF II (1973–9).[33] The then Secretary-General, Kurt Waldheim, formally proposed that the Security Council have ultimate control over peacekeeping missions. This involved initial Security Council authorisation for the mission and subsequent approval of any fundamental changes in its mandate. The Secretary-General would then exercise actual control of the day-to-day operation.[34] This was intended to avoid the difficulties of involving a potentially divided Committee in the detailed activities of an

---

[31] Security Council Resolution 1244, 10 June 1999, para. 5.

[32] J. O. C. Jonah, 'The Management of UN Peacekeeping', in I. J. Rikhye and K. Skjelsbaek (eds.), *The UN and Peacekeeping* (New York: St Martin's Press, 1991), p. 75; and McCoubrey and White, *The Blue Helmets: Legal Regulation of UN Military Operations*, pp. 137–52.

[33] UNEF II was established in October 1973 to supervise the cease-fire between Egyptian and Israeli forces. It ended in July 1979.

[34] For a discussion of the delegation by the Security Council of powers to the Secretary-General, see D. Sarooshi, *The United Nations and the Development of Collective Security* (Oxford: Clarendon Press, 1999), pp. 50–85, esp. p. 63.

operation. This was a valid cause of concern: such a Committee was unlikely to be able to respond quickly to critical situations on the ground. Accordingly, the approach has successfully facilitated the work of subsequent missions. Yet, despite what it has to recommend it, even this system was found to be seriously wanting. During the crisis in the former Yugoslavia, General McKenzie and others were very critical of the lack of support and leadership from UN headquarters in New York.

The precedent established with UNEF II is now well entrenched and all traditional peacekeeping operations, including UNIFIL, have followed its pattern. This is an excellent model when there is general agreement in the Security Council about the political and military goals of the peacekeeping operation, in that the Secretary-General can take the lead without running foul of any member of the Council. In the case of UNIFIL, however, Security Council consensus was inconsistent and, in fact, questionable from the beginning. This often placed the Secretary-General in a difficult and almost untenable position, illustrating that this model has its limitations, even when applied to relatively straightforward peacekeeping operations. These limitations are not of a legal nature and do not reflect a faulty system of command and control. They are political difficulties caused by varying political agendas and different perceptions of the function of peacekeeping operations. Even the best approach cannot withstand the pressures created by ambivalent or divided leadership from the Security Council.

An Under-Secretary-General for peacekeeping operations and a military adviser assist the Secretary-General. In theory, the military adviser should fulfil the function intended for the Military Staff Committee: the position was created by Dag Hammarskjöld in late 1960 to assist in the management of peacekeeping operations.[35] It is essential that the Secretary-General have access to independent military advice relating to proposed or ongoing operations. The role of the military adviser is, as the name suggests, purely advisory. It is the Force Commander who exercises command of peacekeeping operations on behalf of the Secretary-General. In light of this, the Secretary-General, with the approval of the Security Council, appoints the Force Commander. The exact criteria for appointment to this position are unclear, but the post is the most significant link in the chain of command from the

---

[35] I. J. Rikhye, *Military Advisor to the Secretary-General: UN Peacekeeping and the Congo Crisis* (London: Hurst and Co., 1993), pp. 203–20.

Secretary-General to the contingents on the ground. As the Military Staff Committee is essentially out of the picture, the roles of Force Commander and military adviser are crucial to the Secretary-General. It is often said that peacekeeping is more a political than a military mission; consequently, a Force Commander must be as much a diplomat and politician as a military commander. Nonetheless, the inherently military nature of peacekeeping should not be under-estimated even in the more complex multi-dimensional operations of recent years.

The command of UN forces is expressly referred to in the Model Agreement Between the UN and Member States Contributing Personnel and Equipment to UN Peacekeeping Operations,[36] paragraph 7 of which states:

> During the period of assignment to [the UN peacekeeping operation], the personnel made available by [the Participating State] shall remain in their national service but shall be under the command of the UN, vested in the Secretary-General, under the authority of the Security Council. Accordingly, the Secretary-General ... shall have full authority over the deployment, organization, conduct and direction of [the UN peacekeeping operation], including the personnel made available by [the Participating State].

Paragraph 9 reads:

> The functions of [the UN peacekeeping operation] are exclusively international and the personnel made available by [the Participating State] shall regulate their conduct with the interests of the UN only in view. Except on national administration matters, they shall not seek or accept instructions in respect of the performance of their duties from the authority external to the UN, nor shall the government of [the Participating State] give such instructions to them.

Once deployed in the field, the Force Commander assumes main management functions. Nevertheless, despite the clear terms of the troop-contributing state, it would be misleading to suggest that the Force Commander is in command in the sense understood in conventional military operations. A traditional peacekeeping operation has a unique system of dual command, wherein the Force Commander or the equivalent reports directly to the Under-Secretary-General for Peacekeeping Operations. The Force Commander usually has a Chief of Staff to assist

---

[36] UN Doc. A/46/185, 23 May 1991.

in the exercise of military command and authority in the field. However, all peacekeeping operations have a significant civilian component under a Chief Administrative Officer.[37] The Chief Administrative Officer reports to the Force Commander, but he or she also reports directly to Field Operations Division in New York. Given the logistical, administrative and financial aspects of any operation, and the fact that the UN is a civilian and not a military bureaucracy, this is a good idea. Differences have arisen between Force Commanders and the Chief Administrative Officer in the field; however, it is now well established that the Force Commander has overall responsibility for the field management of peacekeeping.[38] In practice, problems can still arise and there is a need for co-ordinating the military and civilian staff responsibilities and efforts. A lot also depends on subjective factors such as personality, but this does not excuse failure to address structural or organisational deficiencies.

In UN peacekeeping and similar operations, as in other military operations, no two situations are identical. The political situation and tactical considerations appropriate in one mission will not necessarily prove relevant elsewhere. There are, nonetheless, certain matters of principle that remain unchanged whenever an international force is deployed. One of the most critical problems facing a senior officer in a UN force is that of command, and the reality that troops under his or her operational control will also remain loyal to their national governments. This potential problem of duality of allegiance is common to all international forces and alliances, but it may be more acute in what can often be an *ad hoc* and hastily established UN force. The growing tendency of some national contingents within a UN force to maintain a back channel communication link with their home governments is a potential problem that may adversely affect the management of peacekeeping operations in the field.[39] For practical reasons, and being aware that it can do nothing to prevent such communications, the UN has not discouraged links between national governments and national contingents. Despite

---

[37] This civilian component should not be confused with the humanitarian workers, human rights and electoral monitors, and nation-building civilians, part of the more recent multi-dimensional peacekeeping operations.

[38] Interviews, Lt-Gen. Walgren and Lt-Gen. Callaghan, former Force Commanders, UNIFIL, 1989 and 1998 respectively.

[39] Jonah, 'The Management of UN Peacekeeping', p. 86; and C. Brady and S. Daws, 'UN Operations: The Political–Military Interface' (1994) 1 *International Peacekeeping* 29–79, esp. 66, 68 and 71.

this position, these communications potentially threaten the operational functions and effectiveness of a peacekeeping force.

National governments have occasionally become aware, prior to UN headquarters in New York, of incidents and operational developments on the ground that involved UNIFIL and other peacekeeping operations.[40] While this may be a reflection on the nature of communication within the UN, it is especially embarrassing when the government concerned seeks a response before New York is formally informed of all the facts. The most serious negative dimension to this ability of contingents to stay in close touch with their respective national governments is when the same government gives what amounts to operational orders to the national contingent that are inconsistent with or even contrary to those of the Force Commander. The following illustrates the problems that can arise:

> Individual contingents remain, as they have been historically, extremely reluctant to accept the chain of command within missions and have placed their loyalty to Force Commanders in doubt by referring matters to national authorities ... [T]he case of Italian 'insubordination' in Somalia ... is merely the most published case. It is well known that French and British soldiers in the former Yugoslavia refer to Paris and London before, if at all, consulting with the UN Secretariat in New York. Among officers serving in Bosnia, the Spanish battalion is known to refer practically all operational issues that arise on the ground to authorities in Madrid. Similarly, Indonesian forces in Cambodia were notorious for their tendency to take directions from the Indonesian Ambassador in Phnom Penh rather than from Lt Gen. John Sanderson, UNTAC's Force Commander.[41]

This undermines the concept of integrated UN command, and it is a serious threat to the proper command and management of peacekeeping operations in the field. It is also inconsistent with the terms of the Model Agreement Between the UN and Member States Contributing Personnel and Equipment to UN Peacekeeping Operations.

Command and control of UN forces in Somalia

Unlike the model prevailing with UNIFIL, the command and control mechanism for the UNOSOM II operation in Somalia was not based on

---

[40] Interviews, Walgren and Callaghan.
[41] M. R. Berdal, *Whither UN Peacekeeping?*, Adelphi Paper 281 (1993), p. 42.

a well-established precedent. In response to a Security Council request, the Secretary-General reported on ways in which the capacity of the UN could be improved with regard to the maintenance of international peace and security. The report, *An Agenda for Peace*, was issued prior to the Somalia crisis and examined the full range of UN peace and security responsibilities as well as the mechanisms available for attaining them.[42] The Secretary-General envisaged a role for the moribund Military Staff Committee in which it would assist in the drafting of agreements with member states under Article 43 of the Charter.[43] One of the more intriguing aspects of the report concerned traditional peace-keeping operations and enforcement action operations pursuant to the collective security provisions of the Charter. In an attempt to reflect the changing nature of maintaining international peace and security, and the *de facto* situation emerging on the ground, the Secretary-General called for the creation of 'peace enforcement' units. The concept was something of a half-way house between traditional peacekeeping and enforcement measures under Chapter VII of the Charter. The units were to be heavily armed and would be deployed with the authorisation of the Security Council and serve under the 'command' of the Secretary-General.

It is easy in hindsight to be critical of proposals that have since failed, but, given the history of command and control mechanisms within UN forces, it was at least overly optimistic to expect that this would be acceptable in practice. Furthermore, once relations between Boutros-Ghali and the United States administration became strained, existing difficulties were exacerbated. A proposal of this kind required the active support of the United States, including a willingness to relinquish some degree of operational command and control to the Secretary-General. This was never a likely prospect, despite the optimism of the time. Identifying what amounted to a form of 'second-generation' peace-keeping and clearing up some of the semantic confusion surrounding

---

[42] UN Doc. A/47/277-S/24111, 17 June 1992.

[43] Art. 43(1) states:

> All Members of the United Nations ... undertake to make available to the Security Council, on its call and in accordance with special agreement or agreements, armed forces, assistance and facilities ... for the purpose of maintaining international peace and security.

L. Goodrich, E. Hambro and A. Simons, *Charter of the United Nations* (3rd edn, New York: Columbia University Press, 1969), pp. 317–26; and B. Simma (ed.), *The Charter of the United Nations: A Commentary* (2nd edn, Oxford: Oxford University Press, 2002), pp. 760–3.

the various concepts was useful. Unfortunately, the issue and complexity of the command and control of these new so-called 'peace enforcement' operations was not appreciated. This soon became evident as UNOSOM I, a more traditional style peacekeeping operation, was being wound down and replaced by the more robust and United States-led UNITAF mission.

The actual idea for a countrywide enforcement operation in Somalia originated with the United States.[44] The Secretary-General favoured UN command of any such operation, but he conceded it was not a realistic option at that time. In fact, the then Chairman of the Joint Chiefs of Staff, General Colin Powell, and other military leaders were insistent that the operation be under the command and control of the United States. This was not surprising and the most the Secretary-General could do was attach as many conditions as possible to ensure some control over the operation by the UN. The Security Council ultimately decided the issue in what was essentially a compromise. Security Council Resolution 794 (1992) implicitly accepted the United States demand to command the operation that was to be known as UNITAF.[45]

Despite this acceptance, the Resolution also authorised the Secretary-General to participate in the necessary arrangements for command and control of the forces.[46] In addition, the Security Council agreed to the establishment of an *ad hoc* commission to oversee the operation, as recommended by the Secretary-General. It declined to place the existing small force, UNOSOM I, under the command of the United States and instead opted to create a formal liaison mechanism between UNOSOM I and the unified command. The Security Council did, however, retain one vital control mechanism: it reserved the right to phase out the UNITAF part of the operation and effectively terminate it, in favour of a more traditional peacekeeping operation.

The initial decision of the Security Council and its general policy regarding UNITAF are important insofar as they indicate a significant departure from previous models for command and control. Superficially, the model seems to resemble the single-state United States-dominated system employed during the Korean operation and, to a lesser extent, the managed coalition model adopted during the First Gulf War. In the debate leading up to the adoption of Resolution 794 (1992), concern was

---

[44] Letter dated 29 November 1992 from the Secretary-General Addressed to the President of the Security Council, SCOR, 47th Session at 1, UN Doc. S/24868 (1992).
[45] S/RES/794 of 3 December 1992.   [46] *Ibid.*, para. 12.

expressed on a number of occasions about the need for the Secretary-General and the Security Council to retain significant political control of the force; this was reflected in the limited but important control retained by the two entities under the Resolution.[47] The United States, then, did not get its own way entirely. A factor that, combined with the evident tension that developed between the US and the UN over the timing of the transition to the second phase of the operation, UNOSOM II, is indicative of how effective this control turned out to be.[48] During the course of the UNITAF phase of the Somalia operation, the United States and the Secretary-General engaged in public debates in the media that reflected in unambiguous terms the level of disagreement between them. In particular, the United States accused the UN of being too slow to assume responsibility for the operation, while the Secretary-General insisted that the United States needed to do more to disarm the violent elements of the population before the UN could assume control. This form of public airing of differences arose as much from the command and control mechanism, as from the nature of the conflict in Somalia. Disagreements of this nature, assuming they did occur, were not aired publicly during the Korean operation, or during the First Gulf War.

The UNOSOM II force of 28,000 personnel, established in March 1993, had many similarities with that of a traditional peacekeeping force. It was commanded by a Turkish General, Cevic Bir, who had contingents from a wide political spectrum under his control. The force was established under Resolution 814 (1993), which included a provision to the effect that the force would be supervised closely by the Secretary-General and the Security Council.[49] In addition, the United States agreed to allow a significant number of its armed forces to participate in the operation.[50] This, not surprisingly, was made subject to a number of conditions, none of which were conducive to a unified system of command and control under the Security Council.

---

[47] SCOR, 47th Session, 3145th Meeting at 17, UN Doc. S/PV 3145 (1992).

[48] See C. O'Cleary, 'US Public Grows Wary of Foreign Entanglements', *Irish Times*, 12 October 1993, p. 11; J. Lancaster, 'United States Beginning Pullout from Somalia: Slow Withdrawal Aimed Partly at Forcing UN to Take Responsibility', *Washington Post*, 19 January 1993, p. A1.

[49] Security Council Resolution 814 (1993), 26 March 1993, paras. 14 and 18.

[50] *Message from the President of the United States – A Report on the Military Operation in Somalia, October 13, 1993* (Washington, DC: US Government Printing Office, 1993).

In the first instance, orders from the UN affecting United States forces were transmitted from the UN Force Commander to the United States troops through the UNOSOM II Deputy Commander, Major General Montgomery, who was a United States army general. General Montgomery was the highest-ranking United States serving officer in the field, and in that capacity he was also the Commander of United States Forces, Somalia (USFORSOM). This was to ensure that a US officer retained full command of United States troops in the country, as General Montgomery reported directly to the Commander in Chief, United States Central Command. In fact, United States Central Command considered that it retained command over the US forces and only delegated 'operational, tactical and/or administrative control of USFORSOM, as required, to support the Commander, UNOSOM II Force Command'.[51] In light of this set-up, it was no coincidence that the Force Commander (Bir) hailed from a NATO member state (Turkey) and that the Secretary-General's Special Representative in Somalia was American, retired Navy Admiral Howe. The Force Commander reported directly to the Special Representative, who in turn reported to the Secretary-General. This gave significant influence to the United States, even if it did not formally command the mission.

What did it all mean in reality and how effective was it as a model for command and control in practice? The United States was adamant that it retained full command of all its forces and it did not even relinquish operational control of combat forces to the Force Commander of UNOSOM II. United States logistic units, there to support the UN operation, were, however, said to be assigned to the Force Commander through the Commander of United States Forces in Somalia for 'operational control'.[52] That meant that, for purposes explicitly agreed in writing between the United States and the UN, the Force Commander may provide them direction in their logistic mission of supporting UN units.

This cumbersome system was further complicated by the US decision to create a Quick Reaction Force. This innovation was justified by reference to the continuing presence of well-armed private militias that 'thwarted the original, lightly armed UN peacekeeping mission (UNOSOM I) as well as the UN's inexperience in conducting a peace enforcement operation'.[53] However, this ignored the United States own lack of experience in UN military operations. The Quick Reaction Force was intended to respond to hostile threats and attacks that exceeded

---

[51] *Ibid.*, p. 18. [52] *Ibid.* [53] *Ibid.*

UNOSOM's military force capabilities. When the security situation improved, it was to move offshore from Somalia and out of the way. Like other United States combat forces, these were not in the UN chain of command. They were under the direct command of the United States Commander in Chief, Central Command. The Deputy Commander of UNOSOM II could have tactical control of the force delegated to him if the situation within Somalia so required. This in effect amounted to the establishment of a parallel United States chain of command that was intended to exist alongside, but independent of, the UN command structure. How this was intended to operate in times of crisis in the context of an already complex multi-dimensional operation involving around thirty nations and many non-governmental organisations, is a question that does not appear to have been addressed seriously by military planners in Washington and the Department of Peacekeeping Operations in New York.

It is difficult to describe this set-up as other than a recipe for confusion and ultimate disaster. It constituted the very antithesis of a unified system of command. It was also a dangerous and deceptive system of command in that it created an illusion of UN control. It would have been preferable to delegate command of the force to the United States as this, at least, would have mirrored reality. Instead, a system was put into place that allowed the United States to control key positions within UNOSOM, while retaining full and operational command of all its combat forces in Somalia. Furthermore, it permitted the United States to retain its special forces on call should the Commander of United States Forces Somalia deem it necessary to deploy them. In addition, the United States deployed a specially constituted 'Task Force Ranger', which remained at all times under the direct command and control of the commander of United States special operations. In Sierra Leone, although British forces were also deployed outside the UN chain of command, inter alia, to support the UN mission, these forces were not intended to adopt a combat role.[54]

Combined with different perceptions among the troop-contributing countries, including the United States, of what the mission actually

---

[54] In the case of British forces in Sierra Leone, the primary task was to train and support the armed forces of the government of Sierra Leone, and evacuate British nationals. See Ministry of Defence Press Release No. 270/00, 10 October 2000 and statement to Parliament by Defence Secretary on Sierra Leone, 15 May 2000; Eighth Report of the Secretary-General on the UN Mission in Sierra Leone (UNMASIL), S/2000/1199, 15 December 2000, paras. 30–2.

entailed, it is not surprising that serious problems arose on the ground.[55] These culminated in the United States' attempt to capture one of the warlords, General Aideed. This effort took place outside the UN chain of command and was, in fact, a unilateral act by the United States using part of the Quick Reaction Force. Among the many consequences of this act was the row between Italy and the UN and that nation's refusal to replace its commander in Somalia. The United States and other contingents could have learned something from the successful deployment of Italian armed forces in and around Beirut as part of the Multi-National Force in the early 1980s.[56] The Italian contingent had nurtured good relations with all parties and the general population in Beirut and had sought successfully to operate as part of the local environment. They departed Lebanon with their reputation enhanced. The British too had tried to establish relations and to liaise with all factions. It kept them in tune with developments on the ground and taught them not to be too closely identified with the Lebanese government and army of the day. The UN's primary complaint seemed to be that the Italian commander in Somalia referred first to Rome before carrying out UN orders. It was acknowledged that Italy had the right to appoint its own general in Somalia, but the UN held the view that it had the right to insist upon a unified disciplined command structure. This would have been a fair argument if it was not for the fact that the UNOSOM II command structure was anything but unified owing to the United States' insistence on maintaining a parallel but independent chain of command, and the problems with the Italians stemmed directly from this situation.

Good relations between a Force Commander and subordinate national contingents are vital. It has been said that officers selected for UN missions should therefore, when possible, be in the Eisenhower rather than the Montgomery or Patton mould.[57] This sentiment has similarly been articulated:

---

[55] *Message from the President of the United States*, pp. 20–1. The United States President also stated at page 2 that 'the US military mission is not now nor was it ever one of 'nation building'. It is difficult to reconcile this statement with the provisions of Security Council Resolution 814 (1993), esp. para. 4.

[56] See generally R. Thakur, *International Peacekeeping in Lebanon* (Boulder: Westview Press, 1987), p. 200; and N. A. Pelcovits, *Peacekeeping on Arab Israeli Fronts* (Boulder: Westview Press 1984), pp. 31–68.

[57] A. J. Wilson, *Some Principles for Peacekeeping Operations: A Guide for Senior Officers*, Monograph No. 2 (Paris: International Information Centre on Peacekeeping Operations, June 1967), p. 2.

> A successful officer in command of a UN force must necessarily possess
> not only a high measure of military skill, stricto sensu, but also well
> developed diplomatic and political skills in dealing with what may be a
> diverse and incohesive multi-national military force.[58]

Ability to compromise and a disinclination to 'rock the boat' are essential qualities. In the normal course of events, the orders of the force commander of a peacekeeping or similarly constituted force will be loyally accepted and executed. National contingents, nevertheless, retain a form of 'right of appeal' to their own governments should a unit or contingent commander feel that the interests of the unit are being unfairly or improperly exploited. Moreover, a proposed strategy or deployment on the ground may not be deemed to be in the best interests of the national government of the unit involved. The command structure imposed by the United States in Somalia was contrary to the concept of a unified command and inconsistent with the principles established in previous operations. While this was not the sole cause of the problems encountered by UNOSOM II, it was a major factor in the lack of cohesion and general confusion associated with the operation.

The prospect of a subordinate officer disobeying a lawful order while serving as part of an international force is always a possibility and, although this is not a frequent occurrence, it happens from time to time.[59] Such events do not always involve high-profile figures who attract media attention, and there may be a range of causes for insubordination. One potential defence to a charge of disobeying a lawful command is to challenge the legality of the order itself. In the context of a UN mission, this may be asserted on the basis that the order is inconsistent with the mandate or even that the Security Council was not competent to adopt a particular resolution in the first place. The matter is most serious if it involves the unit or contingent commander. Consider a hypothetical situation in which an Irish unit commander in UNIFIL is ordered to extend his area of operation and redeploy the troops under his or her command by a certain date.[60] He or she declines because to do so involves exposing the personnel, who are

---

[58] McCoubrey and White, *The Blue Helmets*, p. 143.

[59] In February 1998, an Irish commandant (major) was found guilty of disobeying a lawful order of a superior officer in Lebanon. The incident was minor in nature and it probably should never have gotten that far. See the *Irish Times* and the *Irish Independent*, 5 February 1998.

[60] Although this is a hypothetical example, it is based on an actual incident involving the Irish battalion with UNIFIL in the 1980s.

already over-stretched in the unit's area of operations, to serious risk. Furthermore, the initiative may involve using force against local armed elements in order to establish UN authority in the new area. According to the unit commander's assessment of the situation, this proposal might entail casualties and it would achieve little in the long term.

What are the consequences for the unit commander concerned? There may be none if the force commander decides to take no action. Sometimes a superior officer will evaluate the pros and cons of the situation and may decide that it is in the best interest of all concerned if the matter is allowed to rest. This may not always be an option, though, and is particularly unlikely if the authority and reputation of the commander concerned are at stake. If he or she chooses to take action, the relevant national government or governments will become involved. The national government will either support the unit commander's actions, an option which could ultimately lead to the withdrawal of the whole unit, or the commander will be replaced pending disciplinary action. Events such as these played out in the course of the UNOSOM II mission, when serious differences arose between the commander of the Italian contingent and the overall commander of the force. In that case, the Italian government supported the contingent commander's actions,[61] but the backing of a home government is not something upon which the unit commander can necessarily depend. In its absence, the charge could lead to a court martial for disobeying a lawful order. In such a case, the unit commander could plead that the order was impossible to carry out or that it was not a lawful order in the first instance. With regard to the latter, Resolution 426 (1978) lays down the guidelines and terms of reference for UNIFIL, one of which is that it will not use force except in self-defence.[62] Defence counsel acting on behalf of the officer charged could therefore argue that the proposed action would necessarily have involved the use of force contrary to the mandate.

Another possible defence to a charge of disobeying a lawful order is that no valid chain of command existed between the superior and subordinate officers concerned. The chain of command is one of the essential features of military structures and organisation. It is the

---

[61] *Report of the Commission of Inquiry Established Pursuant to Security Council Resolution 885 (1993) to Investigate Attacks on UNOSOM II Personnel*, S/1994/653, 1 June 1994; and *Irish Times*, 19 July 1993, p. 8.

[62] Security Council Resolution 426, 19 March 1978.

military connection that joins a superior officer to a subordinate for the legal transfer of orders and instructions. An established chain of command is the hallmark of all organised military groups and organisations, and is a prerequisite for the success of any military enterprise, in particular international peacekeeping or similar operations. Once an order or instruction is given, the appropriate legal authority is vested in the recipient to carry out those orders. The chain of command is thus a military hierarchy that is common to all armed forces. It is such an intrinsic part of every military organisation that it is easy to take it for granted, but, in a multi-national force of any nature, it is one of the more sensitive and complex issues that needs to be addressed and agreed upon at an early stage.

In the armed forces of most democracies, it is relatively easy to determine the chain of command from the legislation governing its establishment and operation. It is not a subject that gives rise to difficulties when different elements of a national armed force work together as a cohesive group: laid down in civil and military law; it is emphasised at every level of training and in the daily operational and administrative functioning of the force. Matters can change quickly though, when forces that do not usually share a combined and unified command structure become involved in a common enterprise or mission. This can occur when police and military units come together as part of an aid to the civil power operation, or when units from different countries and different military traditions form part of an international UN force. One of the lessons from the UNOSOM II operation is that, in such scenarios, the issue of command and control is crucial to ensure the overall operational effectiveness and cohesiveness of the combined operation or force. It is unfortunate that this fundamental lesson had to be relearned, and at such a price for all involved.

Command and control of Canadian forces

The organisation of the military forces of Canada and Ireland is based on the British regiment concept. There are, however, several important differences between the two regarding participation in international forces. In almost all cases, Canada deploys entire units on UN service, while, in the case of Ireland, special units are organised and established for peacekeeping duties. Another important difference between Canadian and Irish force participation is in the use of reserve forces for UN deployment. Since 1988, Canada has increasingly applied a concept of 'total force', which structurally integrates regular and reserve units. As a result, any major deployment of Canadian Forces will inevitably involve its reserve forces. To date, Irish reserve units have been precluded from participation in UN operations.

Within the Canadian Forces, the chain of command is a line of authority extending from the Chief of the Defence Staff to the lowest-ranking member of the forces. Under Canadian municipal and military law, its effect is to link a 'superior officer', meaning 'any officer or non-commissioned member who, in relation to any other officer or non-commissioned member, is by [the National Defence Act], or by regulations or custom of the service, authorized to give a lawful command to that other officer or non-commissioned member'.[63] No other person, whether minister or public servant, is part of the chain of command within Canadian Forces, nor does any other person have any command authority.[64] In sum, the chain of command is clearly delineated and does not include anyone outside the armed forces hierarchy. A question that naturally comes to mind, then, is how do Canadian law and the Canadian Forces provide for troops operating as part of an international UN force or as part of NATO.

As articulated, command and control, though intrinsically linked and an essential part of any military organisation or coalition of forces, are not synonymous. Command may be defined as the authority vested in an individual member of the armed forces to direct, co-ordinate and control military forces.[65] Control is the authority exercised by a commander over a part of the activities of subordinate organisations or other organisations not normally under command. The matter of command and control is much more clearly defined under Canadian law than under Irish law although, at first glance, one might form the opposite impression. The Governor General of Canada, as the sovereign's representative, is the overall Commander in Chief of the Canadian Forces. However, civil control of the forces is firmly rooted in the parliamentary

---

[63] Section 2 of the National Defence Act, 'Interpretations'. To paraphrase, an 'officer' is a person who holds Her Majesty's commission in the Canadian Forces, and a 'non-commissioned member' is any other person enrolled in the Canadian Forces.

[64] *Dishonoured Legacy: Report of the Commission of Enquiry into the Deployment of Canadian Forces to Somalia* (Ottawa: Canadian Government Publishing, 1997), Vol. 1, *Structure and Organization of the Canadian Forces*, p. 3.

[65] Department of National Defence (Canada), *Joint Doctrine for the Canadian Forces Joint and Combined Operations*, pp. 2-1 and 2-2. See also *Report of the Canadian Somalia Commission of Enquiry*, Vol. 1, Structure and Organization of the Canadian Forces, 7 and 8.

system and the Cabinet is responsible to Parliament for, *inter alia*, formulating and implementing governmental defence and security policy. Through the National Defence Act, Parliament has set out the basic law governing command of the Canadian Forces. Primary authority rests with the Governor in Council to implement the National Defence Act by regulations for the organization, training, discipline, efficiency, administration and good government of Canadian Forces.[66] Under section 12(2) of the National Defence Act, the Minister of National Defence has the power to regulate the same matters, but subject to any regulation made by the Governor in Council and Treasury Board. The Minister retains one of the key links within the command framework, however, in that he or she has the power to make regulations governing who commands what and whom. Yet the 'exercise' of command is then in the hands of the designated commanders subject to law.

Under section 18(1) of the National Defence Act, the Governor in Council may appoint a Chief of the Defence Staff, 'who shall, subject to the regulations and under the direction of the Minister, be charged with the control and administration of the Canadian Forces'. Furthermore, 'command' of and in the Canadian Forces is confirmed as a military activity that flows through commissioned and non-commissioned officers under section 18(2):

> Unless the Governor in Council otherwise directs, all orders and instructions to the Canadian Forces that are required to give effect to the decisions and to carry out the directions of the Government of Canada or the Minister shall be issued by or through the Chief of the Defence Staff.

The position of the Chief of the Defence Staff is therefore quite powerful, and, in terms of actual command, bestows significant responsibility on the holder of the office. Although he or she is subject to the Minister's direction in exercising general powers, it is evident from the legislation that the responsibilities of the Chief of the Defence Staff are not delegated from the Minister. In fact, the Chief of the Defence Staff has responsibility exclusive of the Minister in three significant areas, the most important of which for our purposes is the conduct of military operations.[67] While the Chief of the Defence Staff may assign some

---

[66] Section 12, National Defence Act.

[67] *Report of the Commission of Enquiry*, Vol. 1, *Structure and Organization of the Canadian Forces*, p. 2. The other two areas are in the promotion of members below the rank of general and in all matters related to aid to the civil power.

command and administrative responsibilities to subordinate officers, these are not to be confused with delegations in law that cannot be further delegated under the maxim *delegatus non potest delegare* (a delegate cannot delegate). The assignment of command is limited by the regulation or custom of the service.[68] One of the central pillars of the command structure and chain of command is that commanding officers at every level are always responsible for the whole of the organisation they command, and they cannot abdicate this overall responsibility by handing it over to subordinates.[69] Within these parameters and framework, the military chain of command is formed.

A significant difference in relation to military command and civil control of the armed forces in Ireland and Canada is in the respective roles of the Canadian Chief of the Defence Staff and the Irish Chief of Staff. Under Canadian law, the Minister has responsibility for the 'management and direction' of the Canadian Forces, whereas the Chief of the Defence Staff has 'control and administration' of the Forces under the direction of the Minister.[70] The distinction between what is meant by management and administration in this context is not clear, but it is evident that Parliament chose to vest 'control' of the Canadian Forces directly in the Chief of the Defence Staff with just one proviso, that it be subject to the direction of the Minister.

The role of the Irish Chief of Staff under the Defence Acts is more circumscribed.[71] Until recently, he or she held a 'principal military office' and, as such, was the head of one of the three primary military branches, namely, the branch of the Chief of Staff. The Defence Act 1954 created two other branches and provided that the respective head of each of the three branches was directly responsible to the Minister for Defence for the performance of such duties as may from time to time be assigned. The purpose of this division of command was to ensure that no one person within the Defence Forces was vested with overall command.

The Defence (Amendment) Act 1998 abolished this three-tier command structure and put in its place a single streamlined system of command which provides that the Chief of Staff only be accountable

---

[68] Section 49 of the National Defence Act (Canada).

[69] Queen's Regulations and Orders for the Canadian Forces, section 4.20(3).

[70] Sections 3 and 4 of the National Defence Act govern the role of the Minister for National Defence, while section 18(1) clearly sets the Chief of Defence Staff apart from the Minister.

[71] Sections 11, 12 and 13 of the Defence Act 1954.

directly to the Minister.[72] It did nothing to address the problem of command within international forces. Although the Minister may also delegate to the Chief of Staff such duties in connection with the business of the Department of Defence as he or she may from time to time determine, the role of the Chief of Staff is of much less significance than that of his or her counterpart in the Canadian Forces. Although the Canadian system vests very significant power in the Chief of the Defence Staff, the holder of this office is directly responsible to Parliament. This system allows for greater parliamentary supervision of the armed forces and ensures that no one minister of a political party in government will exercise too much control. It is superior to that operating in Ireland and could be considered as a model for reform of the structures and legislative framework governing the Irish Defence Forces. The enhanced parliamentary control that the Canadian system provides would be particularly appropriate in Ireland owing to the lack of parliamentary supervision in the role and commitments of the Irish Defence Forces.

Canadian military personnel provided to UN-controlled operations are put under the operational control of the UN Force Commander, or its equivalent, in the field. He or she has authority to task the Canadian troops within agreed terms. Canada, however, retains operational command of its forces at all times. In practice, this does not appear to cause any difficulties. The mission of the UN force is determined by the relevant Security Council, or in some instances General Assembly, resolution. The Force Commander retains the authority to direct and deploy Canadian Forces within the parameters set by the overall mission. Most importantly, the Force Commander has tactical control of the forces on the ground. The concept of operational control is an accepted and convenient tool to apply in multi-national coalitions and international UN forces. It permits a national government to retain overall operational command of its national armed forces, while still placing them under the operational control and tactical management of a military commander outside its national military chain of command.

While seemingly technical, the Canadian system operates smoothly in practice, employing laws that attach greater importance to the distinction between operational command and operational control than is found in Irish law. By contrast, the apparently straightforward Irish approach is fraught with major problems. Irish troops are supposedly

---

[72] Section 4 of the Defence (Amendment) Act 1998, which inserted a new section 13 into the Defence Act 1954.

placed under the command of the UN commander in the field, yet it may be unconstitutional under Irish law to do so.

Constitutional issues arising in the command of Irish forces

The potential problems in relation to the command of an international force outlined above could arise in respect of a unit commander of any nationality. The case of Irish officers serving with UN forces is even more problematic. While the regulations governing peacekeeping forces in the Congo and Cyprus provided that individual national contingents were under the operational command of the UN Force Commander, there was no statutory provision in Irish legislation authorising this position. As a result, a practice arose whereby the Chief of Staff of the Irish Defence Forces issued a directive, on the authority of the Minister for Defence, placing the relevant unit and contingent under the command of the UN Force Commander.[73] There is no statutory basis for this directive, yet this remains the practice today with regard to Irish contingents in UN forces, and in SFOR and KFOR in the former Yugoslavia.

This shortcoming in Irish law was highlighted when the provisions of the Defence (Amendment) Act 1960 were being drafted. The question of whether specific provision should be made in that Act placing the commander of an Irish contingent under the command of the Force Commander of a UN force was then considered. In the event, it was decided not to include such a provision on the grounds that it could be controversial and that the operational command referred to in UN regulations should be distinguished from command in general. The command referred to in the Defence Act 1954 was considered much wider than operational command and included the authority to discipline and punish troops. Any provision for operational command would therefore have to be carefully worded and circumscribed. Furthermore, at that time the Irish authorities were examining the regulations governing the first UN Emergency Force and there was no assurance that subsequent peacekeeping forces would be regulated in a similar manner. Despite the complexities of providing a statutory basis in Irish law for distinguishing between the overall command referred to in the Defence Act 1954 and operational command within the context of a UN force, there is a responsibility on the Irish government to

[73] Interview, Lt-Col. Liddy, former Defence Forces Judge Advocate and Legal Officer, January 1990.

introduce amending legislation. The example of Canada, which provides for Canadian forces to be placed under the operational control of a UN commander in the field, is one model that could be considered. The Minister could incorporate the different levels of command and control, outlined in Defence Force Regulations and in the Defence Act as amended, to provide for elements to be placed under the operational command or the operational control of commanders of international forces organised and established under the authority of the UN. This would provide a legal basis for what is, in reality, established practice.

The command of the Irish Defence Forces is governed by the Irish Constitution, along with legislation and statutory regulations made in accordance therewith.[74] The supreme command of the Defence Forces is vested in the President by virtue of the Irish Constitution.[75] The position of the President in this context appears to be a purely ceremonial one,[76] not unlike that of the Queen under the Canadian Constitution Act 1867.[77] The position of the President as commander is circumscribed by the Constitution as a whole. It would make no sense, legally or otherwise, for the President to play an active part in the command and control of the Defence Forces on a daily basis. While the Defence Act 1954 gives the government command and all its concomitant powers, these too must be exercised in accordance with the Constitution and any laws made thereunder.

Section 17(3) of the Defence Act 1954 empowers the Minister for Defence to make regulations in relation to the exercise of military command by officers. Section 2 of the Act defines the expression 'non-commissioned officer' and the word 'officer', when used without qualification, as referring exclusively to a man of the Defence Forces and a person holding commissioned rank in the Defence Forces respectively. The Force Commander of a UN force is not normally a member of the Defence Forces, although from time to time Irish officers have held such a position. Section 17(3) refers exclusively to officers of the Defence

---

[74] R. Murphy, 'The Legal Framework of United Nations Peacekeeping Forces and the Issue of Command and Control' (1999) 4(1) *Journal of Armed Conflict Law* 41–73; and R. Murphy, 'Legal Issues Arising from Participation in Peacekeeping Operations' (March–May 1994) 3 *International Peacekeeping* 61–5.

[75] The Irish Constitution, Art. 13(4) states: 'The supreme command of the Defence Forces is hereby vested in the President.'

[76] G. W. Hogan and G. White (eds.), *J. M. Kelly: The Irish Constitution* (4th edn, Dublin: Butterworths, 2003), pp. 210–11.

[77] The Act provides that the supreme command is vested in the Queen as 'Commander-in-Chief . . . of all . . . Military Forces'. Constitution Act 1867, Part III, section 15.

Forces. This section empowers the Minister for Defence to make regulations in relation to the exercise of military command by officers.[78] It does not, however, empower the Minister to issue directives or make regulations that authorise persons who are not members of the Defence Forces to exercise command over any part thereof, or persons belonging thereto. Neither the Constitution nor the Defence Act distinguishes operational command from military command. Although the matter has not been judicially considered, there is a strong case to be made that the 'military command' referred to in the Act is an all-embracing concept which includes, *inter alia*, national command and operational command as generally understood internationally. If it were otherwise, then 'military command' under the Act would have little practical significance.

The Irish Constitution also states that all commissioned officers of the Defence Forces shall hold their commissions from the President.[79] The form of commission issued to an officer upon appointment refers to 'such lawful orders and directions as [he or she] shall from time to time receive from the Minister for Defence, or from any of [his or her] superior officers'.[80] Furthermore, section 131 of the Defence Act 1954, which deals with the offence of disobedience to a superior officer, refers to 'a lawful command of a superior officer'.[81] The words 'superior officer' and 'lawful' are very significant in these provisions. An officer of any other national or international force who is not a member of the Irish Defence Forces is not a superior officer for the purposes of the Act and is therefore not vested with any statutory authority to issue a lawful command to Defence Forces personnel. In order to enable the Force Commander of a multi-national UN force to exercise lawful command over that portion of the Defence Forces forming part of the peacekeeping force, it is essential that he or she be vested with lawful command. This is simply not the case under the current procedure, whereby the Chief of Staff issues a directive, at the behest of the Minister for Defence, to a unit commander that purports to place the unit under the operational command of the Force Commander. This tactic is *ultra vires* the Minister, missing, at the very least, statutory authorisation. It

---

[78] These are in the form of Defence Force Regulations or General Routine Orders.

[79] Irish Constitution, Art. 13.5.2°.

[80] This is set out in the Fifth Schedule to the Defence Act 1954.

[81] Section 131 states: 'Every person subject to military law who disobeys a lawful command of a superior officer is guilty of an offence against military law ...'

seems that the Minister has, as a matter of convenience, presumed to define 'military command' in such a way as to delimit its scope and significance.

The situation in Ireland contrasts with that of Germany. Under German law, the question of the scope of command which the Federal Minister of Defence has over German military personnel assigned to a multi-national unit in accordance with Article 65a of the German Constitution is of particular importance.[82] Despite Article 65a, German subordinate military personnel may be ordered by their national superiors to obey the instructions of a foreign directing authority. If a German soldier disobeys a foreign superior's instructions, this constitutes a disciplinary offence against the duty to serve loyally.[83] This means that German soldiers must obey the military directives or orders of a superior officer who is a part of NATO or other multi-national operations, irrespective of the nationality of the superior. There is now a strong body of opinion that, without prejudice to the power of command of the Minister of Defence under the Constitution, foreign commanders of multi-national forces may be included in the chain of command under German military law, provided that certain conditions are met.

It is self-evident that any Irish government minister who acts in an unconstitutional fashion will thereby exceed his or her jurisdiction and authority.[84] Moreover, even if the courts found that the minister was acting constitutionally, a result that would be by no means certain, the question arises whether the minister is acting within powers conferred by statute, in this case the Defence Acts. There have been a number of cases in recent years where the courts have set aside decisions by ministers on the grounds that their actions were not authorised.[85]

---

[82] Art. 65a states: 'Powers of command in respect of the Armed Forces shall be vested in the Federal Minister for Defence.'

[83] *Soldatengesetz* (Soldiers Act), Art. 7. See D. Fleck, 'Multinational Units', in D. Fleck (ed.), *The Handbook of the Law of Visiting Forces* (Oxford: Oxford University Press, 2001), p. 42.

[84] See the comments of Henchy J in *The State (Holland)* v. *Kennedy* [1977] *Irish Reports* 193 at 201 and *The State (Byrne)* v. *Frawley* [1978] *Irish Reports* 326 at 345 and those of Walsh J in *Shelley* v. *Mahon* [1990] *Irish Reports* 36 at 45.

[85] *Meade* v. *Cork County Council*, Supreme Court, 31 July 1974; *Reidy* v. *Minister for Agriculture and Food*, High Court, 9 June 1989; *Devitt* v. *Minister for Education* [1989] *Irish Law Reports Monthly* 696.

Furthermore, the administrative act in question did not appear to be reasonably incidental to or within any implicit powers conferred by statute.[86]

The question of the command of the Defence Forces must be examined in the context of the Defence Act 1954 as a whole. When the importance of command of the Defence Forces is considered along with the lack of control exercised by the Minister for Defence over elements placed under the command of the UN, it follows that neither the Minister nor the Chief of Staff of the Defence Forces has any right to delegate command in the manner currently prescribed.

The question of command was rendered more uncertain in the case of UNIFIL, owing to the fact that there were no regulations published for that force. In 1981, the directive issued by the Chief of Staff was amended to take account of this; however, the fundamental problem outlined remained[87] and could not be circumvented or resolved by what amounted to little more than tinkering with the words. The validity of the directive depends, to some extent, on the existence of a valid parallel UN instrument regulating the designation of the chain of command from the Force Commander. In the absence of this link, it is difficult to see how an identifiable command structure can be maintained. When the matter was queried, the UN Secretariat registered the opinion that the delegation of command within UNIFIL in general was in accordance with normal military custom as applicable to an integrated command. It was considered that a power to determine chain of command was inherent in the Force Commander's exercise of command in the field in accordance with the guidelines laid down and did not require further elaboration.

In fact, the guidelines merely stipulate that a Force Commander will exercise command in the field.[88] It therefore appears that, in the absence of UN regulations for UNIFIL empowering the Force Commander to designate the chain of command and to delegate his authority, the

---

[86] See G. Hogan and D. Morgan, *Administrative Law in Ireland* (3rd edn, Dublin: Round Hall Sweet and Maxwell, 1998), p. 394. The Minister's action in directing the Chief of Staff of the Defence Forces to issue a command directive as outlined may also infringe the principle *delegatus non potest delegare* (a delegate cannot delegate), i.e. a power may only be delegated to a body or persons other than that designated by the *Oireachtas* (legislature) if this is authorised, expressly or by implication, by the legislation in question. It cannot be transferred to any other person or body.

[87] Interview, senior Irish army officer, Army Headquarters, October 1997.

[88] UN Doc. S/12611, para. 4(a).

command structure within the Force had not been formally estab-lished.[89] The fact that this did not cause any particular difficulty in the operation of the force was due to the professionalism of those who served in UNIFIL. A 'gentleman's agreement' or 'understanding' is not a sufficient legal basis for the exercise of command in an international UN force. In the circumstances, it is desirable that the Secretary-General issue regulations for each peacekeeping force that govern the designation of the chain of command and empower the Force Commander to delegate his authority.

The question of command of a UN force as envisaged under the Irish Defence (Amendment) Act 1993 which facilitates participation in peace enforcement missions may be even more problematic than that of a traditional peacekeeping force. In the course of the parliamentary debate on the new legislation, Deputy Taylor-Quinn put the question suc-cinctly when she enquired as to 'what the command structure and rules of engagement will be [for UNOSOM II and] who will be giving the orders?'[90] These matters have been the subject of considerable con-troversy. The issue was most recently evaded in the debate regarding participation in KFOR, with a statement by the Minister that the com-mand and control arrangements for that entity were analogous to that of SFOR in Bosnia-Herzegovina.[91] Yet, what exactly are the arrangements for SFOR? This is the kind of question to which a clear and satisfactory answer is not possible in the present circumstances. The question of command of multi-national forces has been a difficult issue for major powers participating in such forces. While the broader issues of com-mand of international forces are outside the scope and competence of Irish municipal law, the overall uncertainty regarding the command of UN forces is exacerbated in respect of Irish Defence Forces personnel by the failure of successive governments to attempt any resolution of the potential difficulties outlined above.

Conclusion

In the case of UNIFIL, no formal SOFA was concluded until late 1995. The status of the force and other matters relating to its operation and establishment initially had to be interpreted by reference to the terms of reference, general considerations and guidelines for UNIFIL that were

---

[89]   Bowett, *UN Forces*, pp. 115–17.
[90]   Dáil (Parliament) Debates 433 (600–1), 1 July 1993.
[91]   Dáil (Parliament) Debates 507 (852–69 at 857), 1 July 1999.

laid down by the Secretary-General and approved by the Security Council in Resolution 426 (1978). These contained considerably less detail than formal agreements concluded for other peacekeeping forces. Instead, UNIFIL relied on a series of standing operating procedures that provided guidelines and defined the method by which the operation was to be conducted. Although issued on behalf of the Force Commander, their legal basis was questionable. In practice, reference was made to the SOFA and regulations governing the UN force in Cyprus. UNIFIL's own long-awaited SOFA resolved much of the initial legal uncertainty. But the legal obligation on members of the Irish Defence Forces to obey the UNIFIL standing operating procedures was uncertain, as they have no status under Irish military law, and did not form part of the municipal law or military law of contributing states. A similar situation pertains with regard to UN standing operating procedures under Canadian law: they have no legal status and Canadian forces are not obliged to obey them.

One relatively simple method of resolving the legal difficulties created by these standing operating procedures is for the contingent or unit commanders concerned to examine their content and effect. If there is nothing illegal or contrary to the municipal law of the contributing state, the commanding officer should sign them and, in this way, incorporate them into contingent or unit regulations. Few legal problems are amenable to such simple solutions, and, provided that the procedures are not illegal, there seems to be little reason not to incorporate them into unit regulations.

In the aftermath of the UN operation in Somalia, Canada established a Commission of Inquiry into all aspects of its involvement in the mission.[92] The Commission's conclusions were very critical of certain personnel, and the overall 'system' in operation at the time. While some of these criticisms may have been unduly harsh, countries like Ireland could take many of the Commission's recommendations on board. Somalia remains one of the most controversial UN missions in recent times and Ireland is fortunate to have remained unscathed by the controversies that have involved Belgian, Italian and United States armed forces. The reality for all countries involved is that Somalia proved a mission impossible.

---

[92] *Dishonoured Legacy: Report of the Commission of Enquiry into the Deployment of Canadian Forces to Somalia* (Ottawa: Canadian Government Publishing, 1997).

Despite the complexities of providing a statutory basis in Irish law for distinguishing between the overall command referred to in the Defence Act 1954 and operational command, and/or within the context of a UN force, there is a responsibility on the Irish government to revise existing legislation. The example of Canada, which provides for Canadian Forces to be placed under the operational control of a UN commander in the field, is one model that could be considered. Regulations could be introduced by the Minister for Defence providing for different levels of command and control, and the Defence Acts amended to provide for elements to be placed under the operational command or the operational control of commanders of international forces organised and established under the authority of the UN.

In the final analysis, it may be that the problem confronting Canadian and Irish participation in the more pro-active contemporary peacekeeping and enforcement missions is capability and capacity to participate. The current rationalisation and 'downsizing' of armed forces throughout the developed world has impacted on the capacity of countries to participate in UN forces. This may be an even more important determinant of mission success than the nature of the conflict for which intervention is being considered. Canada, despite NATO membership, does not appear to have compromised its status as a 'middle power'. As the European Union moves closer to formal security and defence arrangements, Ireland can look to countries like Canada in order to assess the political and legal implications of such changes.

From the point of view of Ireland, the issue of command and control is even more complex in the context of the peacekeeping missions in the former Yugoslavia. At the time of writing, the highest-ranking Defence Forces officer in Kosovo is currently a Lieutenant-Colonel. The chain of command runs directly from the Force Commander to the commander of the Irish contingent on the ground. This may be unconstitutional, and/or contrary to military law, as the Force Commander is neither a 'superior officer' nor a member of the Defence Forces as required by the Defence Act 1954. In any event, this is an unsatisfactory situation.

The current force in Kosovo is a UN-mandated but NATO-led multinational military force. It is not part of the NATO military command structure. It is more in the nature of an *ad hoc* force created as a NATO crisis-reaction operation or peace-support operation comprising thirty-five states, twelve of which are non-NATO members.[93] However, the

[93] Relevant date, February 2006.

majority of positions at KFOR headquarters are held by personnel from NATO member states. Command and control issues are also foremost in the minds of NATO political and military leaders. For this reason, NATO is alert to the need to 'be careful not to subordinate NATO to any other international body or compromise the integrity of its command structure'.[94] If the NATO-led operation is not subordinate to the UN, then what is its relationship with the Security Council? This depends on where the real concentration of power is based. It is not with the Secretary-General, and nor is it with the Security Council. This is a NATO-led and *de facto* NATO-commanded operation. There is no strategic direction from the Military Staff Committee, and the reality is that the Security Council is merely kept informed.

Revision of the legal framework of UN peacekeeping operations is long overdue. The *ad hoc* and improvised structures and procedures are a source of concern and potential difficulty. Usually these forces have enough to contend with on the ground besides the ineptitude of their own organisation. In all of the Western armed forces, unity of command is an imperative. While it may be difficult to appreciate the full significance of this principle, there is a strong argument to be made that, as long as the UN wishes to use a military force as a peacekeeping or peace enforcement mechanism, the principle must be maintained. It is essential to the success of a military operation that a valid chain of command be authorised. For this reason, there is an onus on the UN Secretariat and the Irish government to resolve the question of command. The situation prevailing for Canadian forces has much merit, and is a pragmatic attempt to balance the needs of the mission with that of the Canadian requirement to retain overall national command of the armed forces. In general, the record in this area with peacekeeping forces seems to be excellent. This owes much to the professionalism and commitment of those involved. However, events in the Congo operation (ONUC, 1960–4), and more recently in Somalia and Kosovo, show that the consensus required in order to maintain this high level of performance in the absence of a clearly delineated and workable structure may not always be present.

---

[94] See Deputy Secretary of State Strobe Talbott on NATO's future 'Strategic Concept', in B. Simma, 'NATO, the UN and the Use of Force: Legal Aspects' (1999) 10 *European Journal of International Law* 1–22 at 15.

4

United Nations peacekeeping in Lebanon, Somalia and Kosovo, and the use of force

Introduction

The principles governing the use of force are fundamental to peacekeeping forces and are one of the characteristics that distinguish peacekeeping from enforcement operations. Although the UN Charter does not specifically provide for peacekeeping operations, their establishment and development is now based upon a number of fundamental principles, adherence to which may well determine the success of a peacekeeping mission.[1] One of these, the prohibition on the use of force, other than in self-defence, is an essential characteristic of traditional peacekeeping operations and is based on practical and doctrinal considerations.[2] Despite these, both the Brahimi Report[3] and the report on the events that led to the fall of Srebrenica[4] question the traditional response of UN forces to the use of force, each advocating the formulation of a more robust doctrine. The UN Secretary-General's report on 'threats and challenges' has referred to the characterisation of peacekeeping missions in terms of 'Chapter VI' or

---

[1] *The Peacekeepers Handbook* (New York: International Peace Academy, 1984), p. 55. The principles include the following:

   (a) negotiation is the primary means of finding solutions;
   (b) suggestion, advice and objective response to courses of action taken by the parties to the dispute rather than direction, imposition and coercion;
   (c) non-use of force except in self-defence, or as a last resort in carrying out the mandate;
   (d) impartiality; and
   (e) recognition of the authority of the host country(s).

[2] See M. Goulding, 'The Use of Force by the United Nations' (1996) 3(1) *International Peacekeeping* 1–18; F. T. Liu, *United Nations Peacekeeping and the Non-Use of Force* (New York: International Peace Academy, 1992), p. 11; and G. van Hegelsom, 'The Law of Armed Conflict and UN Peace-Keeping and Peace-Enforcement Operations' (1993) 6 *Hague Yearbook of International Law* 45–58.

[3] *Report of the Panel on UN Peacekeeping Operations* (Brahimi Report), UN Doc. A/55/305-S/2000/809, 23 August 2000.

[4] See 'Lessons for the Future', in *Report of the Secretary-General Pursuant to General Assembly Resolution 53/35: The Fall of Srebrenica*, General Assembly Doc. A/54/49, 15 November 1999, esp. paras. 502 and 505.

'Chapter VII' operations as somewhat misleading.[5] It acknowledges that there is a distinction between operations in which a robust use of force is integral to the mission and those that involve more 'traditional peace-keeping' in which there is a reasonable expectation that force may not be used. However, in peacekeeping cases – as much as in peace enforcement – it is now the usual practice to adopt a Chapter VII mandate (even if this is not always welcomed by troop contributors). An otherwise benign envir-onment can turn hostile, and it is desirable that there is complete certainty about the mission's capacity to respond with force, if necessary. The experience of UN forces in Somalia, Lebanon and Kosovo shows that traditional limitations on the use of force have proved controversial and difficult to apply in practice, not least because of the correlation to the other characteristics, especially the need to maintain impartiality.[6]

The basic rules for the use of force were established during the first stages of the UNEF I (1956–67)[7] operation, and these set a precedent for several later peacekeeping operations.[8] The Secretary-General then envi-saged that the basic precept of UN operations would always include 'a prohibition against any initiative in the use of armed force', while at the same time permitting a response with force to an armed attack, including attempts to make UN troops withdraw from positions that they occupied under their mandate.[9] After the controversy surrounding

---

[5] *A More Secure World: Our Shared Responsibility: Report of the High-Level Panel on Threats, Challenges and Change*, UN Doc. A/59/565, 2 December 2004, paras. 212–14. See also S. Chesterman, 'The Use of Force in UN Peace Operations', External Study, Best Practices Unit (New York: UN Department of Peacekeeping Operations, 2004), p. 6.

[6] See generally M. von Grunigen, 'Neutrality in Peacekeeping', in A. Cassese (ed.), *United Nations Peacekeeping: Legal Essays* (Dordrecht: Sijthoff and Nordhoff, 1978), pp. 125–53, esp. pp. 137–8.

[7] UNEF I was the first United Nations peacekeeping force and it was established by the first emergency special session of the General Assembly which was held from 1 to 10 November 1956. The mandate of the force was to secure and supervise the cessation of hostilities, including the withdrawal of the armed forces of France, Israel and the United Kingdom from Egyptian territory and, after the withdrawal, to serve as a buffer between the Egyptian and Israeli forces and to provide impartial supervision of the cease-fire. UNEF was withdrawn in May–June 1967, at Egypt's request.

[8] H. Wiseman, 'United Nations Peacekeeping: An Historical Overview', in H. Wiseman (ed.), *Peacekeeping: Appraisals and Proposals* (New York and Oxford: Pergamon Press, 1983), pp. 19–58, esp. p. 33. For a more general discussion on the use of force, see A. James, *The Role of Force in International Order and United Nations Peacekeeping*, Report of a Conference at Ditchley Park, 16–19 May 1969, Ditchley Paper No. 20 (Enstone, Oxfordshire: Ditchley Foundation, 1969).

[9] *Summary Study of the Experience Derived from the Establishment and Operation of the Force*, UN Doc. A/3943, 9 October 1958, para. 179. See R. Siekmann, *Basic Documents on*

the operation in the Congo (ONUC, 1960–4), there was extensive dis-cussion about the use of force.[10] However, there was a significant evolution in the guidelines since UNEF I,[11] and it was the arrangements for UNEF II (1973–9)[12] that marked a turning point in the official UN language, where the authority to use force in self-defence was deemed to include resistance to attempts by forceful means to prevent it from discharging its duties under the mandate. This significantly broadened the definition of self-defence, giving considerably greater latitude to Force Commanders than previously was the case, and became the pre-cedent for all major UN peacekeeping operations thereafter, including UNIFIL.[13] It also allowed the Security Council to assign peacekeeping forces to almost any task, however ill thought out or unrealistic, in the expectation that it could use force under the guise of self-defence and still retain its peacekeeping status.

There are two aspects to the use of force in peacekeeping doctrine. The first is minimum use of force, and the second is the use of force

United Nations and Related Peace-Keeping Forces (2nd edn, Dordrecht: Martinus Nijhoff, 1989), p. 53.

[10] A. James, 'The Congo Controversies' (1994) 1 *International Peacekeeping* 44–58, esp. 51–2; D. W. Bowett, *United Nations Forces* (London: Stevens, 1964), pp. 200–5; M. Harrington Gagnon, 'Peace Forces and the Veto: The Relevance of Consent' (1967) 21(4) *International Organization* 812–36; A. Eide, 'United Nations Forces in Domestic Conflicts', in P. Frydenberg (ed.), *Peacekeeping: Experience and Evaluation – The Oslo Papers* (Oslo: NUPI, 1964), pp. 251–2; N. T. Kassar, 'The Legal Limits to the Use of International Force Through the United Nations Practice' (1979) 35 *Revue Egyptienne de Droit International* 163–234, esp. 195–218; and C. F. Amerasinghe, 'The Use of Armed Force by the United Nations in the Charter Travaux Preparatoires' (1965) 5 *Indian Journal of International Law* 305–33.

[11] T. Findlay, 'The Use of Force in Self-Defence: Theory and Practice', in A. Morrison, D. Fraser and J. Kiras (eds.), *Peacekeeping with Muscle: The Use of Force in International Conflict Resolution* (Clementsport Nova Scotia: Pearson Peacekeeping Centre, 1997), pp. 51–75 at p. 55.

[12] UNEF II was established on 25 October 1973 with the mandate to supervise the implementation of Security Council Resolution 340, which demanded that an immedi-ate and complete ceasefire between Egyptian and Israeli forces be observed and that the parties return to the positions they had occupied at 1650 hours GMT on 22 October 1973. The force was tasked with using its best efforts to prevent a recurrence of the fighting.

[13] Security Council Doc. S/12611, 19 March 1978, para. 4. The paragraph dealing with the use of force stated: 'The Force will be provided with weapons of a defensive character. It will not use force except in self-defence. *Self-defence would include resistance to attempts by forceful means to prevent it from discharging its duties under the mandate of the Security Council.* The Force will proceed on the assumption that the parties to the conflict will take the necessary steps for compliance with the decisions of the Council' See (emphasis added). Findlay, 'The Use of Force in Self-Defence', p. 55.

solely for self-defence.[14] These are not synonymous, in that the first permits the use of force to achieve the military mission or mandate, while the latter restricts the use of force to protection of persons or property. Most of the debate has focused on the use of force for reasons other than self-defence. This is one of the more problematic and controversial issues associated with UN military operations, and it proved especially so in Somalia, Kosovo and Bosnia. During the Bosnian war, the political imperative to be seen 'doing something' led to the creation of 'safe havens', but ignored the wider military implications of the duty to protect those havens.[15] It was not a role that could realistically be undertaken by lightly armed peacekeepers. Although Resolution 836 (1993) delegated the power to member states, acting individually or through regional arrangement, to take military action in Bosnia-Herzegovina to protect safe areas, it remained unclear who should decide when force should be used and for what purpose.[16] The UN will only acknowledge such a duty if member states agree to provide the requisite support and means. The experience of UNIFIL shows that this has also been a difficult problem for traditional peacekeeping operations.[17] In the case of Somalia, the dynamic nature of the humanitarian assistance mandate gradually expanded the authority to use force. Yet, as the objectives changed and the authority to use force altered, the mission became increasingly less impartial.

Since its establishment in 1978, the UNIFIL force has been involved in a number of confrontations involving the use of force.[18] Yet, guidelines governing the use of force have usually been very general in nature,

---

[14] D. Last, *Theory, Doctrine and Practice of Conflict De-Escalation in Peacekeeping Operations* (Clementsport, Nova Scotia: Canadian Peacekeeping Press, 1997), p. 46.

[15] Y. Akashi, 'The Use of Force in a United Nations Peacekeeping Operation: Lessons Learnt from the Safe Areas Mandate' (1995) 19 *Fordham International Law Journal* 312–23. See also *Report of the Secretary-General Pursuant to General Assembly Resolution 53/35 – The Fall of Srebrenica*, General Assembly Doc. A/54/549, 15 November 1999.

[16] D. Sarooshi, *The United Nations and the Development of Collective Security* (Oxford: Clarendon Press, 1999), esp. pp. 72–5, 83–5 and 254–63.

[17] R. Murphy, 'UN Peacekeeping in Lebanon and the Use of Force' (1999) 6(2) *International Peacekeeping* 38–63; and N. D. White, *The United Nations and the Maintenance of International Peace and Security* (2nd edn, Manchester: Manchester University Press, 1997), p. 241.

[18] Liu, *United Nations Peacekeeping and the Non-Use of Force*, pp. 27–35; A. James, *Peacekeeping in International Politics* (London: International Institute for Strategic Studies, 1990), pp. 339–51; and E. A. Erskine, *Mission with UNIFIL, An African Soldier's Reflections* (London: Hurst, 1989), pp. 5–30.

leaving considerable room for interpretation.[19] This is necessary in the operational environment, in which a peacekeeping mission must sometimes perform unclear and possibly unrealistic tasks. Recent UN military operations have blurred the distinction between peacekeeping and peace enforcement, and a broad interpretation of self-defence to include 'defence of the mission' may amount to permitting enforcement of the mandate, even when the operation is authorised under Chapter VI rather than Chapter VII of the Charter.[20] If a peacekeeping force is denied limited *de facto* enforcement powers, this could have the effect of rendering it ineffective for the purpose of fulfilling the mandate. This was especially evident in the case of UNIFIL, and the instances where force was used were, for the most part, as a last resort to prevent the force being rendered ineffective in the face of a lack of co-operation from the parties to the conflict.

This chapter examines the experience of UNIFIL,[21] UNOSOM II and KFOR. The premise of the analysis is that strict adherence to the principle of the use of force in self-defence is the only option available in traditional peacekeeping operations. In support of this premise, it will be shown that the nature of the UNOSOM II mission, which necessitated the adoption of coercive enforcement measures, inevitably led to its role as third-party UN force being converted to that of factional participant. Simply put, the identification of one of the factions as an enemy, and the use of force in pursuit of limited military goals designed to neutralise it, will ultimately escalate rather than decrease the level of conflict. In general, a peacekeeping force should not rely on the use of force to achieve its ends.[22] If it does so, it will lose its status as a peacekeeping mission and cease to be above the conflict it is intended to resolve. However, when a party to the conflict fails to give the required level of co-operation, a decision must be made regarding what degree of force, if any, may be resorted to in the circumstances. In this way, peacekeeping involves novel approaches to crisis resolution that can be

[19] N. J. Weinberger, 'Peacekeeping Options in Lebanon' (1983) 37(3) *Middle East Journal* 341–69, esp. 344.

[20] N. D. White, *The United Nations and the Maintenance of International Peace and Security*, pp. 224–44; J. Fink, 'From Peacekeeping to Peace Enforcement: The Blurring of the Mandate for the Use of Force in Maintaining International Peace and Security' (1995) 19 *Maryland Journal of International Law and Trade* 37–49.

[21] For a list of incidents involving UNIFIL and the use of force, see Liu, *United Nations Peacekeeping and the Non-Use of Force*, pp. 25–35.

[22] B. Urquhart, 'Peacekeeping: A View from the Operational Centre', in H. Wiseman, *United Nations Peacekeeping*, p. 165.

difficult for anyone, including regular soldiers recruited from conventional armies, to understand and apply.[23]

Events in Kosovo, especially during early 2004, show that this is not an easy matter to deal with in practice. The roots of the problems confronting UNMIK and KFOR can be traced to the weak policy adopted in the early stages of deployment which, in turn, was based on a flawed analysis and a fear of taking forceful measures to deal with extremists on all sides. Central to this was a policy of eschewing the use of force in favour of a kid gloves approach that contributed to the breakdown of law and order. Consequently, the protection of vulnerable groups and the creation of a secure environment were not achieved. A worst case scenario presented itself in March 2004, whereby the failure of international security forces to resort to force to protect the minority population was an abdication of their responsibility and a failure to implement the mandate. A combination of factors led to the outbreak of violence. There was the growing frustration among the Albanian population arising from the ambiguous constitutional status of Kosovo itself, and disillusionment with the UNMIK administration.[24] UNMIK is now viewed as an inept and even corrupt international neo-colonial presence that has done little to stem the widespread crime, unemployment and poverty. In addition, whatever respect KFOR commanded has been severely undermined by its uncoordinated response to the outbreak of violence in 2004.

The establishment of peace support operations in Somalia, Lebanon and Kosovo

Somalia

In the case of the initial peace enforcement mission to Somalia (UNITAF), its authorisation to use force was quite novel, as the operation was not in response to an act of aggression.[25] There was no clear

---

[23] Irish troops serving at home are governed by similar rules on the use of force in self-defence as UN peacekeepers. For this reason, they have little difficulty accepting and applying the rules in Lebanon. See *Irish Times*, 31 May 1985, for a comment to this effect by an official army spokesman.

[24] Letter dated 17 November 2004 from the Secretary-General addressed to the President of the Security Council, UN Doc. S/2004/932, 30 November 2004.

[25] Security Council Resolution 751 of 24 April 1992, para. 4. See also *Report of the Secretary-General on the Situation in Somalia*, Security Council Doc. S/23829, 21 April 1992, esp. paras. 22–33 and 62–3; *The United Nations and Somalia 1992–1996* (United

precedent for the type of operations envisaged and the non-consensual intervention by the UN in the affairs of Somalia. The Security Council determined that the situation constituted a threat to international peace and security, and express reference was made to action under Chapter VII to establish a secure environment in order to secure humanitarian relief.[26] Similar to other Chapter VII resolutions, Resolution 794 (1992) did not make express reference to the use of 'force', but referred to the right to 'use all necessary means'.[27] Nevertheless, the clear intent was to permit the use of force if necessary to ensure that the relief efforts were successful. The actual wording of the resolution was remarkably vague in this and other respects. In contrast to Resolution 84 (1950) in respect of the Korea operation,[28] although unified command is mentioned in paragraph 12, it seems that the Security Council gave blanket approval for whatever the Secretary-General and the United States subsequently agreed.

The authorisation to use all necessary means is a typical UN euphemism for the use of force. Despite this, it is still not clear what this means in practice. In the case of Somalia, a great deal of authority seems to have been delegated to a very few to act on behalf of the international community in a way that required little or no accountability.[29] The vague language used also led to uncertainty regarding the UN objectives under the resolution. This was immediately evident from the Secretary-General's letter to President Bush, in which he felt compelled to refer to the need for disarming the factions. A more detailed resolution with clearer aims and objectives, setting down definite parameters for the use of force and clarifying the nature and extent of United States command, would have been preferable.

Although UNITAF did adopt a fairly aggressive stance towards disarming various factions and opening up humanitarian aid routes, there

---

Nations Blue Book Series, 3rd edn, New York: United Nations, 1996), p. 4; and 29(3) *UN Chronicle*, September 1992.

[26] Security Council Resolution 794 (1992), para. 7. For a discussion of Chapter VII and Article 39, see generally L. Goodrich, E. Hambro and A. Simons, *Charter of the United Nations* (3rd edn, London: Columbia University Press, 1969), pp. 290–353, esp. pp. 293–302; and B. Simma (ed.), *The Charter of the United Nations* (2nd edn, Oxford: Oxford University Press, 2002), pp. 701–806.

[27] Security Council Resolution 794 (1992), para. 10.

[28] Adopted 7 July 1950.

[29] For a comprehensive overview of the delegation by the Security Council of its Chapter VII powers, see Sarooshi, *The United Nations and the Development of Collective Security*, esp. pp. 81–2 and 187–91.

was no concerted or even-handed policy.[30] The situation varied from area to area, depending on the national origin of the UN forces. This restrained policy was to change with the deployment of UNOSOM II in March 1993 when Somalia became the testing ground for new peace-keeping and peace-making by the UN, acting under enforcement powers pursuant to Chapter VII.[31] In contrast to UNITAF, UNOSOM II interpreted its mandate as not merely authorising but requiring it to disarm the factions.[32] This involved the selective use of force against one of the factions, Aideed's Somali National Alliance. In adopting such a policy, UNOSOM II broke the cardinal rule when resorting to the use of force by failing to maintain an even-handed and impartial approach; in so doing, it relinquished any pretence of impartiality.

Lebanon

In the case of UNIFIL, one of the major problems confronting the force was the fact that its deployment was based on a number of assumptions, many of which were never fulfilled.[33] In particular, the necessary co-operation of the parties was far from forthcoming.[34] Any decisive action against one of these was liable to escalate and draw UNIFIL into the Lebanese conflict itself. This, in fact, is what later happened to UNOSOM II, and, not unexpectedly, the volunteer contributor states to that mission withdrew their contingents, and, by March 1995, the force ceased to exist.

In the early years of UNIFIL's existence, the Lebanese government looked for a stronger show of force and suggested it be armed with medium and heavy weapons, despite the fact that the force then

[30] Human Rights Watch/Africa, 'Somalia Faces the Future: Human Rights in a Fragmented Society' (1995) 7(2) *Africa Report* 58. In fact, many weapons were moved away from the presence of UN troops to avoid disarmament, with a consequent rise in violence in areas remote from the capital.

[31] S. Makinda, *Seeking Peace from Chaos: Humanitarian Intervention in Somalia* (Boulder and London: International Peace Academy, 1993), p. 76.

[32] See *Report of the Commission of Inquiry Established Pursuant to Resolution 885 (1993) to Investigate Attacks on UNOSOM II Personnel*, UN Doc. S/1994/653, 1 June 1994, reprinted in *The United Nations and Somalia, 1992–1996* (New York: United Nations, 1996), p. 368, esp. pp. 376–7 (hereafter 'UN Commission of Inquiry'), para. 193.

[33] Security Council Doc. S/13026, 12 January 1979, para. 34.

[34] A. James, 'Painful Peacekeeping: The United Nations in Lebanon, 1978–1982' (1983) 38 *International Journal* 613–34, esp. 624; J. F. Murphy, *The United Nations and the Control of Violence* (Manchester: Manchester University Press, 1983), pp. 106 and 57–60; and N. J. Weinberger, 'Peacekeeping Options in Lebanon', p. 344.

possessed a number of heavy weapons that were sufficient to meet the threat from the *de facto* forces and other armed elements.[35] These proposals were not supported by the troop-contributing countries,[36] and, in these circumstances, the Secretary-General chose a cautious policy, adopting guidelines on the use of force applied to previous peacekeeping operations in the region.[37] It is unlikely that the guidelines would have been any different had they been the subject of critical examination and debate, as the Secretary-General had little choice in this matter owing to the urgency of getting UNIFIL deployed in the first place.[38]

Kosovo[39]

The legal basis for the establishment of an international military presence in Kosovo is Resolution 1244 (1999).[40] This sets out the mandate of KFOR and very broadly outlines the responsibilities of the international security presence. These include:

- Establishing a secure environment in which refugees and displaced persons can return home in safety, the international civil presence can

---

[35] UNIFIL already possessed a range of mortars up to 120 mm. The Irish battalion and the French had a number of 90 mm cannons mounted on armoured cars, and the Dutch had TOW missiles.

[36] J. O. C. Jonah, 'Peacekeeping in the Middle East' (1976) 31 *International Journal* 100–22, esp. 155–66.

[37] Security Council Doc. S/12611, 19 March 1978, para. 4. See also N. T. Kassar, 'The Legal Limits to the Use of International Force', pp. 163–236, esp. pp. 214–18. The Secretary-General's outline of the principles of force were more comprehensive for UNFICYP: Security Council Doc. S/5653, 11 April 1964. The guidelines for UNEF II are outlined in *The Blue Helmets* (3rd edn, New York: United Nations, 1996), pp. 60–1. The principles and guidelines for UNEF (Security Council Doc. S/11052/Rev.1) were approved by the Security Council on 27 October 1973 (Resolution 341 (1973)).

[38] Personal interview, Lt-Gen. Erskine, former Force Commander of UNIFIL, Dublin, July 1986.

[39] On NATO intervention in Kosovo, see B. Simma, 'NATO, the UN and the Use of Force: Legal Aspects' (1999) 10 *European Journal of International Law* 1–22; K. Ambos, 'NATO, the UN and the Use of Force: Legal Aspects: A comment on Simma and Cassese' (1999) 2 *Humanitäres Völkerrecht, Deutsches Rotes Kreuz* 114–15; A. Cassesse, 'Ex Iniuria Ius Oritur: Are We Moving Towards International Legitimation of Forcible Humanitarian Countermeasures in the World Community?' (1999) 10 *European Journal of International Law* 23–30; and C. Guicherd, 'International Law and the War in Kosovo' (1999) 41(2) *Survival* 19–34.

[40] Adopted under Chapter VII of the UN Charter, 10 June 1999.

operate, a transition administration can be established, and humanitarian aid can be delivered.

- Ensuring public safety and order until the international civil presence can take responsibility for the task.
- Ensuring the protection and freedom of movement of KFOR itself, the international civil presence, and other international organizations.
- Deterring renewed hostilities.
- Demilitarizing the KLA and other armed Albanian groups.

In effect, Resolution 1244 created an international protectorate. Provision of a secure environment in which to allow UNMIK to perform its multiple tasks was an integral part of the operation. This assignment fell to the 40–50,000 NATO and other troops deployed as part of KFOR. This was a NATO-led international security presence, supposedly under a unified command structure controlled by the commander of KFOR. While KFOR's responsibilities were not as broad as those delegated to the civilian authorities, the mandate to establish 'a secure environment' for refugees and displaced persons in particular left ample scope for NATO to resort to whatever means were necessary to achieve this goal. Although this mandate was intended to apply primarily to Kosovar Albanian refugees, it provided the basis for KFOR's significant role in protecting minorities, especially the Kosovar Serbs.

From the outset, there were security problems in Kosovo and accusations that KFOR was not doing enough to ensure security. Although it did have initial success in the demilitarisation of the KLA and in preventing a civil war, KFOR's initial policy was soft on attacks by Albanian extremists on Serb minorities. The Organization for Security and Co-Operation in Europe (OSCE) found much of the violence to be 'following a systematic pattern, organization and careful targeting of individuals',[41] yet the excuse given by United States military and diplomatic staff was that such attacks were to be expected in the circumstances.[42] Despite the evidence that the KLA were responsible for much of the violence, UNMIK and KFOR and other international bodies continued to deal with its leaders. This had the unfortunate consequence of reinforcing the impression that these were key players which, in turn, marginalised more moderate leaders. Part of the reason for this may

---

[41] *Kosovo-Kosova, As Seen, As Told* (Warsaw: OSCE, Office for Democratic Institutions and Human Rights, 1999), p. xii.

[42] W. O'Neill, *Kosovo – An Unfinished Peace*, International Peace Academy Occasional Paper (Boulder: Lynne Rienner, 2002), p. 46.

have been fear of the KLA. An unforeseen consequence of this policy was that it enabled extremist elements to carve out control of territory and economic assets and, therefore, fuelled the black market and organised crime. Despite a strongly worded warning from then Secretary-General of NATO, George Robertson, that NATO troops would not stand idly by and watch Albanians banish the remaining Serb minority from Kosovo, the assaults on Serbs and other minorities continued.[43] Human Rights Watch and other organisations have been very critical of UNMIK's and KFOR's failure to protect the minorities and, in particular, of their inconsistent responses to abuses committed by the majority Albanian population.[44] On 27 October 1999, an Albanian mob of around one thousand attacked a KFOR-protected convoy of Serbs leaving Kosovo. The fact that the Serbs were leaving in the first place is clear evidence of the failure to provide a secure environment.[45] It is not surprising that there have been calls for KFOR to adopt a more robust interpretation of the mandate and to provide adequate protection for minorities in all parts of Kosovo.[46]

Standing operating procedures and rules of engagement[47]

Despite the fact that the principle of the non-use of force is a long-established element of peacekeeping operations, it is still couched in very

---

[43] Reuters, 22 October 1999.

[44] See, for example, Human Rights Watch, *Abuses Against Serbs and Roma in the New Kosovo* (August 1999). On 27 October 1999, an Albanian mob of around one thousand attacked a KFOR-protected convoy of Serbs leaving Kosovo. Many were injured, and KFOR failed to protect those fleeing as required by Resolution 1244. The fact that the Serbs were leaving in the first place is clear evidence of the failure to provide a secure environment. See also Human Rights Watch, *Failure to Protect: Anti-Minority Violence in Kosovo* (March 2004).

[45] International Crisis Group, *Who's Killing Whom in Kosovo*, Balkans Report No. 78, 2 November 1999, p. 14.

[46] *Ibid.*, p. 17. There were also calls by the ICG for KFOR to clamp down on the remaining structures of the Kosovo Liberation Army, and to monitor closely the KPC.

[47] See generally 'Peace Support Operations', in International Committee of the Red Cross, *Model Manual of the Law of Armed Conflict* (Geneva: ICRC, 1999), paras. 2024–7; G. Bowens, *Legal Guide to Peace Support Operations* (Carlisle, PA: US Army Peacekeeping Institute, 1998), pp. 185–202; J. Simpson, *Law Applicable to Canadian Forces in Somalia 1992/93: A Study Prepared for the Commission of Inquiry into the Deployment of Canadian Forces in Somalia* (Ottawa: Canadian Government Publishing, 1997), pp. 35–9; P. Rowe, 'Maintaining Discipline in United Nations Peace Support Operations: The Legal Quagmire for Military Contingents' (2000) 5(1) *Journal of Conflict and Security Law* 45–62 at 59; *Rules of Engagement (ROE) for Judge Advocates*,

general terms.[48] This can sometimes give rise to controversy regarding its interpretation, although its use under the mandate is subject to the principles of legality, necessity and proportionality.[49] In the course of the UN Transitional Authority in Cambodia (UNTAC, 1991–2), the rules of engagement (ROE) provided for the use of all available means to prevent crimes against humanity. This was interpreted by the Force Commander, Lieutenant-General Anderson (Australia), as permitting the defence of 'anyone going about their legitimate business under the Paris Agreement', including non-uniformed UN personnel and Cambodians.[50] The Special Representative of the Secretary-General, Yasushi Akashi, did not share this broad interpretation. Consequently, UNTAC failed to assert itself when confronted by Khmer Rouge harassment. In one famous incident, both the Special Representative and the Force Commander turned around, rather than press on, when met with a bamboo stick placed across the road by Khmer Rouge fighters. This proved controversial and undermined the morale of UNTAC personnel,[51] and this 'lie down and die' policy changed after the Khmer Rouge decided to boycott the election process.

Likewise, the failure of MONUC (1999) to prevent Bukuvu from being seized by anti-government forces in the Democratic Republic of the Congo in 2004 led to trenchant criticism of the force's failure to protect civilians.[52] Despite the presence of a Uruguayan battalion of MONUC troops, dissident forces took control under the pretext of preventing the 'genocide' of the Banyamulenge population by the pro-government forces. While MONUC did protect significant numbers of civilians, it failed to prevent the seizure of the city and the widespread human rights violations that followed. Troops were not equipped or configured to intervene rapidly to assist civilians in need of protection. Human Rights Watch recommended that MONUC urgently review its ROE to 'ensure a broad interpretation of its Chapter VII mandate to

---

Center for Law and Military Operations (CLAMO), 1 May 2000; *Operational Law Handbook 2002*, International and Operational Law Department, Judge Advocates General's School, US Army (2002), pp. 67–100; and T. Findlay, 'The Use of Force in Self-Defence', pp. 51–75, at pp. 52 and 55.

[48] Security Council Doc. S/12611, 19 March 1978, para. 4.

[49] *Model Manual of the Law of Armed Conflict*, para. 2022.

[50] Chesterman, 'The Use of Force in UN Peace Operations', p. 14.

[51] Interview, former UNTAC officer, Dublin, 2000. Brigadier-General Loridon from France was dismissed after advocating the use of force.

[52] *Fifteenth Report of the Secretary-General on MONUC*, 25 March 2004, UN Doc. S/2004/251, para. 25.

protect civilians'.[53] A report by the Department of Peacekeeping Operations highlighted the discrepancy between the ROE and Resolution 1291 (2000) with respect to the use of force for the protection of civilians.[54] A major problem at the time was the restrictive interpretation of the mandate by the Uruguayan battalion, and an overly cautious interpretation of the ROE and the use of force provisions.

The guidelines for UNIFIL contained no definition of force or of self-defence, but the UN has taken a broad view and self-defence was deemed to include resistance to attempts by forceful means to prevent it from discharging its duties under the mandate. This was open to conflicting interpretations, and a great deal of responsibility was placed on the Force Commander in deciding the degree of force to use when presented with obstacles to implementing the mandate. In order to overcome the difficulties of applying the guidelines to the everyday situation on the ground, a set of standing operating procedures was compiled for UNIFIL that covered, inter alia, the use of force.[55] These provided detailed guidelines for the conduct of day-to-day peacekeeping operations, and also normally granted the military commander on the ground a wide degree of flexibility and discretion in this regard.[56] The policy is to demonstrate a maximum show of force to ensure a minimum use of

---

[53] Human Rights Watch Briefing Paper, *Democratic Republic of Congo: War Crimes in Bukavu* (June 2004), http://www.hrw.org/english/docs/2004/06/11/congo8803_txt.htm.

[54] United Nations, *Operation Artemis: The Lessons of the Interim Emergency Multinational Force* (New York: DPKO, Peacekeeping Best Practices Unit, Military Division, October 2004), p. 8.

[55] For a discussion on standing operating procedures see *The Peacekeepers Handbook*, p. 81. For a copy of the 'Guide to the Use of Force by UNIFIL Personnel', see D. Loomis, *The Somalia Affair: Reflections on Peacemaking and Peacekeeping* (Ottawa: DGL Publications, 1996), pp. 340–2.

[56] Interviews with senior UNIFIL civilian and military officers from April to October 1989, and personal experience of the writer during a tour of duty with UNIFIL at that time. UNIFIL standing operating procedures on the use of force do not define what is meant by armed or unarmed force. There is, however, a brief description of self-defence that repeats part of the guideline laid down by the Secretary-General in 1978. This goes on to say UNIFIL personnel are authorised to use their weapons to defend themselves against direct attacks or threats on their lives, to resist attempts at being disarmed, forcing of UNIFIL positions or forceful entry of the UNIFIL area. The paragraph describing the general guidelines states, *inter alia*, that when fired upon UNIFIL should, as a rule, return fire immediately, though whenever possible inflicting casualties should be avoided. However, weapons should not be used unless no other means are available or they have been exhausted. See also Lt-Col. Vogt, 'Experiences of a German Legal Adviser to the UNOSOM II Mission' (1996) 35 *Revue de droit militaire et de droit de la guerre/The Military Law and Law of War Review* 219 at 223–5.

weapons.[57] In conflict resolution terms, this could be described as a combat or management technique intended to control a violent situation.[58]

From a legal perspective, the early guidelines provided were incomplete and deficient in many regards. They contained inherent ambiguities and did not define certain vital concepts such as 'force' or what constitutes 'an immediate threat to life'.[59] In order to address these deficiencies, the UNIFIL ROE were modified as follows:

Use of armed force
   3. The use of armed force is authorized only:
      (a) in self-defence; or
      (b) in resisting attempts by forceful means to prevent UNIFIL from discharging its duties,
Circumstances under which force may be used
   4. Only minimum force necessary is to be used. The only circumstances under which fire may be opened are:
      (a) Self-defence, including defence against attempts by force to disarm UNIFIL personnel or to prevent it by forceful means from carrying out its tasks;
      (b) In the defence of UNIFIL posts, premises or vehicles under armed attack; and
      (c) In support of other troops of UNIFIL under armed attack.

These were relatively simple and direct guidelines, and they were much less restrictive than those adopted in respect of UNPROFOR in the former Yugoslavia, which for their part stated:

UNPROFOR personnel may use their weapons
   • To defend themselves, other UN personnel, or persons and areas under their protection against direct attack, *acting always under the order of the senior office/soldier at the scene*;

---

[57] Interview, Lt-Gen. Walgren, Force Commander, UNIFIL, October 1989. The standing operating procedures are continuously being examined and reassessed in the light of experience and changing circumstances.

[58] C. Dobbie, 'A Concept for Post Cold War Peacekeeping' (1994) 36(3) *Survival* 20.

[59] Personal experience of the writer from two six-month tours of duty in 1981–2 and 1989 respectively. On the other hand, vague concepts such as the 'minimum force', 'flexible response' and 'the emergency situation' have been omitted. These latter concepts were referred to in the 1980 Standing Operating Procedures and Guidelines on the use of force. The 1990 Guidelines also avoided earlier unrealistic instructions to the effect that fire should be directed low at the legs of the attackers, or that 'minimum casualties and minimum injury to casualties will be caused'.

- To resist attempts by forceful means to prevent the Force from dis-
charging its duties, *acting under the personal authority of the Force
Commander only*; and
- To resist deliberate military and non-military incursions into the
United Nations Protected Areas (UNPA).[60]

In the case of UNIFIL, the standing operating procedures were similar to the Secretary-General's guidelines, as their general nature allowed the respective contingent commanders considerable latitude in deciding on appropriate responses to situations.[61] Not surprisingly, it was difficult to ensure uniform interpretation and application, and practice indicated that these depended very much upon the contingent involved.[62] For this reason, subjective factors such as the personality and training of individual commanders are also of importance when examining responses to operational situations involving the use of force.[63]

In the case of UNOSOM II, the ROE governing the use of force were contained in an operation plan for the force.[64] Their purpose was to provide guidance and instructions to military commanders, within the framework of political directives.[65] ROE define the degree to which and manner in which force may be applied, and are designed so that the application of force is carefully controlled. They are tantamount to orders, but unless carefully drafted they are prone to varying interpretations. ROE are not law or laws in themselves, and to be lawful they must comply with applicable national and international law,

---

[60] Loomis, *The Somalia Affair*, p. 340. Emphasis added.
[61] Personal interviews with a number of former UNIFIL battalion commanders. All operational personnel are briefed on the policy regarding the use of force to resolve any misunderstandings or ambiguities arising from the general nature of the guidelines.
[62] Personal interview, Lt-Col. P. Keogh, Chief Operations Officer, UNIFIL, August 1989.
[63] An examination of the responses of different Irish battalions to harassment and acts of hostility between 1978 and 1990 indicates that the interpretation of the guidelines on the use of force can differ from battalion to battalion. 'Human and institutional' failings were also considered important factors in the failure of the UN to protect Srebrenica: see 'Lessons for the Future', in *Report of the Secretary-General Pursuant to General Assembly Resolution 53/35: The Fall of Srebrenica*, General Assembly Doc. A/54/49, 15 November 1999, para. 485.
[64] The Commission of Inquiry concluded that no terms of reference or standing operation procedures were to be found in UNOSOM II. The main reason for this critical deficiency seemed to be the almost total lack of peacekeeping experience among UNOSOM II ranks and the understaffing of UNOSOM II headquarters during the initial period: UN Commission of Inquiry, para. 258.
[65] Loomis, *The Somalia Affair*, Annex A–F, pp. 644–81; and J. T. Dworken, 'Rules of Engagements: Lessons from Restore Hope' (1994) 74 *Military Review* 27–8.

including international humanitarian law.[66] The interpretation of the ROE changed substantially during the operations in Somalia, in part due to the fact that they were inherently ambiguous and incomplete.[67] In addition, when the security situation changed in May 1993, the Force Commander broadened the ROE, in effect giving UNOSOM II forces a 'blank cheque'.[68] The new rules under Fragmentary Order 39 allowed UNOSOM II to engage without provocation any 'armed militia, technicals and crew served weapons' that were considered 'a threat'.

Peacetime and wartime ROE are mutually exclusive, and apply to different scenarios. When the United States engages in 'non-traditional' operations, these are governed by peacetime rules, or rules derived from peacetime ROE. But, if the underlying legal foundation is ambiguous, it may be difficult to determine the appropriate action under the applicable ROE.[69] In the circumstances, UN forces in general appeared unsure about what their guidelines allowed them to do in response to Somali actions, and disputes about interpretation were inevitable.[70] At one stage, there was a serious dispute between United States and Pakistani troops, when the latter accused the United States marines of being too aggressive and taking too many risks, thereby violating UN ROE.[71]

Despite the fundamental difference in the nature of UNIFIL and UNOSOM II operations, the general nature of the ROEs governing the use of force were very similar. In fact, the UN Under-Secretary-General Marrack Goulding referred to the UNIFIL guidelines in correspondence

---

[66] Simpson, *Law Applicable to Canadian Forces in Somalia*, p. 39. The ROE for the Canadian Joint Force Somalia – Operation Deliverance can be found at pp. 73–80.

[67] Interview, Capt. A. O Murchú, Irish platoon commander with UNOSOM II at the time, August 2000. See also C. Clep and D. Winslow, 'Learning Lessons the Hard Way: Somalia and Srebrenica Compared', in E. Schmidl, *Peace Operations Between War and Peace* (London: Frank Cass, 2000), pp. 93–137 at p. 103.

[68] *Ibid.* See also F. Tanner, 'Weapons Control in Semi-Permissive Environments: A Case for Compellance', in M. Pugh (ed.), *The UN, Peace and Force* (London: Frank Cass, 1996) and 3(4) *International Peacekeeping* 126–45 at 140.

[69] S. Turley, 'Keeping the Peace: Do the Laws of War Apply' (1994) 73 *Texas Law Review* 139 at 166–7.

[70] In *R. v. Mathieu*, CMAC 379, 6 November 1995, the commander of the Canadian Airborne Brigade in Somalia was charged with negligently performing his military duty in issuing an order to subordinates to fire on looters/thieves fleeing Canadian camps, and thereby failing to comply with ROE. See also Chapter 38 of *Dishonored Legacy: Report of the Commission of Inquiry into the Deployment of Canadian Forces to Somalia* (Ottawa: Canadian Government Publishing, 1997).

[71] This arose after an incident where US snipers wounded a medical orderly on the roof of a hospital and apparently killed a pregnant Somali tea seller: see 'US Pulls Somalia Snipers in Dispute with Pakistan', *Chicago Tribune*, 13 January 1994, p. 1.

relating to ROE for UNOSOM, and to 'the overriding principle that force can only be used by a UN operation as a last resort and when all peaceful means have failed'.[72] Ultimately, ROE are interpreted by the commanders on the ground, and the overall strategic direction and policies adopted at a senior level can have a significant bearing on this. In the case of Somalia, once the operation was approved under Chapter VII, this had a significant impact on how UNOSOM commanders and officials viewed their roles. This in turn influenced the application of the ROE, which by their very nature lent themselves to either restrictive or expansive interpretations.

The terms of reference of the Canadian report of the Somalia Commission of Inquiry required an evaluation of 'the extent to which the Task Force Rules of Engagement were effectively interpreted, understood and applied at all levels of the Canadian Force chain of command'.[73] Canadian troops were involved in a number of incidents involving loss of Somali lives.[74] Prior to departure, a government minister was said to have boasted that the soldiers going to Somalia had been provided with ROE that permitted them to shoot first and ask questions later.[75] To reinforce instructions from higher ranks and to render the ROE more comprehensible, soldiers on duty in operational theatre normally carry a condensed version of the ROE.[76] There was more than one version of these 'soldier's cards' circulating in Somalia, and they contained a number of discrepancies.[77] The provisions concerning the resort to force were described differently and yielded significantly dissimilar logical interpretations, depending on the phraseology in a given version.[78]

---

[72] Loomis, *The Somalia Affair*, p. 340.

[73] See 'Rules of Engagement: Confusion and Misinterpretation', in *Dishonored Legacy*, vol. 2, p. 1; and 'Rules of Engagement', in *ibid.*, vol. 5, Chapter 22.

[74] *Ibid.*, Vols. 4 and 5. See also L. C. Green, 'Peacekeeping and War Crimes' (1995) 34 *Revue de droit militaire et de droit de la guerre/The Military Law and Law of War Review* 247–55 at 253.

[75] This was a reference to Barbara McDougall, Secretary of State for External Trade and International Trade, 'Rules of Engagement', in *Dishonoured Legacy*, Vol. 2, p. 5.

[76] It is normally referred to as an aide-memoire, soldier's card, or 'yellow card' in respect of British forces in Northern Ireland, see F. Ni Aolain, *The Politics of Force* (Belfast: Blackstaff, 2000), pp. 84–5 and 129–30.

[77] On 7 August 1993, Lt-Col. Battisti, SSO Current Ops, wrote to all contingent commanders expressing concern that soldiers on duty were 'not clear about ROE as given in the OPLAN'.

[78] For example, one version affirming the application of force depended on necessity and proportionality, while other versions did not mention these elements, stating less clearly the preconditions for using force: *Dishonoured Legacy*, p. 3.

Typically, the ROE were framed in an abstract manner, with no practical examples of situations to assist soldiers in evaluating the degree of force to use. Several contingents had their own ideas on ROE and quickly established themselves as being trigger-happy, a danger to friend and foe alike.[79]

A critical element in the interpretation of the ROEs involved the phrase 'hostile intent', which was defined as 'the threat of imminent use of force'. Any misinterpretation and misapplication of the rules were likely to have serious consequences, as the rules authorised the Canadian Forces to use 'deadly force' in responding to a 'hostile act' or when confronting a 'hostile intent'.[80] Thus there appeared to be no difference between a hostile act and a hostile intent, and many soldiers accepted that this was the case.[81] Furthermore, the issue of the level of threat and the need for a graduated response depending on the severity of the threat encountered was not addressed adequately. The Irish contingent issued its own 'Scale of Force' document.[82] It specified the following graduated responses, but with the proviso that there may be circumstances when the firing of ball ammunition for effect will have to be undertaken as a first reaction:

Scale of Force (In Ascending Order)
a. Physically pushing person(s) away
b. Use of batons
c. Use of CS gas
d. Firing of warning shots
   (1) In front of the feet (where there is soft ground)
   (2) Over the head (where there is no soft ground)
e. Firing for effect
   (1) Firing of ball ammunition for effect (aimed to inflict injury, not death where possible) . . .

The UNOSOM II ROE left the impression that the response to unarmed harassment could be the same as that envisaged for an armed

---

[79] Loomis, *The Somalia Affair*, p. 470.
[80] See generally R. Crabbe, 'Rules of Engagement', in Morrison, Fraser and Kiras (eds.), *Peacekeeping with Muscle*, pp. 123–6 at p. 125; and the testimony of former Deputy Minister Fowler, Canadian Department of National Defence, published by Loomis, *The Somalia Affair*, pp. 332–5.
[81] This is in fact the US position: see Col. C. Dunlap, 'US Legal Issues in Coalition Operations' (1996) 25(5) *Peacekeeping and International Relations* 3–4.
[82] This was a 'restricted' document dated June 1993.

threat, namely, deadly force.[83] Not surprisingly, a policy of shooting thieves was adopted, and this ultimately had tragic consequences.[84] The role of junior non-commissioned officers in the execution of drills and ROE is vital, as it is they that must first react to a problem. As strategic goals were to be achieved by use of force, it became essential to have specific and clear orders available at every level to exercise control over its application. This did not happen.[85]

It is noteworthy that several officers of the United States First Marine Expeditionary Force felt that shows of force in which ring-leaders were shot by snipers had a salutary effect on reducing incidents of violence.[86] But shows of force of this nature did nothing to deter unarmed civilians, who were quick to appreciate their immunity and take advantage of the situation. Moreover, the deterrent effect of such activity is in many respects irrelevant, as the use of force under those circumstances is patently wrong: random acts of theft or low-level violence can never justify firing live ammunition. It is the responsibility of commanders to establish appropriate standing operating procedures, such as the use of sticks or batons. ROEs and the use of force are intended to de-escalate and contain situations, but often, if not clear and resorted to in an undisciplined manner, they can have the opposite effect.

The problem in Kosovo in March 2004 derived from both the actual ROE and the lack of any unified policy for their application. ROE that allow for a gradual response to public order situations should be in place. The KFOR ROE, as outlined on the soldier's card, cover a number of issues (relating to proportionality/minimum force) in addition to outlining when a soldier can open fire. They are written in terms that are

---

[83] The ROE were also silent on the issue of disengagement, and what was an appropriate response when an intruder breaks off an incursion, and the implications for handling detainees were equally uncertain.

[84] Members of the German contingent also had to use 'their hand held weapons to prevent unknown native persons from breaking into the German compound secretly': see Lt-Col. Vogt, 'Experiences of a German Legal Adviser to the UNOSOM II Mission', pp. 219–27 at p. 223. See also *The Public Prosecutors Department and 104 Korad Kalid Omar, Resident in Kismayo, Somalia v. Paracommando*, available in M. Sassoli and A. Bouvier, *How Does Law Protect in War?* (Geneva: ICRC, 1999), pp. 1062–7.

[85] For a detailed account of the background to the adoption of ROE for all three operations in Somalia, see Loomis, *The Somalia Affair*, Chapter 10, pp. 330–82. The US ROE for Operation Restore Hope are at *ibid.*, pp. 349–50.

[86] Last, *Theory, Doctrine and Practice*, p. 85.

intended to be easily understood and followed. While they are intended to be carried at all times for consultation and guidance, they assume a level of training and familiarity so that a soldier presented with a situation requiring an immediate response will do so in a manner consistent with the ROE.

KFOR
Rules of engagement for use in Kosovo
Soldiers Card

To be carried at **all** times

Mission
Your mission is to assist in the implementation of and to help ensure compliance with the Military Technical Agreement (MTA) in Kosovo.

Self-defence
a. You have the right to use necessary and proportional force in self-defence.
b. Use only the minimum force necessary to defend yourself.

General rules
a. Use the minimum force necessary to accomplish your mission.
b. Hostile forces/belligerents who want to surrender will not be harmed. Disarm them and turn them over to your superiors.
c. Treat everyone, including civilians and detained hostile forces/belligerents, humanely.
d. Collect and care for the wounded, whether friend or foe.
e. Respect private property. Do not steal. Do not take 'war trophies'.
Prevent and report all suspected violations of the Law of Armed Conflict to superiors.

Challenging and warning shots
a. If the situation permits issue a challenge:
   In English: 'NATO! STOP OR I WILL FIRE!' or in Serbo-Croat: 'NATO! STANDI ILI PUCAM!'
   (Pronounced as: NATO! STANDI ILI PUTSAM!)
   Or in Albanian: 'NATO! NDAL OSE UNE DO TE QELLOJ!'
   (Pronounced as: NATO! N'DAL OSE UNE DO TE CHILOY)
b. If a person fails to halt, you may be authorised by the on-scene commander or by standing orders to fire a warning shot.

Opening fire

a. You may open fire only if you, friendly forces or persons or property under your protection are threatened with deadly force. This means:

   (1) You may open fire against an individual who fires or aims his weapon at, or otherwise demonstrates an intent to imminently attack, you, friendly forces, or Persons with Designated Special Status (PDSS) or property with designated special status under your protection.

   (2) You may open fire against an individual who plants, throws or prepares to throw, an explosive or incendiary device at, or otherwise demonstrates an intent to imminently attack, you, friendly forces, PDSS or property with designated special status under your protection.

   (3) You may open fire against an individual deliberately driving a vehicle at you, friendly forces, or PDSS or property with designated special status.

b. You may also fire against an individual who attempts to take possession of friendly force weapons, ammunition, or property with designated special status, and there is no other way of avoiding this.

c. You may use minimum force, including opening fire, against an individual who unlawfully commits or is about to commit an act which endangers life, in circumstances where there is no other way to prevent the act.

Minimum force

(a) If you have to open fire, you must:
 – Fire only aimed shots, and
 – Fire no more rounds than necessary, and
 – Take all reasonable efforts not to unnecessarily destroy property, and
 – Stop firing as soon as the situation permits.

(b) You must not intentionally attack civilians, or property that is exclusively civilian or religious in character, except if the property is being used for military purposes or engagement is authorised by your commander.

The ROE issued to Irish soldiers who are part of KFOR are authorised by the North Atlantic Council, the political arm of NATO comprised of all representatives of member states. The ROE permit NATO personnel or friendly forces under NATO authority, and other designated persons, to use minimum force in specified circumstances. These circumstances include, among others, the following:

1. The use of minimum force to prevent any attempts by hostile forces/ belligerents to prevent the KFOR from discharging its duties is permitted.
2. The use of minimum force to defend friendly forces and persons with designated special status against forces demonstrating hostile action is permitted.
3. The use of minimum force to defend friendly forces and persons with designated special status against forces demonstrating hostile intent is permitted.
4. The use of minimum force to prevent the taking possession of or destruction of Force property is permitted.
5. The use of minimum force to prevent the taking possession of or destruction of property with designated special status is permitted. Individual service personnel are to be informed when they are protecting specific property on this basis.
6. The use of minimum force to defend against intrusion by hostile/ belligerents across declared Lines of Separation, Assembly Areas, Military Restricted Areas or other areas designated by an Authorised Commander is permitted.
7. Use of minimum force against any armed individuals who fail to comply with instructions issued for KFOR personnel engaged in the execution of their duties is authorised ...
18. The firing of warning shots is permitted.
19. The use of riot control means against non-belligerents in circumstances deemed appropriate by an Authorised Commander is permitted ...

The ROE go on to provide for circumstances where detention of civilians is permitted, and a range of other circumstances where the use of force is allowed. These ROE do contain an important rider to the effect that the use of lethal force to prevent the taking possession of, or destruction of, force property must include a provision that such hostile action is accompanied by an immediate threat to life (or serious injury).

The United States military commanders consider NATO ROE to be restrictive in nature, unlike the permissive standing ROE which were approved by the Chairman of the Joint Chiefs of Staff for United States forces in October 1994.[87] A review of standing US ROE following the October 2000 attack on the USS Cole docked in Yemen found them adequate against the terrorist threat, but that United States forces

[87] Lt-Col. Stephen M. Womack, 'Rules of Engagement in Multinational Operations', *Marine Corps Gazette*, February 1996, pp. 22–3.

needed to shift from an entirely reactive posture to a posture that more effectively deters terrorist attacks.[88] Permissive ROE allow a military commander to choose the weapon of choice, unless expressly prohibited, tempered only by proportionality and discretion. As a defensive alliance, the use of pre-emptive force to eliminate a threat has been narrowly interpreted by the North Atlantic Council. As ROE are seen as fundamental to the nature of NATO, any amendment requires unanimous consent.

However, in the case of KFOR, the ROE were of little value. Although KFOR forces are said to operate under NATO command and control, and ROE, the reality is different and more complex. Each contingent has its own set of ROE based on the KFOR ROE and standard operating procedures. In this way, they possess modifications reflecting national laws and policies. In 2000, when the Force Commander of KFOR, Major-General Wirth, was asked about the ROE of national contingents, he said that each has its own 'limitations' and was free to define its commitments, within NATO doctrine and standing operating procedures.[89] For this reason, it is essential for a brigade commander to know each contingent's ROE. An international brigade commander can deliberately select and commit a foreign contingent with more flexible engagement constraints than other contingents.[90] The Scandinavian contingents, for example, use dogs in crowd-control situations. This is not permitted under Irish ROE. Similarly, the Irish ROE do not permit the use of CS (tear gas) or similar gas, or rubber/plastic bullets. One senior Irish officer described how he had never heard of the KFOR ROE. There was no mention of these during pre-deployment training in Sweden, and he had not encountered them while on duty in Kosovo.[91] The prevailing situation is that each contingent applied its own national ROE during a wave of anti-minority violence that took place in Kosovo in March 2004 (discussed below), and the overall result was chaotic. Moreover, to designate force protection as the main pillar of your ROE has been described as military cowardice that encourages an overly

---

[88] Ted Westhusing, 'Taking Terrorism and ROE Seriously' (2003) 2(1) *Journal of Military Ethics* 1–24 at 2.

[89] UNMIK Press Release, UNMIK/PR/263, 2 June 2000.

[90] See *Towards a European Vision for Use of Land Forces? Multinationality and Interoperability within the Framework of Operational Missions Ranging from High to Low Intensity (from Combat to Peace Support)* (France: CDES Doctrine Forum, 2001), p. 18.

[91] Personal interview, senior Irish officer, Dublin, September 2004.

defensive and non-deterrent posture.[92] Ultimately, this encourages the more extreme elements to test the parameters of what is acceptable behaviour. Unfortunately, in the aftermath of March 2004, such elements may conclude that they are able to get away with murder.

The UN (and NATO in the case of Kosovo) must shoulder some of the responsibility for this confused state of affairs. The difficulties associated with the military integration of multi-national forces are enormous, but no real effort was made to ensure the uniform adoption and application of ROE among KFOR or UNOSOM II contingents. It is clear that ROE can be different from one nation to another. It is as if NATO has a catalogue in which are listed all the ROE. Finding the lowest common denominator is not enough as there will always be times when a state makes national reservations based on political or similar concerns.[93] Sometimes, differences in interpretation of ROE are more semantic than substantive.[94] General Tieszen, a former military commander in Kosovo, commented that one difference between the United States ROE and others was that the United States emphasised the right of self-protection quickly, without hesitation. They also emphasised the use of direct fire and only such fire as is necessary to defend life. Use of lethal force was also permitted to protect certain designated critical persons other than a member of the American forces which were usually kept classified, and certain designated critical facilities and property.[95] The American contingent was also very constrained in their use of warning shots because of the belief in the propensity of such action to escalate quickly into direct firefights. In fact, the Task Force Hawk (1999) ROE card expressly prohibited the use of warning shots in Kosovo. Meanwhile, some national ROE permitted liberal resort to warning shots, and such behaviour, while complying with the relevant national ROE, made other contingents in Kosovo nervous.

The German contingent with KFOR also encountered difficulties with its ROE and was widely criticised for the way it reacted to the March 2004 riots. At the time, German soldiers were supposed to be able to defend Serbian-Orthodox religious structures only if attacked

---

[92] Analysis of the March 2004 events by a military officer present, entitled "What Went Wrong and Why It Will Happen Again" (anonymous, 2004).

[93] See comments by General Gaviard, *Towards a European Vision for Use of Land Forces?* (France: CDES Doctrine Forum, 2001), p. 47.

[94] See Col. C. Dunlap, 'US Legal Issues in Coalition Operations', pp. 3–4.

[95] See comments by General Tieszen, *Towards a European Vision for Use of Land Forces?* (France: CDES Doctrine Forum, 2001), p. 48.

themselves by the perpetrators of pogroms. In the wake of the riots, a review was conducted which called for a change to the German ROE. Subsequent adaptations to the rules permitted the issuance of tear gas and riot gear, and cleared up ambiguities to ensure that the troops felt able to act forcefully before lives became directly threatened. Under the revised ROE and a new operational concept, access roads to religious sites and to Serbian settlements are blocked so that the protected facility can be approached only with force and a direct attack on the blocking personnel. In addition, Serbian settlements have been declared prohibited military areas.

The Brahimi Report states that UN military units must be capable of defending themselves, other mission components and the mission's mandate.[96] It recommends that ROE should 'not limit contingents to stroke by stroke responses but should allow ripostes sufficient to silence a source of deadly fire that is directed at UN troops or at the people they are charged to protect'.[97] In particular, dangerous situations should not force the UN to cede the initiative to attackers. In essence, the Brahimi Report advocates the adoption of a more robust doctrine and realistic mandates, that should specify an operation's authority to use force.[98] Arising from this and other recommendations, the Secretary-General has reported that guidelines and sample ROE are being drafted, and that these are considered a continuous work in progress, and will be subject to periodic review.[99]

There is an urgent need for the UN to address the inadequacies in this area and formulate generic ROE for all operations based on international law, especially international humanitarian law, and operational considerations.[100] The importance of realistic ROE for troops on the ground cannot be overstated. Mission-specific rules should be drawn up as the need arises. These should be tested, verified and disseminated to

---

[96] Brahimi Report, Part 2, para. 49.   [97] *Ibid.*   [98] *Ibid.*

[99] *Report of the Secretary-General: Implementation of the Recommendations of the Special Committee on Peacekeeping Operations and the Panel on United Nations Peace Operations*, General Assembly Doc. A/56/732, 21 December 2001, para. 70. See also Security Council Resolution 1327, 13 November 2000, Annex II, which refers to the need for appropriate ROE.

[100] A possible example of how this might be done is in the report on *The Basic Principles on the Use of Force and Firearms by Law Enforcement Officers*, adopted by the Eighth Congress on the Prevention of Crime and the Treatment of Offenders, Havana, Cuba, 28 August to 7 September 1990. See also *Report of the Secretary-General on the Implementation of the Recommendations of the Special Committee on Peacekeeping Operations*, A/AC.121/43, 23 February 1999, paras. 9 and 63.

contributing states, and acceptance of them ought to be mandatory for participation. At DPKO, the Best Practices (formerly Lessons Learned) unit should monitor each operation, and propose modifications or amendments based on practical experience in the field. ROE must be accompanied by scenario-based training in the pre- or early deployment stages of an operation. A database of ROE from other countries would assist in this process. While, ultimately, inadequate ROE was just one symptom of more fundamental problems within the UN missions in Kosovo and Somalia, the experience of the missions highlights the fact that this is an issue that contributed to the weakness in their performance and that the matter needs to be properly addressed for the sake of future missions.

Lebanon

When to use force to implement the UNIFIL mandate?

The most controversial element of the guidelines laid down by the Secretary-General is that self-defence includes resistance to attempts by forceful means to prevent UNIFIL from discharging its duties under the mandate.[101] However, on the whole, the mandate was ambiguous and unrealistic from the beginning.[102] This made it difficult to state with certainty the duties of the force under Resolution 425 (1978). Deciding when UNIFIL was being prevented from carrying out its mandate was not always a straightforward task either. Closely linked to these problems was the question of consent to the presence of the force in Lebanon, the lack of any clear definition of the UNIFIL area of operation, and the need to establish freedom of movement. These and other problems were highlighted in the first major confrontation involving UNIFIL and Palestinian forces.[103] In addition to illustrating the lack of planning in the deployment of UNIFIL and major weaknesses in the mandate, the confrontation established an important precedent with

---

[101] Security Council Doc. S/12611, 17 March 1978, para. 4.

[102] B. Urquhart, 'United Nations Peacekeeping in the Middle East', *The World Today*, March 1980, pp. 88–93; and B. Urquhart, 'Peacekeeping: A View from the Operational Centre', in H. Wiseman (ed.), *Peacekeeping: Appraisals and Proposals*, pp. 163–74, esp. p. 164.

[103] A group of armed PLO were challenged by French soldiers when they tried to infiltrate a French position. They opened fire on the French, who responded by returning fire in self-defence. Two infiltrators were killed, and in subsequent clashes three UNIFIL soldiers were killed and fourteen wounded. UN Doc. S/12620/Add.4, 5 May 1978.

regard to the use of force.[104] This had a major influence on the strategy and tactics adopted to deal with harassment in the years ahead.

At this early stage, it became evident that the guidelines of the Secretary-General relating to the use of force were to be restrictively interpreted and applied. The issue at the time was whether UNIFIL was entitled to confront the PLO and to use force to deploy in the Tyre area.[105] A literal interpretation of the relevant guidelines indicated that this would be acceptable activity.[106] In addition, the Lebanese government supported the deployment of UNIFIL in the region, as for some time the PLO was the only real authority there.[107] Thus, the government wanted UNIFIL to adopt a more aggressive policy, in order to implement the mandate, especially in relation to assisting the restoration of its authority in the area.[108] The Lebanese interpretation of what constituted resistance to attempts to implement the mandate was broader than any interpretation made by the different Force Commanders of UNIFIL.[109] Their assessment of the role of UNIFIL was flawed, and indicated a failure to appreciate the constraints under which it operated. However, there were sound military reasons against such action being taken, the primary one being that UNIFIL would most likely lose and sustain significant losses. Moreover, from a political perspective, a more aggressive

---

[104] *Ibid.*, para. 24. Immediately following the confrontation, the Secretary-General emphasised the basic principle that the force was provided only with weapons of a defensive character. They were authorised to use force only in self-defence when attacked or when attempts are made to prevent them performing their duties under the mandate. However, at least two force commanders had looked for more offensive weapons such as tanks: Liu, *United Nations Peacekeeping and the Non-Use of Force*, p. 41.

[105] The initial plan was for the French contingent to deploy and take control in the Tyre region. Personal interview, French officer who served with UNIFIL at the time, Naqoura, Lebanon, August 1989.

[106] The Secretary-General stated self-defence would include resistance to attempts by forceful means to prevent it from discharging its duties under the mandate. Security Council Doc. S/12611, 19 March 1978, para. 4(d).

[107] Personal interview, Lt-Gen. Erskine, former Force Commander of UNIFIL, Dublin, July 1986. The Lebanese resented the presence of the PLO in the south and had agreed to this because there was no real alternative: see W. Khalidi, *Conflict and Violence in Lebanon: Confrontation in the Middle East* (Cambridge, MA: Harvard University Press, 1979), p. 41.

[108] See, for example, Security Council Official Records, 2113 Meeting, 19 January 1979, paras. 185, 208 and 209; Security Council Doc. S/13359, 28 August 1979; and Security Council Doc. S/12384, 5 September 1978.

[109] Personal interviews, Lt-Gen. Erskine and Lt-Gen. Callaghan, both former Force Commanders of UNIFIL, Dublin, 1996 and 1998 respectively.

approach was not universally endorsed: although there were calls from members of the Security Council for a firmer stand and a change in the nature of the mission from one of peacekeeping to peace enforcement,[110] this was not supported by the majority of the members.[111] In the end, UNIFIL bowed to the inevitable and the matter was not pressed.

In the context of a traditional peacekeeping operation, it was important that the force not become involved in functions related to the maintenance of internal law and order. In this regard, the UNIFIL mission was quite unlike that of KFOR in Kosovo. While UNOSOM II had little option, due to the complete breakdown of normal state functions, this was not the case with UNIFIL. Such involvement could have had serious repercussions on the impartiality of the force by involving it in the internal conflict taking place alongside the international crisis caused by the Israeli invasion. In fact, UNIFIL was already bound to be partial to the wishes of the Lebanese government owing to its role under the mandate in assisting 'the Government of Lebanon in ensuring the return of its effective authority in the area'.[112] However, this was ambiguous and interpreted restrictively, and it did not provide any authority for the use of force. The matter of the PLO presence in the Tyre area was linked to this issue. It appeared that the Lebanese wanted UNIFIL to confront the PLO on their behalf while unwilling and unable to do so themselves.[113] Such action was not authorised under the mandate, and would have precipitated a crisis in UN peacekeeping not experienced since the controversy in the Congo. As a peacekeeping force, the strategic use of force to implement the mandate was never considered, but the early attempts to deploy also showed that there was no stomach for the tactical use of force to ensure deployment as required by the mandate. An obvious downside to this approach is that it had a significant effect on the attitude of the Israeli-backed *de facto* forces to the deployment of UNIFIL in areas occupied by them.

---

[110] See, for example, the statements from the representatives of Bangladesh, Security Council Official Records, 2113rd Meeting, 19 January 1979, para. 104; Kuwait, Security Council Official Records, 2147th Meeting, 12 June 1979, para. 57; and Syria, Security Council Official Records, 2148th Meeting, 14 June 1979, para. 110.

[111] Personal interview, Department of Foreign Affairs official, August 2000. The Fijians, the Dutch and, to a lesser extent, the French supported a stronger response by UNIFIL to threats and harassment.

[112] This was required by Resolution 425 (1978).

[113] The attitude of the Lebanese led to exasperation among certain UN officials: see B. Urquhart, *A Life in Peace and War* (New York: Harper and Row, 1987), p. 301.

Escalating the response and the tactical use of force

The next serious test of the credibility of UNIFIL occurred soon after the confrontation, or, more accurately, the lack thereof, with the PLO. Despite the fact that concern was expressed regarding Major Haddad's *de facto* forces prior to the deployment of UNIFIL, there was no contingency plan should these fears that they would not co-operate turn out to be well founded.[114] The terms of reference for UNIFIL and the guidelines on the use of force were too vague to be of much use in the hostile environment that confronted the force. The matter was complicated by the fact that the Lebanese government provisionally recognised Major Haddad's forces.[115]

The effect of this was to deny UNIFIL freedom of movement in a large area that was intended to be part of its area of operation.[116] It appears to have been lured into this situation by the fact that various parties (the PLO, the Israeli forces and Haddad's forces) believed UNIFIL should only be deployed in areas they had occupied and subsequently withdrew from. Because UNIFIL could not deploy without the agreement of these parties on the ground, there was no realistic alternative but to accept this situation.[117] Again, a strict interpretation of this situation in light of UNIFIL's ROE would seem to justify resort to whatever limited force was necessary to fulfil the mandate, but this ignores the realities of the situation in which UNIFIL existed.

Having decided not to confront the PLO nor to press for their own deployment in the Tyre area, UNIFIL was effectively precluded from confronting the *de facto* forces and deploying in the enclave. The use of force to implement the mandate in this instance would have been interpreted by the Israelis as a hostile and non-impartial policy, and would also have been objected to by the United States. Had UNIFIL pressed the issue at the time, it would not have succeeded. The

---

[114] I. J. Rikhye, *Theory and Practice of Peacekeeping* (London: Hurst, 1984), p. 104.

[115] *The Blue Helmets*, p. 91. When Major Haddad refused to co-operate with the Lebanese government and UNIFIL, this recognition was withdrawn: Security Council Doc. S/12834, 5 September 1978, para. 6. See also *Irish Times*, 6, 8, 10 and 13 June 1978.

[116] After the 1982 invasion, the Israelis extended this area and it was referred to as the Security Zone. In 1978, the 'enclave' included an area around the town of Marjuyoun that caused a serious gap in the deployment of UNIFIL and separated the battalion deployed in the north eastern sector from the remainder of the force.

[117] According to its terms of reference, 'self-defence would include resistance to attempts by forceful means to prevent it from discharging its duties under the mandate': Security Council Doc. S/12611, 19 March 1978, para. 4.

co-operation of the *de facto* forces, albeit very limited at times, was essential for the continued existence of the force. Again, it was political and military factors that determined the response adopted by UNIFIL, and not the standing operating procedures and guidelines on the use of force.

The *de facto* forces interpreted UNIFIL's failure to take action as an indication of weakness.[118] They made a number of successful attempts to set up positions within the UNIFIL area, particularly in the Irish area.[119] The standing operating procedures and guidelines on the use of force were of limited use in the circumstances. Resort to the use of force was significantly constrained due to the fact that there were a number of vulnerable positions occupied by Irish UNIFIL troops in the 'enclave' controlled by Major Haddad. By using these as hostages, in a manner not unlike the situation UN personnel found themselves in Bosnia some years later, the *de facto* forces could prevent the use of force by UNIFIL to stop encroachments.[120]

A number of other factors contributed to the apparent ineffectiveness of UNIFIL. In the case of the Irish battalion, its strength was inadequate for the tasks assigned to it. The boundary with the *de facto* forces was twenty-two kilometres in length. There were seven towns situated within a kilometre and a half of that and all were potential targets for a *de facto* forces incursion and takeover. At the same time, the area had to be 'adequately' patrolled and observed to prevent armed elements from infiltrating south towards the Israeli border.[121] This situation permitted

---

[118] There was constant harassment of UNIFIL, and a number of serious incidents occurred. See Security Council Doc. S/13384, 8 June 1979, para. 25; and *The Blue Helmets*, p. 94.

[119] Personal interview, senior Irish officer serving with UNIFIL at the time, April 1984; see also J. Theodorides, 'The United Nations Interim Force in Lebanon' (1981) 20 *Revue de droit militaire et de droit de la guerre/The Military Law and Law of War Review* 309–31, esp. 316–17.

[120] The official UNIFIL policy was also to resolve problems by negotiation. The dilemma facing the Irish UNIFIL troops was evident when the *de facto* forces established a position in a strategic village that was located well within the UNIFIL area. See Security Council Doc. S/13691, 14 December 1979, paras. 40–5. The village was known as Bayt Yahoun.

[121] In a conventional situation, a brigade-level commitment would be required to cover such a large area. The normal level of commitment in a conventional war is a battalion for every one-and-a-half kilometres of front. This would mean that fifteen battalions would have been required to guard the Irish area of responsibility against a full-scale Israeli/*de facto* forces invasion. At the time, the strength of the whole UNIFIL force was roughly that of a brigade (i.e. 5,800).

the *de facto* forces to pick the time and place of any incursion in the knowledge that UNIFIL did not have sufficient troops to adequately patrol the entire 'front'. Protecting the villages themselves was also difficult. According to a strict interpretation of the mandate, this was not the responsibility of UNIFIL. This interpretation was the only realistic policy under the circumstances because it was not possible, in any case, to defend the large number of villages in the area.[122] Despite this, many observers and Irish politicians were critical of UNIFIL and its apparent impotence in this area.[123]

Restraint in the use of force and measured self-protection will generally prevent a situation from escalating further.[124] In the circumstances it is easy to understand why UNIFIL headquarters did not encourage an aggressive military posture.[125] Nevertheless, not all of the criticism of UNIFIL is without foundation. While there were occasions when UNIFIL threatened and used force as a last resort in self-defence,[126] there were other occasions when it failed to do so and invited further harassment. This situation was compounded by the disparate reactions of the various battalions which highlighted the differences in attitude, policy and training among the contingents participating in UNIFIL. The experience of UNIFIL demonstrates that a peacekeeping force encounters great difficulty when operating in a conflict where the political consensus that marks most frontier peacekeeping operations is

---

[122] There were just seventy soldiers available to patrol and observe a front of ten kilometres. Within this area, there were numerous rocky hills, valleys, tracts and roads. The villages and crossroads required patrols or fixed checkpoints. The *de facto* forces were quick to exploit the weakness in such a situation.

[123] *Irish Times* and *Irish Press*, 1 May 1979; *Irish Times*, 14 July 1979; and *Sunday Independent*, 15 July 1979, p. 4. See also 315 Dáil Debates, 14, 12 July 1979, 2261–8.

[124] M. Heiberg and J. J. Holst, 'Keeping the Peace in Lebanon: Assessing International and Multinational Peacekeeping', Norwegian Institute of International Affairs, Working Paper No. 357 (June 1986), p. 3.

[125] The Force Commander and his staff are well aware that some battalions actually disregard the guidelines on the use of force at times. This is another reason for the lack of support from UNIFIL headquarters. M. Heiberg, 'Observations on UN Peacekeeping in Lebanon', Norwegian Institute of International Affairs, Working Paper No. 305, September 1984, p. 34.

[126] UNIFIL used a limited amount of force on a number of occasions, e.g. in the Tyre area in 1978 and to prevent the *de facto* forces' incursion in At-Tiri in 1980. The force also threatened the use of force on a number of occasions: for example, when a number of Finnish soldiers were kidnapped in 1985, the UN Under-Secretary-General, Mr Urquhart, warned that UNIFIL could consider resorting to 'a military option' to secure the release of the men. 32 *Keesing's Contemporary Archives* (January 1986), p. 34129.

absent.[127] This was exacerbated by ambiguities in the mandate, an ambivalent Security Council, and problematic terms of reference.[128]

Confrontation at At-Tiri and the adoption of Resolution 467 (1980)

As the intensity of the harassment by the *de facto* forces increased, the latter became progressively more aggressive, and efforts to expand their area of control culminated in an attempt to take over the village of At-Tiri in 1980.[129] This led to the most serious confrontation between the de facto forces and UNIFIL to date. It would have been a serious setback to UNIFIL if these forces gained control of the village and crossroads. In the words of one Irish officer at the time, had the *de facto* forces taken over the village, 'then Irishbatt and the rest of UNIFIL might as well have packed up and gone home'.[130] In reality, Major Haddad already controlled a larger area than the UN cared to admit. In an effort not to legitimise this situation, the official maps published did not reflect the reality on the ground.[131] UNIFIL had never taken control of the full area intended for its deployment in 1978 and, instead of gradually gaining ground since that time, it in fact lost territory to the *de facto* forces. The situation was then reached where UNIFIL could not afford to lose control of further ground and a firm stance had to be taken if the authority of UNIFIL was to have any significance. The well-documented situation that arose in At-Tiri[132] was one where the level

---

[127] M. Boerma, 'The United Nations Interim Force in Lebanon: Peacekeeping in a Domestic Conflict' (1979) 8(1) *Millennium: Journal of International Studies* 51–63.

[128] See the Secretary-General's criticism of the Security Council in Security Council Doc. S/17965, 9 April 1986, para. 51; and V. Yorke, 'Retaliation and International Peacekeeping in Lebanon' (1978) 5 *Survival* 31.

[129] Security Council Doc. S/13888, 11 April 1980 and Adds.1–3, 16 April and 18 April 1980 respectively. The village at At-Tiri is situated alongside a strategic crossroads. Control of this would have given access to high ground to the north and would have allowed Major Haddad to dominate the whole Irish area.

[130] Personal interview with Irish officer serving with UNIFIL at the time.

[131] See the reports by R. Fisk in *The Times*, 23 and 24 May 1980. In particular, a sketch map in the latter edition reflects the situation at the time. The then Irish Army Chief of Staff is also reported to have commented that the situation on the ground bore little resemblance to 'the maps which look good in New York': *Irish Times*, 2 May 1980.

[132] 'At-Tiri Remembered – 6 April to 13 April 1980', *An Cosantoir*, April 1990, pp. 31–6. Security Council Doc. S/13888, Adds.1–3, dated 11 April 1980, 16 April 1981 and 18 April 1980 respectively. See also Erskine, *Mission with UNIFIL*, pp. 71–87; Security Council Doc. S/13994, 12 June 1980, esp. paras. 44–52; R. Smith, *Under the Blue Flag* (Dublin: Aherlow, 1980), pp. 218–26. See also 319 Dáil Debates 7, 16 April 1980, 1257–74; and 27 *Keesing's Contemporary Archives*, pp. 30919–22.

of harassment and shootings escalated to a situation of almost open warfare between UNIFIL and Haddad's forces. Small arms, heavy machine guns, mortar and tank fire were used against the Irish and other UNIFIL troops. UNIFIL returned fire in a restrained and disciplined fashion. There were casualties and many injuries on both sides.[133] At the end of the day, a firm stand by UNIFIL troops led to the withdrawal of the *de facto* forces from the village and the area immediately around it.

As a result of this incident and a separate event involving the shelling of UNIFIL headquarters by *de facto* forces, the Security Council adopted Resolution 467 (1980).[134] The Resolution commended UNIFIL for its great restraint in very adverse circumstances and called attention to the provisions of the mandate that would allow UNIFIL to use its right to self-defence. This was a significant provision. It was the first occasion on which the Security Council found it necessary to make direct reference to the force's right of self-defence. It constituted retrospective approval of the action taken in At-Tiri. It supported the tactical use of force and it constituted a reminder to all concerned that this was the appropriate action in the circumstances. It also suggested that a more flexible interpretation of the right to use force in self-defence could be considered.[135]

Resolution 467 (1980) could thus have heralded a change in UNIFIL's policy towards the *de facto* forces and armed elements by the Security Council and Secretary-General. The specific reference to the right to use force in self-defence could have provided UNIFIL with the authority to adopt a more robust policy. However, the apparent authority to use force was not reinforced by political will. Despite the reaffirmation of this right in the resolution and its potentially broad interpretation, the Secretary-General was constrained by the political realities of a sometimes-ambivalent Security Council[136] and a clear message from

---

[133] One Irish soldier, Pte Stephen Griffin, and one Fijian soldier were killed and several wounded. One militia man was also killed and at least three wounded. There was no similar incident involving Irish troops in Somalia, though, in one confrontation involving Indian troops and an Irish resupply convoy in March 1994, at least twelve Somalis were killed: see Capt. A. O Murchú, 'Learning from Somalia', *An Cosantoir*, September 1999, pp. 7–11.

[134] Resolution 467 was adopted on 24 April 1980.   [135] *Ibid.*, para. 6.

[136] See Security Council Doc. S/13994, 12 June 1980, para. 69, where the Secretary-General found it necessary to refer to UNIFIL's right to use force in self-defence. In 1986, he was openly critical of the lack of support for UNIFIL by the Security Council: see Security Council Doc. S/17965, 9 April 1986, para. 51.

the contributing countries that they would not support a stronger show of force.[137]

The *de facto* forces obviously believed there would be no real resistance to their attempted takeover of the village. They took full advantage of the presence of isolated Irish UNIFIL troops in observation posts inside the 'enclave'. The Secretary-General's report of the incident is misleading in regard to the use of force. It states that often, during intense small arms fire on Irish positions, the Force Commander 'gave permission to return controlled fire'.[138] In fact, the Irish commander in the area was well aware that he could return fire.[139] He refrained from doing so until his troops were in reasonable positions from which they could return fire and when it became evident there would not be a negotiated solution to the impasse. Then restrained small arms fire was resorted to in self-defence. This escalated to the use of heavy weapons and these too were fired on the order of the local commander.[140]

While criticisms regarding earlier incursions by *de facto* forces were valid,[141] the defence of At-Tiri marked a turning point. The so-called 'kid gloves' approach reportedly favoured by the Irish led to timid responses to encroachments.[142] The provision of the UNIFIL mandate that allowed the force to use its right to self-defence gave each member of the force sufficient scope to use force when he or she considered it

---

[137] Security Council Doc. S/13921, 2 May 1980. Prior to the meeting of troop-contributing countries, the Minister for Foreign Affairs announced that Ireland intended to rely on diplomatic pressure to persuade the Israelis to cease supporting Major Haddad's militia. The communiqué confirmed this policy.

[138] Security Council Doc. S/13888, 11 April 1980, para. 12.

[139] Personal interview, Irish officer serving with UNIFIL at the time, October 1997.

[140] *Ibid.* The heavy weapons in question were the Dutch TOW missiles and the 90mm cannon mounted on a number of Irish armoured cars.

[141] F. McDonald, *Irish Times*, 23 April 1980; R. Fisk, *The Times*, 28 May 1980; *Irish Times*, 26 May 1980; and *Hibernian*, 3 July 1980. See also the leading article in the *Irish Press*, 2 May 1980.

[142] See A. Verrier, *International Peacekeeping* (Harmondsworth: Penguin, 1981), pp. 118–44; and F. McDonald, *Irish Times*, 23 April 1980. There were other criticisms of the tactics employed by UNIFIL. For example, there was a tendency early on in the mission to rely on fixed positions and firepower and to minimise the value of resolute and constant patrolling. The conventional military deployment on high ground and hills was not always the most appropriate method of preventing encroachments. The occupation of such key terrain did not guarantee control of the ground dominated in the conventional manner by these posts. It was often more effective to deploy troops on open, flat and vulnerable ground with the primary purpose of preventing any incursion by the *de facto* forces.

necessary to do so.[143] It was up to each commander to assess every situation and decide the appropriate action in the circumstances. Observers, even with the benefit of hindsight, may not be in possession of all the facts. Furthermore, they have no responsibility and will seldom have experienced the circumstances in which such a decision is made at first hand.

In 1986, a serious confrontation between French UNIFIL troops and members of the Shiite movement Amal highlighted the precarious nature of peacekeeping and how the use of force can create serious problems for the unit concerned.[144] On 11 August 1986, a French sentry shot and killed a local Amal leader and his bodyguard at a checkpoint.[145] Prior to this, UNIFIL had numerous confrontations with local armed elements, but these were diffused by negotiation and compromise. By contrast, in the August 1986 incident, the French made no real attempt to diffuse the situation. This distinction can likely be attributed to the fact that the French sentry involved followed French rather than UNIFIL standing operating procedures.[146] This was in keeping with the French position that their own national military doctrine, ethos and training should not become diluted because they were part of a UN peacekeeping operation. Arguably, the problem at the time would not have become so serious had it arisen in another battalion area. The French have a professional and well-trained army. However, such a conventional army is not always well suited to peacekeeping. The fact that France was involved politically and historically in the affairs of Lebanon and that it is a major power

---

[143] The Secretary-General had stated in the terms of reference that self-defence would include attempts by forceful means to prevent UNIFIL from discharging its duties under the mandate. Security Council Doc. S/12611, 19 March 1978, para. 4(d). When debating the events in south Lebanon in the Dáil, certain Deputies had expressed concern regarding the UNIFIL guide to the use of force and were reassured by the Minister for Defence as follows:

> [T]he guide to the use of force by UNIFIL personnel issued by the Force Commander, gives ample power to local commanders to deal with any situation with which they may be confronted. The circumstances in which unarmed or armed force may be used are well defined, and the decision to use force . . . always rests with the Commander on the spot.

See 320 Dáil Debates 7, 8 May 1980, 1144.

[144] For background to the Amal see generally R. Wright, *Sacred Rage: The Crusade of Islam* (London and New York: Linden Press and Simon and Schuster, 1985), pp. 66–110.

[145] Security Council Doc. S/18348, 18 September 1986, para. 5; Liu, *United Nations Peacekeeping and the Non-Use of Force*, p. 31; and C. Brady and S. Daws, 'UN Operations: The Political-Military Interface' (1994) 1 *International Peacekeeping* 29–79 at 67.

[146] Personal interview, French officer serving with UNIFIL, Naqoura, July 1989.

militates against its suitability for peacekeeping there.[147] It also meant the French were targets for certain Lebanese groups. They were therefore required to take extra security precautions and adopt a more aggressive military posture, though such a posture came naturally to French soldiers anyway. This led to resentment from the local population and a perception that the French were behaving like an occupying force.[148]

Attempts to negotiate a compromise were impeded by the French, who appeared unable to admit that they had made a mistake.[149] UNIFIL's investigation of the incident was also delayed because of French objections. The initial French reaction and the follow-up to it illustrate what can happen when the principles normally adhered to in peacekeeping operations are not followed. The situation would not have become so serious if a less powerful country had been involved, as such an entity would be more likely to seek a genuine resolution of the crisis and be less concerned with loss of face and national pride. In attempting to diffuse potentially violent situations by using maximum restraint and negotiation, UNIFIL risked being accused of backing down and not enforcing the mandate effectively. Yet such solutions were preferable to becoming embroiled in the civil strife taking place in Lebanon, similar to what happened to UNOSOM II, and then being forced to withdraw.

As a result of the clashes that followed the incident involving the French and Amal, the Force Commander undertook measures to improve the security of UNIFIL troops.[150] While certainly a step in the right direction, many of these measures should have been implemented in the first few months of deployment, when it became evident that the parties to the conflict were not going to co-operate. The incident shows how a peacekeeping force is at a distinct military disadvantage in such a situation. UNIFIL did not have the equipment, mobility and supplies to engage in any prolonged hostile action. In simple military terms, it showed that a peacekeeping force is not suitable for offensive action.

---

[147] See the report by R. Fisk, 'Will the UN Be Forced Out of Lebanon', *The Times*, 6 October 1986, p. 12.

[148] Interviews, Lt-Col. P. Keogh, Chief Operations Officer, UNIFIL, July–September 1989.

[149] Interview, senior officer at UNIFIL HQ, October 1989. At one stage, they investigated the possibility of using an aircraft carrier, air support and heavy armour to extricate them from the predicament in which they found themselves. This was confirmed also by French UNIFIL officers.

[150] These measures included, *inter alia*, a crash programme to provide reinforced shelters, the closure of certain vulnerable and exposed positions, redeployment and special precautions against attack. Security Council Doc. S/18348, 18 September 1986, paras. 16–18.

After the incident, the Secretary-General investigated the question of changing the UNIFIL mandate and/or the means provided to the force to carry it out. In a special report, he repeated the basic principles that a peacekeeping force must rely upon:

> UNIFIL cannot use force except in self-defence and is not therefore in a position to enforce the Security Council's will ... [I]ts effectiveness depends on the voluntary co-operation and consent of the parties to the conflict and of the troop contributing governments, the importance of whose role cannot be overemphasised ... [T]he [Security Council] could in theory revise the Force's mandate or terms of reference. In practice, however, the possibilities are very limited.[151]

This particular report is one of the most realistic assessments of the predicament of UNIFIL and the options available to it in the circumstances. The Force Commander made certain recommendations that centred upon a tactical concept of avoiding violence by being able to deploy superior forces if threatened. A number of checkpoints and positions which were of limited operational value and difficult to defend were also closed. This allowed each battalion to concentrate its forces into more easily defended positions that were less vulnerable to attack and harassment by armed elements. It also meant that the problem of having to man vulnerable positions that could be isolated and threatened during periods of tension was reduced as far as possible. Such positions had seriously impeded the ability of Irish battalions to respond to harassment in the early years of UNIFIL's deployment. However, such a plan could not be completely effective, as peacekeeping duty, by its very nature, requires a certain amount of exposure to risk. The crisis also led to the creation of a Force Mobile Reserve, a quasi rapid deployment force, with a mission to demonstrate an international willingness to resist attempts by forceful means to prevent UNIFIL from discharging its duties.[152] Having a large reserve, much bigger than usually retained in conventional military operations, is now recognised as a prerequisite for keeping the peace with force.[153] It may also reduce incidents involving confrontation, as an immediate show of strength may deter parties from

---

[151] *Ibid.*, para. 24.

[152] Personal interview, Lt-Gen. Walgren, Force Commander, UNIFIL, October 1989. This was to be the primary means to enable UNIFIL to deploy superior forces quickly when threatened.

[153] L. MacKenzie, 'Peacekeeping with Muscle: An Oxymoron?', in Morrison, Fraser and Kiras (eds.), *Peacekeeping with Muscle*, pp. 133–7 at p. 136.

further provocative action. Most of all, the 1986 incident highlights the dangers inherent in even limited use of force on traditional peacekeeping operations. While the tactical use of force at At-Tiri in 1980 may have been the appropriate response then, the experience overall is that lightly armed peacekeepers are not in a position to resort to force except in very rare circumstances.

Somalia

The strategic use of force

UNOSOM II has been described as the first peacekeeping operation in UN history that was given the mandate to use force not only in self-defence but also to pursue its mission.[154] While this may not be factually accurate, it does show the degree of confusion surrounding the nature of the operation. It seems that a peacekeeping force with peace enforcement powers was envisaged, along the lines proposed by the Secretary-General in *An Agenda for Peace*.[155] The nature and size of the force reflected the complex and unpredictable nature of the mission.[156] The Secretary-General had looked for combat units from countries that had supplied troops to UNITAF but countries like the United States and Australia declined to provide them. However, the United States ensured that it had people in key positions in order to retain control and it maintained combat-ready troops outside the UN chain of command.

The use of force by UN forces in Somalia was a contentious issue even before the occurrence of the more publicised confrontations involving UNOSOM II. UNITAF forces were accused of indiscriminate shooting, while the policy pertaining to the use of force was described by a United States spokesman as follows: 'American forces . . . are trained to shoot to kill, not wound, whenever they judge there is a threat.'[157] A United States general also described UNITAF's ROE as the 'most liberal' he had

---

[154] Makinda, *Seeking Peace from Chaos: Humanitarian Intervention in Somalia*, p. 76.

[155] *An Agenda for Peace: Preventive Diplomacy, Peacemaking and Peacekeeping: Report of the Secretary-general*, UN Doc. A/47/277, 17 June 1992, p. 26.

[156] Resolution 814 (1993) approved a 20,000 force with a logistical element of about 8,000.

[157] Quoted in M. D. Abdullahi, 'Fiasco in Somalia: US–UN Intervention', Africa Institute of South Africa, Occasional Paper No. 61 (Pretoria: Africa Institute of South Africa, 1995), pp. 18–19. See also Human Rights Watch/Africa, 'Beyond the Warlords: The Need for a Verdict on Human Rights Abuses' (1993) 5(2) *Human Rights Watch Short Report* 1 at 17–18.

seen for a UN-sponsored operation since the Korean conflict.[158] Most remarkable is that there was no attempt to introduce a uniform policy of escalation in degrees of force; the use of weapons in a 'shoot-to-death' policy seemed the reflex action to anything deemed a threat. In an unfamiliar and perceived hostile environment, this was a far-from-ideal crowd-control procedure, and determining what constituted a legitimate threat was fraught with difficulty.

The ROE, as interpreted and applied by the Irish contingent of UNOSOM II, provide an interesting contrast. While fulfilling a support role to the Indian Brigade, convoys were heavily armed, but stringent guidelines were placed on the use of weapons: deterrence through high visibility with weapons and unarmed restraint by weight of numbers was the first line of defence. If this did not work, warning or containing shots were to be fired first, followed by fire at the 'legs and extremities' and, lastly, 'shoot to kill'.[159] In a reflection of United States dominance of the overall operation, however, the United States UNITAF ROE were accepted, with minor modifications, by all participating countries, and later played 'a significant part in the transition to UN-led operations'.[160] But UNOSOM II did not have the cohesion, strength or fire-power of its United States-led predecessor, and there was no critical assessment of the suitability of the transfer of one set of rules for this mission to that of a wholly different operation supposedly under UN control.

As the situation deteriorated, UNISOM II had no alternative but to move beyond humanitarian concerns despite the fact that, if not managed carefully, this was bound to bring it into conflict with local parties. Disarmament was deemed to be one of the keys to success; but, to be effective, the disarmament process would have to be enforceable.[161] It was in an atmosphere of rising tension that the first ever inspection of a Somali National Alliance (a loose coalition led by General Aideed) weapons site was effected on 5 June 1993, over strong objections and warnings by the Somali National Alliance, who considered it

---

[158] Maj.-Gen. L. S. Arnold, 'Somalia: An Operation Other Than War' (1993) 73 *Military Review* 26–35 at 32.

[159] Commandant D. Conway, Officer Commanding Irish Transport Company UNOSOM II, quoted by C. Sears, 'Somalia: Faith, Hope and Charity', *In Dublin*, 11–24 May 1994, pp. 8–13 at p. 12.

[160] Maj.-Gen. W. Freeman, Capt. R. Lambert and Lt-Col. J. Mims, 'Operation Restore Hope: A US Centcom Perspective' (1993) 73 *Military Review* 61–72 at 65.

[161] Security Council Doc. S/25354, 3 March 1993.

provocative.[162] The size and military strength of the inspection teams left no doubt that UNOSOM II had decided to use force if necessary to impose its will. The attempted inspection precipitated a concerted attack against UNOSOM II in Mogadishu that left twenty-four Pakistanis killed, and many wounded and missing.[163] Lack of co-ordination between the military and political divisions and inappropriate political advice contributed to misjudgments of the sensitivity and timing of the inspections.[164] The ensuing confrontation was a sobering experience that highlighted the enormity of the challenge facing the UN in its efforts to forcibly disarm the factions. It also showed the limitations of increased fire-power and heavy weapons. Italian tanks did not come to the rescue as anticipated and helicopters proved a blunt instrument with which to deal with an urban situation.[165] The inadequacy of the equipment and the lack of preparation of UNOSOM II were startling. An additional problem with disarmament was the related issue of consent and confrontation. Somalia illustrated the many potential pitfalls that can befall a UN force in the use of limited force, the most obvious being the likelihood of escalation and loss of any real control, and how easily a situation can slide into combat. It also reiterated many lessons learned in the Congo (ONUC, 1960–4) with regard to the pitfalls of using force, and some new ones as well.

Conflicting interpretations of the concept of operations and the slide into combat

The UN responded to the attack upon UNOSOM II forces with the adoption of Resolution 837 (1993) which included the following operative paragraphs:

> The Security Council ... Acting under Chapter VII of the Charter of the UN,
> 1. Strongly condemns the unprovoked armed attacks against the personnel of UNOSOM II on 5 June 1993, which appear to have been part of a

---

[162] Though the Pakistani contingent were not informed of these warnings: UN Commission of Inquiry, paras. 211 and 215. See also T. Mockaitis, 'Civil Conflict Intervention: Peacekeeping or Enforcement?', in Morrison, Fraser and Kiras (eds.), *Peacekeeping with Muscle*, pp. 31–50 at p. 40.

[163] See UN Commission of Inquiry, paras. 104–24; Human Rights Watch/Africa, 'Somalia Faces the Future: Human Rights in a Fragmented Society' (1995) 7(2) *Africa Watch* at 60–5; Makinda, *Seeking Peace from Chaos: Humanitarian Intervention in Somalia*, p. 80.

[164] UN Commission of Inquiry, para. 221.

[165] Italian helicopters, unable to locate the precise position of machine gun fire, opened fire and injured three UN soldiers. UN Commission of Inquiry, para.116.

calculated and premeditated series of cease-fire violations to prevent by intimidation UNOSOM II from carrying out its mandate as provided for in resolution 814 (1993);

. . .

3. Reemphasizes the crucial importance of the early implementation of the disarmament of all Somali parties, including movements and factions, in accordance with paragraphs 56–69 of the report of the Secretary-General of 3 March 1993 (S/25354), and of neutralizing radio broadcasting systems that contribute to the violence and attacks against UNOSOM II;

. . .

5. Reaffirms that the Secretary-General is authorized under resolution 814 (1993) to take all necessary measures against all those responsible for the armed attacks referred to in paragraph 1 above, including against those responsible for publicly inciting such attacks, to establish the effective authority of UNOSOM II throughout Somalia, including to secure the investigation of their actions and their arrest and detention for prosecution, trial and punishment.[166]

This prepared the ground for a massive demonstration of force by UNOSOM II, and, in what amounted to a direct targeting of the Somali National Alliance's leadership, operative paragraph 6 of the resolution requested the Secretary-General 'to urgently inquire into the incident, with particular emphasis on the role of those factional leaders'. Conclusions were drawn without proper investigation. The Security Council reaffirmed the authority of the Secretary-General 'to use all necessary measures against all those responsible' in order to implement agreements reached, and to arrest, detain, try and punish those who attempted to hinder the realisation of the mandate. Although Aideed was not mentioned, it was clearly directed against him. The effect of this resolution was to authorise punitive action against the Somali National Alliance militia, which in turn would have the effect of precipitating a 'war' with UNOSOM II.[167] This was not a drift into reprisal, such as occurred with United States forces in Beirut a decade before,[168] but a conscious decision to go after Aideed.

---

[166] Security Council Resolution 837, 6 June 1993.

[167] UN Commission of Inquiry, paras. 124–261. A comprehensive list compiled by UNOSOM II showing the military action of both sides was given as Annex 4, and a synopsis of the main incidents is contained in Annex 5 to the report.

[168] The expansion of the military role greatly increased the risk to and adversely impacted on the security of US forces in Lebanon. This ultimately compromised US impartiality in the eyes of Lebanon's various factions. *Report of the Department of Defense*

Aideed's reaction to the conflict with the Pakistani troops is hard to assess, although he outwardly adopted a conciliatory posture and called for an impartial inquiry into the causes of the attacks. Whether this was opportunism or a sincere effort at reconciliation is somewhat academic, however, as UNOSOM II subsequently launched an all-out military operation against him and his followers. This in turn brought simmering tensions to a head between the Italian contingent commander and UNOSOM II officials, with the former opposing the initiative.[169] The row involving the Italians is most instructive, and highlights a fundamental difference of opinion with respect to UNOSOM II's use-of-force policy.[170] The Italians favoured a more restrained approach, and sought the approval of the Italian government before taking any significant military initiative,[171] illustrating the fact that cultural differences between contributing states, or the personality of a particular commander, can be important variables in determining the mode of operation of various missions. Similar differences of policy had occurred with the Italian contingent that was a part of the Multi-National Force in Beirut in the 1980s, and the Italians certainly considered that their approach proved the most successful on that occasion, especially after the attacks on the United States and French contingents there.[172] In the case of Somalia, the Italians ultimately refused to go along with the operations as proposed, and this led to an international incident with recriminations on both sides. Of particular interest was the Italian reoccupation of Strong Point 42 on 9 July 1993 in Mogadishu, which they had previously

---

   Commission on Beirut International Airport Terrorist Attack Act, October 23, 1983, (Washington, DC: Department of Defense, 20 December 1983), Part III, 'The Expanding Military Role'; and R. Thakur, *International Peacekeeping in Lebanon* (Boulder and London: Westview Press, 1987), p. 181.

[169] See C. O'Cleary, *Irish Times*, 15 July 1993. See also the *New York Times* and *Washington Post*, 14 July 1993. The *New York Times* backed the Italians and called for a suspension of military operations to allow the international community to reassess its goal.

[170] See D. Lorch, 'Rifts Among Forces in Somalia Hamper UN Military Effort', *New York Times*, 12 July 1993, pp. 1 and 6; R. Bernstein, 'Italian General to Leave Somalia', *New York Times*, 15 July 1993, p. 4; and A. Cowell, 'Italy, in UN Rift, Threatens Recall of Somalia Troops', *New York Times*, 16 July 1993, pp. 1 and 2. It is noteworthy that the Italian general concerned, General Loi, was also commander of the Italian contingent part of the MNF II operation in Beirut a decade earlier.

[171] Personal interview, senior Italian army officer with UNOSOM II, Pisa, July 1997. See also P. Agnew, reporting from Rome in the *Irish Times*, 16 and 17 July 1993; and Brady and Daws, 'UN Operations', p. 69.

[172] Interview, senior Italian military officer; and R. Thakur, *International Peacekeeping*, pp. 175–202. More than three hundred French and American soldiers were killed in terrorist attacks on their barracks in Beirut on 23 October 1983.

vacated under pressure. Contrary to what was envisaged, they subsequently negotiated with the Somali National Alliance instead of taking the position by force.

The Italians understood the role of a peacekeeping force and the continuum from low-level conflict to armed conflict that exists when such a force adopts a peace enforcement role. It seemed that senior UNOSOM II personnel did not appreciate this and other fundamental principles of peacekeeping operations. Nor was there anyone to teach the basics of peacekeeping to them;[173] rather, it is noteworthy that there was little support for the policy of restraint proposed by the Italians. Among the deficiencies identified as contributing to this state of affairs was the fact that there were no seasoned peacekeepers among the UNOSOM II military leadership to advise on the modalities for UN disarmament inspections and other useful practices. This was a crucial deficit, as the transition from professional soldier to peacekeeper can be difficult, especially for those trained for offensive operations as part of large-scale military forces. The use of force to achieve an objective is central to the ethos of professional soldiering; but, in peacekeeping, this should only be resorted to after all peaceful means have been exhausted.

The Italians required permission from Rome in order to use military force, which often caused delays and was inconsistent with proper command and control doctrine.[174] However, it is hard to blame the Italians for adopting such a policy in the circumstances and, while adding to the multiplicity of chains in the command structure, it did prevent Italy from being dragged into a serious confrontation without adequate consideration of the issues or consequences.

Resolution 837 (1993) was interpreted as authorising the use of force to hunt for the Somali National Alliance leadership, and destroy its power sources, radio base and weapons stores. This was in contrast to the restrained response by UNIFIL to the adoption of Resolution 467 (1980). There was a planned build-up to an offensive operation surpassing any similar UN-commanded operation up to then.[175] As with all such military operations, once action was initiated, the conflict tended to take on a life of its own. This was not the ideal environment for the

---

[173] UN Commission of Inquiry, para. 225.

[174] See Chapter 3, p. 131, above; and P. Diehl, 'With the Best of Intentions: Lessons from UNOSOM I and II' (1996) 19 *Studies in Conflict and Terrorism* 153–77 at 161.

[175] Tanks, attack planes, attack helicopters and armoured personnel carriers had to be brought in to facilitate this operation. UN personnel had to be relocated to safer areas. UN Commission of Inquiry, para. 229.

conduct of such operations. Tanks, helicopters and planes are not weapons for the containment of urban conflict or the conduct of urban warfare, and attempts to reduce collateral damage were bound to be problematic.[176] When all these factors are combined with the use of special forces under a separate chain of command, it was only a matter of time before this led to catastrophe.

An analysis of the period following the attack on Pakistani UNOSOM II forces reveals that the UN initiated almost all of the military action, and that all of the casualties occurred as a result of UNOSOM II operations. Such a situation could not last indefinitely. From early July 1993, UNOSOM II fragmental orders referred to 'enemy forces', and a watershed in tactics occurred with the attack on the Abdi house on 12 July 1993.[177] Unlike similar operations before it, no warnings were given and there were significant casualties.[178] United States helicopters under separate American command attacked the house with missiles and rockets on the ground that it was a command centre of Aideed.[179] This attack was criticised as breaching international humanitarian law and the principle of proportionality and distinction by attacking the house without having confirmed that it was other than it appeared, a civilian villa and not a military command centre.[180] There certainly was a clear alternative to its destruction without warning, a decision that inevitably caused maximum civilian casualties. The problems with the principle of proportionality and the use of force relate to their practical application to situations of conflict. It is easy to state that there must be an acceptable relation between the legitimate destructive effect and undesirable collateral effects.[181] It is an unavoidable consequence of

---

[176] In one well-publicised incident, Pakistani soldiers shot unarmed demonstrators, and the official version of events was contradicted by eyewitness accounts. The Secretary-General expressed regret, but defended the UN role. See Abdullahi, 'Fiasco in Somalia', p. 24. See also U. MacDubhgaill and P. Smyth, Irish Times, 14 June 1993; J. Clayton, Irish Times, 15 June 1993; and David Chazan, Irish Times, 8 June 1993.

[177] See J. Cusack, 'Airborne Strike in Somalia Endangered Irish aid Workers', Irish Times, 13 July 1993, p. 1; and editorial comment, Irish Times, 13 July 1993, p. 13.

[178] UNOSOM estimated the number of dead at 20; the ICRC had figures of 54 killed and 161 injured; while the Somali National Alliance put the number of those killed at 73. UN Commission of Inquiry, para. 154.

[179] It was reported that 16 anti-tank missiles and 2,000 rounds of 20 mm canon were fired at the house, which was destroyed. Keith Richburg, 'UN Helicopter Assault in Somalia Targeted Aideed's Top Commanders', Washington Post, 16 July 1993.

[180] Human Rights Watch/Africa, 'Somalia Faces the Future', p. 63.

[181] Collateral damage is incidental damage to protected persons (e.g. civilians) or protected objects (e.g. religious buildings) which is unavoidable during the course of

armed conflict that innocent people get killed or injured, but a commander must weigh the military advantage of targeting a lawful military objective against the collateral damage most likely to be caused to non-combatants. Failure to do so may render him or her liable to prosecution for war crimes.

The attack was also a major political mistake. It was widely regarded as having targeted civilians and, significantly, many of these were advocates of reconciliation. An unpublished report by the UN Justice Division was very critical of UNOSOM II tactics.[182] Symptomatic of a change in the level of hostilities, attacks became more systematic and involved the use of heavy weapons. There is evidence that militias used women and children to shield them from attack. A UNOSOM II spokesperson is reported to have said '[i]n an ambush there are no sidelines or spectator seats. The individuals on the ground were considered combatants.'[183] Again, this phase of the conflict ended with controversy surrounding the Italian contingent. This centred on the policy in relation to the use of force and the resort to a military solution without exhausting other possibilities. When taking over the Italian position at Strong Point 42, the Nigerian forces were confronted by Somali protestors. The Nigerian response was to open fire, while the Italians began conducting negotiations.[184] The overall picture that emerges from these and other incidents is of a sometimes nervous and even 'trigger-happy' force. UNOSOM II found itself in a hostile and confusing environment, and its leadership seemed intent on finding a solution by resorting to ever increasing degrees of force. The policies adopted were at variance with

---

lawful attacks against military objectives. See Articles 52–6 of Additional Protocol I of 8 June 1977 to the Geneva Conventions of 12 August 1949; and the *Final Report to the Prosecutor by the Committee Established to Review the NATO Bombing Campaign Against the Federal Republic of Yugoslavia*, 8 June 2000, paras. 48–52.

[182] K. Richburg, 'UN Report Criticizes Military Tactics of Somalia Peace Keepers', *Washington Post*, 5 August 1993; and personal interview, Irish UNOSOM official, July 2000. When asked to comment on the attack, Mohamed Sahnoun stated: 'How can you shoot from the air at a villa where people are sitting and meeting, even if they were Aideed's people? … It's absolutely incomprehensible. There were elders at the meeting who might have been doing something useful. The attack was excessive and unjust. You can't explain it to the Somali people or the international community.' Quoted in Abdullahi, 'Fiasco in Somalia', p. 25.

[183] US army spokesman, Maj. D. Stockwell, UPI, 10 September 1993. Aideed claimed 125 were killed, including women and children. This could not be confirmed, but UNOSOM sources accepted that at least sixty people died, Human Rights Watch/ Africa, 'Somalia Faces the Future', p. 65.

[184] UN Commission of Inquiry, paras. 163–5.

those applied in the case of UNIFIL, where successive Secretary-Generals eschewed resort to the use of force and the military option.

The significance of Resolution 837 (1993) cannot be overstated. Nevertheless, it is arguable whether it justified the nature and intensity of the military campaign pursued in its aftermath. The attack by United States-commanded forces culminated in an operation on 3 October that led directly to the United States' decision to withdraw from Somalia.[185] This was the turning point for United States involvement and it ultimately led to the break-up of UNOSOM II, as other countries followed suit. The outcome of the attack was not so surprising: an intelligence assessment in July 1994 noted that operational control of the guerrilla war had passed from the militia leaders to professional soldiers, many of whom had been trained abroad.[186] Aideed's strategy against UNOSOM II forces had been to use isolated attacks around the capital to pin down troops and discourage UN patrols. Targets tended to be opportunistic, with the overall strategy of putting pressure on individual contingents so as to prevent UNOSOM II from launching a cohesive reaction to Somali National Alliance actions. Now full-scale street fighting ensued for control of the city. The United States policy left it open to being depicted as the root cause of all problems in Somalia and as being responsible for provoking punitive attacks on other UNOSOM II contingents.

By January 1994, in the eyes of most Somalis, Aideed had won the battle for Mogadishu and he was then free to concentrate on outlying areas. In February, the Security Council adopted Resolution 897 (1994),[187] after which UNOSOM II was no longer permitted to use force to disarm the factions. The pursuit of a robust peace enforcement strategy had failed and the price paid was very high; large numbers of

---

[185] The debacle of 3 and 4 October is well documented: see Human Rights Watch/Africa, 'Somalia Faces the Future', p. 66–7; and M. Bowden, *Black Hawk Down* (New York: Penguin, 2000). Over 200 Somalis were reported killed, and another 700 or so injured. Eighteen US Rangers died, eighty-four US troops were injured, and one captured. Two helicopters were shot down and three damaged, and a number of armoured vehicles were destroyed. See also the reports by E. O'Loughlin in the *Irish Times*, 29 August and 12 September 1994, and by R. Athkinson in the *Washington Post*, 30 and 31 January 1994.

[186] Personal interview, Irish officer with UNOSOM II at the time, Dublin, October 2000. A senior Pakistani officer, remarking on the heavy casualties they suffered, complained that 'the US is quick to stir up trouble with air strikes, but it is my men and other third world soldiers who always draw the tough assignments on the ground': M. Michaels, 'Peacekmaking War', *Time*, 26 July 1993, p. 36.

[187] Adopted 15-0-0, 4 February 1994.

Somalis and UN personnel were killed and the damage done to the concept of UN peacekeeping operations was enormous. The strategy also left many nations with troops in Somalia exhausted, dismayed and even alarmed.[188] Not surprisingly, when a large number of countries were asked to contribute to the reduced UN operation, the Secretary-General received no positive responses.[189] Resolution 897 (1994) marked a retreat from the aggressive and sometimes combative peace-making operation under Boutros Boutros-Ghali. It is ironic that UNOSOM II then adopted a more cautious impartial role similar to that of UNIFIL, which permitted the use of force only in self-defence, and closely resembled that of UNOSOM I in the first instance. Unfortunately, by this time it was too late, as UNOSOM II forces were regarded as responsible for offences and errors arising from the excessive use of force that thereafter rendered them unacceptable in the eyes of Somalis.[190]

While it would be a serious misrepresentation to suggest that the Irish contribution to UNOSOM II was anything other than miniscule,[191] the contrast between the culture of the United States and that of the Irish personnel was startling. On a visit to Baidoa in the weeks prior to the American withdrawal, US personnel were astounded to find the Irish organising football matches with locals, helping in a local orphanage, and providing welfare services to the local hospital.[192] The difference in approach was obvious, especially to the Americans. They considered the most dangerous part of the mission to be the short drive between various compounds in Mogadishu, and they were openly astonished to learn of the Irish company's weekly convoy schedule to outlying areas. Most United States soldiers admitted to never having engaged an ordinary Somali in conversation, let alone a game of football. The Irish pursued a similar policy in Lebanon, and, while it did not bestow any immunity from attack on Irish solders, it did facilitate the building of relationships with local community leaders. In Somalia, this helped

---

[188] See J. Preston, 'UN Scales Down Mission', *International Herald Tribune*, 7 February 1994, p. 7.

[189] Eur 112, USIA Wireless File, 2 July 1994.

[190] See Abdullahi, 'Fiasco in Somalia', p. 26.

[191] Irish troops did not play any significant role in any combat activities, their purpose being to support the Indian brigade. In March 1994, No. 2 Transport Company was involved in a major incident in which nine Somalis were killed by Indian troops escorting the Irish resupply convoy from Mogadishu to Baidoa.

[192] Interview, Capt. A. O Murchú, September 2000; and Capt. A. O Murchú, 'Learning from Somalia', *An Cosantóir*, September 1999, pp. 7–11.

foster a 'certain grudging tolerance' of the Irish UN presence, as the UN was still regarded by many as just another colonial power. It also meant that, in times of crisis or confrontation, a basic relationship existed with limited lines of communication. Likewise with the Canadian contingent who, despite the crimes of a few, not all of which were committed in Somalia, performed a difficult task in a restrained manner without engaging in enforcement action and 'over the top' military action.[193]

Kosovo

In March 2004, the long-simmering tensions beneath the surface in Kosovo boiled over into large-scale civil unrest and violence. In this case, the target of the Albanian groups was not just the minority Serb community, but also the UN personnel and equipment. Rioting mobs of youths were responsible for nineteen deaths and over 900 injuries, as well as the displacement of some 4,500 people.[194] In addition, sixty-five international police officers, fifty-eight Kosovo Police Service (KPS) officers and sixty-one members of KFOR suffered injuries. The implications for the future of Kosovo are very serious. The UNMIK and KFOR response showed a lack of resolve, and the lessons of these events were not lost on extremists in Kosovo and the neighbouring region. There have been warnings that Kosovo may well become a European West Bank or Colombia.

There was a creeping erosion of the authority of KFOR almost from the first days of deployment. In early February 2000, tensions between the Serb and Albanian communities erupted in violence. There were a number of incidents involving loss of life, including the injuring of French KFOR troops by sniper fire. In response, KFOR launched a multi-national operation (Operation Ibar) under French command the primary aim of which was to search for weapons. Although reported by KFOR as successful, this assessment is open to question. For a start, the operation illustrated some significant tensions among the troop-contributing countries. In a well-publicised incident, after a knife-wielding Serb threatened to kill an American soldier, a United States company participating in the operation was ordered to withdraw from Mitrovica in the face of a stone-throwing

---

[193] Loomis, *The Somalia Affair*, Chapter 17, pp. 608–34.
[194] There were 730 Serb, Ashkali and Roma homes damaged or destroyed, up to ten public buildings, and thirty Serbian churches and two monasteries damaged or destroyed. UN Doc. S/2004/348, *Report of the Secretary-General on the United Nations Interim Administration Mission in Kosovo*, 30 April 2004, para. 3.

crowd of Serbs. It was then reported that the Chairman of the Joint Chiefs of Staff in the United States, General Hugh Shelton, complained to NATO Supreme Commander, General Wesley Clark, about sending American troops to volatile areas such as Mitrovica, asserting that other contributing countries should send more troops to Kosovo before United States troops are deployed in such areas.[195]

In addition, the French were criticised for their failure to act appropriately in attempting to prevent Serb demonstrators from attacking Albanians, an assessment the French forcefully rejected.[196] The argument was made that protecting property is not a priority of the KFOR mission and that, for this reason, it would have been wrong to use deadly force for this purpose. The French interpretation of the mandate and ROE was narrow and controversial. The contingent's priority in Mitrovica was force protection, protection of the local population, and protection of KFOR installations and equipment. KFOR ROE appear to allow, under certain circumstance, the use of force against civilians engaged in demonstrations or riots or who commit or threaten to commit serious crimes in the presence of KFOR forces, or who pose a threat to the security of individuals or to the property of persons connected with KFOR or the international civilian missions in Kosovo.

Many international workers were critical of a perceived unwillingness by French KFOR troops to provide them with sufficient protection (their facilities and vehicles in particular had been the object of attack). In a thinly veiled criticism of KFOR, the head of the UNHCR operations in Kosovo asserted that international workers should not be 'sitting ducks' and threatened to withdraw if UNHCR continued to be targeted by the local population.[197] UN police were also often critical of the lack of support they received in carrying out their policing duties.

The level of violence had been increasing steadily since the end of 2003. Under pressure to show some progress in the overall political situation, UNMIK and KFOR facilitated the creation of an illusion of normalisation.[198] Despite this, the outbreak of violence over the

---

[195] J. Perlez, 'Joint Chiefs Chairman Protests Troops' Mission to Kosovo Town', *New York Times*, 1 March 2000.

[196] International Crisis Group, *Kosovo's Linchpin: Overcoming Division in Mitrovica*, Balkans Report No. 96, 31 May 2000, p. 10.

[197] Reuters, 'UN Agency Threatens to Suspend Operations in Kosovo Area', *New York Times*, 4 May 2000.

[198] International Crisis Group, *Collapse in Kosovo*, Europe Report No. 155, 22 April 2004, p. 17.

two-day period from 17 to 18 March 2004 did not come as a surprise. It was said at the time that KFOR and UNMIK very nearly lost control of Kosovo. UNMIK established a Crisis Management Review Body to examine how it dealt with the situation and to determine how it might do better. But allegations of a cover-up quickly emerged.[199] Members of the minority population were evacuated, but their homes and property were then destroyed. KFOR was unable or unwilling to respond appropriately; there were no apparent standing operating procedures or contingency plans to cope with the situation that arose. The use-of-force ROE proved unworkable, and KFOR failed to provide the secure environment it was charged with creating and maintaining.

What should have been done to avert, or at least to mitigate, the crisis? The two major flashpoints – the main bridge dividing Mitrovica and the Calgavica main road blockade – could have been contained had KFOR and the police been alert and had they responded appropriately. Notably, however, there was a failure to anticipate the trouble, despite evidence that individual military and police officers could see what was coming. In addition, no reinforcements were sent to support those deployed at the bridge, and the so-called chain of command failed to function. Sheer numbers were also a problem: KFOR had been reduced from around 45,000 to 17,500, with further troop cuts planned, and so fixed positions such as checkpoints had been replaced by less labour-intensive mobile patrols. Moreover, many duties formerly undertaken by UNMIK police were delegated to the Kosovo Police Service, which was just not ready for the job.

Numbers were also asserted to have played a part when it was widely reported that French KFOR troops failed to protect the village of Svinjare, a few hundred metres from their logistical base.[200] Despite having received a two-hour warning, the French subsequently claimed that they had too few troops to respond; as a result, Serb property was either looted or destroyed. In Prizren, German KFOR troops were unable to prevent the Orthodox churches, seminary buildings and monasteries from being laid waste. Individual Serb houses were also destroyed. The nature of many of the locations targeted did make them exceptionally difficult to protect, whereas the village of Svinjare could

---

[199] *Ibid.*, p. 19.

[200] See Jean-Endes Barbier, 'Smouldering Serb Village in Kosovo Gutted in Sight of NATO Peacekeepers', Agence France Presse, 21 March 2004. N. Wood, 'Kosovo Smoulders After Mob Violence', *New York Times*, 24 March 2004, p. 10.

have be defended with relative ease. It seemed that the rioters knew exactly how far to go without provoking the German soldiers into shooting.

The legacy of the March 2004 violence was not just the loss of credibility by UNMIK and KFOR, but also the bitter recriminations that followed between the various branches of the UN operation. Reference was made to the 'Srebrenica syndrome' amongst KFOR troops, to the effect that, if you do not have enough troops, you just give in instead of standing your ground. This begs the question, what military commander ever considered he or she had sufficient troops or resources?

KFOR lost face in Kosovo and in the eyes of the international community as a whole. In response to intimidation and the threat of violence, the international security presence relinquished a significant amount of its authority to the extremists. Another consequence of the March rioting and the failure to respond appropriately is that KFOR was left a much less unified force. The French found themselves working in close proximity to armed Serb civilians in northern Mitrovica. United States KFOR elements forged strong ties with Kosovo Liberation Army's successor organisation, the Kosovo Protection Corps (KPC). They even mounted joint patrols for a time, thereby bestowing legitimacy on the KPC that had previously been denied to them. United States KFOR Multinational Brigade East had a long history of partnership with the KPC. They and the German KFOR contingent of the Multinational Brigade South-East used the KPC to contain the violence. By contrast, the Scandinavian Multinational Brigade Centre has the reputation for retaining its own security-independence at almost all costs.[201] It declined KPC assistance as it did not want to give the impression that it could not handle the situation. In the Irish area of responsibility, members of minority communities were given reassurances by KFOR troops and stayed put. In this instance, KFOR did fulfil its mandate to protect such communities. Although unlikely, it is not inconceivable that KFOR forces could find themselves on opposing sides in any future conflagration in Kosovo. These developments compromise the long-term impartiality of KFOR. However, it may be necessary for some contingents to forge such links with local forces, as the long-term presence of a large number of international troops cannot be guaranteed.

---

[201] International Crisis Group, *Collapse in Kosovo*, p. 23.

Extremists and criminals have seen the vulnerability of KFOR. UNMIK and KFOR now operate in a quasi-hostile environment. KFOR was shown not to be able to protect the Serb minority and a 'humanitarian intervention' by Serbian forces to protect this group must be considered a future possibility. UNMIK and KFOR need to assess their mission and role in Kosovo. The international presence was intended to keep the peace until the final status issue could be determined. The International Crisis Group has concluded that UNMIK is no longer an efficient or stabilising factor but, rather, attracts a dangerous level of hostility.[202] Both KFOR and UNMIK have failed to implement the mandate. This is unexceptional in the context of UN missions, but Kosovo remains a pot on the boil, ready at any time to spill over and spread violence throughout the region.

There was a significant contrast between the policy adopted by the French and that adopted by some other contingents. In essence, other national contingents did not adopt such a restrictive interpretation of the mandate. The British contingent adopted a flexible but aggressive no-nonsense approach. They worked on the ground in small units, an approach that maximises visibility amongst the local population and confers a degree of autonomy on relatively low-ranking personnel, enabling them to respond immediately and appropriately to whatever situation arises. This concept of operations retained the option of deploying a stronger, more concentrated force when necessary. In contrast, the French have the reputation for inconsistency. When they decide to respond to situations of tension or crisis, they are generally effective; however, they are often too eager to return to the *status quo*, even where it is premature to do so. They have acted against demonstrators, but they have failed to halt the harassment of minorities by Serbs in northern Mitrovica and have notably failed to take action against the local 'bridge watchers' who act as vigilantes to prevent non-Serbs returning to their former homes or entering the Serb-controlled area.

KFOR's problems in Mitrovica, of course, extend beyond the French. American forces observe the classic military doctrine of placing the highest priority on the security of their own force. They also deploy overwhelming, and occasionally effective, force. However, such tactics are often inappropriate when a threat is relatively small and involves minor actors. It is also a blunt instrument with which to deal with civil

---

[202] *Ibid.*, p. 36.

disturbances and riots. The British contingent, possibly due to the lessons learned from mistakes in Northern Ireland and elsewhere, appears to have adopted the best overall approach.

The difference in philosophies has been compounded by command and control problems which have beset KFOR from the outset in the broadest sense. Resolution 1244 made the military and civilian components distinct but equal partners in the international community's efforts to create a functioning democratic administrative structure in Kosovo. It requires the Special Representative of the Secretary-General, as overall head of the civil presence, to co-ordinate closely with the international security presence to ensure that both presences operate towards the same goals and in a mutually supportive manner. The responsibility of KFOR expressly includes supporting as appropriate, and co-ordinating closely with the work of the international presence. This is the only guidance on the nature and extent of the relationship between UNMIK and KFOR. Although established under the auspices of the UN, it is not a typical UN peace support operation. It is not subject to the Secretary-General or his representative in Kosovo, and it does not have the command and control structure of other UN operations.[203] This may have appeared to be a good idea on paper, but the practical implications for an operation as complex as that in Kosovo were not considered in full. The language of mutual co-operation between UNMIK and KFOR may read well in Resolution 1244, but the consequences for achieving the overall objective of the mission are still being felt on the ground. This supposedly symbiotic relationship has not facilitated accomplishing the mission; instead, it has created serious challenges to both UNMIK and KFOR.

The separation of civilian and military roles contrasts with the successful model adopted with the creation of the UN Transitional Administration for Eastern Slavonia (UNTAES). This mission was under overall UN control and was comprised of a civil affairs and multi-national military components. A key element in the success of the UNTAES operation was the appointment of a Transitional Administrator with overall control of both military and civil affairs. The Transitional Administrator used the military component to good effect in the maintenance of law and order, in the

[203] D. Marshall and S. Inglis, 'The Disempowerment of Human Rights-Based Justice in the United Nations Mission in Kosovo' (2003) 16 *Harvard Human Rights Journal* 107–46 at 108.

provision of security in areas of ethnic unrest, and in the arrest of war criminals.

Moreover, even if one were to leave the UNMIK–KFOR dichotomy out of the equation, different military doctrines, cultures and styles have worked against the attainment of a cohesive and unified approach to implementing the mandate within KFOR itself. The German commander of KFOR, General Klaus Reinhardt, expressed his view of this problem rather bluntly when he said, 'one of the most important things that I have learnt in Kosovo is that the man who is KFOR commander, in fact doesn't have anything to command'.[204]

Over the course of the two-day period in March 2004, the security forces in Kosovo, i.e. KFOR, UMMIK and the Kosovo Police Service, almost lost control of the province. The rioting and attacks on the minority community were spontaneous yet organised. In many locations, every single Serb, Roma and Ashkali home was burned, while Albanian homes alongside these remained untouched. This can only be described as a gigantic failure by the security forces to enforce the mandate and to provide the required level of security. French, German and Italian KFOR troops merit special criticism. Career-conscious commanders were afraid to make decisions that could impact negatively on their future advancement. The fact that conventional military tactics are useless in a security environment such as exists in Kosovo also contributed to the problem. In addition, there is an obvious need for troops and a police force trained for crowd control and riot situations in order to address the threat to the minority communities and to the security forces themselves. Moreover, while there was little likelihood of an invasion prior to the March 2004 violence, the failure of KFOR to adequately respond to it may provide the Serbian authorities in Belgrade with an excuse and some encouragement to intervene in the future. The situation was summed up by a senior UNMIK official when he said:

> We always knew that Kosovo would not be invaded. KFOR is in Kosovo to protect from civil violence, civil disturbance and ethnic violence. They don't need tanks, but riot gear and shields, and soldiers trained in dealing with public disorder. If KFOR was not prepared for such civil disorder, then why the heck not? What did they think they were in Kosovo for?[205]

---

[204] *Die Welt*, 19 June 2000.
[205] Senior UNMIK official quoted in Human Rights Watch, *Failure to Protect: Anti-Minority Violence in Kosovo*, March 2004, p. 1.

Armoured fighting vehicles are almost useless in situations of civil disturbance. As KFOR does not have sufficient numbers, the very least it can be provided with is adequate equipment and training for the mission. There is need for a complete review and overhaul of the security structures currently in place in Kosovo. Conventional armies are reluctant to adopt a role in quelling riots and similar internal security matters. Nevertheless, this is the primary threat in Kosovo. As a result, the training, role and mission of KFOR are in need of special attention. KFOR must also put in place standing operation procedures common to all contingents and brigade areas, and national governments must not be allowed to dictate policies that ultimately undermine the unity and cohesion of KFOR. Relations between KFOR, UNMIK and the Kosovo Police Service, which were not good in the first place, were ultimately further undermined. Human Rights Watch has called for KFOR 'to develop a unified command structure and a common response system to violence in Kosovo, abandoning the decentralised structures and disparate national doctrines that contributed to the chaos of March 17 and 18'.[206]

The final paragraph of the Secretary-General's report to the Security Council for the period in question thanks KFOR; it also expresses gratitude to NATO for the swift deployment of additional troops and to UNMIK for their commitment and professionalism in carrying out their duties.[207] While the British deserve credit for the prompt and effective deployment of the Over the Horizon Forces, such diplomatic language is otherwise farcical in the context of the abject failure of so many elements to perform their missions and fulfil their responsibilities. A special internal report more accurately portrays a mission in crisis. Many on the ground in Kosovo believe that, if the rioting had lasted an additional day, the mission would have collapsed.[208] In fairness, a number of measures have been taken to address the inadequacies evident after the March 2004 riots. Local and minority involvement in the security process is now being facilitated through Local Crime Prevention Councils established at municipality level, and the Kosovo Security Advisory Group at the central level. The Local Crime Prevention

---

[206] Human Rights Watch, *Failure to Protect: Anti-Minority Violence in Kosovo*, March 2004, p. 2.

[207] UN Doc. S/2004/348, *Report of the Secretary-General on the United Nations Interim Administration Mission in Kosovo*, 30 April 2004, para. 62.

[208] See C. Jennings, 'NATO Peacekeepers "Unable" to Keep Lid on Violence in Kosovo', *Scotsman*, 2 September 2004.

Councils are working as consultative bodies, bringing together representatives of each ethnic community, religious leaders, representatives of the board of education as well as the police, KFOR, the Organization for Security and Co-operation in Europe and all those with a stake in the overall security situation. The Kosovo Security Advisory Group was intended as a confidence-building measure. Its main purpose is to facilitate dialogue between communities on issues related to security and freedom of movement, the primary concern of vulnerable groups wherever located. However, opposition from Belgrade is hindering this initiative and it remains to be seen if it will fulfil its purpose.

There is now better co-ordination between UNMIK and KFOR. Joint contingency plans have been created and joint operations to improve communication, command and control have taken place. KFOR also established small mobile liaison and monitoring teams for each municipality. These are the eyes and ears of KFOR on the ground, and reflect a tactical change from static positions to less predictable and more responsive patrolling involving a special focus on liaison with local communities and the monitoring of vulnerable areas. An essential element in their job is establishing contact with local religious, political and village leaders, police, and similar persons. Having observed these operating in the Irish area in December 2004, they proved highly effective. This owed a great deal to the commitment and professionalism of the teams involved, so great care must go into their actual selection. The Kosovo Police Service is now better equipped and trained to deal with crowd control and public order, and special units have been set up for this purpose. The police now have inter-ethnic officers appointed to police stations, and Minority Issues Officers to regional police headquarters. Although all of these have yet to be tested in practice, there is a realisation that the events of March 2004 must never be allowed to reoccur.

Conclusion

The litmus test for determining the nature of a UN operation, whether peacekeeping or peace enforcement, remains the ability and willingness to resort to the use of force. Despite this, the dividing line between the use of force in self-defence on traditional peacekeeping operations, and that in peace enforcement operations, is not so clear in practice. Much will depend on subjective variables that are difficult to predict; and these may influence the way in which a mandate is interpreted and applied. (Who, for example, has the authority to determine what defence of the mandate or mission means in practice?) For this reason, it is more than a coincidence that the commanders of traditional peacekeeping forces are more often than not selected from neutral or non-aligned nations, and that the first commander of UNOSOM II was a general from a NATO member country.

International law relating to the use of force under the authority of the UN has evolved with the practice of the Security Council during recent conflicts, and the norm for non-intervention under Article 2(7) of the UN Charter had been diminished by the intervention in, *inter alia*, Somalia, Kosovo and Iraq. There was no clear precedent for the non-consensual intervention and the type of operations envisaged by the UN in the affairs of Somalia. *An Agenda for Peace*[209] provides some doctrinal clarity, but fails to deal with the situation wherein a peacekeeper's right to use force extends beyond the accepted boundaries of self-defence and strays into the realm of peace enforcement. Allowing a force to take positive action in defence of its purpose is little different from allowing it to enforce its purpose.[210]

In Kosovo, NATO's strategy was restricted by the need to maintain unity within the alliance. The threat and then use of force in the early stages did not produce the desired result. In fact, the evidence leads to the conclusion that the use of violence actually exacerbated the situation and precipitated further atrocities. Furthermore, while the air campaign did not cause widespread civilian casualties, it did have a severe impact on daily civilian life.

In a more contrite view in the Supplement to *An Agenda for Peace*, the Secretary-General noted that, in some cases, peacekeeping forces are delegated tasks that 'can on occasion exceed the mission of peacekeeping forces and the expectations of peacekeeping force contributors'.[211] It would appear that the Secretary-General's analysis that peace enforcement is a viable option for coalitions of the willing, but not

---

[209] *An Agenda for Peace: Preventive Diplomacy, Peacemaking and Peacekeeping: Report of the Secretary-General*, UN Doc. A/47/277, 17 June 1992.

[210] N. D. White, 'The UN Charter and Peacekeeping Forces', in Pugh (ed.), *The UN, Peace and Force*, pp. 41–63 at p. 53.

[211] *Supplement to An Agenda for Peace* (New York: United Nations, 1995), para. 35. For an analysis, see M. Reisman, 'Peacemaking' (1993) 18 *Yale Journal of International Law* 415.

UN-controlled missions, is a realistic assessment of the political and military reality of UN peace support operations.[212]

It is sometimes claimed that soldiers are not always concerned with legal niceties surrounding the use of force, and the whole debate may be somewhat 'academic', but such assertions miss the point.[213] Although UNIFIL's right to use force in defence of the mandate allowed for flexible ROE, one of the lessons to be drawn from the UNIFIL and UNOSOM II experiences is that the tactical use of force by UNIFIL in self-defence or to defend the mandate was significantly different from the strategic use of force employed by UNOSOM II.

Consent and co-operation of all parties to a conflict remains a fundamental characteristic of traditional peacekeeping operations. Linked to this is the need for impartiality in all UN operations. The Brahimi Report has noted that, while this means adherence to the principles of the Charter and to the objectives of a mandate, it is not the same as equal treatment of all parties in all cases for all time, which can amount to appeasement.[214] In situations of contemporary conflict, local parties may 'not consist of moral equals but of obvious aggressors and victims, and peacekeepers may not only be operationally justified in using force, but morally compelled to do so'. Genocide in Rwanda was able to go as far as it did in part because of a failure of the international community (through the auspices of the UN) to oppose obvious evil. Ethnic cleansing of the remaining minority population in Kosovo must be prevented. However, permitting one country to determine the nature and extent of the use of force is not likely in the best interests of the UN, and allows a degree of 'limited liability' for that country in the event of things going wrong.[215] When this happened in Somalia, the United States extricated itself with relative ease, while the UN was used as a scapegoat for the manner in which events unfolded. The need for the formulation of a doctrinal basis for robust peacekeeping operations is more imperative than ever if the UN is to implement the recommendations of the

---

[212] D. Daniel, 'Wandering Out of the Void? Conceptualizing Practicable Peace Enforcement', in Morrison, Fraser and Kiras (eds.), *Peacekeeping with Muscle*, pp. 1–15 at p. 10.

[213] See T. Mockaitis, 'Civil Conflict Intervention', p. 47. Such claims also do not take account of potential criminal liability for breaches of international humanitarian law: see below, Chapter 5.

[214] Brahimi Report, Part 2, para. 50.

[215] The term was first used with reference to 'superpower' support for peacekeeping by N. A. Pelcovits, *Peacekeeping on Arab-Israeli Fronts: Lessons from the Lebanon and Sinai* (Boulder and London: Westview Press, 1984), p. 84.

Brahimi Report and still have a future in the terrain between traditional peacekeeping and war fighting.[216]

Military elites usually identify narrow concrete objectives to serve as the focal point for operations,[217] but the situation in Somalia was not amenable to narrowly defined goals. It has been said that disarmament can never be a military option, but must be a voluntary affair.[218] While there is truth in this assertion, it can also be used to detract from other major factors at play in the context of Somalia. It was not the use of force *per se* that brought the demise of the UN operation, but a combination of factors, one of which was the selective and excessive use of force.

The recommendations of the Brahimi Report are commendable, especially the need to provide mission leadership with strategic guidance. But this is a high-reaching goal, given the fact that UN-controlled forces are generally not even given adequate capabilities to intimidate or enforce. Another UN report is unlikely to change this historical fact. The British 'Wider Peacekeeping' concept is one of the more lucid explanations of the use of force and permits its initiation in circumstances other than in self-defence.[219] However, it must be proportional, applied impartially, and have the consent of a majority of the significant parties.[220] It must also contribute to the accomplishment of the mandate in the longer term.

The resolutions in respect of UNITAF and UNOSOM II expressly referred to Chapter VII, and permitted the use of force without further authorisation. Even though such action may be legal, it is often controversial and the foreign policies of contributing states must be taken into account. This is especially so when peacekeepers adopt peace enforcement roles. The use of force also has serious training, operational and logistical implications.[221] The Lebanon and Somalia operations illustrate that problems arise when missions are ill-defined, and this uncertainty was compounded, in the case of Somalia, by a dispute regarding the authority to use force. What was an acceptable level of

---

[216] J. G. Ruggie, 'The UN and the Collective Use of Force: Whither or Whether?, in Pugh (ed.), *The UN, Peace and Force*, pp. 1–20 at p. 11.

[217] C. Kupchan, 'Getting In: The Initial Stage of Military Intervention', in Ariel E. Levite *et al.* (eds.), *Foreign Military Intervention* (New York: Columbia University Press, 1992), p. 249.

[218] Ambassador Jesus of Cape Verde, quoted in Brady and Daws, 'UN Operations', p. 77.

[219] See United Kingdom Army Field Manual, *Wider Peacekeeping* (5th Draft Rev. 1994).

[220] See Last, *Theory, Doctrine and Practice*, pp. 50–4.

[221] Fink, 'From Peacekeeping to Peace Enforcement', p. 42.

force to remain within the parameters set by 'all necessary means'? This may be an impossible question to answer in the abstract, but this does not excuse the subsequent failure to establish clearly articulated ROE and authority for the use of force.

In the course of the UN operation in the Congo in the 1960s, the principle of the non-use of force except in self-defence was also applied.[222] In that instance, some critics concluded that the emphasis on self-defence was too rigid in view of the functions of the mission and that, in practice, it could not be followed.[223] The broad terms of the resolutions dealing with the Congo are somewhat similar to those of UNOSOM II and UNIFIL, insofar as all three sets give rise to conflicting interpretations. An additional parallel between the Congo and Somalia missions may be drawn in that the lack of clarity as to the specific functions of each force resulted in serious disputes.[224] The ground rules for the use of force in the Congo changed as the mission progressed and in this way it could be described as the first instance of 'mission creep'. The right to use force was extended, but the exact limitations on it were unclear. However, despite authorisation to use force in the prevention of civil war 'as a last resort', and in the apprehension of foreign mercenaries, the UN still considered itself bound by respect for state sovereignty.[225] Moreover, unlike UNOSOM II, the authorisation to use force was not interpreted or applied as a sanction against the Congolese people. The Somalia mission allowed the Security Council to give almost any task, however ill thought out or unrealistic, to a peace-keeping force, in the expectation that it could use force under the guise of self-defence and still retain its peacekeeping status. The situation with regard to UNIFIL was more straightforward, and the fundamental principle that the only use of force permitted in peacekeeping action is that of self-defence was not altered.

During the Congo operation, the Secretary-General was criticised for his failure to appreciate the essential link between the right of

---

[222] R. Higgins, *The United Nations Operation in the Congo (ONUC) 1960–1964* (London: Royal Institute of International Affairs, 1980), pp. 44–53, 57–61, 348 and 384–7.

[223] D. W. Bowett, *United Nations Forces*, pp. 200–5; and G. I. A. D. Draper, 'The Legal Limitation upon the Employment of Weapons by the United Nations Force in the Congo' (1963) 12 *International Comparative Legal Quarterly* 387–413 at 406.

[224] R. Higgins, *The United Nations Operation in the Congo*; and R. Higgins, *The Development of International Law through the Political Organs of the United Nations* (Oxford: Oxford University Press, 1963), pp. 228–35.

[225] Kassar, 'The Legal Limits to the Use of International Force', p. 208.

self-defence and the right to freedom of movement. The same criticism might be made in relation to UNIFIL. When the 1978 Israeli redeployment plan was completed, each party either restricted or blocked UNIFIL's movements, sometimes seriously enough to jeopardise the mandate. In order to be successful, UNIFIL needed freedom of movement and, to achieve this, it was entitled to use the minimum force required.[226] This would not have involved taking the military initiative and adopting an offensive strategy. On the other hand, some have been quick to judge UNIFIL for occasions in which the force sustained punishment and did not resist violations and thereby proved its weakness. Such criticism, however, is not necessarily well founded as it often fails to take into account the constraints under which the force operated.

The UN Secretary-General had overall responsibility for the conduct of the peacekeeping mission in Lebanon and, later, overall 'command' of UNOSOM II, and in each capacity he had to be mindful of the views of the troop-contributing states.[227] Without their support in the first instance, it would not have been possible to field or maintain a UN force on the ground. In Somalia, when the United States decided to withdraw, this had a knock-on effect on the whole operation, and there was little the Secretary-General could do to retrieve the situation.

In 1986, the Secretary-General considered various alternatives in respect of UNIFIL.[228] One of these would have required the force to control the movement of heavy weapons only, while another was to reduce the force's area of operation in order to eliminate the overlap between it and the security zone, or to convert the force into an observer group. These proposals, if implemented, would have reduced the risks of confrontation with armed elements. They would also have curtailed the role and ability of the force in exercising control over the level of hostilities in the area. Reducing the size of the area of operation was likely to be perceived as a victory for the Israelis and their proxy forces in Lebanon. It would also have been inconsistent with Resolution 425 (1978) and therefore was unacceptable to the Lebanese and others.

---

[226] Security Council Doc. S/12611, 19 March 1978.
[227] *Ibid*. See also B. Skogmo, *International Peacekeeping in Lebanon, 1978–1988* (Boulder and London: Lynne Rienner, 1989), pp. 131–62; and Sarooshi, *The United Nations and the Development of Collective Security*, p. 69.
[228] Security Council Doc. S/18348, 18 September 1986, paras. 23–8.

When these factors are taken into account, there was little prospect of such changes taking place.

After the 1982 Israeli invasion, the Lebanese government again called for a re-examination of the mandate because of the failure to stem the Israeli advance.[229] In the circumstances, UNIFIL had no alternative but to show token resistance, as any show of force would have been crushed by the overwhelming superiority in numbers and equipment of the Israeli Defence Forces. The question of UNIFIL's freedom of movement was never resolved satisfactorily until the Israeli withdrawal in 2001. This indicates that it was not essential in the first place. In the field of UN peacekeeping, there are few absolute rules. The Lebanese government was not alone in calling for firmer action by UNIFIL. However, it wanted action taken against the Israeli-backed *de facto* forces, while the Israelis sought action against the PLO.[230] Both were selective and partial assessments of the role of UNIFIL. The Lebanese position was opportunistic and difficult to maintain as it expected UNIFIL to take action against those it was unwilling to confront itself.

Peacekeeping operations can be a frustrating experience for the military personnel involved.[231] There are political ramifications to all decisions made by them and issues are seldom black and white. The Force Commander must ensure that his or her interpretation of the mandate and the guidelines on the use of force conform to that of the Secretary-General. The lack of consensus in the Security Council hampered the degree of support given to UNIFIL as it meant the Secretary-General was allowed greater discretion in the day-to-day running of the force than should have been the case. In this regard, the difficulty of implementing a deliberately vague mandate added to the problem of political control. It is not surprising that the Secretary-General did not undertake any bold or radical initiatives in relation to UNIFIL. This contrasted with the policy adopted in respect of UNOSOM II

---

[229] *Monday Morning*, Beirut, 28 June–4 July 1982, Vol. 11, p. 523. In 1985, the Lebanese government appeared to accept that UNIFIL's role and policy would not be changed. Security Council Doc. S/17063, 27 March 1985.

[230] Personal interview, Lt-Gen. Erskine, former Force Commander of UNIFIL, Dublin, July 1986.

[231] M. Heiberg and J. J. Holst, 'Peacekeeping in Lebanon: Comparing UNIFIL and the MNF', Norwegian Institute of International Affairs, Working Paper, 1986, pp. 399–421, esp. pp. 414–15. The extreme restraint that UNIFIL has generally exercised has often resulted in frustration and bitterness among soldiers who are trained in the offensive spirit of traditional military operations.

where the failed attempt at enforcement through peacekeeping was predictable.[232]

The incidents involving UNIFIL show that the principle of non-use of force has been controversial and difficult to apply in practice. It places an onerous responsibility on military commanders involved in peace-keeping operations to appreciate the wider political and other ramifications of their actions, and shows that the most important considerations can frequently be non-military in nature.[233] In theory, military weakness should be non-threatening and an asset during traditional peacekeep-ing; in practice, this may not be the case. At an early stage it was decided that operational effectiveness would be curtailed in order to adhere to the principle of non-use of force. This reflected sound judgment by those responsible and derived from the experience of the limitations of the use of force in international peacekeeping. In this regard, the At-Tiri incident involving the use of force in 1980 is best regarded as *sui generis*. In a situation as volatile as Lebanon, the continued existence of the peacekeeping force reflected the realism and political astuteness of the Secretary-General and military commanders on the ground. The debacle of the Multi-National Force's (MNF) involvement in Beirut during 1983,[234] and the failure of the more recent robust peacekeeping in Somalia, has vindicated this policy.

In analysing the respective roles of UNIFIL and UNOSOM, it must be borne in mind that the purpose of UNIFIL was not to create a military obstacle to the aims of belligerent parties, but to facilitate a peaceful resolution of an international crisis. This contrasted with that envisaged for UNOSOM II, which all sides acknowledged would involve peace enforcement based on express reference to Chapter VII. While the non-confrontational nature of peacekeeping is well established, it is not so clear where peace enforcement fits in the context of traditional peace-keeping and enforcement action, and no clear parameters are set as to when and to what extent the use of force is permissible. In this way, the real controversy in Somalia was not about the right to use force, but how

---

[232] J. Ciechanski, 'Enforcement Measures under Chapter VII of the UN Charter: UN Practice after the Cold War', in Pugh (ed.), *The UN, Peace and Force*, pp. 82–104 at p. 90.

[233] R. W. Nelson, 'Multinational Peacekeeping in the Middle East and the United Nations Model' (1985) 61(1) *International Affairs* 67–89.

[234] More than three hundred French and American soldiers were killed in terrorist attacks on their barracks in Beirut on 23 October 1983. See generally Thakur, *International Peacekeeping*, esp. 175–202.

this was interpreted and applied in practice. The United States interpreted the UNITAF mission restrictively and declined to disarm the factions or engage in any significant form of enforcement measures. Later, UNOSOM II embarked upon enforcement measures, but the indiscriminate use of force even in Chapter VII operations can result in crossing the line from that which is acceptable to achieve the mandate, and that which is indistinguishable from all-out war.

UNOSOM II's experience provides a salutary lesson on the limits of the use of force, and a willingness to accept the responsibilities arising from such action. While some countries are not prepared to take part in enforcement operations,[235] it is also evident from Somalia that, unless the vital interests of the United States are at stake, there is little point in committing American forces to combat roles abroad. Most of all, UNOSOM II shows the need to set clear objectives when resorting to the use of force; and, for the United States and UN, there were lessons on what could or would work in the future.[236] The Secretary-General's report on the fall of Srebrenica concluded that the cardinal lesson of that awful sequence of events is that 'a deliberate and systematic attempt to terrorize, expel or murder an entire people must be met decisively with all necessary means', and it accused the UN of 'pervasive ambivalence ... regarding the role of force in the pursuit of peace; [and] an institutional ideology of impartiality when confronted with an attempted genocide'.[237] This view is consistent with the robust doctrine advocated in the Brahimi Report. However, the UN Commission of Inquiry on events in Somalia recommended that the UN refrain from taking peace enforcement actions within the internal conflicts of states.[238] Are these conclusions contradictory? The answer must surely be no. When confronted with crimes of the magnitude of what took place at Srebrenica, there can be no room for ambivalence. This raises the question whether the UN should undertake peacekeeping and peace enforcement as part of the one mission. UNIFIL shows that it is possible to use force in self-defence and retain impartiality. But enforcement

---

[235] See G. Anderson, 'UNOSOM II: Not Failure: Not Success', in D. Daniel and F. Hayes (eds.), *Beyond Traditional Peacekeeping* (New York: St Martin's Press, 1995), p. 274.

[236] R. Oakley, 'Somalia, Lessons of a Rescue', *International Herald Tribune*, 22 March 1994.

[237] See 'Lessons for the Future', in *Report of the Secretary-General Pursuant to General Assembly Resolution 53/35: The Fall of Srebrenica*, General Assembly Doc. A/54/49, 15 November 1999, paras. 502 and 505 (hereafter 'Report on Srebrenica').

[238] UN Commission of Inquiry, para. 270.

action of any kind is inconsistent with the principles of peacekeeping, and Chapter VI operations should not have elements of enforcement in the mandate that could lead to the incremental adoption of a Chapter VII strategy. The quasi-enforcement approach in peacekeeping does not work; apart from its poor track record due to weak judgment and inadequate resources, it is inherently flawed. In this way, when not to use force is as crucial a question as when to use it.

The ongoing violence in Kosovo, and the killings of members of both communities with impunity, highlights the serious deficiencies in the security environment provided by KFOR. There is an urgent need to find some consistent policy to address the small armed groups from both communities that are behind these acts. This requires a change of policy regarding the use of force and in the interpretation of the ROE. But such a change requires the consent of contributing states. The actual ROE provide ample opportunity and legal justification for resort to force when necessary. What is needed is the will to do so. Had a firm and consistent policy been adopted in the early stages of deployment by UNMIK and KFOR, many believe the violence and ethnic tensions endemic to Kosovo could have been reduced significantly. The separate KFOR brigades are controlled like independent fiefdoms, with little or no central command, and significant variations in policy and procedures. There is no real effort to subordinate the military operation to NATO procedures or command. Even within brigade areas there are no common standing operations procedures, and national policies take precedence. Deploying conscript soldiers with little experience and inadequate training for the situation in Kosovo is part of the problem. Some contingents should not be there, and those that are must have proper training and equipment.

Deploying lightly armed peacekeepers like UNPROFOR creates expectations that cannot be fulfilled. It is also risky for the peacekeepers and for those who seek their protection. In Bosnia, Serb war aims were ultimately repulsed on the battlefield.[239] Yet the UN Secretariat had convinced itself early on that this kind of response was not an option. Writing about the predicament of UNPROFOR, Yasushi Akashi (former Special Representative of the Secretary-General in Cambodia and in the former Yugoslavia) remarked that a peacekeeping force will face serious constraints on what it will be able to achieve if it takes place in an area where the interests of the Security Council members (especially the

---

[239] Report on Srebrenica, para. 497.

permanent members) are engaged and when there is no consensus among those members.[240] Somalia, on the other hand, illustrated that a UN force engaged in robust peacekeeping will face serious constraints on what can be achieved if the national interests of the major contributors are not engaged, and the required political will to persevere is not there.

[240] Akashi, 'The Use of Force in a United Nations Peacekeeping Operation', p. 313.

5

UN military operations and international humanitarian and human rights law

Introduction

> Here is hand to hand struggle in all its horror and frightfulness: Austrians and Allies trampling each other under foot, killing one another on piles of bleeding corpses, felling their enemies with their rifle butts, crushing skulls, ripping bellies open with sabre and bayonet. No quarter is given; it is sheer butchery, a struggle between maddened beasts with blood and fury. Even the wounded fight to the last gasp. When they have no weapons left, they seize their enemies by the throat and they tear them with their teeth.
>
> Henry Dunant, *A Memory of Solferino*

This quote may seem at first to be somewhat out of place in a chapter dealing with UN peacekeeping and related military activity. Yet recent UN operations have had more in common with the operation conducted in Korea, or the enforcement measures carried out in the Congo during the 1960s, than with the more traditional peacekeeping prevalent during the 1970s and 1980s. When one looks at the actual combat engaged in by the United States Rangers in Mogadishu during their attempt to capture one of the leading warlords, General Aideed, or the coalition forces during the Gulf wars of 1991 and 2003, then Dunant's scenario may not be so far from the reality for the soldiers involved at first hand.

This chapter examines the applicability and relevance of international humanitarian law (humanitarian law) and international human rights law to all types of military action undertaken by or on behalf of the UN.[1] Owing to the controversy surrounding action by UNOSOM forces in Somalia, the question of respect for the principles of humanitarian law by UN forces has been the subject of controversy and

---

[1] Humanitarian law denotes the whole body of law applicable during armed conflict, often referred to as the law of armed conflict (*jus in bello*). See C. Greenwood, 'Historical Development and Legal Basis', in D. Fleck (ed.), *Handbook of Humanitarian Law in Armed Conflicts* (Oxford: Oxford University Press, 1995), pp. 8–12.

debate.[2] Although the reasons for this turn of events are a source of regret, the heightened awareness is welcome. The less controversial traditional peacekeeping missions can also involve important issues of humanitarian law, as is illustrated by the situation that UNIFIL found itself in after the Israeli invasion of 1982. One of the major stumbling blocks for peace-keeping troops is that the relevant principles are enshrined in international instruments governing the conduct of combatants engaged in armed con-flict of an international or non-international character. To use a military metaphor, the target of these rules is the combatant or participator, not the peacekeeper or observer.

Although originally there was some doubt about the applicability of humanitarian law to UN forces, it is now generally accepted that UN forces are bound by humanitarian law, whether performing duties of a peace-keeping or enforcement nature.[3] The UN has declared its commitment to the application of humanitarian law to peacekeeping operations, but has consistently taken the position that UN forces cannot be considered a 'party' to the conflict, nor a 'Power' within the meaning of the Geneva Conventions. To accept that peacekeepers are parties to a conflict would at the very least mean a loss of impartiality. The UN also lacks the requisite structures for dealing with violations of humanitarian law and it does not possess the competence to recognise that an armed conflict invoking such law exists.[4] The concept of armed conflict is discussed below, but its nature and existence is determined by the level of violence and the parties involved.

A further obstacle confronting those charged with ensuring UN force compliance with humanitarian law norms is to make the rules accessible to those most responsible for their implementation, i.e. the soldiers on the ground. The language of the international instruments in question

---

[2] See, for example, U. Palwankar (ed.), *Report on a Symposium on Humanitarian Action and Peacekeeping Operations*, June 22–24, 1994, Geneva (Geneva: ICRC, 1994) (hereafter '*Symposium*'); Martin Meijer, Notes on the Conference on "The UN and International Humanitarian Law", Geneva, 19–20 October 1995' (1995) 2(6) *International Peacekeeping* 136–8 at 137; and 'Report on the International Workshop: "Towards a Future for Peacekeeping: Perspectives of a New Italian/German Co-operation", Pisa, 17–18 November 1995' (1995) 2(6) *International Peacekeeping* 138.

[3] C. Greenwood, 'Scope of Application of Humanitarian Law', in Fleck (ed.), *Handbook of Humanitarian Law*, pp. 39–49 at p. 46. This is not just a practical necessity, but may arise from obligations of states 'to respect and ensure respect' for the Geneva Conventions and Protocols 'in all circumstances'. See also B. Tittemore, 'Belligerents in Blue Helmets: Applying International Humanitarian Law to United Nations Peace Operations' (1997) 33 *Stanford Journal of International Law* 61–117 at 107.

[4] S. Turley, 'Keeping the Peace' (1994) 73 *Texas Law Review* 158.

is often obtuse and unintelligible. The principles enshrined in these instruments, when combined with a 'dumbed down' approach for classroom instruction, are often presented in a half-hearted and 'touchy feely' way that makes the instructors and principles involved appear out of touch with reality. Best has described the situation as follows:

> It cannot be said that books in this field are lacking. The international law of war ... has become something of a boom industry in the legal realm and raises a regiment of professional experts. The way in which those experts write about it and debate it among themselves, however, is not often directly communicable to all the others who also have pressing interests of their own in the subject and who, some of them, also write and confer increasingly about it, conscious that, beyond the legal experts with whom they may happily have contact, are many from whom they are cut off.[5]

In considering the applicability of humanitarian law and human rights law to UN operations, a number of questions arise: (i) What international law applies to the conflict or situation in the country where the UN force is deployed? (ii) What international law regulates the conduct of the UN force itself and how is this determined? (iii) What can or should the UN force do when it becomes aware that parties in the country where it is deployed are violating applicable international law? (The answer to this question will be dependent in part on the mandate of the force.) The question may also be posed as to whether there is any useful purpose served in applying humanitarian law to peacekeeping and similar forces whose mission is to restore or maintain a peaceful environment in a crisis area. And, if these principles of law have a role, how can this be evaluated and improved to make it an accepted part of the conduct of all those involved, even if not actually participating in armed conflict? The answer to these questions is of direct relevance to troops participating in peacekeeping, as it will determine the standards that they will be required to uphold in order to comply with the relevant international obligations.[6] There is also the issue of the appropriate use of force and rules of engagement, and in what circumstances could the use of force constitute a grave or other breach of the Geneva Conventions and/or Additional Protocols, or a violation of international

---

[5] G. Best, *War and Law Since 1945* (Oxford: Oxford University Press, 1994), p. 10.
[6] J. Simpson, *Law Applicable to Canadian Forces in Somalia 1992/93* (a study prepared for the Commission of Inquiry into the Deployment of Canadian Forces to Somalia, Ottawa: Minister of Public Works and Government Services, 1997), p. 23 (hereafter '*Simpson Study*').

human rights principles. These are real issues confronting today's peace-keepers, but especially those participating in the so-called 'robust' peace-keeping operations similar to that of UNOSOM II in Somalia. A failure to comply with applicable humanitarian law could result in an Irish, British or Canadian soldier being tried by an appropriate national court, a foreign national court or an international tribunal on criminal charges or for war crimes, irrespective of the categorisation of the conflict as internal or international in character.[7]

Human rights and humanitarian law

Human rights and humanitarian law have different historical and doctrinal origins.[8] Although it has become increasingly important in the regulation of internal armed conflict, humanitarian law was initially intended to govern situations of armed conflict between states.[9] Human rights law, on the other hand, originated in the intra-state relationship between the government and the governed. Its primary focus is the protection of the individual; it is not dependent upon victim nationality[10] and is not princi-pally concerned with the punishment of those who are guilty of violations.

Human rights law is applicable both pre- and post-armed conflict, times during which humanitarian law clearly does not apply; but the query as to which set of laws will apply in a conflict situation is not always easily discerned. It was historically assumed that only one of the two regimes could be applicable in a conflict situation, and that the choice between the two would depend upon the categorisation of the conflict.[11] The problem with this position, however, is that a dangerous

---

[7] See Institute of International Law, 'The Application of International Humanitarian Law and Fundamental Human Rights, in Armed Conflicts in Which Non-State Entities Are Parties' (Fourteenth Commission, Berlin Session, 25 August 1999), p. 3.

[8] T. Meron, 'The Protection of the Human Person under Human Rights and Humanitarian Law' (1992) *UN Bulletin of Human Rights* 91/1 33–45. See also L. Doswald-Beck and S. Vite, 'International Humanitarian Law and Human Rights Law' (1993) *International Review of the Red Cross* No. 293; and *Minimum Humanitarian Standards: Report of the Secretary-General*, UN Doc. E/CN.4/1998/8, 5 January 1998.

[9] C. Greenwood, 'Scope of Application of Humanitarian Law', pp. 39–49; and D. Schindler, 'The Different Types of Armed Conflicts According to the Geneva Conventions and Protocols' (1979) 163 *Recueil des cours* 153–6.

[10] T. Meron, *Human Rights in Internal Strife: Their International Protection* (Cambridge: Grotius, 1987), p. 29.

[11] T. Meron, 'On the Inadequate Reach of Humanitarian and Human Rights Law and the Need for a New Instrument' (1983) 77 *American Journal of International Law* 580–606 at 602.

lacuna may exist if the applicability of both regimes is denied.[12] Substantively, the two regimes overlap, as humanitarian law protects basic human rights in armed conflict and other situations of violence. In so doing, humanitarian law may provide more expansive protection than human rights law in that it regulates beyond state activity; armed groups – state led or otherwise – and individuals belonging to them are constrained by its provisions.[13] The application of such principles in non-international armed conflicts is not linked to the legitimacy of armed groups.[14] The International Committee of the Red Cross (ICRC) has held that humanitarian law principles, recognised as part of customary international law, are binding upon all states and all armed forces present in situations of armed conflicts.[15] In addition, recent Security Council resolutions have called upon 'all the parties to the conflict' to respect humanitarian law.[16] The UN Secretary-General has also issued a Bulletin averring that the fundamental principles and rules of humanitarian law are applicable to UN forces when they are actively engaged as combatants in situations of armed conflict.[17] However, in situations where that law does not apply, the international accountability of such groups for human rights abuses

---

[12] *Ibid.*; see also Meron, *Human Rights in Internal Strife*, pp. 3–49; T. Meron and A. Rosas, 'A Declaration of Minimum Humanitarian Standards' (1991) 85 *American Journal of International Law* 375–81; and Commission on Human Rights, *Minimum Humanitarian Standards: Report of the Sub-Commission on Prevention of Discrimination and Protection of Minorities*, UN Doc. E/CN.4/1998/87, 5 January 1998.

[13] See 'Armed Conflicts Linked to the Disintegration of State Structures: Preparatory Document for the First Periodical Meeting on International Humanitarian Law' (Geneva: ICRC, 19–23 January 1998), p. 8; and C. Greenwood, 'International Humanitarian Law and United Nations Military Operations' (1998) 1 *Yearbook of International Humanitarian Law* 3–34 esp. 7–9.

[14] It is the identification of the relevant legal prescription in the given context that is of central concern: see H. McCoubrey and N. White, *International Organizations and Civil Wars* (Aldershot: Dartmouth, 1995), p. 67.

[15] D. Shraga and R. Zacklin, 'The Applicability of International Humanitarian Law to United Nations Peacekeeping Operations: Conceptual. Legal and Practical Issues', in *Symposium* (note 2 above), p. 40. See also F. Kalshoven, 'The Undertaking to Respect and Ensure Respect in All Circumstances: From Tiny Seed to Ripening Fruit' (1999) 2 *Yearbook of International Humanitarian Law* 3–66, esp. 38ff; and ICRC Resolution XXXVII of the XXth International Red Cross Conference (Vienna, 1965), in D. Schindler and J. Toman, *The Laws of Armed Conflicts: A Collection of Conventions, Resolutions and Other Documents* (3rd edn, Dordrecht: Martinus Nijhoff, 1988), p. 259.

[16] For example, see Resolution 814, 26 March 1993, para. 13 (Somalia); and Resolution 788, 19 November 1992, para. 5 (Liberia).

[17] Secretary-General's Bulletin on Observance by UN Forces of International Humanitarian Law, UN Doc. ST/SGB/1993/3, 6 August 1999.

remains unclear (although such acts would be criminalised under domestic criminal law).[18]

The International Court of Justice in the *Advisory Opinion on Nuclear Weapons* addressed the relationship between humanitarian law and human rights law.[19] The Court affirmed that they are two distinct bodies of law and that human rights law continues to apply in time of war unless it has been lawfully derogated from. It went on to state the relevance of humanitarian law:

> In principle, the right not arbitrarily to be deprived of one's life applies also in hostilities. The test of what is an arbitrary deprivation of life, however, then falls to be determined by the appropriate *lex specialis*, namely, the law applicable in armed conflict.[20]

The effect of this is that humanitarian law is to be used to interpret a human rights rule and, conversely that, in the context of the conduct of hostilities, human rights law may not be interpreted differently from humanitarian law.[21] In this way, there has been a significant overlap and convergence in humanitarian and human rights law. Human rights are a key issue in guaranteeing consistent and effective peacekeeping.[22] Their neglect discredits UN operations while undermining other advances and damaging the reputation of states contributing troops. Up to the debacle of events in Somalia, Canada had an excellent reputation as a

---

[18] The International Criminal Court (ICC) and related issues are discussed later. See also D. Robinson and H. von Hebel, 'War Crimes in Internal Conflicts: Article 8 of the ICC Statute' (1999) 2 *Yearbook of International Humanitarian Law* 193–209.

[19] *Legality of the Threat or Use of Nuclear Weapons*, Advisory Opinion of 8 July 1996, (1996) ICJ Reports 226. See generally L. Boisson de Chazournes and P. Sands (eds.), *International Law, the International Court of Justice and Nuclear Weapons* (Cambridge: Cambridge University Press, 1999); and a number of articles in (1997) *International Review of the Red Cross*, No. 316, esp. C. Greenwood, 'The Advisory Opinion on Nuclear Weapons and the Contribution of the International Court of Justice to International Humanitarian Law', 65–75.

[20] Para. 25 of the judgment.

[21] L. Doswald-Beck, 'International Humanitarian Law and the Advisory Opinion of the International Court of Justice on the Legality of the Threat or Use of Nuclear Weapons' (1997) *International Review of the Red Cross* No. 316, 35–55, esp. 45.

[22] Diego Garcia-Sayan, 'Human Rights and Peace-Keeping Operations' (1994) 29 *University of Richmond Law Review* 41–65 at 45. This article deals primarily with the UN mission to El Salvador (ONUSAL). See also D. Forsythe, 'Human Rights and International Security: United Nations Field Operations Redux', in Castermans, van Hoof and Smith (eds.), *The Role of the Nation State in the 21st Century* (Dordrecht: Kluwer, 1998), pp. 265–76.

contributor to peacekeeping operations.[23] Despite their importance, human rights are not expressly mentioned in the model Status of Force Agreement (SOFA) between the UN and the host state. As this chapter reveals, such protections are vital, and nothing can be more contradictory than a UN force transgressing international humanitarian law or human rights standards that have been gradually and painstakingly agreed upon during the last sixty years.

Humanitarian law and armed conflicts

The status of a UN or similar force depends on the underlying authority upon which the force is present in the receiving state as well as the nature and mission of the force.[24] Under existing law, a UN peacekeeping operation is considered a subsidiary organ of the UN, established pursuant to a resolution of the Security Council or General Assembly. As such, it enjoys the status, privileges and immunities of the Organization provided for in Article 105 of the UN Charter, and the UN Convention on the Privileges and Immunities of the UN of 13 February 1946.[25] The legal framework for UN forces is usually made up of the following:

- a resolution of the Security Council or the General Assembly;
- a Status of Force Agreement between the UN and the host state;

---

[23] See *Dishonoured Legacy: Report of the Commission of Enquiry into the Deployment of Canadian Forces to Somalia* (Ottawa: Canadian Government Publishing, 1997); and *Africa Rights Report, Somalia – Human Rights Abuses by the UN Forces* (London: Africa Rights, July 1993); and M. Huband, 'UN Troops Opened Fire on Protestors in Mogadishu Pakistani vs. Somalia Fighters', *Guardian*, 31 December 1993, p. 6. The Africa Rights report documents a number of grave breaches of the Geneva Conventions by a number of contingents in Somalia. Most disturbing is the conclusion that these were 'not cases of undisciplined actions by individual soldiers, but stem from the highest echelons of the command structure' (p. i). Italy and Belgium also established inquiries into the conduct of their respective armed forces in Somalia: see Amnesty International, 'AI Concerns in Europe: January–June 1997', AI Index EUR 01/06/97 (1997), p. 1; and Amnesty International, 'Italy: A Briefing for the UN Committee Against Torture', AI Index EUR 30/02/99 (May 1995), p. 10.

[24] See W. G. Sharp, 'Protecting the Avatars of International Peace and Security' (1996) 7 *Duke Journal of Comparative and International Law* 92–183 at 112–43.

[25] In addition, the Secretary-General endeavours to conclude Status of Force Agreements with the host state governments. This is not always possible: for example, none was concluded in Somalia, and it took nearly twenty years to conclude a Status of Force Agreement in respect of UNIFIL. See generally D. Fleck and M. Saalfeld, 'Combining Efforts to Improve the Legal Status of UN Peacekeeping Forces and Their Effective Protection' (1994) 1(3) *International Peacekeeping* 82–84.

- an agreement by exchange of letters or a memorandum of understanding between each of the participating states and the UN; and
- regulations for the force issued by the Secretary-General.

However, as UN forces generally tend to be deployed in situations of conflict, determining what situations constitute 'armed conflict' under international law, and the laws governing UN and other forces present or participating as combatants in such situations, is a vital issue. Humanitarian law will also provide a certain level of protection to UN forces, depending on the degree of involvement and the nature of the conflict.[26]

The norms regulating armed conflict are not only of ancient origin, but are also found in diverse cultures on many continents. After the piecemeal development of humanitarian law at the end of the nineteeth and the start of the twentieth centuries,[27] the experience of the Second World War made the shortcomings in the legal regulation of this field all too apparent. This realisation led to the adoption in 1949 of four conventions in which most of humanitarian law is now codified.[28] The adoption of the 1949 Conventions, coupled with the earlier body of Hague law governing the conduct of hostilities, meant that traditional inter-state wars (or 'armed conflicts' to use the language of the Geneva Conventions)

---

[26] This is outlined by Greenwood, 'International Humanitarian Law and United Nations Military Operations', pp. 30–1; see also A. Roberts and R. Guelff (eds.), *Documents on the Laws of War* (3rd edn, Oxford: Oxford University Press, 2000), p. 623. Article 8(2)(d)(iii) of the Statute of the International Criminal Court (ICC) also prohibits attacks on peacekeepers 'so long as they are entitled to the protection given to civilians or civilian objects under the international law of armed conflict': see O. Triffterer (ed.) *Commentary on the Rome Statue of the International Criminal Court* (Baden-Baden: Nomos, 1999), pp. 277–8; and the 'ICRC Reference Document to Assist Preparatory Commission to Assist in Its Work on Elements of Crimes for the ICC', para. 1.3.3.4, 'General Points Common to the Offences under Article 8(2)(e) of the ICC Statute (1999)'.

[27] 1899 saw the adoption of a treaty that made the principles of the 1864 treaty applicable to the wounded and shipwrecked at sea. In 1906, the 1864 treaty was revised, and in the following year the 1899 treaty was amended along the same lines. In 1926, a convention on the treatment of prisoners of war was adopted. See Kalshoven, *Constraints on the Waging of War*, pp. 9–10.

[28] Geneva Convention for the Amelioration of the Condition of the Wounded and Sick in Armed Forces in the Field 1949 ('Geneva I'); Geneva Convention for the Amelioration of the Condition of Wounded, Sick and Shipwrecked Members of Armed Forces at Sea 1949 ('Geneva II'); Geneva Convention Relative to the Treatment of Prisoners of War 1949 ('Geneva III'); and Geneva Convention Relative to the Protection of Civilian Person in Time of War 1949 ('Geneva IV').

were now (at least theoretically) well regulated.[29] The phrase 'armed conflict' was employed to make clear that the Conventions apply once a conflict between states employing the use of arms has begun, whether or not there is a formal declaration of war.[30] The Conventions do not however, provide, for situations involving an armed conflict between the UN and a state, or between organised groups within a state.

The UN system was carefully designed to make war illegal and unnecessary;[31] nowhere in the UN Charter is the concept of war mentioned. Having rendered the concept of the classical 'war' redundant, it might have seemed unduly pessimistic for the UN to set about regulating that which purportedly no longer exists. It is not surprising, then, that the International Law Commission of the UN declined to resurrect the concept when it considered the codification of humanitarian law in 1949. It was believed that, if the Commission were to undertake this study at its outset, public opinion might equate this with a lack of confidence in the efficiency of the means at the disposal of the UN for maintaining peace.[32] As a result, the responsibility for codifying and improving the principles of humanitarian law fell upon the ICRC.

As the majority of armed conflicts in the Cold War period did not approximate to inter-state wars of the kind envisaged by traditional humanitarian law, certain obvious gaps in the legal regulation governing armed conflicts remained.[33] The adoption of the Conventions marked a break with the past in that Article 3, which is common to all four Conventions, seeks to establish certain minimum standards of behaviour 'in the case of armed conflict not of an international character' which reaches an undefined level of intensity. While of modest scope,

---

[29] Art. 2 common to all four Geneva Conventions of 1949. *The Geneva Conventions of 12 August 1949 – Commentary: IV Geneva Convention* (Geneva: ICRC, 1958), pp. 20–1.

[30] See Greenwood, 'Scope of Application of Humanitarian Law', pp. 42–3.

[31] Thomas M. Franck and Faiza Patel, 'Agora: The Gulf Crisis in International and Foreign Relations Law: UN Police Action in Lieu of War: "The Old Order Changeth"' (1991) 85 *American Journal of International Law* 63. For general background on the UN and humanitarian law, see C. Bourloyannis, 'The Security Council of the United Nations and the Implementation of International Humanitarian Law' (1993) 20(2) *Denver Journal of International Law and Policy* 335–55; and G. Abi-Saab, 'The United Nations and International Humanitarian Law: Conclusions' (1996) *Actes du Colloque International de l'Universite de Geneve*.

[32] S. Bailey, *Prohibitions and Restraints on War* (Oxford: Oxford University Press, 1972), p. 92.

[33] The 1999 report of the Secretary-General on the protection of civilians in armed conflict makes depressing reading: see *UN Secretary-General's Report on the Protection of Civilians in Armed Conflict*, UN Doc. S/1999/957, 8 September 1999.

this was a radical development.[34] Unfortunately, limitations in its application remain as states often maintain that the conflict in question is not one that was intended to be governed by the Conventions. In the alternative, states are likely to deny that their internal disturbances meet the required level of 'armed conflict', and Article 3 is not instructive in this regard as it does not attempt to define the requisite level of intensity for its application.[35] Additional Protocols I and II were adopted in 1977 to address some of these deficiencies, but they too do not take into account Security Council-authorised deployment of UN or multi-national forces.[36]

Protocol I brought what were often referred to as 'wars of national liberation' within the definition of international conflicts.[37] Protocol II, on the other hand, did not apply to all non-international armed conflicts, but only to those that meet a new and relatively high threshold test.[38] Despite the time and effort that went into the drafting of the Protocols, the result was less than satisfactory, especially with regard to assistance in the classification of armed conflicts to determine which Protocol, if any, applies in a given case. The applicability of Protocol II is far too narrow, and this helps to explain in part why so many states are party to it. Whereas, prior to 1977, guerrilla or non-conventional wars were governed only by common Article 3, after the adoption of the Protocols these might fall into one of three (partly overlapping) categories. Struggles against colonialism, racist regimes and alien

---

[34] G. Aldrich, 'The Laws of War on Land' (2000) 94 *American Journal of International Law* 42–59 at 59.

[35] See G. Aldrich, 'Human Rights in Armed Conflict: Conflicting Views' (1973) 67 *American Society of International Law Proceedings* 141 at 142; and R. Baxter, 'Some Existing Problems of Humanitarian Law', in *The Concept of International Armed Conflict: Further Outlook 1* (Proceedings of the International Symposium on Humanitarian Law, Brussels, 1974).

[36] See generally *Commentary on the Additional Protocols of 8 June 1977 to the Geneva Conventions of 12 August 1946* (Geneva: ICRC, 1987), p. 33.

[37] Protocol Additional to the Geneva Conventions of 12 August 1949, and Relating to the Protection of Victims of International Armed Conflict ('Protocol 1'), Art. 1(4). This saved captured guerrilla fighters who met certain conditions from trial and potential execution for actions committed in the course of liberation wars, by granting such captives prisoner-of-war status.

[38] Protocol Additional to the Geneva Conventions of 12 August 1949, and Relating to the Protection of Victims of Non-International Armed Conflicts ('Protocol II'), Art. 1(1). See B. De Schutter and C. Van De Wyngaert, 'Coping with Non-International Armed Conflicts: The Borderline Between National and International Law' (1983) 13 *Georgia Journal of International and Comparative Law* 279 at 285.

occupation, as defined in Protocol I, are now subject to the rules of international armed conflict. Other conflicts which meet the high threshold of Protocol II are governed both by that Protocol and by common Article 3; while conflicts which reach a certain level of intensity, but fall below the Protocol II threshold, are governed solely by common Article 3.

A fourth category can be noted, that of 'internal disturbances or tensions', which is mentioned, though not substantively legislated for, in Protocol II.[39] This category covers situations involving significant political violence such as occurred in Albania,[40] where the threshold of common Article 3 is not reached. Many have considered that a dangerous lacuna can exist in such circumstances: human rights law may be extensively derogated from while the relevant situation falls beyond the reach of humanitarian law.[41] In an attempt to address this issue, a number of declarations and codes of conduct have been proposed but no substantial progress has been made.[42]

When the broader picture of the development of humanitarian law over the last two decades is examined, it is evident that, in addition to their contribution to the regulation of non-conventional warfare, the 1977 Protocols are significant in two other respects. First, Protocol I represents the interweaving of Hague law and Geneva law, in that it includes provisions designed to protect the civilian population and

---

[39] Protocol II.

[40] See D. Kritsiotis, 'Security Council Resolution 1101 (1997) and the Multi-National Protection Force of Operation Alba in Albania' (1999) 12 *Leiden Journal of International Law* 511–47.

[41] See Meron, 'On the Inadequate Reach of Humanitarian and Human Rights Law', p. 589.

[42] See, for example, H. P. Gasser, 'A Measure of Humanity in Internal Disturbances and Tensions: Proposals for a Code of Conduct' (1988) 38 *International Review of the Red Cross* 262. See also the 'Oslo Statement on Norms and Procedures in Times of Public Emergency or Internal Violence' (1987) and the adoption of the 'Declaration of Minimum Humanitarian Standards' at Turku/Åbo, Finland, 1990 (sometimes referred to as the 'Turku/Abo Declaration'). The text of the Oslo Statement is included in the pamphlet *Declaration of Minimum Humanitarian Standards* (Turku: Åbo Akademi University Institute for Human Rights, 1991), pp. 13–16. The text of the Declaration is appended to T. Meron and A. Rosas, 'A Declaration of Minimum Humanitarian Standards' (1991) 85 *American Journal of International Law* 375. In 1994, an amended version of the Turku/Åbo document was adopted, which received a degree of validation from both UN and OSCE mechanisms. The text of the document is appended to A. Eide, A. Rosas and T. Meron, 'Combating Lawlessness in Gray Zone Conflicts Through Minimum Humanitarian Standards' (1995) 89 *American Journal of International Law* 215.

those *hors de combat*,[43] and sets out new rules on the conduct of hostilities based on the principle of proportionality.[44] Secondly, both Protocols represent a degree of merger of humanitarian law with its younger cousin, international human rights law, in that they incorporate detailed and explicit human rights guarantees, drawn directly in some instances from the International Covenant on Civil and Political Rights.[45] As a result, the Additional Protocols have blurred the distinction between what was traditionally seen as humanitarian law – with its emphasis on generic rights determined according to the status of certain participants or other groups caught up in an armed conflict – and the more individual-based rights, which form the core of international human rights law.

None of the existing Conventions or Protocols addresses the specific issue of UN forces, or forces acting on the authority of the UN, in situations of armed conflict. It could be said that this situation leaves such forces in somewhat of a grey area. However, the Institut de droit internatonale has confirmed that the rules of the 'law of armed conflict' apply as of right and must be complied with in every circumstance by UN forces engaged in hostilities.[46] If the UN is considered the sum of its parts, then it comprises states. In this way, a conflict involving the UN must also engage individual states acting for or on its behalf. While the UN is clear that it is capable of being responsible for an internationally wrongful act,[47] the obligation to comply with the Conventions could be viewed as falling simply on the states concerned. It does not seem correct to allow the organisation, under whose control and upon whose authority and behalf the states are acting, to evade

---

[43] See, for instance, Arts. 52–56.   [44] See especially Arts. 57 and 58.

[45] For instance, the fair trial guarantees in Art. 75 of Protocol 1 and Art. 6 of Protocol II are clearly based upon, though are not identical to, those in Art. 14 of the ICCPR. For a discussion of this point, see S. Stavros, 'The Right to a Fair Trial in Emergency Situations' (1992) 41 *International and Comparative Law Quarterly* 343.

[46] (1951) 54-II *Annuaire de l'Institut de droit international* 466, and (1975) 56-II *Annuaire de l'Institute de droit international* 541. See also Institute of International Law, 'The Application of International Humanitarian Law and Fundamental Human Rights, in Armed Conflicts in Which Non-State Entities Are Parties' (Fourteenth Commission, Berlin Session 1999, 25 August 1999), p. 4; and D. Schindler and J. Toman (eds.), *The Laws of Armed Conflicts* (Dordrecht: Martinus Nijhoff, 1988), pp. 903 and 907.

[47] See R. Dupuy (ed.), *A Handbook on International Organizations* (2nd edn, Dordrecht: Martinus Nijhoff, 1998), p. 887; and *Secretary-General's Report on Administrative and Budgetary Aspects of the Financing of United Nations Peacekeeping Operations*, UN Doc. A/51/389, 20 September 1996, reproduced in 37 *International Legal Materials* (1998) 702, para. 4.

responsibility.[48] There should be no doubt that an organisation is responsible for the illegal acts committed by that organisation, but not all acts or conduct can be attributable to the organisation. Unlike a state, it must be kept in mind that an international organisation's capacity to act is functional, not sovereign.[49]

International human rights law

The law relating to human rights can be seen to have influenced certain aspects in the development of humanitarian law. This is evidenced by the human rights language used in such instruments as common Article 3 of the Geneva Conventions, Article 75 of Protocol I and Article 4 of Protocol II. As human rights law came into being, humanitarian law was being refined, and the former has undergone a steady progression since then. Among the more important human rights instruments are the Universal Declaration of Human Rights[50] and the International Covenant on Civil and Political Rights (ICCPR).[51] While the Universal Declaration of Human Rights is not a binding legal instrument, many of its provisions are also enshrined in the ICCPR, Article 7 of which states that 'no-one shall be subjected to torture or to cruel, inhuman or degrading treatment or punishment'. Moreover, the ICCPR defines this right as being non-derogable, including in times of public emergency that threaten the life of a nation.

The Convention Against Torture and Other Cruel, Inhuman or Degrading Treatment or Punishment (CAT)[52] details provisions of redress for victims of an act of torture and outlines duties and obligations on states parties in preventing torture. Article 2(1) requires each state party to prevent acts of torture in any territory under its jurisdiction. Article 2(2) provides that no exceptional circumstances whatsoever, whether a state of war or a threat of war, internal political instability or any other public emergency, may be invoked as a justification for torture.

[48] See generally C. F. Amerasinghe, *Principles of the Institutional Law of International Organization* (Cambridge: Cambridge University Press, 1996), pp. 223–48.
[49] Dupuy (ed.), *A Handbook on International Organizations*, p. 888.
[50] Universal Declaration of Human Rights (UDHR), GA Res. 217 A (III), UN Doc. A/810/71 (1948).
[51] International Covenant on Civil and Political Rights (ICCPR), GA Res. 2200 A (XXI), 16 December 1966, 21 UN GAOR Supp. (No. 16) 49, UN Doc. A/6316 (1966), 993 UNTS 3, entered into force 3 January 1976.
[52] Convention Against Torture and Other Cruel, Inhuman or Degrading Treatment or Punishment (CAT), GA Res. 39/46 10 December 1984, 39 UN GAOR Supp. (No. 51) 197, UN Doc. A/39/51 (1984), entered into force 26 June 1987.

Armed conflict and civil disorder are often characterised by the deliberate targeting of women. Although the 1979 Convention on the Elimination of All Forms of Discrimination Against Women (CEDAW)[53] provides some degree of protection for women, this group remain vulnerable to physical and sexual abuse, torture, slavery, rape and other crimes against humanity. Women also constitute the greatest numbers of refugees and displaced persons and, as such, they are often subjected to violence, discrimination and exploitation.

In addition to the protection provided under CEDAW, Security Council Resolution 1325 of 31 October 2000 on Women, Peace and Security[54] calls on all parties to armed conflict to take special measures to protect women and girls from gender-based violence, particularly rape and other forms of sexual abuse, and all other forms of violence in situations of armed conflict. It further emphasises state responsibility to end impunity and to prosecute those responsible for genocide, crimes against humanity and war crimes, including those relating to sexual and other violence against women and girls. There is also special protection provided for children under the 1990 Convention on the Rights of the Child (CRC)[55] and Optional Protocols, in addition to that provided under Article 24 of the ICCPR. The extra-territorial application of these human rights treaties is well established in the jurisprudence of the UN Human Rights Committee.[56] In 2004, the Committee stated:

---

[53] Convention on the Elimination of All Forms of Discrimination Against Women (CEDAW), GA Res. 34/180, 34 UN GAOR Supp. (No. 46) 193, UN Doc. A/34/46, entered into force 3 September 1981. In December 1993, the UN General Assembly adopted a Declaration on the Elimination of Violence Against Women; the UN has also appointed a Special Rapporteur and the General Assembly adopted an Optional Protocol providing for an individual complaint mechanism.

[54] S/RES/1325 (2000). See *Women, Peace and Security: Study submitted to the Secretary General pursuant to Security Council Resolution 1325* (New York: United Nations, 2000); and the Declaration on the Protection of Women and Children in Emergency and Armed Conflict, GA Res. 3318 (XXIX), 29 UN GAOR Supp. (No. 31) 146, UN Doc. A/9631 (1974).

[55] Convention on the Rights of the Child (CRC) GA Res. 44/25, 44 UN GAOR Supp. (No. 49) 167, UN Doc. A/44/49 (1989), entered into force 2 September 1990.

[56] Human Rights Committee, Comments on United States of America, para. 19, UN Doc. CCPR/C/79/Add.50 (1995); and J. Cerone, 'Reasonable Measures in Unreasonable Circumstances: A Legal Responsibility Framework for Human Rights Violations in Post-Conflict Territories under UN Administration', in N. D. White and K. Klassen (eds.), *The UN, Human Rights and Post-Conflict Situations* (Manchester: Manchester University Press, 2005), pp. 42–80 at 46.

> A State party [to the ICCPR] must respect and ensure the rights laid down
> in the Covenant to anyone within the power and effective control of that
> State party, even if not situated within the territory of that State party . . .
> This principle also applies to those within the power or effective control
> of a State party acting outside its territory, regardless of the circumstances
> in which such power or effective control was obtained, such as forces
> constituting a national contingent of a State party assigned to a national
> peace-keeping or peace-enforcement operation.[57]

The Committee also expressed concern about the conduct of Belgian
forces part of UNOSOM II. The Covenant creates a duty on a state party
to ensure that members of the armed forces participating in 'peacekeeping missions or NATO military missions' are trained appropriately
and familiar with the relevant human rights provisions.[58]

There are also a number of important regional treaties and other instruments dealing with human rights.[59] Among these is the European
Convention on Human Rights, which has been ratified by all member
states of the Council of Europe and is applicable to everyone within its
jurisdiction.[60] The Convention is interpreted and applied in the jurisprudence of the European Court of Human Rights, and the Court's
pronouncements with regard to jurisdiction have important implications
for European states participating in peacekeeping operations. According
to the *Bankovic* decision (concerning claims by relatives of those killed
in the bombing of the Serbian television station in Belgrade by NATO
during the Kosovo campaign in 1999), when a state party finds itself in
'overall effective control of an area', it is in a position to secure the entire

---

[57] General Comment No. 31, UN Doc. CCPR/C/2/1/Rev.1/Add.13 (2004), para. 10.

[58] Concluding Observations of the Human Rights Committee: Belgium, 19 November
1998, UN Doc. CCPR/C/79/Add.99, para. 14; and Concluding Observations of the
Human Rights Committee: Belgium, 12 August 2004, UN Doc. CCPR/C/81/BEL,
para. 10.

[59] European Convention for the Prevention of Torture and Inhuman or Degrading
Treatment or Punishment, entered into force 1 February 1989, Doc. No. H (87) 4,
1987, ETS No. 126; Inter-American Convention on the Prevention, Punishment and
Eradication of Violence Against Women, entered into force 3 March 1995, reprinted in
33 ILM 1534 (1994); Inter-American Convention to Prevent and Punish Torture,
entered into force 28 February 1987, OASTS 67, GA Doc. OEA/Ser.P, AG/doc.2023/
85 rev.I (1986). American Convention on Human Rights (Pact of San José), entered into
force 18 July 1978, OASTS 36, OAS Off. Rec. OEA/Ser.L/V/11.23, Doc. 21, rev.6 (1979).

[60] European Convention for the Protection of Human Rights and Fundamental Freedoms,
213 UNTS 221, entered into force 3 September 1953. See also the African Charter on
Human and Peoples' Rights, entered into force 21 October 1986, OAU Doc. CAB/LEG/
67/3 Rev.5.

range of Convention rights and obligations.[61] The inconsistencies in the jurisprudence of the European Court of Human Rights was highlighted in the England and Wales High Court and Court of Appeal decisions in the *Al Skeini* case (dealing with allegations that British forces in Iraq had violated the United Kingdom Human Rights Act 1998 when the United Kingdom was recognised as an occupying power there during 2003).[62] The High Court held that, 'although there was common ground both that the Convention's reach is essentially territorial and that there are exceptions to the basic principle of territoriality, there is complete disagreement as to the width, nature, rationale and applicability of the exceptions'.[63] It seems from the *Bankovic* and *Al Skeini* decisions that public powers must be exercised in order to create responsibility under the European Convention. This can arise when a state is in control of territory as a result of military occupation, or through the consent, acquiescence or invitation of the government of the territory. It follows that the extra-territorial principle may also arise when control is exercised pursuant to a UN mandate. Such a conclusion represents a far more conservative approach than that employed by the Inter-American Commission on Human Rights, one of two bodies in the inter-American system for the promotion and protection of human rights. The Commission has found for the extra-territorial application of human rights law in circumstances where the state merely has control over the individual complaining of a violation.[64] These regional systems have provisions governing the right to life, prohibitions on torture, cruel and inhuman treatment and also violence in general, and specifically as against women and children. The question posed is to what extent, if any, these can be enforced against UN peacekeeping forces. This is especially relevant in Kosovo, where regulations promulgated by UNMIK grant

---

[61] *Bankovic and others v. Belgium and others* (App. No. 52207/99), ECtHR, 12 December 2001. The European Court of Human Rights held that the claims against NATO states for violation of human rights were inadmissible on the basis that the bombing occurred in territory outside the legal space of the ECHR.

[62] *R. (on the application of Mazin Jumaa Gatteh Al-Skeini and others) v. Secretary of State for Defence* [2004] EWHC (Admin) 2911; [2005] EWCA Civ 1609, 21 December 2005. The judgments decided that the scope of the European Convention is essentially territorial but also extends exceptionally to the case of outposts of the United Kingdom's authority abroad such as embassies and consulates and, in this case, a prison in Iraq operated by British forces.

[63] *R. (on the application of Mazin Jumaa Gatteh Al-Skeini and others) v. Secretary of State for Defence* [2004] EWHC (Admin) 2911, para. 109.

[64] *Coard and others v. United States*, Case 10.951, Report No. 109/99, 29 September 1999.

immunity from any legal process to UNMIK itself, and UNMIK and KFOR personnel.[65] The establishment of the Human Rights Advisory Panel in March 2006 is a welcome initiative and precedent, but this has a limited remit and there is still no real international mechanism to review acts of UNMIK or KFOR.[66]

As the UN is not a state, the source of its obligation to observe human rights is not without controversy.[67] Although not a party to the major human rights treaties, it remains a subject of international law. One way around the problem of applying human rights norms to the UN itself is to regard the UN Charter and its accompanying instruments as forming a constitution. In this way, the relevant treaties and related instruments govern UN as well as state activities.

Sexual abuse and peacekeeping operations

The issue of accountability and the conduct of peacekeeping and humanitarian workers have been simmering in the background for a number of years, but recently has been acknowledged as a serious problem.[68] Complaints emerged from Cambodia, Bosnia, Macedonia, Mozambique, West Africa, the Democratic Republic of the Congo, Eritrea and Kosovo. Following the publication of several reports, it has emerged that sexual exploitation, rape and trafficking in persons are a common consequence of the deployment of peacekeeping troops and civilian police forces.[69]

In late 2001, a report commissioned jointly by the UN High Commissioner for Refugees and Save the Children United Kingdom alleged that sexual violence and exploitation was widespread among the refugee and internally displaced person communities in the West

---

[65] UNMIK Regulation No. 2000/47 of 18 August 2000.

[66] UNMIK Regulation No. 2006/12 of 23 March 2006. The findings and recommendations of the Human Rights Advisory Panel are submitted to the Special Representative of the Secretary-General who has exclusive authority and discretion to make decisions on them: see http://www.unmikonline.org/human_rights/index.htm.

[67] N. D. White and K. Klassen, 'An Emerging Legal Regime', in White and Klassen (eds.), *The UN, Human Rights and Post-Conflict Situations*, p. 7; and B. Kondoch, 'Human Rights Law and UN Peace Operations in Post-Conflict Situations', in the same book, at p. 36.

[68] F. Hoffmann and F. Mégret, 'Fostering Human Rights Accountability: An Ombudsperson for the United Nations?' (2005) 11 *Global Governance* 43–6.

[69] See UN Doc. E/CN.4/2001/73, 23 January 2001; and UN Doc. A/51/306, 9 September 1996.

African countries of Guinea, Liberia and Sierra Leone.[70] The perpetrators of these abuses were said to include members of UN peacekeeping forces and humanitarian aid workers – the very people who had been designated to protect these vulnerable communities. The publicity surrounding the publication of the report prompted an investigation by the UN Office of Internal Oversight Services (OIOS).[71] Efforts to combat such misconduct have been undertaken and include the establishment of Codes of Conduct, the adoption of Security Council Resolution 1325 (2000), the Secretary-General's Bulletin on Special Measures for Protection from Sexual Exploitation and Sexual Abuse (2003),[72] and an emphasis on a policy of 'zero-tolerance' towards sexual exploitation and abuse by UN staff. In the aftermath of these, 2005 saw members of the UN peacekeeping mission in the Democratic Republic of the Congo (MONUC) facing 150 charges of sexual exploitation and abuse. These include allegations of paedophilia, rape and solicitation for prostitution, and several investigative teams have been sent to review what may turn out to be the worst sex scandal that the UN has ever had to face. Furthermore, from 1 January 2004 to 9 December 2005, investigations against 278 peackeeping personnel were carried out, resulting in the dismissal of 16 civilians and the repatriation, on disciplinary grounds, of 16 members of formed police units and 122 military personnel (including six commanders).[73] Despite these developments, there is a widespread perception that peacekeeping personnel are not accountable for their conduct and that there is a *de facto* tolerance for and immunity from prosecution for such behaviour.[74]

In a press release on 19 November 2004, Kofi Annan acknowledged the existence of proof that sexual exploitation and abuse had been committed by peacekeepers in the Democratic Republic of the Congo:

---

[70] UNHCR and Save the Children UK Report, *Sexual Violence and Exploitation: The Experience of Refugee Children in Guinea, Liberia and Sierra Leone* (2002) (hereinafter 'UNHCR/Save the Children Report').

[71] *Report of the Secretary-General on the Activities of the Office of Internal Oversight Services Investigation into Sexual Exploitation of Refugees by Aid Workers in West Africa*, UN Doc. A/57/465, 11 October 2002, para. 3.

[72] UN Doc. ST/SGB/2003/13, 9 October 2003.

[73] UN Doc. A/60/640/Add.1, 29 December 2005, Implementation of the Recommendations of the Special Committee on Peacekeeping Operations, para. 42.

[74] *Report of the Secretary-General: A Comprehensive Strategy to Eliminate Future Sexual Exploitation and Abuse in United Nations Peacekeeping Operations*, UN Doc. A/59/10, 24 March 2005 ('Zeid Report'), para. 66.

> I am afraid that there is clear evidence that acts of gross misconduct have taken place. This is a shameful thing for the UN to have to say, and I am absolutely outraged by it . . . We cannot rest until we have rooted out all such practices from MONUC, from any other peacekeeping operation, and indeed anywhere in the Organization that they might occur. And we must make sure that those involved are held fully accountable.[75]

An OIOS investigation into these allegations was launched in May 2004, and a special investigation team was later sent by the Department of Peacekeeping Operations to examine possible further cases. While investigation of such allegations is important, the effectiveness and consequences of an OIOS investigation is seen by many as insufficient. Unfortunately, the UN has no legal authority to prosecute those against whom they find evidence of wrongdoing. At most, the UN can repatriate a peacekeeper to his or her country of origin, but cannot ensure the prosecution of that person once he or she has returned home. Violations of human rights and abuse by UN and humanitarian personnel, whether in the form of sexual exploitation or otherwise, must not be tolerated. It violates the very core of the UN.

The general response has been to promulgate codes of practice and to revise training programmes and guidelines, efforts that are welcome, but insufficient. To be fair, the UN has made repeated calls on troop-contributing states to investigate and prosecute all allegations of human rights violations by peacekeepers and to report back to the UN.[76] But the UN itself is bound by the terms of its agreement with troop contributors and the Status of Force Agreements, and it has no authority to insist on more. The situation is exacerbated in places like Kosovo, where the UN is entrusted with the administration of the entire territory. A system must be put in place where anyone employed by or affiliated with the UN will be held accountable and, when the circumstances so warrant, prosecuted.[77] For this reason, the report undertaken by the Secretary-General's adviser on sexual exploitation and abuse by UN peacekeepers, Prince Zeid of Jordan, is an important analysis of the problem and includes practical recommendations outlined below aimed at eliminating such practices.[78]

---

[75] UN Press Release SG/SM/9605 AFR/1069 PKO/115, 19 November 2004.

[76] UN Doc. A/55/163-S/2000712, 19 July 2000.

[77] *Report of the Secretary-General on the Activities of the Office of Internal Oversight Services Investigation into Sexual Exploitation of Refugees by Aid Workers in West Africa*, UN Doc. A/57/465, 11 October 2002, para. 3.

[78] Zeid Report (note 74 above).

The situation pertaining to UN operations is further complicated by the fact that contemporary missions may have up to five different categories of participating personnel. The largest group are usually the so-called 'blue helmets' or members of national military contingents supplied to the UN for a specified duration (usually six or twelve months). There are also civilian police from various police forces around the world, civilian staff, UN volunteers and military observers. Yet the Secretary-General's Bulletin prohibiting exploitation does not apply to all categories, an unsatisfactory state of affairs that has yet to be rectified, despite the recommendation in the Zeid Report calling for its universal application.

After media reports in early 2004 noted the recurrence of acts of sexual exploitation and abuse of Congolese women and girls by UN peacekeepers, the OIOS conducted an investigation in Bunia between May and September of that year. The investigation uncovered evidence of regular and widespread sexual contact by peacekeepers with underage girls, although many of the allegations could not be substantiated owing to their non-specific nature. Further obstacles, such as the passage of time, the fact that numerous rape victims were too traumatised to be pressed for evidence and the age of younger victims hindered the investigation of individual cases; nevertheless, cogent evidence of a pattern of sexual exploitation was found.

The subsequent report issued by the OIOS declared, among other things, that:

> In many cases of the interviews conducted by the investigation team during its four months of field work, particularly of the younger girls, aged 11 to 14 years, it became clear that for most of them, having sex with the peacekeepers was a means of getting food and sometimes small sums of money. The boys and young men who facilitated sexual encounters between peacekeepers and the girls sometimes received food as payment for their services as well. In addition to the corroborated cases reported . . . interviews with other girls and women indicated the widespread nature of the sexual activity occurring in Bunia.[79]

This was consistent with other reports from the region. Human Rights Watch found that MONUC's credibility had been undermined by the exploitative and abusive behaviour of some of its own staff.[80] Girls as

---

[79] *Ibid.*, para. 11.
[80] Human Rights Watch Statement to Committee on International Relations, US House of Representatives, Washington, DC, 1 March 2005.

young as 13 years of age reported that they had been raped by MONUC soldiers. Other girls between the ages of 12 and 15 had engaged in what is commonly referred to as 'survival sex' – sexual relations engaged in so as to obtain some food, money or protection. Relations of this nature are inherently exploitative and relatively easy to establish in post-conflict environments where women and girls often find themselves in vulnerable positions.

The Secretary-General's Bulletin on special measures for the protection from sexual exploitation is binding on all staff of the UN,[81] and its provisions are similar to those contained in the MONUC Code of Conduct. Likewise, the Bulletin prohibits military forces under UN command and control from committing acts of sexual exploitation.[82] These documents expand on the standards found in the Code of Personal Conduct for Blue Helmets. Section 1 of the Bulletin defines sexual exploitation as follows:

> any actual or attempted abuse of a position of vulnerability, differential power, or trust, for sexual purposes, including, but not limited to, profiting monetarily, socially or politically from sexual exploitation of another.

Sexual abuse is defined as 'actual or threatened physical intrusion of a sexual nature, whether by force or under unequal or coercive conditions'. Section 2 of the MONUC code of conduct contains similar provisions. It expands on the definition of sexual abuse and provides that abuse and exploitation of this nature include any sexual misconduct that has a detrimental effect on the image, credibility, impartiality or integrity of the UN.

The Secretary-General's Bulletin on the observance by UN forces of humanitarian law is also relevant.[83] Section 7 governs the treatment of civilians and persons *hors de combat* and prohibits acts of abuse or exploitation. It contains the following express provisions which create a duty to protect women and children from exploitation:

---

[81] *Secretary-General's Bulletin on Special Measures for the Protection from Sexual Exploitation and Sexual Abuse*, ST/SGB/2003/13, 9 October 2003, Section 2.1.

[82] *Ibid.*, Section 2.2.

[83] *Secretary-General's Bulletin on Observance by UN Forces of International Humanitarian Law*, UN Doc. ST/SGB/1993/3, 6 August 1999. See M. Zwanenburg, 'The Secretary-General's Bulletin on Observance by United Nations Forces of International Humanitarian Law: Some Preliminary Observations' (1999) 5 (415) *International Peacekeeping* 133–9.

Section 7.3 Women shall be especially protected against any attack, in particular against rape, enforced prostitution or any other form of indecent assault.

Section 7.4 Children shall be the object of special respect and shall be protected against any form of indecent assault.

The UN personnel in the DRC abused the vulnerability of the local population and exploited the most vulnerable for sexual purposes. The conduct was prohibited and was a clear violation of the duty to protect the most vulnerable members of Congolese society.[84] The majority of victims were between the ages of twelve and sixteen years and were extremely vulnerable. They were very poor and illiterate; many had lost close family members and were traumatised by the sexual and other violence that characterised the conflict. Although the investigation focused on three UN contingents, it cannot be assumed that other contingents did not engage in similar improper activities. Among the factors facilitating a lack of accountability among peacekeepers was the regular troop rotations and the lack of a prevention programme aimed at stopping such abuse, despite the fact that this is a requirement of the Under-Secretary-General for Peacekeeping Operations and the Special Representative of the Secretary-General for MONUC. Few military or civilian staff seemed aware of the existence or applicability of directives, policies, rules and regulations aimed at governing their sexual conduct. This was also the case with troops serving with the UNMEE mission in Eritrea. The level of ignorance is perhaps best illustrated by the fact that the investigation team in Bunia found evidence of ongoing sexual contact while the investigation was taking place.

While there is a consensus that such conduct is reprehensible and should be prevented, there is also an acknowledgment that it is widespread during UN peacekeeping operations. The Special Representative of the Secretary-General for MONUC provided the following insight into how to deal with such behaviour:

I believe that emphasis needs to be placed on the accountability of the officers of contingents to which the perpetrators belong, from contingent to company and platoon commanders. It is clearly evident that while there has been no shortcoming insofar as disseminating the code of

---

[84] *Report of the Secretary General on the Activities of the Office of Internal Oversight Services Investigation into Sexual Exploitation of Refugees by Aid Workers in West Africa*, UN Doc. A/57/465 [3], 11 October 2002, para. 22.

conduct and the Secretary-General's zero tolerance policy on matters of sexual exploitation and abuse, the same cannot be said for enforcement of this. In certain instances, it is apparent that the feeling of impunity is such that not only have the policies not been enforced, but the command structures have not always given investigators their full cooperation. I also consider it imperative that the results of Member States' actions against the perpetrators of these abuses be made available to the UN and that the Mission highlight to incoming commanders the gravity and extent of the problem and underscore the commanders' responsibility to prevent similar acts during their mandate. Only such stern deterrents, in my view, will enable us to stamp out sexual exploitation and sexual abuse in the peacekeeping environment.[85]

In order to address the issue of sexual exploitation by UN forces, no further regulations or directives are required. Zero tolerance of this and any related activity must involve holding perpetrators and their superiors responsible. The most effective way to achieve this is to ensure national prosecutions take place. That being said, superior officers cannot be held responsible for all acts of their subordinates, but the principles of command responsibility under international humanitarian law provide a template. Superiors or commanders must be accountable for action when they knew, or ought reasonably to have known, or, in the case of civilians, consciously disregarded information which clearly indicated subordinates were engaging in such activities. Failure to co-operate with implementation and investigation should not be tolerated.

The Zeid Report made recommendations for action on four broad fronts:

> Rules against sexual exploitation and abuse must be unified for all categories of peacekeeping personnel. A professional investigative process must be established and modern scientific methods of identification must be utilized. A series of organizational, managerial and command measures must be instituted to address sexual exploitation and abuse. A number of recommendations are made to ensure that peacekeeping personnel . . . are held individually accountable . . . and that they are held financially accountable for the harm they have done to victims.[86]

Allegations of sexual abuse of minors and local women were also made against Irish soldiers serving with the UN mission in Eritrea

---

[85] *Ibid.*, para. 46.   [86] Zeid Report (note 74 above), para. 94.

(UNMEE).[87] These were investigated and a number of Irish soldiers disciplined. However, the initial investigation by Italian Carabinieri was flawed and conclusions were drawn on the basis of unreliable identification evidence. Allegations of sexual relations with minors proved difficult to substantiate, as it was not possible to establish with certainty the age of the victims. The disciplinary hearings took place in Ireland, as the soldiers involved had completed their tour of duty by the time action was taken. This is a common problem with most troop-contributing states. If soldiers are rotated every six or twelve months, requiring disciplinary hearings to be held in the mission area is not always practical. The procedures put in place to investigate and prosecute wrongdoing must also ensure that the good name and reputation of innocent personnel is protected.

There seems little alternative to the present system whereby the only possibility for the prosecution of UN forces lies with their respective states. No UN mechanism for prosecuting UN forces exists and contributing states are unlikely to agree any proposal for such an arrangement. The real problem is to ensure that national prosecutions do take place. Establishing a central monitoring system adopted to track the process and outcome is one means of addressing this problem. This could incorporate a system whereby states that failed to co-operate or to follow through with prosecutions could be 'named and shamed' similar to what happens under UN human rights monitoring mechanisms. The Secretary-General's 2003 Bulletin on sexual misconduct should be binding on all categories of peacekeepers and any transgression should constitute 'serious misconduct'. This, and the relevant rules and code of conduct, should be made available in the language of all those participating in peacekeeping operations. In addition, in order to prosecute successfully, while at the same time respecting the rights of those against whom inaccurate or false allegations may be made, it is of the utmost importance to establish a professional investigative process.[88]

On-site courts-martial should be standard. However, regular rotations of military personnel may mean that this is not a practical option. Disciplinary measures should involve financial penalties for transgressions, and the fines paid into a trust fund for victims. Although the UN does encounter difficulty obtaining troop contributions from states from time to time, this should not influence the decision to

---

[87] Interviews, Irish officers who served with UNMEE, July/August 2005.
[88] Zeid Report (note 74 above), pp. 30–1.

impose conditions on troop-contributing countries. The selection process at national level for UN service is often inadequate or non-existent, and this has contributed to problems of corruption and improper behaviour in the mission area.[89]

The Office of the High Commissioner for Human Rights has developed an important human rights training programme for peacekeepers. This 'training for trainers' is a vital element in promoting the human rights agenda in peacekeeping and, with that, an awareness of the broader context in which sexual exploitation may occur. Training strategies of this nature should be combined with practical measures in the field. In this regard, the Zeid Report appropriately recommends adding benefits and burdens for those working in the field. While living conditions of those in mission areas should be enhanced by improved access to internet and international telephone facilities, curfews should also be designated and certain areas deemed out of bounds.

Each UN SOFA should contain an express reference to relevant international human rights instruments. Access to such materials is also important; otherwise there is a risk of paying lip-service to the relevant provisions. This was sorely lacking in the EU SOFA with Macedonia, which refers to the protection of the environment and cultural heritages, yet makes no mention of human rights.[90] Surely people should outrank places in terms of priority and protection.

International and non-international armed conflicts

Although it may be argued that the distinction between international and non-international armed conflict has lost much of its significance,[91] this is an overly optimistic assessment. Determining whether a conflict can be characterised as internal or international can still be critically important,[92] as the rules which apply during internal conflicts remain

---

[89] Interview, senior staff member, DPKO, New York, May 2005.

[90] Agreement between the European Union and the Former Yugoslav Republic of Macedonia on the Status of the European Union-Led Forces in the Former Yugoslav Republic of Macedonia, *Official Journal of the European Union*, 29 March 2003, L 82/46–51.

[91] See D. Schindler, 'Significance of the Geneva Conventions for the Contemporary World' (1999) *International Review of the Red Cross* No. 836, 715–29.

[92] See T. Meron, 'War Crimes in Yugoslavia and the Development of International Law' (1994) 88 *American Journal of International Law* 78–83 at 80; and C. Byron, 'Armed Conflicts: International or Non-International?' (2001) 6(1) *Journal of Conflict and Security Law* 63–90.

rudimentary and skeletal compared to those applicable to international conflicts.[93] When a conflict is regarded as international in character, the whole *jus in bello* (justice in war) principles of the Geneva Conventions (some 400 articles) apply. However, the protection afforded under common Article 3 and Protocol II governing non-international armed conflicts is much more limited in scope. The International Court of Justice decision in the *Nicaragua* case illustrates how far the evaluation of conflict status has shifted from dependence on the classification by the sovereign state alone towards neutral external measurement by international bodies.[94] Distinguishing between international and non-international armed conflict in contemporary situations remains difficult,[95] however, as is evidenced by the contradictory decisions of different trial chambers of the International Criminal Tribunal for the Former Yugoslavia on the nature of the conflict in the former Yugoslavia.[96] Ironically, though, two opinions rendered by the Appeals Chamber of the Tribunal are of the most significance in this context.

---

[93] Greenwood, 'International Humanitarian Law and United Nations Military Operations', pp. 3–34 at p. 9; and D. Schindler, 'The Different Types of Armed Coflicts According to the Geneva Conventions and Protocols' (1979) 163 *Recuil des Cours* 116–63. For an overview of the international law applicable to armed conflicts to which non-state entities are parties, see Institute of International Law, 'The Application of International Humanitarian Law and Fundamental Human Rights, in Armed Conflicts in Which Non-State Entities Are Parties' (Fourteenth Commission, Berlin Session 1999, 25 August 1999), pp. 3–5.

[94] *Military and Paramilitary activities (Nicaragua v. United States)*, (1986) ICJ Reports 4, paras. 219 and 220. The ICJ contrasted the conflict between the Contras and the Sandinista government with that between the US and Nicaragua. The first, as internal, was governed by common Article 3 only; the second, as international, fell under the rules governing international armed conflicts. The Court also affirmed that the fundamental general principles of humanitarian law (common Article 3, in the opinion of the Court) belong to the body of general international law, in other words, that they apply in all circumstances for the better protection of the victims, regardless of the legal classification of armed conflicts. See G. Abi-Saab, 'Humanitarian Law and Internal Conflicts: The Evolution of Legal Concern', in A. Delissen and A. Tanja (eds.), *Humanitarian Law of Armed Conflict: Essays in Honour of F. Kalshoven* (Dordrecht: Martinus Nijhoff, 1991), pp. 209–23.

[95] See generally M. Sassoli and A. Bouvier, 'The Law of Non-International Armed Conflict', in M. Sassoli and A. Bouvier, *How Does Law Protect in War* (2nd edn, Geneva: ICRC, 2006), Vol. II, pp. 252–70; and the 'ICRC Reference Document to Assist Preparatory Commission to Assist in Its Work on Elements of Crimes for the ICC', para. 1.3.3.4, 'General Points Common to the Offences under Article 8(2)(e) of the ICC Statute (1999)'.

[96] See T. Meron, 'The Humanization of Humanitarian Law' (2000) 94 *American Journal of International Law* 239–78 esp. 261.

The first is the opinion in the *Tadic* case to the effect that many principles and rules previously considered applicable only in international armed conflict are now applicable in internal armed conflicts, and serious violations of humanitarian law committed within the context of such internal conflicts constitute war crimes.[97] Secondly, on the issue of jurisdiction in the same case, the Appeals Chamber defined 'non-international armed conflict' as 'protracted armed violence between governmental authorities and organised armed groups or between such groups within a state'.[98] In this way, the Appeals Chamber has encouraged the blurring of the distinction between international and non-international armed conflicts, shifting the traditional focus on state sovereignty towards a human rights approach to international problems.[99] One potential drawback to this aspect of the *Tadic* decision is that it could have been interpreted as creating another category of armed conflict, i.e. where protracted armed violence occurs. This would have added a further complication to the already difficult topic of determining the nature and categorisation of armed conflicts. The same kind of reasoning was later adopted by the International Criminal Tribunal for Rwanda in the *Akayesu* case.[100] Fortunately, subsequent decisions of the Yugoslav Tribunal have clarified this potential anomaly.[101]

In all of these developments, the impact of humanitarian law on UN forces does not seem to have been given serious consideration.[102] While

---

[97] *Prosecutor* v. *Tadic*, Appeal on Jurisdiction, No. IT-94-1-AR72 (2 October 1995), 105 ILR 417, para. 70, reprinted in 35 ILM 32 (1996). See P. Rowe, 'The Substantive Jurisdiction of the Tribunal' (1996) 45 *International and Comparative Law Quarterly* 696–701; and C. Greenwood, 'International Humanitarian Law and the *Tadic* Case' (1996) 7 *European Journal of International Law* 265–83 esp. 276.

[98] *Ibid.*, para. 70. See also T. Meron, 'Classification of Armed Conflict in the Former Yugoslavia: *Nicaragua*'s Fallout' (1998) 92 *American Journal of International Law* 236–42.

[99] The Statute of the ICC has also tended to blur the distinction: see Meron, 'The Humanization of Humanitarian Law', pp. 262 and 275.

[100] *Prosecutor* v. *Akayesu*, ICTR, Case No. ICTR-96-4-T, 2 September 1998, paras. 619–21. It is noteworthy that the language of Article 8(2)(f) of the Statute of the ICC is similar to that used in the *Tadic* decision and refers to 'protracted armed conflict': see Triffterer (ed.), *Commentary on the Rome Statute*, pp. 284–6.

[101] For example, *Prosecutor* v. *Tadic*, Judgment, Appeals Chamber (15 July 1999), paras. 68–162 esp. paras. 80–97. See also *Prosecutor* v. *Blaskic*, Judgment, Trial Chamber (3 March 2000), paras. 63–72 and 75–123; and *Prosecutor* v. *Aleksovski*, Judgment, Appeals Chamber, No. IT-95-14/1-A (24 March 2000), paras. 120–2.

[102] But it is noteworthy that in the *Tadic* case (*Tadic*, Decision on the Defence Motion for Interlocutory Appeal on Jurisdiction, Case No. IT-94-1-AR72 (2 October 1995)), the Appeals Chamber referred to the ICJ decision in the *Nicaragua* case that Article 1 of the

the intensity and classification of the conflict are fundamental determinants of the application of humanitarian law where UN forces are deployed, they can also be an important determinant of UN military involvement in intra-state conflicts in the first place. Serious levels of violence and widespread or systematic attacks on civilians may provoke an international response. As Somalia and Lebanon show, such conflicts are often not amenable to simple 'quick fix' solutions. UN forces can find themselves deployed in complex political situations where the international legal framework within which they must operate is anything but clear. Despite claims to the contrary, this is all the more likely when it is considered that humanitarian law does not apply to most kinds of UN military activities.[103] Recent UN operations have involved authorised and mandated operations mounted in situations of conflict where clashes involving local actors or parties and UN soldiers were inevitable. These have left casualties on both sides and have involved both combatant and non-combatant alike. Often the parties to such conflicts have undergone a sustained period of bitter and bloody conflict. Many combatants are not soldiers of regular armies but are members of militias or groups of armed civilians with little discipline and an ill-defined command structure.[104] Fighters of this nature do not always fit easily into the matrix of humanitarian law combatant status. There is also the vexed question of responsibility for the actions or omissions of UN soldiers in the field, specifically, what ought to be done when confronted by human rights abuses on a large scale. In this way, the matter of the applicability of humanitarian law to UN forces is of much more than academic interest. It is directly relevant to those states contributing contingents, and to the UN itself, even if it is not formally a party to the relevant international treaties.

Humanitarian law and UN operations

UN forces can take on many different forms, and the status and nature of a force is important in evaluating the applicability of humanitarian law

---

four Geneva Conventions 'lays down an obligation that is incumbent, not only on states, but also on other international entities including the UN' (para. 93).

[103] P. Rowe, 'Maintaining Discipline in UN Peace Support Operations: The Legal Quagmire for Military Contingents' (2000) 5 (1) *Journal of Conflict and Security Law* 45–62 esp. 50–8.

[104] United Nations, *The Blue Helmets: A Review of United Nations Peacekeeping* (3rd edn, New York: United Nations, 1996), p. 4.

principles. The difference between peacekeeping and enforcement action operations is fundamental, but second-generation operations, while not constituting enforcement action as originally envisaged under the UN Charter, possess characteristics of both types of operations.[105] There is also the problem of distinguishing between UN-mandated operations and those merely authorised to be carried out by coalitions of the willing. While these issues are important in determining the extent of the application of humanitarian law to UN forces, the fundamental issue remains the existence of an armed conflict. Ultimately, it is the fact of participation in hostilities, not the existence of authority to do so, that is significant.[106]

In recent years, the Security Council has authorised groups of states to organise 'peace enforcement' operations with specific goals. The United States has been at the forefront of these operations in, *inter alia*, Somalia, Haiti and the former Yugoslavia. The operations in question, while not constituting enforcement action as originally envisaged under the Charter, owed much to the half-way house suggested by Boutros Boutros-Ghali in his original *An Agenda for Peace* document.[107] In all cases, the relevant resolutions of the Security Council drew upon Chapter VII of the Charter, with subsequent military action conducted by states outside of their own national borders, in the territory of a foreign country and with UN authorisation. In this way, the activity could not be said to constitute aggression or the illegal use of force contrary to international law. The military operations were similar to conventional operations involving coalition forces under a complex but essentially unified operational command structure and were intended to be governed by the Geneva Conventions and Additional Protocols and the international law of armed conflict as a whole.[108]

In addition, it is an accepted principle that humanitarian law applies in equal measure to all parties involved irrespective of any other consideration, including the issue of the legality and objective of the resort to the use of force. There is broad agreement that humanitarian law norms apply to UN military operations,[109] a view supported by the

---

[105] See Chapter 1, p. 8, above.
[106] Greenwood, 'International Humanitarian Law and United Nations Military Operations', p. 11.
[107] UN Doc. A/47/277-S/24111, June 1992.
[108] Interviews, UN official and senior military officer seconded to UN DPKO, New York, 1998.
[109] K. Okimoto, 'Violations of International Humanitarian Law by United Nations Forces and Their Legal Consequences' (2003) 6 *Yearbook of International Humanitarian Law*

terms of the relevant Conventions. In particular, there is no doctrine of ends and means in the application of humanitarian principles, and the Geneva Conventions affirmatively require that 'the High Contracting Parties undertake to respect and ensure respect for the present Convention in all circumstances'.[110] While not every armed confrontation triggers the application of humanitarian law, states involved are obliged to ensure its strict implementation once the threshold of 'armed conflict' has been reached.

The most contentious missions, from both a legal and a political perspective, will probably be those operations where the peace is most precarious. These may take place during international or non-international armed conflicts. Such operations go well beyond traditional peacekeeping precepts and often slip from peace to conflict and from Chapter VI to Chapter VII of the Charter, even in the course of a single mission. However, classifications are needed and standards must be sought.[111] While it is acknowledged that every deployment of troops outside their own territory is subject to international political and legal ramifications, clarification of what these are is needed, especially when the UN troops involved are likely to be engaged in hostilities with local actors.

D. W. Bowett addressed the issue of the application of the law of armed conflict to operations by UN forces by examining two preliminary questions: first, what functions a UN force may assume; and, secondly, which types of command structure may be adopted for a UN force.[112] An analysis of the different functions that may be entrusted to UN forces suggests that the application of the laws of armed conflict may

---

199–238; H. McCoubrey, 'International Law and National Contingents in UN Forces' (1994) 12 *International Relations* 39–50 at 46; Greenwood, 'International Humanitarian Law and United Nations Military Operations', p. 18; and M. Bothe, 'Peacekeeping', in Simma (ed.), *The Charter of the United Nations*, p. 648. See also two resolutions adopted by the Institut de Droit International: Resolution on the Conditions of Application of Humanitarian Rules of Armed Conflict to Hostilities in Which UN Forces May Be Engaged, adopted in Zagreb in 1971, (1971) 54-II *Annuaire de l'Institut de droit international* 465; and Resolution on the Conditions of Application of Humanitarian Rules of Armed Conflict to Hostilities in Which UN Forces May Be Engaged, adopted in Wiesbaden in 1975, (1975) 56 *Annuarire de l'Institut de droit international* 540.

[110] Article 1 of First Geneva Convention of 1949; and the Preamble to Additional Protocol I of 1977.

[111] T. Pfanner, 'Application of International Humanitarian Law and Military Operations Undertaken under the UN Charter', in *Symposium* (note 2 above), p. 50.

[112] D. W. Bowett, *United Nations Forces* (London: Stevens, 1964), pp. 484–5.

be relevant to certain types of functions but not to others. The most fundamental difference to identify in the first instance is between that of enforcement action under Chapter VII of the Charter and traditional peacekeeping, though, as previously stated, in recent years the distinction between the two has become less clear. Bowett's two questions are also inextricably linked, as the command structure will largely depend on the function of the force.[113] A further complication arises by virtue of the kind of operations conducted under Chapter VII and intended to be enforcement action in nature, despite the failure to conclude the requisite agreements with the UN under Article 43 of the Charter. The issue of who commands the force, the UN or the states concerned, is especially relevant in operations involving 'coalitions of the willing'.

More significantly, from the point of view of the applicability of humanitarian law, nowhere in Chapter VII, and Article 42 in particular, is 'war' mentioned. It refers to 'such action by sea, air or land forces as may be necessary ... [and] may include demonstrations, blockade, and other operations by air, sea or land forces of members of the UN'. The obvious implication of this is that military action taken by the UN is not to be regarded as 'war', and this was the commonly accepted view of the UN action in Korea. Given the intensity of the hostilities during the Korean conflict, this point may seem somewhat academic to the ordinary person on the street, or to the soldier acting under UN 'command' in the midst of the hostilities.[114] The tendency to view conflicts of this nature as other than war may also confuse the issues somewhat and have its origins in the old just war theory. The problem with this is that it may justify the use of violence on a massive scale and, indirectly, undermine humanitarian law principles by failing to view those against whom the military action is being taken as equally deserving of their protection.

Writing in 1964, Bowett stated that 'there [was] no known case in which the UN Command ever claimed exemption from any of the accepted rules of the laws of war, customary or conventional'.[115] In fact, there appears to be no record of the UN ever claiming that

---

[113] Ibid., pp. 487–8. Bowett identified three types of command structure: (i) command delegated to a state or group of states by the UN; (ii) command entrusted to an individual appointed by and responsible to the UN, but lacking disciplinary authority; and (iii) command entrusted to an individual appointed by and responsible to the UN and having disciplinary authority.

[114] See R. Murphy, 'The Legal Framework of UN Peacekeeping Forces and the Issue of Command and Control' (1999) 4(1) Journal of Armed Conflict Law 41–73.

[115] Bowett, United Nations Forces, p. 56.

humanitarian law does not apply to operations authorised by or undertaken on behalf of the Organization. But the policy of the UN with regard to the applicability of humanitarian law to forces under its command or operational control is still ambivalent.

Not surprisingly, the matter of enforcing humanitarian law is left to the contributing states. Theoretically, given the universal nature of the principles, this should not prove problematic; but, in practice, a lot will depend on the country concerned and the level of importance attached to dissemination and training among the armed forces. As a result, such an arrangement cannot be regarded as satisfactory and raises the issue of UN responsibility for violations of international law in such instances.

While there can be no doubt that the UN is a subject of international law and capable of possessing international rights and duties, an analysis of the jurisprudence of the International Court of Justice reveals that it is impossible to categorically address the legal consequences of personality for international organisations.[116] The issue is currently being examined by the International Law Commission.[117] The UN is, however, a separate legal person from and additional to its member states, and is not simply an aggregation of those states. Once the existence of international personality and rights is conceded, it is not difficult to infer that this will also entail obligations, a position specifically supported in the *WHO Agreement* case by the International Court of Justice with regard to the existence of obligations under customary international law for international organisations.[118] That there are situations where the UN will be responsible under customary international law for acts of persons or armed forces acting under its control is beyond dispute.[119] In fact, states have brought claims

---

[116] Amerasinghe, *Principles of the Institutional Law*, pp. 92–3. See also B. Tittemore, 'Belligerants in Blue Helmets', pp. 92–5.

[117] See International Law Commission, *Special Report on Responsibility of International Organizations*, UN Doc. A/CN.4/541, 2 April 2004. On the issue of the relationship between the attribution of conduct to an international organisations and the attribution of conduct to a state, the Special Rapporteur states (*ibid.*, paras. 7 and 9):

> Attribution of conduct to an international organization does not necessarily exclude attribution of the same conduct to a State; nor does, vice versa, attribution of conduct to a State rule out attribution to an international organization ... It seems reasonable to envisage that, if an international organization aids or assists, or directs or controls, a State in the commission of a wrongful act, or coerces a State to commit it, the organization shall be held responsible under conditions similar to those of a State.

[118] (1980) ICJ Reports 67 at 90.

[119] Amerisinghe, *Principles of the Institutional Law*, pp. 240–1.

against the UN arising from violations of international law during the ONUC (Congo) operation and these were later settled by negotiation.[120]

This is not an aberration, as the UN has generally accepted responsibility for illegal acts that may have been committed by armed forces (belonging to member states) acting under its control.[121] Such liability is possible when national contingents become organs of the UN by being placed under its authority and control. This does not happen when a country or countries retain control of a military force, as in the First Gulf War, even if acting in the execution of a UN decision. Where national contingents come together to form 'coalitions of the willing' but remain outside of any UN command and control framework, in such cases the UN cannot be held responsible for their acts.[122] Rather, the acts of military forces remain the responsibility of the states concerned. However, definitive statements remain problematic due to the complex issues surrounding the command and control of UN forces discussed in Chapter 3, and a lot will depend on the facts of a case. In the meantime, the effective control test retains its central role in determining liability, and in some cases may even allow for concurrent responsibility because of a limbo status involving an ill-defined form of dual control.[123]

The United Nations position

In 1994, as Serb troops advanced on the UN declared 'safe area' of Bihac, the municipal hospital stood in the middle of their line of advance.[124]

---

[120] See UN Doc. A/CN.4/195 and Add.1, 7 April 1967. The principal claimant was the Belgian govenment. Despite the nature of the authorisation to use force in the ONUC operation, the ICJ found that it 'did not involve "preventive or enforcement" measures against any State under Chapter VII': Advisory Opinion, *Certain Expenses of the United Nations*, (1962) ICJ Reports 177. See Bowett, *United Nations Forces*, pp. 175–80.

[121] Amerasinghe, *Principles of the Institutional Law*, p. 242; and Dupuy (ed.), *A Handbook on International Organizations*, p. 891. The UN has acknowledged liability for activities carried out by both UNEF and ONUC.

[122] Amerasinghe, *Principles of the Institutional Law*, p. 243; and F. Seyersted, 'United Nations Forces: Some Legal Problems' (1961) 37 *British Yearbook of International Law* 362 and 421.

[123] See *Nissan v. Attorney General* [1968] 1 *Queen's Bench* 286; [1969] 1 *All England Reports* 629; I. Brownlie, 'Decisions of British Courts During 1968 Involving Questions of International Law' (1968–9) 42 *British Yearbook of International Law* 217; and *Secretary-General's Report on Administrative and Budgetary Aspects of the Financing of United Nations Peacekeeping Operations*, UN Doc. A/51/389, 20 September 1996, para. 18.

[124] R. Gutman, 'The UN and the Geneva Conventions', in R. Gutman and D. Reif (eds.), *Crimes of War* (New York: Norton and Co., 1999), pp. 361–4.

The Canadian commander of the UN forces showed no sign of taking any action to protect the hospital. The UN civil affairs officer urged that the hospital should be protected owing to its special status under the Geneva Conventions and that UNPROFOR had a duty to protect it.

> [The civil affairs officer] drafted a memo to this effect, and his superior in Sarajevo, a Russian, issued a formal request. 'The Geneva Conventions stipulate that hospitals shall not be attacked ... the support and concurrence of UNPROFOR military will also be needed. Please immediately pursue the plan with Bihac military commander', it said. Acting on the memo, the commander instructed Bangladeshi troops to drive their armoured personnel carriers onto the hospital grounds. The Serbs refrained from attacking the hospital and the ground attack was halted. Bihac, a town of seventy thousand, was saved.[125]

A short time later, the UN Office of Legal Affairs issued a statement to set the record straight and ensure that the 'Bihac incident' did not create a precedent for the future. UN forces are bound only by their Security Council mandate and are not legally obligated to uphold the Geneva Conventions, as obligations arising under humanitarian law are only binding on states. Moreover, Article 103 of the UN Charter may also be relied upon to support the argument that the obligations arising under the UN Charter on member states (including those arising from Security Council resolutions) take precedence over other international treaties, including the Geneva Conventions and Additional Protocols.[126] The role of the UN is to carry out the will of the international community as expressed by the Security Council.[127] When states assign troops to peacekeeping duties, they are theoretically under the command or operational control of the Security Council. As this work has demonstrated, however, the reality is much more complex. Few states ever relinquish full operational control to the UN.[128] The 'Bihac incident' illustrates the UN's ambivalent attitude towards humanitarian law. This

---

[125] *Ibid.*, p. 361.

[126] See B. Simma (ed.), *The Charter of the United Nations* (2nd edn, Oxford: Oxford University Press, 2002), pp. 1292–302; and L. M. Goodrich, E. Hambro and A. P. Simons, *Charter of the United Nations* (3rd edn, London: Columbia University Press, 1969), pp. 614–17. See also B. Tittemore, 'Belligerents in Blue Helmets', esp. pp. 101–8.

[127] Statement attributed to S. Katz, Office of Legal Affairs official, in R. Gutman, 'UN and the Geneva Conventions', in Gutman and Rieff (eds.), *Crimes of War*, pp. 361–4 at p. 361.

[128] See R. Murphy, 'The Legal Framework of UN Peacekeeping Forces', pp. 41–73.

has been a source of tension between the ICRC and the UN, the ICRC adopting a much broader interpretation of the application of humanitarian law to UN forces, as discussed below. Although the UN has declared its commitment to the application of humanitarian law to peacekeeping operations, it has consistently taken the position that UN forces act on behalf of the international community and, therefore, they can be considered neither a 'party' to the conflict, nor a 'Power' within the meaning of the Geneva Conventions. The mere presence of UN peacekeeping soldiers in an area of conflict or a theatre of war, while performing a humanitarian or diplomatic mission, does not necessarily mean that humanitarian law binds these troops.[129]

In addition, the UN is not in a position to become a party to the Geneva Conventions or the Additional Protocols, as this would entail binding the Organization to detailed provisions that are aimed at states, and do not fit the role and function of an international organisation.[130] Notwithstanding its international legal personality, the UN is not a state and, thus, does not possess the juridical or administrative powers to discharge many of the obligations laid down in the Conventions.[131] This does not, however, mean that the conduct of hostilities by UN forces will be free from humanitarian constraints or that humanitarian law considerations will not apply.[132] While a relevant factor in determining how UN forces will implement humanitarian law, it is not a reason for concluding that it cannot be applicable to them.[133]

The ICRC has been instrumental in obtaining agreement from the UN that international forces acting under UN authority do so in

---

[129] This position has not altered with the *Secretary-General's Bulletin on Observance by UN Forces of International Humanitarian Law*, UN Doc. ST/SGB/1993/3, 6 August 1999.

[130] On the question of treaty-making powers, see Amerasinghe, *Principles of the Institutional Law*, pp. 102–3.

[131] *Reparations Case* (1949) ICJ Reports 174. From a formal point of view, the UN cannot become a party to the Conventions because their final clauses do not provide for the participation of international organisations such as the UN: see *Symposium* (note 2 above), p. 43. In addition, '[t]he UN, as such, had no judiciary [sic] system, no legal basis on which it could try individuals': Mr B. Miyet, Under-Secretary-General for Peacekeeping Operations, quoted in (1997) 34(3) *UN Chronicle* 39. As a result, UN soldiers involved in child prostitution while they were part of the UN operation in Mozambique were repatriated.

[132] It is widely accepted that the 'laws of war remain directly relevant to such forces': A. Roberts and R. Guelff (eds.), *Documents on the Laws of War* (3rd edn, Oxford: Oxford University Press, 2000), p. 721.

[133] Greenwood, 'International Humanitarian Law and United Nations Military Operations', p. 15.

accordance with the 'principles and spirit' of relevant law.[134] In this regard, the relatively recent UN Model Agreement with troop-contributing states and the Model Status of Force Agreements between the UN and host states now include an express provision to this effect.[135] Under that provision, the UN undertakes that the operations of the force in question will be conducted with full respect for the principles and spirit of the general international conventions applicable to the conduct of military personnel. However, incorporation of a provision to this effect in the regulations governing the force and in the agreements with troop contributing states does not entail the direct responsibility of the UN to ensure respect for humanitarian law by members of its forces.

Thus, while these developments are welcome, they fail to address the fundamental questions, and, more importantly, seem to suggest that the UN does not have a duty to monitor the behaviour of third parties. The official statement issued after the 'Bihac incident' already referred to confirms this policy.[136] This is crucial, as the military culture requires that such duties be spelt out in clear terms. There is, however, a lack of consistency in this regard, as UNIFIL did monitor the behaviour of a third party in Lebanon after the 1982 Israeli invasion.[137] Faced with an untenable position when Israeli forces occupied its area of operations, UNIFIL adopted a role of monitoring Israeli forces as part of its *de facto*

---

[134] U. Palwankar, 'Applicability of International Humanitarian Law to UN Peacekeeping Forces' (1993) *International Review of the Red Cross* No. 80 227–40 at 229–33. A provision to this effect was incorporated into the UNEF, ONUC and UNFICYP Force Regulations. As no Regulations were adopted in respect of UNIFIL, no such provision exists for that force.

[135] Shraga and Zacklin, in *Symposium* (note 2 above), p. 44. The Model Agreement with troop contributors contains the following provision:

> [The UN peacekeeping operation] shall observe and respect the principles and spirit of the general international conventions applicable to the conduct of military personnel. The international conventions referred to above include the four Geneva Conventions of 12 August 1949 and their Additional Protocols of 8 June 1977 and the UNESCO Convention of 14 May 1954 on the Protection of Cultural Property in the event of armed conflict. [The participating state] shall therefore ensure that the members of its national contingent serving . . . be fully acquainted with the principles and spirit of the conventions.

[136] R. Gutman, 'The UN and the Geneva Conventions', in Gutman and Reif (eds.), *Crimes of War*, pp. 361–4. There were also claims that UN forces in Bosnia-Herzegovina ignored evidence of human rights abuses elsewhere.

[137] Interview, T. Goksel, UNIFIL spokesman, Naqoura, Lebanon, 1998; and personal experience of the writer.

mission. The predicament of UNIFIL at the time is discussed below, but its policy had some success in restraining the actions of the Israeli forces.

The recent Secretary-General's Bulletin on the observance by UN forces of humanitarian law makes some headway in addressing these problems.[138] It adds significant weight to the ICRC position which is at variance with that of the UN and is important in terms of legal certainty by giving substance to certain obligations. Bulletins of this nature are intended to be legally binding on UN personnel, in this case UN forces.[139] Section 1 of the Bulletin states that:

> The fundamental principles and rules of international humanitarian law set out in the present Bulletin are applicable to UN forces when in situations of armed conflict they are actively engaged therein as combatants, to the extent and for the duration of their engagement. They are accordingly applicable in enforcement actions, or in peacekeeping operations when the use of force is permitted in self-defence.

The categorisation of UN troops as combatants in certain instances may seem unusual, especially to troop-contributing states. Moreover, this Bulletin must be judged in the context of the 1994 Convention on the Safety of UN and Associated Personnel, which results in a problematic overlap in the respective regimes.[140] The two are incompatible because they are based on fundamentally different principles. The objective of the Convention is to protect UN personnel and ensure immunity from attack for those not engaged in enforcement operations under Chapter VII involving combat against organised armed forces; the remit of humanitarian law is much broader and respects the combatant's privilege to attack enemy forces once the general rules of international law are

---

[138] *Secretary-General's Bulletin on Observance by UN Forces of International Humanitarian Law*, UN Doc. ST/SGB/1993/3, 6 August 1999. See M. Zwanenburg, 'The Secretary-General's Bulletin on Observance by United Nations Forces of International Humanitarian Law: Some Preliminary Observations' (1999) 5(4/5) *International Peacekeeping* 133–9; and Rowe, 'Maintaining Discipline in UN Peace Support Operations', p. 52.

[139] Personal interview with an official of the UN Legal Division, New York, December 2000. Bulletins were described as part of the UN 'internal law, binding within the Organization's own legal system'.

[140] The 1994 Convention entered into force on 15 January 1999, and has been ratified or acceded to by seventy-nine states (January 2006). It is discussed in greater detail herein. The key provisions of the Convention require parties to take all appropriate measures to ensure the safety of UN and associated personnel.

followed, and is based on the cardinal principle that combat forces are treated equally.

The Secretary-General's Bulletin is a significant development and appears to declare that, when UN forces, for whatever reason, are required to resort to the use of force in armed conflict situations, humanitarian law applies. The degree, intensity and duration of force required are unclear, but some threshold must exist and be crossed before triggering the application of humanitarian law. Under this approach, commanders and soldiers will still find themselves in a kind of legal no man's land trying to determine in the first instance if the situation can be classified as one of armed conflict, and then whether the use of force is sufficient to change their status from that of peacekeeper or peace enforcer, to that of combatant. No pocket book of humanitarian law of the kind usually supplied to military personnel will supply easy answers to these questions. Nevertheless, paragraph 9(4) of the Bulletin seems to provide an answer to those who would see the UN stand by in situations such as arose in Bihac. Under these provisions, the UN shall in all circumstances respect and protect medical personnel and the wounded,[141] placing a clear onus on peacekeepers to intervene and actively accept responsibility for the protection of these persons.

The Bulletin also commits the UN to ensuring that members of military peacekeeping contingents are fully acquainted with the rules of humanitarian law. It accepts co-responsibility with the contributing states for this whether or not there is a Status of Force Agreement in place. The potential liability of the UN for breach of this duty is unclear. Most importantly, however, section 4 of the Bulletin establishes that it is the responsibility of national courts to prosecute military personnel for violations of humanitarian law. Accordingly, the UN is not required to establish a special tribunal to consider violations of humanitarian law by UN troops; the *status quo ante* remains.[142]

---

[141] Paragraph 9.4 states: 'The UN shall in all circumstances respect and protect medical personnel exclusively engaged in the search for, transport or treatment of the wounded or sick, as well as religious personnel.' Paragraph 9.5 states: 'The UN shall respect and protect transports of wounded and sick or medical equipment in the same way mobile medical units.'

[142] On 22 December 2000, the Security Council proposed that the Special Court for Sierra Leone have jurisdiction over crimes committed by peacekeepers or related personnel, where the state that had sent the relevant personnel was unwilling or genuinely unable to carry out an investigation or prosecution: see Amnesty International, *Sierra Leone: Renewed Commitment Needed to End Impunity*, 24 September 2001, para. 3.6.

The practical effect of the Bulletin on UN forces on the ground, and on the policy of contributing states, remains to be seen. Does it impose a wider duty to intervene in order to prevent violations of humanitarian law by third parties in the absence of a specific provision to this effect in the mandate? Common Article 1 of the Geneva Conventions provides that 'the High Contracting Parties undertake to respect and to ensure respect for the present Convention in all circumstances'.[143] It can be argued that this, and a similar provision in Protocol 1, places a duty on UN forces to take action to prevent such violations.[144] Although this may not have been the original intention of the negotiators of the Conventions[145] and Protocol, is such an interpretation supported by the agreement to respect and observe the 'spirit and principles' of humanitarian law and the recent Secretary-General's Bulletin? It would seem that the UN remains reluctant to acknowledge a duty to intervene in such circumstances,[146] and that the Bulletin acknowledges such a duty in very limited circumstances. In this way, as the law currently stands, a UN force is not under a general legal duty to intervene on behalf of victims of violations of applicable law in its area of operations, unless the mandate of the force provides otherwise.

The real problem for the UN is that acknowledging a duty to intervene creates an onus to give the force(s) the capacity to do so without exposure to unnecessary risk.[147] If a force cannot intervene directly without exposing troops to significant danger, the duty of a commander must first be to the safety of his or her personnel. Most lightly armed peacekeepers will not be in a position to prevent large-scale abuses by a party to the conflict, and this was the predicament of the Dutch

---

[143] See Pictet, *Commentary: Geneva Convention IV Relative to the Protection of Civilian Persons in Time of War* (Geneva: ICRC, 1958), p. 16.

[144] See Greenwood, 'International Humanitarian Law and United Nations Operations', pp. 9 and 32–3.

[145] A. Roberts, 'The Laws of War: Problems of Implementation', in *Law in Humanitarian Crises* (Brussels: European Commission, 1995), p. 13 at pp. 31–2.

[146] For a discussion of this issue, see R. Weiner and F. Ni Aolain, 'Beyond the Laws of War: Peacekeeping in Search of a Legal Framework' (1996) 27 *Columbia Human Rights Law Review* 293 at 312–20.

[147] *Report of the Panel on UN Peacekeeping Operations* (Brahimi Report), UN Doc. A/55/305-S/2000/809, 23 August 2000, recommended that UN peacekeepers – troops or police – be authorised to stop violence against civilians, within their means, in support of basic UN principles. At present, this has no legal status, but it is a significant acknowledgment of the duty to intervene. See generally R. Marx, 'A Non-Governmental Human Rights Strategy for Peacekeeping' (1996) 14 *Netherlands Quarterly of Human Rights* 126–45.

contingent at Srebrenica.[148] But this will not relieve them of responsibility to take some action within the means available, as protests on the ground and later through higher channels can have a positive effect and do not generally incur exposure to risk. A fear by UN commanders of taking a stand and the possible consequences that may follow this is the kernel of the dilemma and in these circumstances there is a likelihood that some commanders will hide behind the cloak of preserving force security to excuse their failure to protect. It can also be argued that intervention in such circumstances will compromise the impartiality of the force, but, if the policy adopted by the UN is applied in a consistent and impartial manner, this argument may be rebutted. Acknowledging that such a duty exists by expressly providing for it in the mandate of the force may make the mission more difficult, but it cannot be right to allow a UN force to stand idly by in circumstances where breaches of humanitarian law and human rights take place in their area of operations.[149]

The ICRC position

Having rendered the concept of the classical 'war' redundant, the UN considered that it could not now set about regulating its conduct, and the responsibility to codify and improve the principles of humanitarian law fell upon the ICRC. The question of the applicability of humanitarian law to UN forces was raised for the first time during the Korean conflict. This highlighted a fundamental problem for the UN in regard to ensuring compliance with the principles involved. When requested by the ICRC to apply *de facto* the humanitarian law principles protecting war victims, especially common Article 3 of the Geneva Conventions, the UN commander replied that his instructions were to abide by the humanitarian principles of the 1949 Geneva Conventions, particularly common Article 3, and by the detailed provisions of the Geneva Convention relating to prisoners of war.[150] The importance of the latter convention may have arisen from the need to ensure that all prisoners were treated equally, whereas, in the case of common Article 3, the

---

[148] See R. Siekmann, 'The Legal Position of Dutchbat vis-a-vis Srebrenica' (1998) 1 *Yearbook of International Humanitarian Law* 301–12.

[149] See generally O. Ulich, 'Peacekeeping and Human Rights: Is There a Duty to Protect' (Spring 1996) *International Human Rights Advocacy*.

[150] Shraga and Zacklin, in *Symposium* (note 2 above), pp. 39–48 at p. 39.

principles concerned represent a compulsory minimum to be applied irrespective of the nature of the conflict or the issue of reciprocity.[151] However, as the UN commander, he claimed that he did not have the authority to accept, or the means to ensure the accomplishment of, responsibilities incumbent upon sovereign nations under the detailed provisions of the other Geneva Conventions. Since then, the ICRC has drawn the attention of the Secretary-General to the application of humanitarian law to the forces at his disposal, and to the desirability that they be provided with adequate instruction in this area.[152]

The essence of the ICRC position is that humanitarian law principles, recognised as part of customary international law, are binding upon all states and upon all armed forces present in situations of conflict.[153] If these rules are binding on all states, they must also bind an international organisation that resorts to the use of force on their behalf. This is especially so when this organisation is an independent subject of international law and was established by those states bound by the principles in the first place. In this context, the status of the parties or the legality of the use of force are not issues that will determine the applicability of humanitarian law. Recognising that the UN is not a party to the Conventions, and, given the nature of the Organization, it is accepted that humanitarian law principles would need to be applied *mutatis mutandis* to the Organization.[154]

When member states are authorised by the Security Council to intervene in a conflict such as that in Somalia, the basic character of the conflict remains internal.[155] However, the forces of the participating member states are carrying out an international mission on the basis of

---

[151] Common Article 3, referred to as the mini-convention, is contained in all four Geneva Conventions. It applies to armed conflict 'not of an international character'. See Pictet, *Commentary: Geneva Convention IV*, pp. 25–44. The ICJ has deemed that 'certain general and well recognised principles', including those contained in common Article 3, reflect the 'elementary considerations of humanity': the *Corfu Channel Case*, (1949) ICJ Reports 4 at 22.

[152] Both the ICRC and the International Conference of the Red Cross and Red Crescent on many occasions expressed their opinion on the applicability of international humanitarian law to peacekeeping forces: see Palwankar, 'Applicability of International Humanitarian Law', pp. 230–1.

[153] Shraga and Zacklin, in *Symposium* (note 2 above), p. 43.

[154] Thus rules pertaining to prisoners of war or penal sanctions could not apply, whereas rules pertaining to methods and means of combat, categories of protected persons and respect for recognised signs, would be fully applicable. Statement by the ICRC at the 47th Session of the General Assembly on 13 November 1992.

[155] Pfanner, in *Symposium* (note 2 above), pp. 49–59 at p. 55.

a UN resolution. In the relations between the 'UN forces' and the parties to the conflict, the rules applicable to international armed conflict must be applied. While it is acknowledged that the application of the rules of humanitarian law in their entirety is problematic as this was intended for conflict between states,[156] it would be a denial of the clear international dimension of such missions if humanitarian law were to be restricted to common Article 3 or Protocol II to the Geneva Conventions.

It is apparent that the adoption of military measures under Chapter VI or VII of the Charter is likely to call for the application of humanitarian law under various profiles. Action against the illegal use of force has historically involved the use of force by the UN or states acting on its behalf. Action of this nature operates in situations where humanitarian law calls for the application of its *jus in bello* rules.[157] In regard to peace-keeping operations, it is commonly accepted that deployment in situations constituting a threat to international peace and security may also call for preventive measures involving the use of force. If and when armed conflict does break out and humanitarian law is applicable, it makes little sense to argue that UN forces on the ground are not bound by these same principles.[158] Adherence to these principles will also assist in facilitating a restoration of the peace, the ultimate goal of all UN forces.

The 1994 Convention on the Safety of UN and Associated Personnel[159]

An effort to address some of the issues surrounding the protection of UN forces resulted in the adoption of the 1994 Convention on the Safety of UN and Associated Personnel ('the Convention'). The declared purpose of the Convention is to protect UN and associated personnel from becoming the object of attack by purporting to criminalise attacks on

---

[156] *Ibid.*

[157] P. Benvenuti, 'The Implementation of International Humanitarian Law in the Framework of Peacekeeping Operations', *Law in Humanitarian Crises* (Brussels: European Commission, 1995), Vol. 1, pp. 83–120 at p. 85.

[158] Both the ICRC and the International Conference of the Red Cross and Red Crescent on many occasions expressed their opinion on the applicability of international humanitarian law to peacekeeping forces: see Palwankar, 'Applicability of International Humanitarian Law', pp. 230–1.

[159] An Optional Protocol to the Convention, which will provide legal protection for UN and associated personnel in peacebuilding missions going beyond peacekeeping operations was recommended to the General Assembly by the Sixth Committee on 16 November 2005. GA/L/3291, 16 November 2005.

peacekeeping troops. Its key provisions require parties to take all appropriate measures to ensure the safety of protected personnel and to prosecute or extradite offenders. The Convention clarifies the protective duties of the receiving or host state, and this is a welcome initiative; but, in the context of UN enforcement measures and humanitarian law, the Convention raises some interesting issues. The outcome, in terms of what has been achieved, may in some ways be described as the proverbial camel created by a committee established to design a horse.[160]

Taking into account its Preamble, it is evident that concerns over the scale and frequency of attacks on peacekeeping forces provided the impetus for the drafting of the Convention. Its opening acknowledges the contribution of UN personnel in the fields of preventive diplomacy, peace-making, peacekeeping, peace-building and humanitarian and other operations, yet, notably, makes no specific mention of 'peace enforcement' operations. Rather, the importance of the traditional characteristics of peacekeeping operations is emphasised as is the non-use of force except in self-defence and the policy of impartiality.[161] Significantly, the Convention contains a number of 'savings clauses' which note, *inter alia*, that nothing shall affect the applicability of humanitarian law and universally recognised standards of human rights to UN operations and personnel, or their responsibility to respect humanitarian law and human rights standards.[162] One of the interesting features of this provision is that it merely states that the law is applicable but, given the complexity of the issue, and the haste with which the Convention was drafted,[163] fails to outline the circumstances as to when

---

[160] See W. G. Sharp, 'Protecting the Avatars of International Peace and Security' (1996) 7 *Duke Journal of Comparative and International Law* 93–183. Sharp is very critical of the Convention, and he suggests the adoption of an Additional Protocol III instead. Greenwood replied to Sharp's article in C. Greenwood, 'Protection of Peacekeepers: The Legal Regime' (1996) 7 *Duke Journal of Comparative and International Law* 185–207.

[161] Article 6 of the Convention calls on UN personnel to respect the laws of the host state and to refrain from any action or activity incompatible with the impartial and international nature of its duties. Article 20 and the Preamble emphasise the issue of consent, while Article 21 refers to the right to use force in self-defence.

[162] Article 20(a) of the Convention.

[163] It would seem that the Convention was adopted with undue haste. The Sixth Committee adopted draft resolution A/C.6/49/L.9 by consensus on 16 November 1994. Resolution 49/59 adopting the Convention and declaring it open for signature and ratification was adopted by the General Assembly by consensus on 9 December 1994. See generally P. Kirsch, 'The Convention on the Safety of UN and Associated Personnel' (1995) 2(5) *International Peacekeeping* 102–6.

and where this is so. It is, however, unfortunate that an opportunity to clarify and even expand on this area was not availed of.

The Convention provides that UN personnel, including those involved in maintaining peace and security, or providing emergency humanitarian assistance, are protected from attack.[164] The negotiators realised that it was necessary to have a clear separation between situations where the Convention will apply and those wherein humanitarian law is applicable, so that UN and associated personnel and those who attack them are covered by one regime or the other, but not both.[165] An important reason for this is not to undermine the Geneva Conventions, which rely in part for their effectiveness on all forces being treated equally. If it became a crime to engage in combat with UN forces acting as combatants, this could have a dramatic impact on a party's willingness to adhere to accepted principles of humanitarian law.

Article 1 of the Convention is central to its applicability and scope. The text provides for a two-fold definition. The operation must be established by a competent organ of the UN, in accordance with the Charter and under UN authority and control. In addition, one of two further conditions must be met, namely:

1. the operations must be for the purpose of maintaining or restoring international peace and security; or
2. where the Security Council or General Assembly has decided for the purposes of the Convention, that there exists an exceptional risk to the safety of the personnel participating in the operation.

This means that operations authorised, as opposed to mandated by the Security Council, but carried out under the command and control of

---

[164] E. Bloom, 'Protecting Peacekeepers: The Convention on the Safety of UN and Associated Personnel' (1995) 89 *American Journal of International Law* 621–31 at 623–4. In essence, it covers two types of personnel who carry out activities in support of the fulfilment of the mandate of a UN operation. In the first category are those directly engaged as part of a UN-mandated operation whether in a military, police or civilian capacity. The second category covers 'associated personnel', i.e. persons assigned by the Secretary-General or an intergovernmental organisation with the agreement of a competent organ of the UN. For example, NATO forces asked to assist UNPROFOR in Bosnia-Herzegovina and US assistance under UNITAF in Somalia would fall within this element of the definition.

[165] *Ibid.*, p. 625. However, Article 20(a) of the Convention, a 'savings clause', indicates that the special protective status given to non-combatant UN forces neither derogates from those provisions of humanitarian law that would protect such forces, nor removes the responsibility of non-combatant UN forces to respect the law.

one or more states are outside the scope of the Convention. The Convention also provides further evidence that enforcement measures by the UN are subject to humanitarian law. In particular, Article 2(2) is entirely consistent with this contention and, in defining the scope and application, establishes that it:

> shall not apply to a UN operation authorised by the Security Council as an enforcement action under Chapter VII of the Charter of the UN in which any of the personnel are engaged as combatants against organised armed forces and to which the law of international armed conflict applies.[166]

Chapter VII operations are thus excluded from the scope of the Convention upon the fulfilment of this cumulative list of conditions.[167] Even if only part of the operation fulfils these conditions, all of the UN elements participating in that operation will be excluded from its protection.

Initially, the ICRC and some states had concerns regarding the reference to international armed conflict, but the wording of Article 2(2) proved acceptable in the end because it was generally agreed that it was impossible for the UN to be involved in internal armed conflict. Once UN or associated personnel intervene or became engaged in a conflict with a local force (as opposed to acting merely in self-defence), the conflict becomes, by definition, 'international' in character. Identifying whether any of the personnel are engaged as combatants against organised armed forces and whether the operation is one to which humanitarian law applies is more problematic. The formulation was designed to be consistent with common Article 2 of the Geneva Conventions and, thus, the point of analysis is whether the operation involves combat during an international armed conflict, thereby triggering the application of Article 2 while excluding the application of the UN Convention. This element will prove difficult to interpret in practice and the fact that there is no agreement on which provisions of humanitarian law apply to UN personnel, and in what circumstances, will only add to the confusion. It is also predicted that the UN and troop-contributing states will be reluctant to recognise that the Convention has ceased to

---

[166] This should be read in conjunction with Article 1 (definitions) of the Convention.

[167] M. C. Bourloyannis-Vrailas, 'The Convention on the Safety of UN and Associated Personnel' (1995) 44 *International Comparative Law Quarterly* 560–90 at 567.

apply and that this policy will inflate the level of conflict required before acknowledging that 'armed conflict' is taking place.[168]

Another interpretation is that humanitarian law continues to apply to UN personnel when, in the conduct of a Chapter VII mandated operation, they are actively engaged in a combat mission, regardless of whether the armed conflict is international or internal in character. Humanitarian law would also be applicable in peacekeeping operations, which, however peaceful and consensual they may theoretically be, may in practice give rise to situations where UN personnel can resort to the use of force in self-defence or to resist attempts to prevent them carrying out their mandate.[169] However, in most traditional peacekeeping operations, situations where force is used in self-defence are short and cannot be described as involving sustained periods of fighting. Incidents of this nature do not by themselves remove the protection offered by the Convention because the UN troops involved are not necessarily engaged as combatants.

Under the Convention traditional peacekeeping forces enjoy a protected status similar to that of non-combatants. It effectively repeals the combatant's privilege: soldiers in the field who attack UN military personnel pursuant to the orders of their commanders are deemed to be committing a crime for which individual criminal responsibility is established.[170] It has been argued that in effect the Convention changes humanitarian law by criminalising attacks on UN forces and modifying the combatant's privilege as it applies to such attacks, without a concomitant recognition that the UN is governed in such situations by specific norms of the same body of law.[171] This conclusion is flawed. Under humanitarian law, where only non-combatants are protected from attack, UN personnel acting as combatants are bound both to apply these rules and to invoke their protection when appropriate. In this way, the Convention and humanitarian law are mutually exclusive: the former regime applies to non-conflict situations and the latter to any situation of a sufficient degree of armed conflict.

---

[168] See C. Greenwood, 'Protection of Peacekeepers: The Legal Regime', pp. 200–2.

[169] Shraga and Zacklin, in *Symposium* (note 2 above), pp. 46–7. See R. Murphy, 'UN Peacekeeping in Lebanon and the Use of Force' (1999) 6(2) *International Peacekeeping* 38–63.

[170] Article 9 of the Convention.

[171] R. Glick, 'Lip Service to the Laws of War: Humanitarian Law and UN Armed Forces' (1995) 17 *Michigan Journal of International Law* 53–107 at 81–96.

The exact scope and nature of UN operations covered by the Convention are matters on which there is a divergence of opinion. Originally, the Convention was to be limited to operations 'established pursuant to a mandate approved by a resolution of the Security Council'.[172] A broader material scope of application of the Convention was eventually agreed.[173] The view that the Convention applies to most kinds of UN operations which fall short of enforcement action is the dominant opinion, although the protection provided thereunder might not extend to all stages and components of the military operation.[174] The confusion arises primarily from the different perspectives among countries as to the actual purpose of the Convention. Many were critical of the scope and expansion of the Security Council's activities, but were powerless to prevent it. They saw the approval of a Convention covering traditional peacekeepers as a means to reign in the Security Council. As a result, arguing that the instrument should only apply to traditional peacekeeping operations somewhat misses the point. It is precisely because of Somalia-type operations that pressure was brought to bear to deal with the legal deficiencies which exist in the international regime.[175]

The end result remains unsatisfactory in that the difficulty of distinguishing between peacekeeping and enforcement operations, while making provision for hybrid operations involving both, has not been properly taken into account. This crucial issue, like the question relating to the applicability of humanitarian law to UN operations, continues to be unresolved. Why is the Convention so replete with references to the characteristics of traditional peacekeeping duties, i.e. impartiality, host state consent and the non-use of force except in self-defence? The outstanding issues relate to when and who determines that a confrontation between UN troops and others reaches the threshold that the participants may be regarded as combatants under Article 2(2) of the

---

[172] UN Doc. A/AC.242/L.2, proposal by New Zealand and Ukraine, Article 1, paragraph 2. Civilian UN personnel were also unhappy with the original proposals: interview, Ambassador P. Kirsch, former chairman of the negotiations on the Convention, Galway, August 2000.

[173] For background see A. Bouvier, 'Convention on the Safety of UN and Associated Personnel' (1995) *International Review of the Red Cross* No. 309, 638–66.

[174] Shraga and Zacklin, in *Symposium* (note 2 above), p. 46. S. Lepper, 'War Crimes and the Protection of Peacekeeping Forces' (1995) 28 *Akron Law Review* 411–15 at 415.

[175] Interview, Ambassador Kirsch. There was also concern among some states to avoid condoning the possible future presence of NGOs on their territory, and the issue of consent to the presence of UN forces in the first instance.

Convention. Did Aideed's forces in Somalia constitute 'organised forces' for the purposes of the Convention? These are not straightforward matters. It is evident from the foregoing that the Convention is a poorly drafted document that was heavily influenced by political factors. As a compromise document, governments like that of Canada and Ireland may take some solace from the fact that the troops serving with missions in Kosovo and Bosnia-Herzegovina are protected by the terms of the Convention. But how this will work in practice is anyone's guess and it presents a potential nightmare for a prosecutor seeking to invoke the terms of the Convention.

There is also the issue of European and Western neo-colonialism acting under the cloak of UN activity.[176] How will the Convention operate in a situation like Somalia, when a major contributor to the UN force decides to target a clan or militia leader, and sometimes operates outside of the UN command structure? The problem with accepting that peace enforcement operations come within its remit is that the Convention seeks to criminalise action by military forces against UN mandated or authorised peace enforcement operations. What happens when these operations are outside the formal framework of the organisation, and come under the umbrella of traditional and reciprocal inter-power relations to which the humanitarian law of armed conflict naturally applies? During wartime combat operations or hostile acts engaged in during an armed conflict, combatants do not commit crimes by killing or wounding the 'enemy' if this is carried out in a manner that does not conflict with the rules of humanitarian law.[177] It cannot be correct that military action at the behest of political or other leaders, which is otherwise in accordance with humanitarian law, could render the combatants concerned liable to prosecution under the Convention. Such a scenario would place these forces in an invidious position, which, it is submitted, is neither the intention nor the effect of the Convention.

---

[176] Some states have reviewed their positions and expressed reservations about the Security Council's use of Chapter VII: see J. Ciechanski, 'Enforcement Measures under Chapter VII of the UN Charter: UN Practice after the Cold War', and D. Daniel and B. Hayes, 'Securing Observance of UN Mandates Through the Employment of Military Force', in M. Pugh (ed.), *The UN, Peace and Force*, pp. 82–104 at 97, and pp. 105–25 at 106, respectively.

[177] Under the Geneva Conventions Relative to the Treatment of Prisoners of War of August 12, 1949, 75 UNTS 135 (Third Geneva Convention), prisoners of war, that is, captured enemy combatants, cannot be prosecuted or punished for having fought in accordance with humanitarian law.

Doubts have been expressed about the Convention's usefulness and the question was raised whether it did not rather belong to *jus ad bellum* (right to war) – as it contains the prohibition to wage war at the UN – than to *jus in bello*.[178] The Convention does address what was a significant gap in international law as, prior to the coming into effect of the Statute of the International Criminal Court in July 2002,[179] no international instrument prohibited or provided legal remedies for attacks upon traditional peacekeeping forces acting in that role. However, the Convention does not have a significant impact on the humanitarian law implications of UN operations and its adoption marks a lost opportunity to clarify rather than further obfuscate the question. It also avoids the thorny issue of the consequences if the procedure and/or the adoption of UN resolutions authorising or mandating certain kinds of peace enforcement operations are themselves not in accordance with the UN Charter and international law. In short, the Convention bears all the scars of a behind-the-scenes battle regarding the separate but linked issue of the expanded powers of the Security Council.

Humanitarian law and UN forces in Lebanon and Somalia

The Predicament of UNIFIL

As UNIFIL was being established, the President of the ICRC wrote to the Secretary-General, drawing his attention to the necessity for forces placed at the disposal of the UN to comply with the Geneva Conventions.[180] Later, the Secretary-General wrote to the troop-contributing states advising that, in situations where members of UNIFIL have to use weapons in self-defence, the principles and spirit of humanitarian law 'as contained, *inter alia*, in the Geneva Conventions . . . [and] the Protocols . . . shall apply'. Troop-contributing states were obliged to ensure that their troops fully understood the principles of humanitarian law. For its part, the UN consented to undertake, 'through the chain of command, the task of supervising the effective compliance with the

---

[178] See comments to this effect in the Notes on the Conference on 'The UN and International Humanitarian Law', Geneva, 19–20 October 1995, in M. Meijer, (1995) 2(6) *International Peacekeeping* 136–8 at 137.

[179] Article 8(2)(d)(iii) of the Statute of the ICC prohibits attacks on peacekeepers 'so long as they are entitled to the protection given to civilians or civilian objects under the international law of armed conflict': Triffterer (ed.), *Commentary on the Rome Statue of the International Criminal Court*, pp. 277–8.

[180] U. Palwankar, 'Applicability of International Humanitarian Law', pp. 227–40 at 230.

principles of humanitarian law by the contingents of its peacekeeping forces'.[181] But no system for monitoring such activity was ever put in place. Similarly, relevant training seemed to be conducted on an *ad hoc* basis and did not always achieve the desired level of knowledge.[182]

When the Israeli forces invaded and subsequently occupied most of south Lebanon in 1982, UNIFIL was presented with a number of serious challenges. It was never envisaged that the force would find itself alongside non-Lebanese forces within UNIFIL's area of operations. In the circumstances, UNIFIL was unable to enforce its standing operating procedures or to make any serious attempt to carry out its mandate. Not surprisingly, UN officials used every means at their disposal to justify the continued presence of UNIFIL in such an adverse situation.

The legality of Israeli actions in Lebanon received little public attention up until the report of the International Commission established to enquire into reported violations of international law by Israel during its 1982 invasion.[183] In the absence of an official UN investigating authority, it was considered essential to establish an independent international tribunal or commission to investigate complaints against Israel.[184] The Commission dealt comprehensively with a wide range of matters arising from Israeli policy throughout Lebanon and concluded that Israel had violated a number of international legal principles and conventions governing the laws of war.

The question of the Israeli treatment of Lebanese civilians in the aftermath of the invasion was first brought before the Security Council in 1984[185] in response to two draft resolutions introduced by the Lebanese government to the Security Council calling on Israel to comply with the provisions of the Fourth Geneva Convention and the regulations annexed to the Hague Convention of 1907. UNIFIL was thus

---

[181] *Ibid.*, pp. 232–3.
[182] This conclusion was arrived at from a visit to UNIFIL in 1998, and discussions with a number of contingent commanders.
[183] *Israel in Lebanon: Report of the International Commission to Enquire into Reported Violations of International Law by Israel During Its Invasion of the Lebanon* (London: Ithaca Press, 1983). See also Human Rights Watch, *Civilian Pawns: Laws of War Violations and the Use of Weapons on the Israeli-Lebanon Border* (New York: Human Rights Watch, 1996).
[184] *Ibid.*, Preface, pp. xi–x. The Commission was comprised of Mr S. MacBride (Chairman), Professor R. Falk, K. Asmal, Dr B. Bercusson, Professor G. de la Pradelle and Professor S. Wild.
[185] UN Doc. S/16713, 24 August 1984, letter from the representative of Lebanon to the Council President. The four Geneva Conventions of 1949 were ratified by Lebanon and Israel in 1951. Neither was party to the Additional Protocols of 1977.

inadvertently presented with an opportunity to play a role in ensuring Israeli observance of these Conventions.[186] While the Security Council prevaricated over what to do about the peacekeeping force, the role of safeguarding the rights of a civilian population under occupation provided a reasonable solution to the problem in the short term. This policy was a reaction to events rather than a carefully planned response.

Since the invasion undermined the whole *raison d'être* of the force, adopting such a role provided an interim solution to the total disregard of UNIFIL's authority by Israel. However, the force could do little to influence the major events taking place elsewhere in the country, and unless it was prepared to intervene within its own area it risked being held responsible for Israeli actions there.[187] Faced with an impossible situation, UNIFIL did perform a worthwhile function in highlighting breaches of humanitarian law but, more importantly, it ensured compliance with fundamental principles that seemingly would otherwise have been disregarded. This aspect of UNIFIL's presence at the time should not be underestimated: even those Lebanese who were often critical of the force's failure to carry out its mandate agreed that it played an important role during the period. However, the situation presented particular difficulties for UNIFIL that deserve closer analysis.

Israeli forces adopted what became known as an 'iron fist' policy during 1984 to deter further attacks, putting UNIFIL in an impossible position.[188] In the changed situation, there was an urgent need to define

---

[186] The Lebanese draft resolution called upon Israel as the Occupying Power, to respect strictly the rights of the civilian population in the area under its occupation and to comply strictly with the provisions of the Fourth Geneva Convention. The vote on the text (S/16732) was fourteen in favour, to one against (the United States); there were no abstentions. The draft resolution was not adopted due to the negative vote of the United States. See also SCOR, 2552th Meeting, 29 August 1984, to 2556th Meeting, 4 September 1984.

[187] There were also grave risks for UNIFIL of being caught in crossfire or being deliberately targeted by parties to the conflict: see D. Turns, 'Some Reflections on the Conflict in Southern Lebanon: The "Qana Incident" and International Humanitarian Law' (2000) 5 *Journal of Conflict and Security Law* 177–209.

[188] Beginning in February 1984, the policy involved, *inter alia*, the deportation of Lebanese from their home villages, expulsions of local inhabitants, curfews, mass arrests, internment, the transfer of suspects and the increased destruction of homes belonging to suspected resistance fighters. The plan was reportedly sanctioned by the Israeli Defence Minister and was likened to that used in the Gaza Strip in the early 1970s to curtail Palestinian unrest: see R. Fisk, *The Times*, 15 February and 21 February 1985. For a more extensive account by the same author, see R. Fisk, *Pity the Nation* (London: Andre Deutsch, 1990), especially pp. 243–81.

the policy that UNIFIL should adopt and, in response, the Secretary-General issued the following statement:

> [A] new situation has developed in southern Lebanon ... UNIFIL is now stationed in an area where active resistance against IDF is in progress, and in which the latter is engaged in active countermeasures. UNIFIL, for obvious reason, has no right to impede Lebanese acts of resistance against the occupying force, nor does it have the mandate or the means to prevent countermeasures ... It seems to me that the only course for UNIFIL is to maintain its presence and to continue within its limited means to carry out its existing functions in the area.[189]

This highlighted the dilemma facing UNIFIL as it had neither the means nor the authority to prevent resistance attacks against Israeli forces and the subsequent countermeasures by Israel. It remained unclear as to how UNIFIL was to distinguish between Palestinian guerrillas and local resistance groups attempting to infiltrate by night through UNIFIL lines, and the Secretary-General's call to carry out existing functions was not elaborated upon. In attempting to monitor the Israeli raids on villages, UNIFIL sometimes appeared to be in collusion with the occupiers. The sight of UNIFIL soldiers alongside Israeli soldiers created the illusion and belief that UNIFIL was helping to carry out the raid.[190] The policy also meant that UNIFIL avoided the potentially difficult issue of which, if any, resistance groups were entitled to recognition.

Notwithstanding the position adopted, a number of confrontations occurred when UNIFIL denied unauthorised armed personnel passage through its checkpoints. An incident in the Irish area in November 1985 demonstrates UNIFIL's dangerous predicament, highlighting the ease with which armed elements could mobilise and the consequent vulnerability of UNIFIL personnel.[191] It could be argued that the armed elements should have been granted total freedom of movement. While this would have been consistent with the Secretary-General's policy statement, UNIFIL had to draw the line somewhere. Had it allowed unauthorised Lebanese armed

---

[189] UN Doc. S/17093, 11 April 1985, para. 24.

[190] The leader of Amal, Mr. Nabbi Berri, accused UNIFIL of helping the Israelis on occasions: *The Irish Times*, 23 January 1985. Other groups made similar accusations, *The Times*, 22 February 1985.

[191] UN Doc. S/17684, 16 December 1985, para. 7. A confrontation developed when Irish soldiers apprehended four armed men. A UNIFIL patrol dispatched to the scene was intercepted and detained by armed elements. Other Irish positions were quickly surrounded by armed elements and UNIFIL reinforcements fired on. Fire was returned and the situation was later resolved by negotiations with senior Amal personnel.

elements complete freedom of movement, it would have relinquished the last vestiges of authority that it possessed in the area. As it was, the policy of co-operating with the moderate Shiite movement, Amal, allowed the group's members considerable scope in the area.

The situation deteriorated as the Israeli Defence Forces redeployed in 1985 and clashes occurred with UNIFIL troops. The French battalion in particular adopted a more forceful stance than many of the other UNIFIL contingents.[192] Irish UNIFIL troops also clashed with the Israelis, especially during raids on the Shiite village of Yatar.[193] But UNIFIL's policy of monitoring and reporting did little to instil confidence among the population who accused it of being 'both the observer and protector of the [Israeli] invasion army'.[194] UNIFIL policy appeared to be accomplishing little, leading to the aforementioned allegations of collusion.[195] Such conclusions are both ironic and unfair: UNIFIL personnel sent to monitor Israeli operations often placed themselves in danger in attempting to mitigate the excessive behaviour of the Israelis and their allies. UNIFIL was, in effect, placed in a 'no-win' situation and, perhaps predictably, a serious threat was made against UNIFIL by one of the resistance groups soon after the 'iron fist' policy began.[196] In such circumstances, it was difficult to determine whether UNIFIL's accomplishments justified its continued presence in south Lebanon. Its function was rendered unclear and its overall predicament unsatisfactory. In fact, reports to the Security Council in 1985 and 1986 were very pessimistic and displayed little hope for improving the situation. However, the Secretary-General continued to recommend extensions of the mandate.

---

[192] In one incident, the French became involved in a fist-fight with the Israelis whilst trying to prevent the latter from blowing up houses. They were also reported to have laid the French Tricolour at the entrance to a village, threatening to shoot the first Israeli to drive over it. The Israelis are reported to have retreated. R. Fisk, *The Times*, 28 February 1985.

[193] In the first joint Israeli/'South Lebanon Army' operation, during which the latter forces played the leading role, an attempt to forcefully evict Irish troops from their post was successfully resisted. See R. Fisk, *Irish Times*, 8 March 1985. The report was confirmed by Commandant B. McKevitt who was then serving with 56 Infantry Battalion. The Israelis used the South Lebanon Army to extend the 'security zone' and push the Irish back from certain posts in their way. The Irish refused to move from posts such as 'Charlies Mountain' (Al Yatun) despite Israeli demands to do so. *Irish Times*, 21 and 22 March 1985 and 1 April 1985; and *Guardian*, 21 March 1985.

[194] Personal interview, senior Irish officer who served with UNIFIL at the time, Dublin, June 1998.

[195] R. Fisk, *The Times*, 22 February 1985.

[196] *Ibid*. The threat was made by the Shia Muslim organisation, Hizbollah.

The anomalous position of UNIFIL was evident during a serious incident in February 1986 when Israeli forces and their surrogates in the so-called 'South Lebanon Army' were ambushed near the village of Kunin in the Israeli-controlled 'security zone'.[197] Two Israeli soldiers were abducted, leading to a series of Israeli cordon and search operations. UNIFIL monitored the situation as closely as possible and tried to prevent acts of violence against the local population[198] and, in so doing, put themselves at risk, especially with regard to the less disciplined 'South Lebanon Army'. The Secretary-General's report of the incident states that UNIFIL personnel

> observed some cases of what appeared to be unacceptable treatment of prisoners by IDF/SLA [Israeli Defence Force/South Lebanon Army] personnel. The UNIFIL reports of the incidents were transmitted immediately to the Israeli authorities and their comments invited.[199]

As a result of the operation, a number of local civilians registered complaints regarding the treatment they received.[200] The most serious of these was that the Israeli forces attempted to expel all of the locals from the village of Kunin in retaliation for the abductions and that Israeli actions violated a number of provisions of the Fourth Geneva Convention.

While the Israeli anger is understandable, its response was disproportionate;[201] the attempt to expel all of the Shiite residents of Kunin could

---

[197] UN Doc. S/17965, 9 April 1986, para. 21.

[198] UNIFIL reported that six persons, including one Israeli soldier, were killed in the operation, ten more were wounded and about 150 others were taken prisoner by the Israeli/'South Lebanon Army' forces. Eighty of the detained were released soon afterwards; however, the other sixty were held indefinitely.

[199] *Ibid.* Israel claimed that its forces had received clear instructions on how to behave towards the local civilian population before and during the operation, and that follow-up investigations of all Israeli army units involved had found no deviation from these instructions.

[200] Personal interview with senior Lebanese Red Cross official, 19 September 1989, and local civilians from villages affected, September and October 1989. The Secretary-General's report states that, following the incident, an Israeli force of about three mechanised battalions, accompanied by members of the SLA and supported by tanks and helicopter troop-carriers and gunships, carried out a series of cordon-and-search operations in the UNFIIL area from 17 to 22 February. UN Doc. S/17965, 9 April 1986, para. 21.

[201] Those detained were blindfolded and had their hands tied behind their backs. Many of the suspects were beaten. Personal interviews with UNIFIL officers who witnessed such events at the time. For an account of Israeli Defence Forces actions in Lebanon, see D. Yermiya, *My War Diary: Israel in Lebanon* (London: Pluto Press, 1983). The pamphlet,

be justified on neither military nor security grounds.[202] Rather, the large number of civilians detained indicates that the follow-up operation was retaliatory and intended to coerce information from the detainees. There was a similar threat to other villages in the UN area but these were thwarted by UNIFIL intervention. As a result, the peacekeeping force is owed some credit for protecting the civilian population in the area.[203]

The Israelis faced a dilemma insofar as their tactics alienated the population and incurred international condemnation. In addition, they remained apparently unable to defeat the resistance groups and Israelis themselves began to question whether the tactics adopted were compatible with the so-called 'purity of arms' doctrine.[204] In fact, the policy was so evidently self-defeating that it was difficult to discern any coherent long-term goal. Many of the Shiite villages that suffered most during this period were strongly opposed to the Palestinian presence prior to the invasion. Their hatred subsequently switched to the Israelis and attempts to have the 'South Lebanon Army' adopt a more prominent role only made matters worse. Figures compiled by the UN in 1985 indicate that the 'iron fist' policy failed. Daily attacks on Israeli soldiers increased considerably and, in one well-publicised suicide attack by a Shiite resistance fighter, twelve Israeli soldiers were killed.[205] It was the eighth attack of its kind and the Israeli response was predictable. True to form, a major operation was launched against a number of villages.

Operation Iron Fist: Israeli Policy in Lebanon, published by the League of Arab States (London, May 1985), gives a somewhat biased chronology of events.

[202] Article 49(2) of the fourth Geneva Convention states: 'the Occupying Power may undertake total or partial evacuation if the security of the population or imperative military reasons so demand'. Neither justification was applicable in this instance: see Pictet, *Commentary: Geneva Convention IV*, pp. 277–83.

[203] Israeli tactics led to widespread and unnecessary damage being caused to the property and personal belongings of villagers, contrary to Article 53 of the fourth Geneva Convention: UN Doc. S/17965, 9 April 1986, paras. 13–15; and interviews with local inhabitants living in the areas searched at the time, July to October 1989. When the Israeli troops were assisted or followed by the *de facto* forces, the damage caused to property was much worse and the operation frequently turned into one of terrorising and ill-treating villagers. The 'South Lebanon Army' also engaged in looting, and harassment of UNIFIL troops. The Israeli troops made no attempt to restrain them from the excesses despite their responsibility under Article 29 and Section III of the fourth Geneva Convention respectively.

[204] The doctrine is known as Tohar Haneshek and penetrates all aspects of Israeli Defence Forces life: see K. A. Gabriel, *Operation Peace for Galilee: The Israeli PLO War in Lebanon* (Toronto: Collins, 1985), paras. 171–6.

[205] *Irish Times*, 11 March 1985.

leaving at least thirty-two dead. Throughout 1985, numerous cordon and search operations were carried out and Israeli forces frequently shelled villages, particularly in the Irish area. During this period, the Israelis continued their efforts to impose the 'South Lebanon Army' on the people of the south while dangerous confrontations ensued when UNIFIL tried to curtail the activities of this militia.[206]

This state of affairs caused many things to unravel: maintenance of the security zone effectively precluded UNIFIL from carrying out patrols in the battalion sectors, for fear of being mistaken for resistance fighters by the 'South Lebanon Army'. In addition, many vulnerable checkpoints and observation posts were closed, diminishing the effectiveness of the force considerably. This led to criticism of the manner in which Irish soldiers fulfilled their peacekeeping role and there were a number of controversial incidents in the Irish sector,[207] in particular the abduction of local resistance leaders from the Irish area of operations in December 1988. Some supposed Irish collusion in the affair and, as a result, a checkpoint was overrun on the next day and three Irish soldiers kidnapped by armed elements. With the help of Amal, the soldiers were found alive and well,[208] yet the whole affair highlighted a number of weaknesses in the UNIFIL and Irish performance in Lebanon.[209] Why were the Israelis able to enter the area in daylight and abduct civilians? What was UNIFIL's function if it could not, or would not, prevent such abductions? In March 1989, the resistance movement exacted further revenge for the perceived collusion when three Irish soldiers were targeted and killed by a land mine.[210]

The most serious aspect for UNIFIL as a whole, however, was its reliance upon the Amal movement to resolve the affair. While there were some confrontations with Amal since the Israeli redeployment, UNIFIL's

---

[206] UN Doc. S/17684, 16 December 1985, paras. 2–7. The Norwegian battalion had particular difficulty with these groups when restrictions were imposed on the movement of UNIFIL personnel.

[207] See for example the comments in (1998) 11 *International Defence Review* 1434.

[208] See Secretary-General's report, UN Doc. S/20416, 24 January 1989. An extremist group intended to take the soldiers to Beirut.

[209] It was even said that 'Irish soldiers now see their prime task as staying alive until the end of their period of duty'. This is hardly surprising given the relatively high number of Irish casualties in Lebanon to date and the lack of co-operation from the parties to the conflict.

[210] This conclusion is based on conversations with local resistance fighters during 1989; see also H. McDonald, *IISHBATT: The Story of Ireland's Blue Berets in the Lebanon* (Dublin: Gill and Macmillan, 1993), pp. 116–17.

general relations with the movement gradually improved and, in due course, the level of co-operation between the two amounted to an unofficial alliance. This can be explained in that there was no effective governmental authority in the south and Amal was the closest thing to some form of authority. In addition, there were rival governments in Beirut for a prolonged period while Amal's leader remained minister for the south. The movement also had considerable support in the area and was pro-UNIFIL, while the alternative was Hizbollah, which did not support the force's presence in Lebanon. Nonetheless, the level of co-operation between UNIFIL and Amal risked compromising impartiality. This was one of the most serious threats to UNIFIL's precarious position as regards general acceptability in the area.

Summary

The degree of control exercised by Israel before and after the 1985 redeployment was sufficient to justify the UN's decision to treat the Israeli forces as an Occupying Power under international law and this, in turn, determined the nature of UNIFIL's response. However, there is no escaping the inconsistency between the UNIFIL policy regarding the Occupying Power and the indigenous resistance movements and its original mandate and terms of reference. In granting the Israelis the rights and privileges of an Occupying Power, while at the same time deliberately avoiding impeding acts of resistance, the peace-keeping force made no progress whatsoever in confirming the Israeli withdrawal or bringing about a cessation of hostilities. Nonetheless, the performance of humanitarian tasks as an interim measure was worthwhile insofar as it eased the plight of the local population and maintained goodwill towards UNIFIL. Its additional accomplishment is that it undermined Hizbollah leaders and others within Lebanon who sought to discredit the force as a 'tool of American imperialism'. However, the good achieved does not justify the continued presence of a 6,000-strong peacekeeping force in what was effectively occupied territory, unable to perform any of its original tasks laid down by the Security Council. Whether UNIFIL would have achieved as much or even more by withdrawing at the time will never be known. The government of the Netherlands obviously thought so when it decided to withdraw the Dutch contingent. In the long term, an alternative peacekeeping force could have been deployed under a more realistic mandate in circumstances more conducive to the conduct of peacekeeping.

The presence of UNIFIL rendered the Israeli occupation of south Lebanon unique and less harsh than otherwise would have been the case. UNIFIL gave the local population support and protection by intervening to prevent, by non-violent means, the demolition of public and private property and the ill-treatment of civilians. A major achievement during this period was the ability to hinder Israeli consolidation of its occupation of Lebanon. Some commentators were critical of the policy of treating the Israeli forces as an Occupying Power, owing to the presence of UNIFIL as the legitimate military power in its area of operation.[211] However, it was neither an instrument of the Lebanese government nor a replacement for the Lebanese Army. It is true that there was a lack of consistency among the different UNIFIL battalions in their policy towards the Israeli forces and the 'South Lebanon Army'. The peacekeeping force had no option but to accept the reality of its predicament, 'without the mandate or firepower to do more, UNIFIL found itself in the unenviable position of watching the rockets and shells fire back and forth overhead, while on occasion falling victim to direct hits itself'.[212] The real shame is that the Security Council did nothing to change this, and that UN forces were sidelined to fulfil a role essentially as witnesses and protestors to violations of humanitarian law.

Somalia

Somalia, on the other hand, shifted from a traditional peacekeeping mission to one of robust peace enforcement and seemingly little attention was paid to the political and legal consequences of this escalation. The consequent situation, therefore, provides a stark example of UN military forces operating in the twilight zone between peace and armed conflict or war. In this intervening no man's land, '[a] clear demarcation between a state of war and a state of peace no longer exist[ed], if it ever

---

[211] M. Heiberg and J. J. Holst, 'Keeping the Peace in Lebanon: Assessing International and Multinational Peacekeeping' Norwegian Institute of International Affairs, Working Paper No. 357, 1986, pp. 13–14. See also M. Heiberg and J. J. Holst, 'Peacekeeping in Lebanon: Comparing UNIFIL and the MNF', Norwegian Institute of International Affairs, Working Paper, 1986, p. 406. It was submitted that, since UNIFIL continued to operate as a legitimate military authority, inside the area of operation, the IDF did not exert exclusive control and therefore should not have been regarded as an Occupying Power.

[212] Human Rights Watch, *Civilian Pawns*, p. 35.

did'.[213] This is problematic in that, in the theatre of military operations, the determination as to which rules apply depends on the level of conflict, as this 'dictates the nature of the law applicable ... either the internal law of the state or international humanitarian law'.[214] In short, in order to understand and abide by the rules of the game, participants must first know what those rules are; but the situation in Somalia did not enable this. Despite the level of hostilities, the reported body count, and the armed confrontations and shooting, a definitive characterisation of the conflict remained elusive and, accordingly, so did the determination of applicable law. This gave rise to the assertion that the application of the Geneva Conventions and Additional Protocols to the situation merely demonstrated the inadequacies in the international legal regime with regard to meeting the complexities presented by peacekeeping operations.[215] Nevertheless, in the relations between UNITAF forces and the parties to the conflict, it must surely be the case that the rules of humanitarian law were applicable. To accept anything less would be to adopt a minimalist view that denies the clear international character of the mission.

The problem of determining which set of rules in international law is applicable to peace operations is not unique to UNIFIL or UNOSOM II: the issue has arisen in other contexts, such as the court-martial of a United States army officer, Captain Lawrence P. Rockwood. A member of the United States-led Multinational Force in Haiti,[216] Captain Rockwood was convicted of felony charges arising from his unauthorised human rights inspection of Haiti's National Penitentiary in September 1994. In determining Rockwood's fate, the military trial judge ultimately refused to instruct the court-martial of the applicability of international law, telling the members of the court that they should bear in mind that expert witnesses could not agree on the parameters of international law applicable to the case. The outcome of this case supports the notion that peacekeepers have a limited remit: it emphasises the preservation of peace to the detriment of a potential role in the protection of the local population. However, peacekeeping also involves

---

[213] P. Zengel, 'Assassination and the Law of Armed Conflict' (1992) 43 *Mercer Law Review* 615 at 644.

[214] R. Kiwanuka, 'Humanitarian Norms and Internal Strife: Problems and Prospects', in F. Karlhoven and Y. Sandoz (eds.), *Implementation of International Humanitarian Law* (Dordrecht and London: Nijhoff, 1989), pp. 229–34.

[215] Turley, 'Keeping the Peace', p. 156.

[216] *United States* v. *Captain L. P. Rockwood II*, (1998) 48 MJ 501.

positive duties on behalf of the military personnel involved. This is where humanitarian law has a role to play. First and foremost, however, the responsibilities of the military must be spelt out in clear terms, preferably in the mandate, in order to be useful in a military culture. In this regard, the adoption of the role of Protecting Power by traditional peacekeepers is one option that could be examined.[217] However, it is not appropriate for peace enforcement operations as the requisite neutrality would not exist.

The issue of the applicability of humanitarian law was considered by a military court with regard to the activity of Canadian forces in Somalia in *R. v. Brocklebank*.[218] The case arose from the capture while attempting an intrusion into a UNITAF camp and torture to death of a sixteen-year-old Somali civilian at the hands of Canadian forces part of the UNITAF mission in March 1993.[219] These events ultimately led to a military Board of Inquiry, several courts-martial and appeals, and the establishment of a civilian Commission of Enquiry into the deployment of Canadian forces to Somalia ('the Commission'). Although the Commission discussed the issue specifically of the applicability of the Geneva Conventions and Protocols, it did not reach any firm conclusion in this regard. This is unfortunate, but it is also preferable to making decisions on matters that it may not have felt competent or able to decide in the circumstances.

The decision in *Brocklebank* concerned, *inter alia*, the applicability of the Unit Guide to the Geneva Conventions, which imposes on members of Canadian forces at all times a duty to safeguard civilians in Canadian forces custody, whether or not these civilians are in that member's custody. The court concluded that, as there was no declared war or

---

[217] A Protecting Power was anticipated in the Geneva Conventions as a state that is a neutral party to a conflict, instructed by the belligerent parties to protect the interests of warring states' nationals, 'protected persons' and those detained in an armed conflict. See Article 8 common to Geneva Convention I, II and III.

[218] Court Martial Appeal Court of Canada, (1996) 134 DLR (4th) 377. Private Brocklebank was arrested for aiding and abetting the torture of Shidane Arone, a Somali teenager who entered the Canadian Forces compound and was tortured and beaten to death while in custody. See K. Boustany, 'Brocklebank: A Questionable Decision of the Court Martial Appeal Court of Canada' (1998) 1 *Yearbook of International Humanitarian Law* 371–4; and J. Holland, 'Canadian Courts Martial Resulting from Participation in the UNITAF Mission in Somalia' (1994) 1(4) *International Peacekeeping* 131–2.

[219] See R. M. Young and M. Molina, 'IHL and Peace Operations: Sharing Canada's Lessons Learned from Somalia' (1998) 1 *Yearbook of International Humanitarian Law* 362–70 at 370.

armed conflict in Somalia, and as the Canadian forces deployed as part of the UNITAF mission were performing peacekeeping duties, they were not engaged in an armed conflict. In the circumstances, the court held that Private Brocklebank had no legal obligation to ensure the safety of the prisoner, as neither the Geneva Conventions nor Additional Protocol II applied to Canadian forces in Somalia. Furthermore, neither the Conventions nor Protocols applied to a peacekeeping operation.

This analysis is flawed in a number of respects, some of which may spring from an inherent misunderstanding of the nature of the mission at hand. The judgment makes numerous references to the fact that the Canadian forces were, at the relevant point in time, involved in a 'peace-keeping mission'. This is simply not the case, as the UNITAF mission was authorised by the Security Council under Chapter VII. The circumstances indicate that the peacekeeping mission of UNOSOM I was replaced by a peace enforcement operation comprising a coalition of nations. Moreover, it is worth noting that Security Council Resolution 794 (1992) which established UNITAF vigorously condemned all violations of humanitarian law committed in Somalia.[220] This was a clear recognition by the Security Council that the conflict in Somalia was of a sufficient degree of intensity to trigger the application of humanitarian law. Despite this, Decary JA for the majority found that there was no evidence of an armed conflict. The court does not appear to have heard any evidence of the level of killings among the armed factions and the casualties among other contingents of UNITAF. Cognisance does not appear to have been taken of the reports of the Secretary-General on the situation in Somalia, up to and during this period. The judgment also seems to have placed too much emphasis on the need for a certificate from the Canadian Secretary of State for External Affairs stating that at a certain time a state of war or international or non-international armed conflict existed.[221] However, no authority in the Canadian government can make a decision which effectively exempts Canadian forces from the application of humanitarian law if it applies under international law. Not surprisingly, the *Brocklebank* decision has been questioned, most notably in the Simpson Study on the Law Applicable to Canadian Forces in Somalia 1992/93, which makes a strong case that the decision of the

---

[220] Adopted 3 December 1992.
[221] Pursuant to section 9 of the Geneva Conventions Act of 1956. See *Simpson Study* (note 6 above), pp. 26–8.

court appears to have been, at least partly, based on the wrong provisions of the Fourth Geneva Convention and Protocols.[222]

The difficulty surrounding this issue was evident in the inconclusive findings of the Commission and the diverse views of other commentators.[223] It is noteworthy that a Belgian military court, acting as the Court of Appeals, also concluded that the four Geneva Conventions of 1949 and the two Additional Protocols of 1977 were not applicable to the armed conflict in Somalia.[224] In addition, members of UNOSOM II could not be considered 'combatants' since their primary task was not to fight any of the factions, nor could they be said to be an 'occupying force'. An Italian Commission of Inquiry also had difficulty grappling with this issue, and it failed to make any legal evaluation of the facts, especially from the perspective of humanitarian law.[225]

Another view proffered is that the situation in Somalia was not an international or non-international armed conflict within the established treaties.[226] However, a number of the relevant international instruments contain a substitute principle, the Martens Clause, which holds that, in cases not explicitly covered by treaty law, civilian persons and combatants remain under the protection and authority of the principles of international law.[227] It has also been argued that the provisions of the

---

[222] *Ibid.*, pp. 30–3. The Court Martial Appeal Court may have failed to properly consider the relevance of Articles 4 and 27 of the fourth Geneva Convention. The Canadian Forces may arguably have been a party to the conflict or may have been occupying part of Somalia within the meaning of the fourth Convention. If so, this would create a group of 'protected persons' that the court failed to recognise. The decision was also questioned by Boustany, 'Brocklebank: A Questionable Decision', p. 371; and Young and Molina, 'IHL and Peace Operations', pp. 365–7.

[223] Although the Commission avoided reaching a firm conclusion, a number of senior members of the Canadian Forces testified at the Commission's hearings that they thought the law of armed conflict applied in Somalia: *Simpson Study* (note 6 above), p. 27; and *Dishonoured Legacy* (note 23 above).

[224] Judgment of the Belgian Military Court regarding violations of IHL committed in Somalia and Rwanda, No. 54 AR 1997, 20 November. 1997. Published in *Journal des tribunaux*, 24 April 1998, pp. 286–9 (French language); and Comment by M. Cogen, (1998) 1 *Yearbook of International Humanitarian Law* 415–16.

[225] See N. Lupi, 'Report by the Enquiry Commission on the Behaviour of Italian Peacekeeping Troops in Somalia' (1998) 1 *Yearbook of International Humanitarian Law* 375–9.

[226] D. Hurley, 'An Application of the Laws of Armed Conflict', in Smith (ed.), *The Force of Law: International Law and the Land Commander* (Canberra: Australian Defence Studies Centre/Australian Defence Forces Academy, 1994), pp. 179–87 at p. 182. Col. Hurley commanded the 1st Royal Australian Regiment in Somalia.

[227] T. Meron, 'The Martens Clause, Principles of Humanity, and Dictates of Public Conscience' (2000) 94 *American Journal of International Law* 78–89; A. Cassese, 'The

Hague Rules, the Fourth Geneva Convention, and customary rules concerning an 'occupying power', could have applied in Somalia.[228] The policy of the United States is also interesting, in that, while applying the provisions of common Article 3 (internal armed conflicts), it made it clear that it did not consider the Fourth Geneva Convention applied during the UNITAF deployment. Despite the outcome of the *Brocklebank* decision, and whatever the category or qualification given to the situation in Somalia, it is difficult not to conclude that Private Brocklebank failed in a duty incumbent upon any soldier in the circumstances. There can be no grey areas when confronted with such blatant human rights abuses. Cognisance should have been taken of the Martens Clause as it imposes at all times the minimal but over-riding obligation to act in accordance with the laws of humanity and the dictates of public conscience.[229] No relativity such as that suggested by the majority decision of the court should be allowed in this regard.

Summary: practical difficulties applying the Conventions in Somalia

The most important determinant of the applicability of the humanitarian law is the level of hostilities, and Somalia presents no exception to this general rule. Common Article 2 of the Geneva Conventions states that they '[s]hall apply to all cases of declared war or any other armed conflict, which may arise between two or more of the High Contracting Parties, even if a state of war is not recognised by one of them'. One of the major difficulties with this provision is the ill-defined nature of what constitutes 'any other armed conflict'. It fails to address in clear

---

Martens Clause: Half a Loaf or Simply Pie in the Sky?' (2000) 11 *European Journal of International Law* 187–286; and G. Abi-Saab, 'Humanitarian Law and Internal Conflicts: The Evolution of Legal Concern', in A. Delissen and G. Tanja (eds.), *Humanitarian Law of Armed Conflict* (Dordrecht: Martinus Nijhoff, 1991), p. 222.

[228] M. J. Kelly, *Restoring and Maintaining Order in Complex Peace Operations* (The Hague: Kluwer, 1999), esp. pp. 111–182, and M. J. Kelly, 'Legal Regimes and Law Enforcement on Peace Operations', in Smith (ed.), *The Force of Law: International Law and the Land Commander*, pp. 189–204 at p. 193.

[229] This clause had previously been recognised as proof that under international law war does not totally negate the protection accorded to the civilian population: *Finta*, High Court of Justice, Canada, 10 July 1989, 82 ILR 435. Furthermore, in the *Corfu Channel Case* (Merits) (1949) ICJ Reports 22, the ICJ refers to the terms of the Martens clause as corresponding to what it had earlier identified under 'elementary considerations of humanity, even more exacting in peace than in war'.

legal terms at what stage the level of violence is sufficient to constitute armed conflict.[230] In this way, it may be described as humanitarian, but hardly definitive.[231] Its deliberately expansive nature is geared to ensuring that the humanitarian protections afforded by the Conventions are applicable in cases which fall short of declared war. In one sense this ambiguity may be described as a positive attribute, as it enables protections to be invoked in circumstances that could not have been envisaged at the time of drafting. However, this lack of precision can also be a major weakness in that the discretion bestowed on states may be abused.[232] The need for recognition by one of the relevant states is also a problem; it does not make allowances for situations in which none of the parties acknowledges that a state of war exists.[233] Not surprisingly, there is considerable support for the view that 'armed conflict' should be given a broad interpretation and that the existence of international armed conflict should not be regarded as contingent upon hostilities reaching a particular level of intensity.

The requirement of state recognition is especially problematical for UN military operations, as the UN is neither a party to the Conventions nor a state. It does not have the competence to recognise that an armed conflict exists and is therefore incapable of invoking the application of the Geneva Conventions. The Additional Protocols of 1977 were intended to address some of the more apparent deficiencies in the current system, but these too do not take into account the deployment of UN forces or multi-national forces authorised by the Security Council.[234] Protocol I appears to have no application to Somalia, as

---

[230] Although 'war crimes' are defined in Article 8 of the Statute of the ICC, these too are linked to the existence of an armed conflict situation: see Triffterer (ed.), *Commentary on the Rome Statue*, pp. 173–288; and W. A. Schabas, *An Introduction to the International Court* (2nd edn, Cambridge: Cambridge University Press, 2004), pp. 51–66.

[231] R. Miller, *The Law of War* (Lexington, MA, Lexington Books, 1975), p. 275. This is also the position of the ICRC.

[232] C. Nier, 'The Yugoslavian Civil War: An Analysis of the Applicability of the Laws of War Governing Non-International Armed Conflicts in the Modern World' (1992) 10 *Dickley Journal of International Law* 303 at 317.

[233] The drafters of the Hague Convention on the Protection of Cultural Property amended the phrase to read 'even if a state of war is not recognised by one or more of them'.

[234] Protocol I refers to struggles 'in which people are fighting against colonial domination and alien occupation and against racist regimes in the exercise of their right of self-determination': see *Commentary on the Additional Protocols of 8 June 1977 to the Geneva Conventions of 12 August 1946* (Geneva: ICRC, 1987), p. 33.

the clan fighting and conflict in general do not qualify as a struggle for self-determination, or a struggle against a racist regime.[235]

Protocol II, by contrast, applies only when there is a conflict between the armed forces of a High Contracting Party and dissident groups within the same territory. However, as regards Somalia, it is not possible to determine which faction, if any, could be deemed the 'lawful government'. A strong case can be made that Aideed's force fulfilled a number of important requirements to be regarded as a dissident organised force in control of a defined area, but the issue is so legitimately debatable that definitive conclusions are problematic. The level of fighting could also be regarded as having exceeded that regarded in other cases as sufficient to amount to armed conflict, and it meets the criteria suggested by Pictet and the Appeals Chamber of the International Criminal Tribunal for the Former Yugoslavia in the *Tadic* case.[236] The experiences of Bosnia-Herzegovina and Somalia, however, indicate that NATO and the UN adopt a certain *à la carte* policy when it comes to determining the existence of 'armed conflict' and whether they are parties thereto. It would also seem that the threshold for triggering armed conflict is higher in the case of military operations authorised or mandated by the UN.

The United States had the opportunity to recognise that an armed conflict took place in Somalia, but it pointedly declined to do so. The Clinton administration refused to declare it a war zone, arguing that, even after thirty United States solders had been killed and nearly two hundred wounded, and with many hundreds more Somali casualties, there had yet to be an event 'that makes it clear to everyone that this is combat, not peacekeeping'.[237] The lack of an authoritative method for determining when a situation justifies the application of humanitarian law remains a significant weakness in the contemporary legal framework governing situations of conflict. Basing a finding of the existence of war or armed conflict in a material sense, *inter alia*, on the duration of the conflict merely serves to facilitate the exclusion of short-term hostilities

---

[235] An interesting aspect to the applicability of Protocol I, and some other relevant treaties, is that not all states have ratified it, and this could give rise to the situation where different contingents in a unified force are governed by different principles of law. This situation arose in respect of the NATO forces engaged in the Kosovo conflict during 1999.

[236] See note 97 above; and Pictet, *Commentary: Geneva Convention IV*, pp. 17–44.

[237] Cited in Turley, 'Keeping the Peace', p. 136. For an account of US military action in Somalia, see M. Bowden, *Black Hawk Down* (New York: Penguin, 2000).

such as occurred in Somalia and elsewhere. Surely it would be preferable if measures were taken to ensure that humanitarian law applies to conflict situations, especially those involving UN military forces, as a matter of law, rather than upon the finding of the existence of material war or armed conflict. Somalia also raises issues of international human rights law. In response to international pressure and resolutions of the Security Council and the General Assembly, a programme was instigated for the investigation of human rights abuses. This led to the adoption of standing operation procedures for UNOSOM detentions to ensure compliance with relevant international standards. Up until that development, the systems in place had serious deficiencies.[238]

Kosovo

In the UN Secretary-General's Report of 12 July 1999, UNMIK's obligations to protect and promote human rights pursuant to Resolution 1244 were interpreted as a requirement that it be guided by internationally recognised human rights standards in the exercise of its authority. The UN administration of Kosovo, however, falls to a large extent outside the human rights implementation mechanisms that exist at an international level; as such, there is no framework within which aggrieved persons can enforce those rights.[239] In providing a secure environment, adherence to human rights norms by KFOR is especially important. KFOR also exercised a number of powers normally associated with police activity. In June 1999, civil authority did not exist and there was no legitimate criminal justice system, no law enforcement authority, and no judicial or penitentiary system. In the circumstances, it was essential that the commander of KFOR have the authority to detain individuals in order to accomplish his mission. Such decisions were military rather than judicial in nature and were made on a case-by-case basis. Persons were detained if they were deemed to constitute a threat and the civilian authorities were unable or unwilling to take authority for the matter.

Amnesty International repeatedly raised concerns about instances in which individual NATO-led peacekeeping forces in Kosovo and

---

[238] M. Kelly, 'The UN, Security and Human Rights: Achieving a Winning Balance', in White and Klassen (eds.), *The UN, Human Rights and Post-Conflict Situations*, pp. 118–48 at p. 130.

[239] M. Cordial, 'Outline of Presentation of Situation in Kosovo', in A. Faite and J. L. Grenier (eds.), *Expert Meeting on Multinational Operations, Geneva, 11–12 December 2003* (Geneva: ICRC, 2004), pp. 49–58 at p. 50.

Bosnia-Herzegovina failed to adhere to international human rights law and standards regarding detention.[240] Alleged violations included incidents of illegal and arbitrary arrest, ill-treatment and failure to protect the rights of those in custody. These shortcomings were attributed to a lack of civilian control and a lack of real accountability. What democratic control exists is exercised by the national governments over their respective contingents and this has exacerbated the situation. UNMIK had neither the legal jurisdiction nor the mandate to conduct investigations into KFOR activities, and NATO does not have an independent investigation mechanism for such purposes either. Amnesty also considered that the detention of people without review by a judicial body violated international law and standards.

Although KFOR's police role was gradually reduced in favour of the UNMIK police and the Kosovo Police Service, it still maintains checkpoints where people may be searched and may also be involved in house searches and detentions. In the circumstances, it is important to establish a mechanism with which to oversee such actions and to facilitate complaints from individuals whose rights may have been violated. As Serbia and Montenegro consented to the presence of international forces as part of a UN-mandated mission in Kosovo, the laws of occupation were not applicable *de jure* since there was no 'occupation' by hostile forces in the strict sense of that term.[241] Although the 'consent' was controversial, the military presence was approved by the Security Council and was consistent with the UN Charter.

The first UNMIK Regulation made domestic law applicable only insofar as it was compatible with human rights standards. It required all persons undertaking public duties or holding public office to observe international human rights standards. The matter of determining what law was applicable in Kosovo, crucial to establishing the rule of law, was problematic from the start. It was an issue, however, that needed to be resolved efficiently: in the absence of a generally accepted and understood legal framework, the situation would quickly have become chaotic. To prevent this, the Special Representative of the Secretary-General declared at an early stage that all legislative and executive authority with

---

[240] Letter from Amnesty International concerning lack of accountability of KFOR and SFOR, 20 October 2003.

[241] Faite and Grenier (eds.), *Expert Meeting on Multinational Operations*, p. 16; and M. Sassoli, 'Outline of De Jure and De Facto Applicability of the Law of Occupation to United Nations-Mandated Forces', pp. 33–4.

respect to Kosovo was vested in UNMIK.[242] He also made a controversial ruling that the applicable law in the territory of Kosovo was that which applied prior to 24 March 1999, the first day of the NATO intervention. As a result, the laws of the Federal Republic of Yugoslavia and of the Republic of Serbia were deemed applicable, insofar as these did not conflict with internationally recognised standards, with the mandate given to UNMIK, or with any Regulation issued by UNMIK.[243] In this way, the Special Representative established the supremacy of his office and that of UNMIK Regulations over existing laws. Not surprisingly, the restoration of the old laws was strongly opposed by the Albanians, and an amending Regulation soon followed, mandating the application of prior Kosovar laws.[244]

The Ombudsperson of Kosovo criticised the Regulation on several grounds. He found that, while the seldom-applied secondary source of the Kosovo law was subject to a review for compatibility with internationally recognised human rights standards, the two primary sources of law were exempt. This is contrary to the intent of Resolution 1244, and created uncertainty about the role of international human rights standards in the legal regime.[245] He also observed that the promulgation of a law limiting the effect of binding international human rights standards to selected parts of domestic law significantly devalued the standards themselves.

It was ultimately found that the UNMIK Regulation did not adequately entrench international human rights standards in the legal system of Kosovo. Amnesty International also raised concerns with regard to the accountability of the authorities under the human rights treaties. In spite of Regulations requiring that international human rights instruments be observed, no account was taken of the important distinction between self-executing and non-self-executing international principles. As a result of the lack of incorporation of international human rights instruments into domestic law, the remedies or claims procedures of some of these are not available to the people of Kosovo

---

[242] UNMIK/REG/1999/1, 25 July 1999, section 1, para. 1, amended by UNMIK/REG/2000/54, 27 September 2000.

[243] UNMIK/REG/1999/1, 25 July 1999, section 3.

[244] UNMIK/REG/1999/24, 12 December 1999, on the Law Applicable in Kosovo.

[245] Ombudsperson Institution in Kosovo, *Special Report No. 2 on Certain Aspects of UNMIK Regulation No. 2000/59 Amending UNMIK Regulation No. 1999/24 on the Law Applicable in Kosovo* (27 October 2000), para. 10.

making human rights protection appear like an 'empty shell'.[246] In 2002, the Council of Europe's Commissioner for Human Rights provided the following assessment:

> [I]t is clear that the very structure of the international administration, as well as certain powers retained by its various branches, substantially deviate from international human rights norms and the accepted principles of the rule of law.[247]

He recommended that, as a minimum, UNMIK and KFOR should be bound by those human rights documents to which the state of the Former Republic of Yugoslavia (Serbia and Montenegro) is a party. Yet, the unique situation in Kosovo was one in which 'the legal responsibility, and the main political responsibility for the respect of human rights standards in Kosovo lies, for the time being, with UNMIK'.[248] The application of international human rights law to an international organisation that cannot accede to the principal conventions is problematic.[249] While Article 1.3 of UNMIK Regulation 1999/1 states that, in exercising their functions, all persons undertaking public duties or holding public office shall observe the major international human rights instruments,[250] UNMIK Regulation 2000/47 provides immunity 'from

---

[246] S. Vité, 'The Applicability of International Human Rights Law in Kosovo', in A. Faite and J. Labbe Grenier (eds.), *ICRC Report on the Applicability of International Humanitarian Law and International Human Rights Law to UN Mandated Forces* Genera: ICRC, (2004), p. 88.

[247] Alvaro Gil-Robles, Council of Europe Commissioner for Human Rights, *Kosovo: The Human Rights Situation and the Fate of Persons Displaced from Their Homes* (Strasbourg: Council of Europe, 16 October 2003), Introduction, para. 3.

[248] *Ibid.*, para. 34.

[249] Customary law and 'general principles recognised by civilised nations' may bind the UN in its peacekeeping capacity: see C. Bongiorno, 'A Culture of Impunity: Applying International Human Rights Law to the United Nations in East Timor' (2002) 33 *Columbia Human Rights Law Review* 623–92 at 641.

[250] As reflected, in particular, in the 1948 Universal Declaration of Human Rights, the 1950 European Convention for the Protection of Human Rights and Fundamental Freedoms and the Protocols thereto, the 1966 International Covenant on Civil and Political Rights and the Protocols thereto, the 1966 International Covenant on Economic, Social and Cultural Rights, the 1965 Convention on the Elimination of All Forms of Racial Discrimination, the 1979 Convention on the Elimination of All Forms of Discrimination Against Women, the 1984 Convention Against Torture and Other Cruel, Inhuman or Degrading Treatment or Punishment and the 1989 International Convention on the Rights of the Child. See United Nations, Human Rights Committee, *Report Submitted by the United Nations Interim Administration Mission in Kosovo to the Human Rights Committee on the Human Rights Situation in Kosovo Since June 1999*, UN Doc. CCPR/C/UNK/1, 13 March 2006, paras. 110–24.

any legal process' to KFOR and UNMIK personnel.[251] Such blanket immunity is difficult to justify and inconsistent with the spirit and purpose of the relevant human rights instruments.

Immunity for international organisations in such contexts has many precedents.[252] The privileges and immunities of UN personnel are generally limited by the principle of functional necessity: UN personnel are only immune to the extent necessary to discharge their duties. Human rights violations that are committed outside the scope of official duties should not be amenable to a plea of immunity. In Bosnia, however, the functional limitations on peacekeepers' immunity have been ignored and International Police Task Force officers have been shielded from prosecution.[253] In Kosovo, like Bosnia, the immunity given to peacekeepers is in the interests of KFOR and UNMIK, and not for the benefit of individuals within the organisation. The primary issue is not the criminal or other liability of individuals, but whether the acts of the respective organisations are in conformity with relevant human rights obligations. The UN Secretary-General has the right and duty to waive immunity in respect of UNMIK personnel where such a shield would impede the course of justice. This has occurred on a number of occasions. KFOR personnel remain subject to the military law and criminal code of their sending states.

The Venice Commission was mandated to look into the human rights situation in Kosovo with a view to designing a mechanism or mechanisms that will allow for adequate remedies in respect of alleged breaches of human rights. The lack of a functional system of oversight in respect of acts or omissions of UNMIK and KFOR was seen as a serious deficiency. Although Serbia and Montenegro has ratified the European Convention on Human Rights, since the adoption of Resolution 1244 it does not exercise 'jurisdiction' over Kosovo within the meaning of Article 1 of the Convention. In this way, the country cannot be held accountable for acts of KFOR or UNMIK that are outside its control. While a Human Rights Oversight Committee and an Inter-Pillar

---

[251] Sections 2 and 3 of UNMIK Regulation 2000/47 of 18 August 2000.

[252] European Commission for Democracy Through Law (Venice Commission), *Opinion on Human Rights in Kosovo: Possible Establishment of Review Mechanisms*, Opinion No. 280/2004 (Strasbourg: Council of Europe, 11 October 2004), p. 14.

[253] J. Murray, 'Who Will Police the Peace-Builders? The Failure to Establish Accountability for the Participation of United Nations Civilian Police in the Trafficking of Women in Post-Conflict Bosnia and Herzgovina' (2003) 34 *Columbia Human Rights Law Review* 475–527 at 508.

Working Group on Human Rights were established in June 2002, neither was a properly constituted independent review body.

Although UNMIK, as a UN entity established under Chapter VII of the UN Charter, does not generally come within the jurisdiction of the European Convention on Human Rights (even if individual contributing states are a party to the Convention), the situation pertaining to KFOR is more complex. KFOR is not a UN peacekeeping mission and it is not a subsidiary organ of the UN. Under international law, acts by KFOR, including violations of human rights, are not attributable to the UN as an international legal person. NATO accountability for acts or omissions of KFOR is more complex. NATO is not a party to the European Convention on Human Rights and, despite aspiring to a unified command and control system, the KFOR reality is much different. The commander of KFOR could be described as more of a co-ordinator than a military commander in the traditional sense. For this reason, an action to establish the accountability of individual troop-contributing states is more likely to succeed, especially if the relevant state is a member of the Council of Europe, than any such action against NATO. However, the issues remain complex.[254]

Much of what UNMIK has attempted has been controversial, especially the problem of the judiciary. Judges serve at the effective pleasure of the administration in defiance of basic separation-of-powers doctrine. In order to overcome some of the legal obstacles, it has been proposed to extend the jurisdiction of the European Court of Human Rights to both UNMIK and KFOR. This too is not without its problems, as the European Convention on Human Rights is a regional treaty intended to bind states, not organisations. Amending the Convention would require the agreement of member states and a modification to the Statute of the Council of Europe. This is not a practical option. The Venice Commission concluded that the best option is to develop specific mechanisms to facilitate independent review of UNMIK Regulations and the acts of UNMIK and KFOR.

The Venice Commission proposed the establishment of two human rights mechanisms for Kosovo. In the short term, it recommended setting up an independent internal advisory review mechanism. The more medium-term recommendation, the establishment of a Human Rights Court for Kosovo, presupposes that UN/UNMIK and NATO/KFOR possess a treaty-making power to enable its creation. Although it

---

[254] *Ibid.*, p. 18.

is foreseeable that such a proposal might not find favour, it is hard to see how the provision of an effective legal remedy would hinder the respective organisations in the performance of their tasks.[255] Internal review mechanisms, especially within military organisations, can be limited owing to command structures and hierarchy. This can be mitigated by augmenting such bodies with independent lawyers from outside the military or administrative chain of command. In the circumstances, it is not surprising that UNMIK is considered to have failed to clearly establish the supremacy of international human rights standards as the framework within which UNMIK and KFOR should determine the extent and quality of their actions.[256] This failure threatens the transition process underway in Kosovo, as well as the legitimacy of the international presence there.

Conclusion

It is undisputed that the UN has international legal personality and that it is a subject of international law.[257] Although it is arguable that the UN is capable of possessing both rights and duties, it does not automatically follow that all the rules of international law, in particular those relating to humanitarian law, apply to the Organization. The arguments that the UN cannot be bound by such rules owing to their specific nature and structure, and that it does not possess the necessary internal structure, are not compelling. In fact, the structures and resources of the UN are superior to many smaller states. When the UN was established, it became part of the existing international legal order. It was created by the common accord of states within the system. It is not within the powers of those states to create a functional international institution that is outside the framework of the pre-existing international legal order. There are of course practical difficulties for the UN in ensuring troops under its command or operational control do not infringe any of the applicable rules of international law, not the least being the fact that

---

[255] *Ibid.*

[256] D. Marshall and S. Inglis, 'The Disempowerment of Human Rights-Based Justice in the United Nations Mission in Kosovo' (2003) 16 *Harvard Human Rights Law Journal* 95–148 at 96.

[257] *Reparations Case* (1949) ICJ Reports 174. See also Michael Bothe, 'Peacekeeping and International Humanitarian Law: Friends or Foes?' (1996) 3 *International Peacekeeping* 91–5 at 94.

no troops have ever served under the full command and control of the UN, and it is unlikely that they will do so in the foreseeable future.

The UN has obligations under international human rights law that it has not formally acknowledged up to very recently. Despite the adoption of Security Council Resolution 1325 (2000) and the Secretary-General's Bulletin on Special Measures for Protection from Sexual Exploitation and Sexual Abuse (2003), serious problems have arisen in the Democratic Republic of the Congo and elsewhere. The technical co-operation between the Office of the High Commissioner for Human Rights and the Department of Peacekeeping Operations as part of a policy of 'mainstreaming' international human rights standards into UN activities does not empower human rights components of peacekeeping operations. In order to remove uncertainty surrounding the human rights obligations of UN peacekeeping operations, an explicit and binding commitment to such standards must be made. A broad 'Peacekeeping Bill of Rights' could be formulated and applied selectively to the functions that individual missions undertake.[258]

In addition to such an instrument, another suggestion is the establishment of a UN Ombudsperson. Such tools are indispensable in providing good governance and accountability mechanisms.[259] An institution of this kind would have to be given real powers to avoid the scenario that befell the Ombudsperson Institution in Kosovo, which was often ignored or merely tolerated rather than supported by the UN. As the UN is not technically a party to the major human rights instruments and treaties, none of the treaty bodies charged with reviewing compliance was ever called to examine the conduct of the UN from a human rights perspective. However, UNMIK is to present a report on the implementation of the International Covenant on Civil and Political Rights in Kosovo to the relevant UN committee during 2006. When the Human Rights Committee and the Committee Against Torture had the opportunity to examine the role of the UN in Somalia indirectly through the reports of states whose troops had been involved in violations of international human rights standards while serving there, no reference was made to UN responsibility.

---

[258] C. Bongiorno, 'A Culture of Impunity: Applying International Human Rights Law to the United Nations in East Timor' (2002) 33 *Columbia Human Rights Law Review* 623–92 at 679.

[259] Hoffmann and Mégret, 'Fostering Human Rights Accountability: An Ombudsperson for the United Nations?', pp. 43–63 at p. 53.

The more specific problem of sexual exploitation has been outlined in the Secretary-General's report on a comprehensive strategy to eliminate future exploitation.[260] Many of the recommendations have merit and should be implemented without delay, especially those relating to the individual disciplinary, financial and criminal accountability of all UN staff. One recommendation calls for the development of an international convention that would cause UN personnel to be subject to the jurisdiction of states parties for specified crimes. Among the difficulties with such a proposal are that it would apply only to the parties to the convention and that finding consensus in drafting an effective convention could prove challenging. Admittedly, the adoption of a convention with inconsistencies and loopholes that creates an illusion of protection and accountability, similar to that of the Convention for the Safety of UN Personnel, could easily undermine the value of the instrument. However, retaining a system where prosecutions for such actions are 'fortuitous' is unsustainable.[261]

The *Bankovic* decision of the European Court of Human Rights has delimited the extra-territorial reach of the European Convention.[262] Its protection is principally confined to the territories of contracting states, and applicable only in exceptional circumstances to territories of non-contracting parties. The extra-territorial reach of this and similar regional provisions cannot replace the protective regime imposed by international humanitarian law in situations of armed conflict. The parties to the Geneva Conventions are bound to respect the provisions in all circumstances if they are engaged in armed conflict, whether within or outside their territory. Vulnerable persons may qualify as 'protected persons' 'in the hands of' a party to the conflict. This is given a broad meaning under the Conventions.

While the principles and basic rules of humanitarian law may represent fundamental values that have received almost universal acceptance, peacetime efforts to implement them at the national level are nonetheless insufficient. In fact, it is often a marginal item in military training programmes.[263] Consequently, these rules of law are not as well known

---

[260] Report of the Secretary-General, *A Comprehensive Strategy to Eliminate Future Sexual Exploitation and Abuse in United Nations Peacekeeping Operations*, UN Doc. A/59/10, 24 March 2005.

[261] *Ibid.*, para. 88.

[262] *Bankovic and Others v. Belgium and Others* (App. No. 52207/99), ECtHR, 12 December 2001.

[263] See generally D. Lloyd Roberts, 'Training the Armed Forces to Respect International Humanitarian Law: The Perspective of the ICRC Delegate to the Armed and Security

or understood as they should be by those who must apply them, especially members of the armed forces. However, the conduct of Canadian and other contingents part of UNOSOM II highlights the need for training in this area.[264]

After the capture of a United States helicopter pilot shot down over Mogadishu, it was said that the United States recognised too late that there was no international law to protect him.[265] A gap was discerned in international law; in the absence of an international armed conflict, the Geneva Convention protecting prisoners did not apply. But, to rely upon humanitarian principles in a conflict, both parties must be prepared to demonstrate willingness to respect those principles. Reciprocity, while not a legal requirement, is a practical necessity. A primary consideration in developing principles of humanitarian law is the self-interest of the most protected class of person under the original rules, the combatant. States, and in particular the United States, sought to fill a perceived gap in international law by way of the Convention on the Protection of UN Personnel. This Convention is far from perfect, however, and may not alter the risk to which UN personnel will be exposed. Categorising those who oppose or threaten UN personnel as criminals or outlaws carries certain dangers and, if not implemented with caution and skill, could be associated with a new kind of colonial mentality.[266]

With regard to the initial question posed as to the relevant applicable law to situations where UN forces are deployed, this will depend largely on the nature and extent of the conflict. Nevertheless, there appears to be little doubt that those provisions of humanitarian law that have customary status will apply to UN forces. Such provisions bind all states, and may reasonably be suggested to apply to the UN itself. The most difficult question arises in respect of those rules that have not yet

Forces of South Asia' (1997) *International Review of the Red Cross* No. 319, 433–46; F. de Mulinen, *The Law of War and the Armed Forces*, Series Ius in Bello, No. 1 (Geneva: Henry Dunant Institute, 1992); and Y. Sandoz, 'Respect for the Law of Armed Conflict: The ICRC's Observations and Experiences', *International Seminar on International Humanitarian Law in a New Strategic Environment: Training of Armed Forces*, Stockholm, 17–18 June 1996.

[264] Though this need was recognised much earlier by some: see L. C. Green, 'Humanitarian Law and the Man in the Field' (1976) 14 *Revue de droit militaire et de droit de la guerre/ The Military Law and Law of War Review* 96–115.

[265] S. Lepper, 'War Crimes and the Protection of Peacekeeping Forces' (1995) 28 *Akron Law Review* 411–15 at 415.

[266] A. Roberts, *Humanitarian Action in War*, Adelphi Paper 305 (Oxford: Oxford University Press, 1996), p. 70.

attained customary status. There seems little sense in a system where combatants engaged in conflict are subject to humanitarian law when they are acting as members of national armed forces, whereas members of armed forces in the same armed conflict acting as peacekeepers are exempt from the obligation to respect the rights of protected persons. This is all the more absurd when these soldiers represent the organisation charged with upholding and promoting the fundamental human rights that humanitarian law seeks to protect. The application of humanitarian law to UN forces will not compromise the mission to promote peace. Moreover, as the declared aim of such operations is the restoration of international peace and security, it is surely not the case that it can be based on action in violation of existing principles of law.

What can or should a UN force do when it becomes aware that parties in the country where it is deployed are violating applicable international law? Unless the mandate of a force states otherwise, there is no present legal duty to protect victims of such violations. However, international military and civilian field personnel cannot be silent witnesses to gross violations of international human rights or humanitarian law. Nor do they wish to be. The legal obligations of peacekeeping and other UN military forces should reflect the notion that they will affirmatively seek to prevent abuses. The Brahimi Report suggests a more assertive and interventionist approach in such cases and states that 'UN peacekeepers – troops or police – who witness violence against civilians should be presumed to be authorised to stop it, within their means'.[267] If a force cannot intervene directly without exposing troops to significant danger, then the duty of a commander must first be to the safety of his or her personnel. Most lightly armed peacekeepers will not be in a position to prevent large-scale abuses by a party to the conflict. The Brahimi recommendations are a welcome initiative, but they presuppose that UN personnel will be in a position to act when appropriate, a presumption that requires the means and capacity to do so, factors that have not necessarily been present in the past.

Enforcement of international humanitarian law and human rights law is especially problematic in respect of UN forces. Relying on the disciplinary regimes of contributing states to enforce municipal law is one solution; but this requires the co-operation of those states concerned and an appropriate legal structure to deal with such offences.

---

[267] *Report of the Panel on UN Peacekeeping Operations* (Brahimi Report), UN Doc. A/55/305-S/2000/809, 23 August 2000, Executive Summary, p. 3.

Brocklebank, Rockwood and similar trials make clear that there is significant confusion regarding the applicability of international law to the different kinds of UN military operations. Yet courts-martial or their equivalent within contributing states remain the most likely fora for dealing with relevant disciplinary matters. While the independence of municipal legal regimes and disciplinary procedures must be respected, the current confusion is militating against a uniform and agreed formula for determining the applicability of international law to such operations.

The establishment of the International Criminal Court (ICC) is the most significant recent development in this regard. Once a state has ratified the Statute, all of the nationals of that state are subject to its provisions.[268] Concern about implementing humanitarian law was one of the driving forces behind proposals for the new court's establishment. The United States was most concerned about the impact this might have on participation in multi-national and peacekeeping operations.[269] However, the ICC is not a serious alternative to the present system of criminal jurisdiction over peacekeepers. The Preamble to the ICC Statute states that the Court shall be complementary to national criminal jurisdictions.[270] In stark contrast to the Statutes for the Yugoslav and Rwanda Tribunals, the Statute of the ICC acknowledges the primacy of national authorities, unless the latter are unable or unwilling to adequately investigate and prosecute alleged offences. In addition, Article 8 of the Statute, which deals with war crimes, is also linked to the notion of armed conflict (international and internal), and is dependent on the existence of a minimum threshold of conflict before the relevant provisions can apply.[271] The Statute of the ICC emphasises the prosecution of war crimes on a large scale, whereas the crimes

---

[268] See generally Triffterer (ed.), *Commentary on the Rome Statute*, pp. 180–288; Schabas, *An Introduction to the International Court*, pp. 1–25; M. C. Bassiouni, *The Statute of the International Criminal Court: A Documentary History* (New York: Transnational, 1998); R. Lee (ed.), *The International Criminal Court: The Making of the Rome Statute* (Dordrecht: Kluwer, 1999), pp. 79–126; L. Caflisch, 'Toward the Establishment of a Permanent International Criminal Jurisdiction' (1998) 4(5) *International Peacekeeping* 110–15; and http://www.igc.org/icc/.

[269] M. Zwanenburg, 'The Statute for an International Criminal Court and the United States: Peacekeepers under Fire?' (1999) 10 *European Journal of International Law* 124–43 at 126.

[270] ICC Statute, Preamble, para. 10, and Articles 1, 12–15 and 17–19: see Triffterer, *Commentary on the Rome Statute*, pp. 15 and 59–61.

[271] Triffterer (ed.), *Commentary on the Rome Statute*, pp. 180–288, esp. pp. 264–78; Schabas, *An Introduction to the International Court*, pp. 51–66; and Lee (ed.), *The International Criminal Court*, pp. 103–26. Lee notes that the Statute contains a

committed by peacekeepers have been isolated and not part of a plan or policy sanctioned by higher authorities. Despite this, the possibility of a prosecution for a single act constituting a war crime still exists, and contrasts with the threshold level of gravity for a crime against humanity under the Statute.[272]

Clarifying which laws apply in a conflict situation is not as simple a task as it may first appear. Troops involved in the same operation may be subject to different rules, owing to dissimilar obligations undertaken by contributing states. For example, Canadian and German members of IFOR, SFOR and the current KFOR are subject to Protocol I, while United States and French troops were not (though France has since ratified Protocol I). This problem is mitigated somewhat by the fact that many of the relevant norms are part of customary international law which binds all states.[273] Requiring all UN personnel to be educated and trained in human rights and humanitarian law is essential. Instruction in humanitarian law is a legal obligation on states party to the Geneva Conventions and its Additional Protocols. In addition, the UN and the ICRC should agree on the rules applicable to military operations conducted on behalf of or by the UN. There is an urgent need for codification of the law as 'ambiguity is always a fault in legal norms and in international humanitarian law it is potentially a source of disaster'.[274] Several commentators have called for the formation of an independent body to police the application of humanitarian law and to recommend revisions where necessary. Despite the universality of the Geneva Conventions, not all of the details of their provisions are declaratory of customary law. The situation is even more uncertain in regard to Protocol I; moreover, not all customary rules may be applicable to operations carried out by UN forces.

---

substantially lower threshold for internal armed conflict than that laid down in Protocol II (*Ibid.*, p. 125).

[272] M. Arsanjani, 'The Rome Statute of an International Criminal Court' (1999) 93 *American Journal of International Law* 33. Article 7(1) of the Statute provides that particular acts must have been committed as part of a 'widespread or systematic attack directed against any civilian population': Triffterer (ed.), *Commentary on the Rome Statute*, pp. 126–7.

[273] In the case of Ireland, Protocols I and II became part of municipal law and binding on Irish soldiers with the passing of the Geneva Conventions (Amendment) Act 1998.

[274] H. McCoubrey, *International Humanitarian Law* (Aldershot: Dartmouth, 1990), p. 18. Although McCoubrey was addressing the confusion surrounding internal and international armed conflicts, the basic logic applies to all issues concerning humanitarian law.

It is an unavoidable flaw that, in relation to the purposes and functions of the UN, humanitarian law plays only a secondary role. Furthermore, states perceive criminal jurisdiction over their nationals as part of their jealously guarded sovereignty, and considerable national sensitivities are associated with participation in UN military operations.[275] The creation of a special tribunal or court to deal with such matters is one potential solution, but the fact that few if any countries actually place their forces under the full command of the UN could be problematic. It would also create constitutional difficulties for some countries. The matter would be complicated in respect of those countries with dualist legal regimes that do not automatically incorporate international provisions into their domestic legal systems. Given the Secretary-General's Bulletin regarding the application of humanitarian law to UN forces and the number of references to it in Security Council resolutions as a 'body of law' to be applied 'in all circumstances', it may be argued that humanitarian law is a peremptory norm of international law and part of *jus cogens* (i.e. a fundamental principle of international law that binds all states).[276]

In most instances, the task of applying theoretical principles of international law to specific cases becomes the responsibility of armed forces on the ground. There are a number of measures that contributing states could take to improve the current situation. Up until recently, United States policy was linked to the notion of armed conflict such that its military were obliged to comply with humanitarian law in conducting military operations in times of armed conflict. However, military regulations are silent on when an engagement reaches the level of armed conflict, or as to what demarcates the point at which the laws of armed conflict apply. These distinctions are crucial to peacekeeping operations, and neither the recent Secretary-General's Bulletin nor the Convention on the Protection of UN Personnel shed much light on this area. In 1996, the United States Chairman of the Joint Chiefs of Staff issued an instruction that extended the application of 'the law of war principles during all operations that are characterized as Military Operations

---

[275] H. McCoubrey, 'International Humanitarian Law and United Nations Military Action in the "New World Order"' (1994) 1 *International Law and Armed Conflict: Commentary* 36 at 45.

[276] See comments to this effect in M. Meijer, 'Notes on the Conference on "The UN and International Humanitarian Law", Geneva: 19–20 October 1995' (1995) 2(6) *International Peacekeeping* 136–8 at 137. The Secretary-General issued his Bulletin on 6 August 1999: UN Doc. ST/SGB/1999/3.

Other Than War'.[277] This effectively covers every conceivable military operation. Most significantly, there is no triggering event wedded to the notion of armed conflict, which is a prerequisite for the application of these principles under international law. This is a welcome initiative but, from a legal perspective, it too has deficiencies in that the instruction refers to principles of war, but gives no indication of what these might be.

Humanitarian law represents the fundamental principles of humanity imposed on all of us, including the Security Council and agents of the UN. It must be respected in all circumstances, regardless of the existence or nature of the armed conflict. A solution ought to be for an acknowledgment and declaration that humanitarian law binds UN personnel, and that UN military and other personnel will be educated, trained and monitored in this regard. Ensuring the universality of the treaties on humanitarian law, including the Statute of the ICC, would serve as an additional guarantee of compliance. After one hundred years of lawmaking, the primary objective must not be new law, but ensuring compliance with and effective implementation of the laws already in existence.[278] It is the responsibility of the UN and all countries contributing troops to UN operations to ensure that personnel undergo systematic training in international human rights and humanitarian law, and that standing operating procedures be created in order to deal with violations when they occur.

---

[277] 'USA: International and Operational Law Note: When Does the Law of War Apply? Analysis of Department of Defense Policy on Application of the Laws of War', reprinted from *The Army Lawyer*, Department of the Army, June 1998, in (1998) 1 *Yearbook of International Humanitarian Law* 617–19.

[278] C. Greenwood, *International Humanitarian Law and the Laws of War: Preliminary Report for the Centennial Commemoration of the First Hague Peace Conference 1899* (May 1999), p. 3, para. 1.6, quoting Sir Franklin Berman. The report was reprinted in F. Kalshoven (ed.), *The Centennial of the First International Peace Conference: Reports and Conclusions* (The Hague, Boston and London: Kluwer Law International, 2000), pp. 161–259.

6

Conclusion

The need for UN reform

> The problem is a lack of vision, the opportunity is to provide that vision – the
> challenge is to promote the view that can see pragmatic idealism prevail over
> rather stale realism ... [which] is often a euphemism for a short-sightedness
> and policies lacking in the necessary courage and vision.[1]

In recent years, the UN has faced a series of financial crises that have
threatened its existence. The availability of troops from developed
countries for peacekeeping in Africa and elsewhere remains a major
problem,[2] but a more serious threat is posed by the self-serving agenda
pursued by the permanent members of the Security Council. It is they
who are responsible for 85 per cent of global arms exports, while at the
same time charged with primary responsibility for the maintenance of
international peace and security. The victors of World War II have
arrogated the crucial power within the Security Council, making full
use of its inherently undemocratic structure and procedures. This ruling
oligarchy represents one of the major obstacles to the proper functioning of the UN and is a major impediment to peace based on justice and
universal suffrage. The legitimacy of the Security Council derives from
the commitment of all member states to confer primary responsibility
for international peace and security on a body of limited membership.
There must be balanced and fair representation, reflective of the global
membership of the UN and the realities of regional and global power.
The organisation should not be a tool for enhancing pre-existing hegemonic power; if anything, it should curtail and control the potential
abuse inherent in the possession of such power. The recent *High-Level*

---

[1] B. Urquhart, 'The United Nations in 1992: Problems and Opportunities' (1992) 68(2)
International Affairs 311.

[2] *Report of the Secretary-General: Implementation of the United Nations Millennium
Declaration*, UN Doc. A/58/323, 2 September 2003, para. 36.

Panel Report on Threats, Challenges and Change calls for enlargement and reform, but makes no recommendations as to how to deal with this divisive issue.[3] Unfortunately, such reforms are unlikely to produce a less divisive Council.

At the same time, there are issues and events that it is not acceptable to remain neutral in respect of – genocide, ethnic cleansing, mass rapes, and other crimes against humanity or war crimes. The duty to act as responsible members of the international community endures and is compelling, in particular, given the shameful record of European countries throughout the Yugoslav conflict. The reality is that it took a NATO-led force to impose some measure of peace and to prevent the seemingly endless slaughter of so many innocent civilians. In April 2005, the NATO Secretary-General called for closer NATO–UN co-operation,[4] but, at the same time, NATO powers have left the UN bereft of resources and unable to act. The unilateral NATO response to the Kosovo crises may provide a more accurate insight into the true nature and purpose of these forces. NATO makes for an unpredictable bedfellow: it once gave the UN full co-operation as part of peacekeeping and enforcement missions in Bosnia-Herzegovina, yet later it seemed to be competing with the UN in Europe. This may suit a financially constrained UN in the short term, but what of NATO's plans outside its own area of operations and without UN authorisation? Where do the interests of smaller states lie in such a scenario? The lessons of history are clear: their interests lie with the UN, collective security and international law.

In the current climate of rationalisation and reduction in the size of armed forces, the capacity of many traditional contributors to peace-keeping operations in today's robust and complex missions is being challenged. This can have a qualitative impact on the composition of a multi-national force and thereby influence the outcome of the mission. Events in Somalia, Lebanon and Kosovo highlight the deficiencies in international institutions and organisations. The UN, the European Union and the African Union have all found that responding effectively to internal or intra-state conflicts is difficult. Critics of the UN have noted the Organization's use of rhetoric over much-needed decisive

---

[3] *A More Secure World: Our Shared Responsibility: Report of the High-Level Panel on Threats, Challenges and Change*, UN Doc. A/59/565, p. 2 December 2004, paras. 244–60. E. Luck, 'How Not to Reform the United Nations' (2005) 11 *Global Governance* 407–14.

[4] P. Ames, 'NATO Chief Calls for More UN Cooperation', Associated Press, 14 April 2005.

action and leadership. Its bulging bureaucracy often seems to epitomise inefficiency and inertia.[5] In the former Yugoslavia, the UN was exposed as the paper tiger so many believe it to be. The peacekeeping operation was unsustainable as there was no peace to keep, while enforcement action was unsustainable due to a lack of political will among the permanent members of the Security Council. The successes of the UN are often neglected or ignored, while criticisms abound. Although the latter are often legitimate, the blame normally lies not with the UN, but rather with its membership as a whole.

Intervention

Former United States President, Bill Clinton, said that the UN cannot engage in all of the world's conflicts and that it must learn when to say no;[6] but who is to distinguish those causes that are worthy from those that should be ignored? Rwanda was a disaster waiting to happen and, even if the international community was willing to intervene, who would decide when, where and how? In the case of Rwanda, unlike Bosnia, there was no pretence. Although the French ultimately responded, the nation's efforts were too late to prevent the genocide and the intervention was primarily motivated by French national interest. Yet France, a permanent member of the Security Council, was one of the main suppliers of weapons to the perpetrators of the genocide and continued to lend support to those militias in exile.[7]

One of most serious deficiencies in the UN system is its inability to respond effectively to crises involving violent intra-state or internal conflicts. Traditional inter-state war of the scale that led to the First Gulf War and Operation Desert Storm is quite rare. The reverse is true of conflicts within states. Africa and many parts of the world are comprised mostly of artificially drawn state boundaries that often divide traditional political, ethnic and national groups. Multi-nation states are far more common than homogenous states. Ethnic and religious differences are

---

[5] See comments by Boutros Boutros-Ghali, 'Empowering the United Nations' (1992/3) 71 *Foreign Affairs* 100, to the effect that 'duplication is widespread; co-ordination is often minimal; bureaucratic battles aimed at monopolizing a particular subject are rife; and organizational objectives are sometimes in conflict'.

[6] President Clinton, Address to the UN General Assembly, New York, 27 September 1993, US Department of State *Dispatch*, Vol. 4, No. 39, p. 652.

[7] Human Rights Watch, *Rearming with Impunity: International Support for the Perpetrators of the Rwandan Genocide*, Human Rights Watch, May 1995.

not the primary cause of conflict, no more than bad weather and crop failure are the sole causes of famine and starvation. In order to respond to the problem of intra-state conflict, there is need for reform of doctrinal foundations and to develop long-term strategies for the post-military intervention phase. Intervention in any internal conflict is fraught with uncertainty, as was demonstrated by the initial setbacks of the UN mission in Sierra Leone (1999–2005). Success there may not have been unqualified, but lessons were learned. The near collapse of the mission in 2000 brought into question the viability of all UN peace-keeping operations, requiring an intervention by British forces to turn things around.[8] Not all missions of this nature encounter such difficulties and the United Nations Observer Mission in El Salvador (ONUSAL, 1991–5) is evidence that such operations can succeed. The *An Agenda for Peace* report, not unlike the rhetoric of most national governments, pays lip-service to non-governmental actors. But, of the many lessons to be learned from Somalia, one is that non-governmental players, whether clan, community, tribal or nation-based, and international NGOs can play a significant role in preventing a country or society from imploding. First, this role must be recognised: those involved in non-governmental work are often most aware of what is happening on the ground. Therefore, proposals for deploying early-warning monitors to potential trouble spots make no sense when the existing knowledge base on the ground is ignored. Policies must be changed, but the attitudes of those that frame them must be altered as well.

Events in Somalia, and more recently those in Haiti (resulting in MINUSTAH, 2004), cannot be said to have posed a significant threat to international peace and security. Nevertheless, the Security Council decided to intervene. This reflects a growing sense of responsibility for the protection of vulnerable populations, also evident when NATO intervened in Kosovo. Security Council Resolution 1296 (2000) on the protection of civilians in armed conflicts invokes the primary responsibility of the Council for the maintenance of international peace and security. In so doing, it notes that 'the deliberate targeting of civilian populations ... and the committing of systematic, flagrant and widespread violations of international humanitarian and human right law' may constitute a threat to peace and security.[9] In this context, the *Report*

---

[8] M. Doyle, 'UN Troops Bid Farewell to Freetown', BBC News, 15 December 2005.
[9] Security Council Resolution 1296, 19 April 2000, reaffirmed by Resolution 1674, 28 April 2006.

of the High-Level Panel on Threats, Challenges and Change acknowledges that regional organisations can be a vital part of the multilateral system, noting that any action taken should be within the framework of the Charter and should not facilitate the creation of a *de facto* class system of regional responses. Despite this, it recognises that urgent situations may require a regional organisation to seek retroactive approval from the Security Council.[10] But countries of the global South have legitimate fears that humanitarian intervention may be used as a pretext or Trojan horse for destabilising selected governments or regimes. A more representative Security Council might allay some of these fears, yet agreeing on a need for reform of the UN and finding the consensus to implement change are two different things. Nevertheless, a global society based on universal sovereignty and respect for fundamental human rights has the potential to provide all peoples with legitimate involvement in issues affecting the world as a whole.

Who is to blame for the debacles in Rwanda, Somalia and the former Yugoslavia? To some extent the whole international community of states and peoples share responsibility. However, the Security Council set up all three UN missions. Each was ill-conceived and short-sighted, and essentially placed the peacekeepers in an impossible situation. The Council hesitated and prevaricated when faced with starvation in Somalia and genocide in Rwanda, and it refused to give UNPROFOR the resources required to protect itself, let alone the people whose very existence depended upon its protection. At the same time, the cosy consensus surrounding the UN response to Iraq's unlawful invasion of Kuwait was a sham. There was no mention of the economic intimidation that was imposed on the more vulnerable states of the South in order to secure their support or silence.[11]

Operational and legal issues

There are many less aspirational matters concerning peacekeeping operations that need attention. While the UN has improved its

[10] *Report of the High-Level Panel on Threats, Challenges and Change* (note 3 above), para. 272.

[11] P. Bennis, 'Blue Helmets: For What? Under Whom?', in E. Childers (ed.), *Challenges to the United Nations* (New York: St Martin's Press, 1995), pp. 152–75 at 156; and personal interview, Mr E. Childers, former UN civil servant and Senior Advisor to the UN Director-General for Development and International Economic Co-operation, Galway, 1995.

peacekeeping capacity and procedures,[12] a revision of its legal frame-work is long overdue. The *ad hoc* and improvised structures and proce-dures of the UN have long been a source of concern and difficulty, and forces on the ground have enough to contend with besides the inepti-tude of their own organisation. The Somalia operation shows that it is essential that a valid and unified chain of command be authorised. There is also an urgent need to clarify the relationship between the Security Council and 'coalitions of the willing', especially with regard to the relevant command and control mechanism adopted.[13] NATO is alert to the need not to subordinate itself to any other international body, but where does this leave the UN?[14] The current force in Kosovo is a UN-mandated but NATO-led and *de facto* NATO-commanded operation involving no strategic direction from any UN body.

A key determinant in distinguishing peacekeeping from peace enfor-cement is the ability and willingness to use force. The Security Council had no hesitation in giving UNOSOM II a peace enforcement mandate and granting the Secretary-General overall control. In contrast, the Council and the Secretary-General were at all times clear that UNIFIL was a peacekeeping mission and, as such, would not be permitted to adopt a peace enforcement role, incrementally or otherwise. The adop-tion of resolutions invoking Chapter VII and phrased in such overtly militaristic terms has the potential to escalate the level of violence unless strictly controlled. This is what happened in Somalia. By operating outside of the formal UN chain of command, it could be said that the United States 'hijacked' the mission and pursued an agenda not always consistent with UN objectives.[15] The abandonment of impartiality, and the consequent loss of credibility by both the United States and the UN (it being increasingly difficult to distinguish between them), proved a recipe for disaster. Although operating outside of the formal UN com-mand system on peacekeeping operations is usually ill-advised and counter-productive, in exceptional circumstances it may prove success-ful if the mission is of limited scope and duration. This was so when, in

---

[12] D. C. Jett, *Why Peacekeeping Fails* (New York: Palgrave, 2001), p. 172.

[13] D. Sarooshi, *The United Nations and the Development of Collective Security* (Oxford: Clarendon Press, 1999), pp. 247–85.

[14] Deputy Secretary of State Strobe Talbott on NATO's future 'Strategic Concept', in B. Simma, 'NATO, the UN and the Use of Force: Legal Aspects' (1999) 10 *European Journal of International Law* 1–22 at 15.

[15] See J. Cox, 'Watershed in Somalia', in Morrison, Fraser and Kiras (eds.), *Peacekeeping with Muscle*, pp. 127–32 at p. 130.

2000, British forces in Sierra Leone were deployed outside of the UN chain of command to, *inter alia*, support the UN mission there.[16]

A clear lesson is that UN peacekeeping or peace enforcement operations alone cannot end a war nor will the robust interpretation of a mandate provide the solution to intra-state conflict. The use of force by or on behalf of the UN, whatever the circumstances, must be resorted to only in the context of an overall political strategy with clearly defined political goals. While military force is the best way to achieve exclusively military objectives, using force to obtain a mix of military and political objectives is more problematic. It was not the use of force that brought about the demise of the UN operation in Somalia, but a combination of factors, including selective and excessive use of force. The Brahimi Report, while calling for more robust mandates, fails to address the issues raised by regional peacekeepers or coalitions of the willing acting under the authority of the UN. The recommendations of the report make interesting reading, but UN-controlled forces are generally not given adequate capabilities to intimidate or enforce. Another UN report is unlikely to change this historical fact.

Unrealistic expectations

Much criticism of operations has arisen from unrealistic expectations over what a UN military operation, whether traditional peacekeeping or peace enforcement, can achieve in the context of ongoing hostilities. The UN Commission of Inquiry on events in Somalia recommended that the UN refrain from taking peace enforcement actions within the internal conflicts of states.[17] But UN forces should never be deployed in a situation where they are forced to play the role of witness to gross violations of international human rights or international humanitarian law. This raises the question of whether the UN should undertake peacekeeping and peace enforcement as part of one mission. This

---

[16] Though in the case of British forces in Sierra Leone they were not intended to adopt a combat role: the primary task was to train and support the armed forces of the government of Sierra Leone, and to evacuate British nationals. See Ministry of Defence Press Release No. 270/00, 10 October 2000, and statement to Parliament by Defence Secretary on Sierra Leone, 15 May 2000; *Eighth Report of the Secretary-General on the UN Mission in Sierra Leone*, UN Doc. S/2000/1199, 15 December 2000, paras. 30–2.

[17] *Report of the Commission of Inquiry Established Pursuant to Resolution 885 (1993) to Investigate Attacks on UNOSOM II Personnel*, UN Doc. S/1994/653, 1 June 1994, para. 270.

amalgamation caused doctrinal confusion and contributed to mission failure in Somalia. The UNIFIL experience, on the other hand, demonstrates that it is possible to use force under limited circumstances (in self-defence) and still retain impartiality. However, at an early stage in the mission it was decided that operational effectiveness would be curtailed in order to adhere to the principle of non-use of force. The debacle of the Multi-National Force's (MNF) involvement in Beirut during 1983, and the failure of the intervention in Somalia, vindicated this policy.

All three operations examined highlight the need for support from the members of the Security Council, irrespective of the particular nature of the mission. They also illustrate that problems arise when missions are ill-defined; moreover, this was compounded in the case of Somalia by a dispute about the authority to use force, and in Kosovo by uncertainty regarding the future status of the province. What is an acceptable level of force within the parameters set by 'all necessary means'?

Distinguishing between 'victim' and 'aggressor' in many contemporary conflicts is fraught with problems, and making such a judgment may not always be consistent with the principles of the UN Charter. The failure of MONUC to halt the seizure of Bukavu in the Democratic Republic of the Congo in early 2004 led to violent demonstrations and attacks against the UN forces and agencies across the country.[18] MONUC was blamed for not using force to carry out its mandate. The human rights violations that occurred at the time prompted a demand for a tougher response from the UN and facilitated a review of the mandate that led to UN military operations against armed militias.

Lack of accountability

The UN has created a range of accountability mechanisms at the international level, from international tribunals to special courts and truth commissions. However, the UN also has obligations that it has not acknowledged in full. The dismissive attitude with which the UN has sometimes dealt with allegations of sexual exploitation and related activities may now be at an end. However, UN codes of conduct and a Secretary-General's Bulletin are impotent mechanisms and reliance continues to be placed on national authorities, despite the fact that

---

[18] *Report of the Secretary-General on MONUC*, 25 March 2004, UN Doc. S/2004/251, para. 25.

these have proved inadequate to date. A broad 'Peacekeeping Bill of Rights' could be formulated and carefully applied to the functions that individual missions undertake in order to remove uncertainty surrounding the human rights obligations of such operations.[19] This could be augmented by the establishment of an Ombudsperson or Inspector-General to oversee all UN activities. Ironically, dealing with transgressions by civilian UN personnel, who fall outside military rules, is currently proving more problematic. Disciplinary procedures will also have to conform to international standards, and take into account national constitutional principles. The proposal to conduct courts-martial in the country where the abuse occurs is not such a novel idea; many courts-martial already take place in the country of deployment. However, it may not be practical to do so once a contingent has departed the mission area, something which is a regular feature of UN missions.

It is hard not to see this problem as linked to the overall failure of gender mainstreaming in peace operations, and a failure to acknowledge the rights and interests of women in post-conflict situations in general.[20] Some commentators have called into question the role of MONUC and similar peacekeeping operations in this regard. That accusations of sexual abuse are tools in the arsenal of those who seek to undermine the role of the UN in general cannot be overlooked. The UN needs to take urgent and adequate action to deal with those accused of sexual abuse, both to bring a halt to the transgressions and to ensure that the issue does not overshadow the important role that the UN plays in its efforts to bring about peace.[21] The bleak reality of the situation is embodied in the reported statement of a Congolese woman: 'Yes it's true that some girls have been raped by UN soldiers, but so many more have been brutally raped by other armed groups. Please focus on stopping this as it brings us so much pain and suffering.'[22] While UN troops must be held accountable, it is also important to make all perpetrators of sexual violence accountable and to keep in

---

[19] C. Bongiorno, 'A Culture of Impunity: Applying International Human Rights Law to the United Nations in East Timor' (2002) 33 *Columbia Human Rights Law Review* 623–92 at 679.

[20] Windhoek Declaration: The Namibia Plan of Action on 'Mainstreaming a Gender Perspective in Multinational Peace Support Operation's, Windhoek, 31 May 2000; and European Parliament Resolution on Participation of Women in Peaceful Conflict Resolution (2000/2025(INI)), A5-0308/2000, 30 November 2000, para. O.

[21] Human Rights Watch Statement to Committee on International Relations, US House of Representatives, Washington DC, 1 March 2005 (making this observation regarding the activities of MONUC in the Democratic Republic of the Congo).

[22] Ibid.

mind that this is primarily a human rights issue. Programmes to assist those subject to exploitation are necessary, and need to include emergency medical care and psychological counselling and advice.

In September 2005, the UN announced that it would replace the Ukraine contingent of the UN force in South Lebanon due to 'significant financial misconduct'.[23] Similarly, repercussion should follow for those countries whose troops have been engaged in sexual misconduct: at a minimum, these contingents should be named and all internal reports made publicly available. The Organization is consistently short of peacekeepers for various missions, but this does not mean that it must accept troops whose behaviour is far more serious than financial misconduct. If proper measures are not taken by national authorities to address and prevent such misconduct, the countries involved must not be allowed to act in any capacity that provides an opportunity for further exploitative behaviour.

Ensuring compliance with international humanitarian law norms on peacekeeping operations remains problematic. There are, of course, practical difficulties for the UN in ensuring that troops under its command or operational control do not infringe any of the applicable rules of international law. Among these unresolved issues is the fact that no troops have ever served under the full command and control of the UN, and it is unlikely that they will do so in the foreseeable future. Enforcement of humanitarian law is especially problematic in respect of UN forces, and it is evident that there is significant confusion regarding the applicability of international humanitarian law to the different kinds of UN military operations. Relying on the contributing states to use their civil or military legal regimes to enforce municipal law is one solution, but this requires the co-operation of those states concerned and the existence of an appropriate legal structure with which to deal with such offences. While the independence of municipal legal regimes and disciplinary procedures must be respected, the current confusion militates against a uniform and agreed formula for determining the applicability of international law to such operations.

The application of international humanitarian law to UN forces will enhance rather than compromise the mission to promote peace. In addition, the legal obligations of peacekeeping and other UN military forces should reflect the notion that they will affirmatively seek to prevent abuses. This is best achieved by an express provision to this

---

[23] Agence France-Press (AFP) report, 6 September 2005.

effect in the mandate. Mandatory training for all UN personnel in this area is essential.

The 1994 Convention on the Safety of UN and Associated Personnel has complicated the matter somewhat. As it stands, the Convention is a poorly drafted and ill-thought-out document that was heavily influenced by political factors. It is unlikely that the Convention will have any impact on the creation of a safe environment within which peacekeepers may operate. Troop-contributing states would be advised not to place too much store in its ability to protect UN persons, and prosecutors should be circumspect regarding efforts to invoke its terms.

The UN, NATO and Kosovo

The states that bear primary responsibility for the deployment of a peace-keeping force are often the same states engaged in political manoeuvres that ignore or undermine the UN mission. UNIFIL, with its flawed mandate and unrealistic goals, was one such mission. In examining the crisis confronting the interpositionary peacekeeping force deployed to monitor the cessation of hostilities between Ethiopia and Eritrea (UNMEE, 2000) in 2005, it is evident that lessons that should have been learned from the UNIFIL experience were ignored. In late 2005, a major threat to the UNMEE operation arose after Ethiopia failed to accept a decision of the Permanent Court of Arbitration concerning disputed territory with Eritrea.[24] Eritrea responded by demanding a withdrawal of certain contingents from its territory. Unfortunately, the European Union and the United States failed to put sufficient pressure on Ethiopia to respect the arbitration decision, thereby undermining the overall UN mission.

In addition, the evolving *ad hoc* nature of international administration poses a threat to UN legitimacy, and to peacekeeping operations linked thereto. Territory administered by the UN should be a showcase of accountability and democratic governance in accordance with the principles associated with the integrated mission concept. Kosovo does not provide such an example; rather, in the absence of clear rules governing their conduct, international officials find themselves endowed with more or less absolute power.[25] UN involvement does not guarantee the benevolent exercise of power. Neither the Secretary-General nor the Security Council appears to

---

[24] *The Economist*, 29 October 2005, p. 48; and BBC News, 7 and 8 December 2005.
[25] E. Mortimer, 'International Administration of War-Torn Societies' (2004) 10 *Global Governance* 7–14 at 13.

have the will or mechanism to examine the conduct of an administration in detail. Resolution 1244 (1999), despite advocating the protection of human rights, did not create any mechanism for enforcing such rights against UNMIK or KFOR.

According to the Independent International Commission on Kosovo, there are four essential elements to be borne in mind for the future of the province.[26] These are: the relationship of the province to the Federal Republic of Yugoslavia (FRY); the relationship of Kosovar institutions of self-government to a continuing UN administrative presence and to the international security presence; the nature of Kosovo's borders and its relationship to neighbouring states; and the definition of Kosovo as an entity within the international community. The Commission's report considered a number of options for the future, such as UN protectorate status, partition into two entities, full independence, and substantial autonomy and self-government within the FRY. Ultimately, it settled on 'conditional independence' as the best possible long-term option, and at the time of writing this remains the optimum solution.[27]

In Kosovo, NATO's strategy was restricted by the need to maintain unity within the alliance. The threat and then use of force in the early stages did not produce the desired result. In fact, the use of violence may have exacerbated the situation and precipitated further atrocities. Furthermore, while the air campaign did not cause widespread civilian casualties, it did have a severe impact on daily civilian life. The debacle of United States involvement in Somalia was uppermost in the minds of the Clinton administration, and it wanted to avoid at all costs having young Americans coming home in body bags.

It may be argued that the NATO intervention in Kosovo was selective. However, this does not take account of the fact that the situation arose in a region that had an organisation with the capacity to take action against the systematic abuse of human rights at a time when the events surrounding the conflict in Bosnia-Herzegovina were still fresh in people's minds. Nor may it be denied that the resort to violence in the struggle for self-determination was a pivotal factor in the case of Kosovo.

The NATO campaign did allow the return of one million refugees and displaced persons to their homes. It also gave a clear message that the West will defend Muslim communities, and some lessons were learned from the

---

[26] Independent International Commission on Kosovo, *Kosovo Report: Conflict – International Response – Lessons Learned* (Oxford: Oxford University Press, 2000), p. 259.

[27] July 2006.

Bosnian conflict. However, NATO later presided over the ethnic cleansing of Serbs and failed to protect other vulnerable communities in Kosovo. The credibility that the initial intervention earned for NATO has since been undermined. The KLA has retained its structures in the Kosovo Protection Corps, and this is linked to serious criminality in the province. On the ground, there is insufficient operational planning and joint strategies between the UNMIK pillars. Much of what UNMIK has attempted has been controversial. Ambiguity surrounding UNMIK's powers in relation to public assets has hindered efforts at economic development. You cannot force populations that have endured centuries-old animosities and recent oppression to live together in harmony. It is not the multi-ethnic society that was intended. Stability remains fragile and depends on effective institutions of government. The premature reduction in the international presence there could precipitate another major crisis with more serious consequences than occurred in Timor-Leste (formerly East Timor) during 2006. While the UN's role in Cyprus and the Middle East has been blamed, perhaps legitimately, for the failure of the parties to find a workable agreement, Kosovo presents a unique challenge to the European Union and the UN for which there is no quick fix. What may be needed in Kosovo is a General MacArthur or a Paddy Ashdown figure, unafraid to govern and not seeking a populist agenda or the adulation of Kosovars.

Minority protection is at the heart of the human rights agenda in Kosovo. The freedom of movement of those who live in enclaves is significantly curtailed owing to the threat of violence. To date, UNMIK has not been able to effectively redress these problems. The emphasis on return of property and reconstruction is important, but it is of little long-term value without a proactive policy with regard to fair employment, access to education and essential services for minorities. The existence of the legal protection framework has not led to substantial improvement in the everyday life of minorities. As a result, many minorities (mostly Serbs) boycott the UN system and instead avail of the parallel institutions of Serbia. UNMIK regards the dissolution of these parallel structures as a further step towards gaining public confidence in UN institutions and unifying the population of Kosovo. However, this policy emphasises the symptoms and neglects to address the root causes of the problem. The termination of the parallel structures will not automatically bring an end to violence and enhance freedom of movement for the minorities. In order to improve the situation, it is necessary to gain the support of prominent Albanian and Serbian leaders. The most the UN can hope to achieve in the future is to facilitate an agreement between the parties that they will be willing to implement themselves. The achievement of such a goal is not likely in the foreseeable future.

There is a need to develop meaningful local government that provides vulnerable communities, especially the Serbs, with more authority. The group also needs effective mechanisms to promote and protect their identity; it would be foolhardy to transfer governance to Kosovar institutions without retaining a strong and effective intervention and sanctions policy to ensure performance.[28] UNMIK and KFOR will have to retain primary responsibility for security. While the Kosovo Police Service is developing more capacity, it still has some way to go. Under Resolution 1244 (1999), the primary responsibility for the provision of a secure environment rests with UNMIK and KFOR. It is likely that the European Union will eventually take the international lead role and assume most responsibility for Kosovo. It must exert enough pressure on the Albanians to respect and facilitate the presence of minorities, along with OSCE capacity-building measures.[29] In the meantime, it is imperative that the six-nation contact group – the United States, the United Kingdom, France, Germany, Italy and Russia – agree upon a road-map and timeframe to resolve the issue of status. This could be linked to the drafting of a constitution for Kosovo guaranteeing future status and minority protection, but with a European Union or similar international monitoring mission.

Lessons for the future

An unforeseen consequence of the failure of intervention in Somalia has been the creation of an environment where Al-Qaeda operatives and similar extremists function with relative impunity.[30] Most contemporary peacekeeping operations require a long-term commitment to post-conflict peace-building. There is no 'quick fix' solution or universal template that can be transposed from one situation to another. The short-term missions, like that in Albania (Operation Alba, April to August 1997), are the exception rather than the rule. Strict compliance with the golden rules of consent, impartiality and non-use of force was

---

[28] Letter dated 6 August 2004 from the Secretary-General addressed to the President of the Security Council, UN Doc. S/2004/932, 30 November 2004, referring to Kosovo Provisional Institutions.

[29] Letter dated 17 November 2004 from the Secretary-General addressed to the President of the Security Council, UN Doc. S/ 2004/932, 30 November 2004, para. 65.

[30] International Crisis Group, *Counter-Terrorism in Somalia: Losing Hearts and Minds?*, ICG Africa Report No. 95, 11 July 2005.

crucial in Albania, but will not always be appropriate in other situations. In order to contain a variety of crises on the African continent, the UN must be prepared for long-term engagement.[31]

The long-term strategy in Somalia was unclear at the time of inception and, by the end of the operation, was non-existent, and it is not true to say that the UN broadened the mandate against the wishes of the United States. Where the peace is imposed, as in the case of the former Yugoslavia post-Dayton, the price to be paid is that of adequate resources and a long-term commitment to political rehabilitation. What efforts that were made at rebuilding the war-torn society were inept and imposed without sufficient attention to indigenous political, cultural and social traditions. Instead of seeking to marginalise all of the major warlords, the UN targeted Aideed. The unfolding events showed that the United States and the UN forces failed to appreciate the contradictions and inconsistencies in their confused roles of peacekeeping, peace-making and peace enforcement. When this was combined with United States domination and key positions that were held by difficult personalities, it is hardly surprising that UNOSOM II became a major protagonist in the conflict it was supposed to help resolve.

These issues did not arise in the case of UNIFIL, as this was an operation with an almost exclusively military focus. The political objectives were clear, but they were never intended to be the responsibility of UNIFIL; the force was meant to facilitate their achievement by international diplomacy. Nor was there a civil component to the mission. However, in the case of both UNIFIL and Somalia, the Security Council acted as if the mandate would be self-executing once the troops were deployed. The crises arising from armed conflict between Israel and the Lebanese Shia Islamic group Hizbollah during the summer of 2006 indicated that the lessons of UNIFIL were not learned. The leaders of the G-8 industrial nations and the UN Secretary-General called for the swift deployment of international troops in southern Lebanon to end the escalating violence.[32] Among the suggestions made was one from French President Chirac who called for the setting-up of a border surveillance 'cordon sanitaire' along the Israeli–Lebanese armistice line and a mandate that included disarming the Hizbollah militia. It seemed to be forgotten initially that there was already a UN peacekeeping force present in south Lebanon and that it had been there since 1978.

[31] UN Security Council Press Release SC/6410, 14 August 1997.
[32] Reuters, 19 July 2006.

Before deploying a UN authorised or commanded force, it is essential that there first be some kind of cease-fire agreement. As UNIFIL discovered to its cost, even agreement by leaders or governments does not always translate into co-operation on the ground. UNIFIL did not have an agreed area of operations at the outset and this significantly impeded its deployment in the early days. It is unlikely that this basic lesson was even considered by those advocating a new force for south Lebanon in 2006. Other more fundamental issues were also not addressed. UN Resolution 1559 (2004) called for the disbanding and disarmament of all Lebanese and non-Lebanese militias (a clear reference to Hizbollah).[33] It also supports the extension of the control of the government of Lebanon over all Lebanese territory. A new UN force could not ignore this resolution, but it constituted an impossible task in the circumstances. How was the proposed international force to disarm Hizbollah? Any attempt to do so would bring it into direct conflict with a party to the conflict. The Israeli Defence Forces had shown complete disregard for the safety of UN peacekeepers in the past and there was no reason to assume that this had changed. What responsibility would such a force have in regard to the protection of civilians? This is one of the most controversial developments in peace support operations in recent years. If Israel could not stop Hizbollah continuing rocket attacks on Israel, how was it hoped that a UN force could do so? A worst case scenario was the presence of an emasculated international force while Israeli forces and Hizbollah continue to reign terror on the civilians of Lebanon and Israel respectively.

There are similarities between the United States/UN-led mission in Somalia and the British army deployment in Northern Ireland in August 1969.[34] At first, both forces received a friendly reception from the local population, but relations soured when perceptions of their role changed and they failed to take account of its contradictions and inconsistencies. Likewise, in the 1980s, Indian intervention in Sri Lanka and United States intervention in Lebanon involved a similar confusion in roles and a practical incompatibility in their intervention.[35] After the death of over one thousand

---

[33] S/Res/1559(2004), adopted 2 September 2004.

[34] R. Murphy, *Ireland, Peacekeeping and Policing the 'New World Order'* (Belfast: Centre for Research and Documentation, 1997), pp. 25–44; and generally F. Ní Aolain, *The Politics of Force* (Belfast: Blackstaff, 2000); R. Evelagh, *Peace Keeping in a Democratic Society: The Lessons of Northern Ireland* (London: Hurst and Co., 1978); D. Hamill, *Pig in the Middle: The Army in Northern Ireland* (London: Methuen, 1985); and E. McCann, *War and an Irish Town* (3rd edn, London: Pluto Press, 1993).

[35] A. James, *Peacekeeping in International Politics* (London: Macmillan, 1990), pp. 131–3.

Indian peacekeepers in Sri Lanka, the soldiers were withdrawn as their presence presented an obstacle to achieving a peaceful resolution of the conflict. In Lebanon, despite the United States possessing the weaponry of a superpower, marines were reduced to that of a militia in Beirut.

There are aspects to the UN operation in Somalia that are especially reprehensible. The defence offered to claims of excessive zeal in the use of force has an all-too-familiar ring: provocateurs mingled in the crowds and fired first; collateral damage was minimal and civilian casualties exaggerated; the 'terrorists' used women and children as shields etc. Reputable organisations like the ICRC disputed the UN version of events. In addition, hundreds of Somalis were held in administrative detention. The scale of intensity and the frequency of the use of force converted UNOSOM II into a hostile army of occupation in the eyes of many Somalis, and endangered all those participating in the operation. What made matters worse is that this was done on behalf of the international community by the very Organization committed to setting, promoting and enforcing human rights standards by state governments. Apart from the loss of life on all sides, the tragedy of Somalia is the legacy of failure created when, in fact, the UN was called upon to do a range of impossible and confused tasks.

When it becomes evident that a mandate cannot be fulfilled, the UN faces the dilemma of withdrawing and abandoning the mission (with the consequent loss of credibility), or remaining in a situation on the ground that is unsustainable. Leadership, both political and military, is an often overlooked variable in the peacekeeping equation. The military in particular must be prepared to change. According to the former UN commander in Rwanda, General Roméo Dallaire, 'the era of a general who knows how to fight is gone, especially with the middle powers'.[36] A general must know how to be a diplomat and a humanist, skilled in the politics and nuances of nation-building. Although recent mandates have attempted to reflect the complex nature of most current missions, demanding clear mandates and timeframes is just not always realistic. This is an age of complexity and ambiguity and, if particular leaders cannot function in such an environment, those individuals should not be a part of the process. The early stages of UN missions in Sierra Leone (UNAMSIL) and the Democratic Republic of the Congo (MONUC) and Sudan (UNMIS) indicate that the problems associated

---

[36] C. Offman, 'Everything Humanly Possible', *Financial Times Magazine*, 12 March 2005, pp. 14–15.

with planning, logistics and training of peacekeepers remain and that little has been done to overcome the operational deficiencies evident in the case studies examined here. The High Level Panel on Threats, Challenges and Change was very critical of the 'glacial speed' at which the UN and member states responded to attacks on civilians in Africa, especially compared with the rapid response to the September 11 attacks in the United States.[37] The UN Peacebuilding Commission may remedy some of the inter-agency rivalry and duplication, but it must not be allowed to become just another layer of UN bureaucracy or a 'hostage to the prerogatives of the Security Council'.[38]

In deciding whether or not to initiate enforcement action or launch a peacekeeping operation, the criteria must be objective. The response should be graduated and proportionate and the mission must retain the support of the international community as a whole. It is a mistake to assume that the square peg of UN humanitarian intervention will fit into the round hole of either peacekeeping or enforcement operations. UN peacekeeping has serious operational and legal limitations, but it remains one of the more successful multilateral attempts to maintain peace and security. Compared with other interventions, peacekeeping offers the best return on investment.[39] Alternatives to the UN in this field are often much more expensive and much less capable. Despite setbacks, there is no reason why the UN cannot regain much of its lost credibility and adapt to the changed international environment. It is too easy to be cynical and to view the UN as a vehicle for the exercise of self-interest and realpolitik. Its founders intended that it embody a higher morality than that which determined the responses of individual states. Like democracy itself, the UN is an imperfect system, but there are few visions of a more effective alternative.

---

[37] *Report of the High-Level Panel on Threats Challenges and Change* (note 3 above), paras. 41–2.

[38] Maged Abdelaziz, Egyptian Ambassador to the United Nations, quoted by W. Hoge, 'UN Creates Commission to Assist Nations Recovering from Wars', *New York Times*, 21 December 2005.

[39] J. Guéhenno, 'A Continent Is Crying for Peacekeepers', *International Herald Tribune*, 15 October 2004; and J. Dobbins, S. G. Jones, K. Crane, A. Rathmell, B. Steele, R. Telschik and A. Timilsina, *The UN's Role in Nation Building: From Congo to Iraq* (Santa Monica, CA: Rand Corporation, 2005).

APPENDIX 1
RESOLUTIONS OF THE SECURITY COUNCIL: UNIFIL

Resolution 425 (1978) of 19 March 1978

The Security Council,

Taking note of the letters from the Permanent Representative of Lebanon and from the Permanent Representative of Israel,

Having heard the statements of the Permanent Representatives of Lebanon and Israel,

Gravely concerned at the deterioration of the situation in the Middle East and its consequences to the maintenance of international peace,

Convinced that the present situation impedes the achievement of a just peace in the Middle East,

1. *Calls* for strict respect for the territorial integrity, sovereignty and political independence of Lebanon within its internationally recognised boundaries;
2. *Calls upon* Israel immediately to cease its military action against Lebanese territorial integrity and withdraw forthwith its forces from all Lebanese territory;
3. *Decides*, in the light of the request of the Government of Lebanon, to establish immediately under its authority a United Nations interim force for Southern Lebanon for the purpose of confirming the withdrawal of Israeli forces, restoring international peace and security and assisting the Government of Lebanon in ensuring the return of its effective authority in the area, the force to be composed of personnel drawn from Member States;
4. *Requests* the Secretary-General to report to the Council within twenty-four hours on the implementation of the present resolution.

[Adopted at the 2,074th meeting by twelve votes to none, with two abstentions (Czechoslovakia and the Union of Soviet Socialist Republics).]

Resolution 467 (1980) of 24 April 1980

The Security Council,

Acting in response to the request of the Government of Lebanon,

Having studied the special report of the Secretary General on the United Nations Interim Force in Lebanon of 11 April 1980 and the subsequent statements, reports and addenda,

Having expressed itself through the statement of the President of the Security Council of 18 April 1980,

Recalling its resolutions 425 (1978), 426 (1978), 427 (1978), 434 (1978), 444 (1979), 450 (1979) and 459 (1979),

Recalling the terms of reference and general guidelines of the Force, as stated in the report of the Secretary General of 19 March 1978 confirmed by resolution 426 (1978), and particularly:

a. That the Force 'must be able to function as an integrated and efficient military unit',
b. That the Force 'must enjoy the freedom of movement and communication and other facilities that are necessary for the performance of its tasks',
c. That the Force 'will not use force except in self defence',
d. That 'self defence would include resistance to attempts by forceful means to prevent it from discharging its duties under the mandate of the Security Council',

1. *Reaffirms* its determination to implement the above-mentioned resolutions, particularly resolutions 425 (1978), 426 (1978) and 459 (1979), in the totality of the area of operation assigned to the United Nations Interim Force in Lebanon, up to the internationally recognised boundaries;
2. *Condemns* all actions contrary to the provisions of the above-mentioned resolutions and, in particular, strongly deplores:
   (a) Any violation of Lebanese sovereignty and territorial integrity;
   (b) The military intervention of Israel in Lebanon;
   (c) All acts of violence in violation of the General Armistice Agreement between Israel and Lebanon;
   (d) Provision of military assistance to the so-called *de facto* forces;
   (e) All acts of interference with the United Nations Truce Supervision Organisation:
   (f) All acts of hostility against the Force and in or through its area of operation as inconsistent with Security Council resolutions;
   (g) All obstructions of the ability of the Force to confirm the complete withdrawal of Israeli forces from Lebanon, to supervise the cessation of hostilities, to ensure the peaceful character of the area of operation, to control movement and to take measures deemed necessary to ensure the effective restoration of the sovereignty of Lebanon;
   (h) Acts that have led to loss of life and physical injuries among the personnel of the Force and of the United Nations Truce Supervision Organisation, their harassment and abuse, the disruption of communication, as well as the destruction of property and material;
3. *Condemns* the deliberate shelling of the headquarters of the Force and more particularly the field hospital, which enjoys special protection under international law;

4. *Commends* the efforts undertaken by the Secretary General and by the interested Governments to bring about the cessation of hostilities and to enable the Force to carry out its mandate effectively without interference;

5. *Commends* the Force for its great restraint in carrying out its duties in very adverse circumstances;

6. *Calls attention* to the provisions in the mandate that would allow the Force to use its right to self-defence;

7. *Calls attention* to the terms of reference of the Force which provide that it will use its best efforts to prevent the recurrence of fighting and to ensure that its area of operation will not be utilized for hostile activities of any kind;

8. *Requests* the Secretary General to convene a meeting, at an appropriate level, of the Israel–Lebanon Mixed Armistice Commission to agree on precise recommendations and further to reactivate the General Armistice Agreement conducive to the restoration of the sovereignty of Lebanon over all its territory up to the internationally recognised boundaries;

9. *Calls upon* all parties concerned and all those capable of lending any assistance to co-operate with the Secretary General in enabling the Force to fulfil its mandate;

10. *Recognises* the urgent need to explore all ways and means of securing the full implementation of resolution 425 (1978), including enhancing the capacity of the Force to fulfil its mandate in all its parts;

11. Requests the Secretary General to report as soon as possible on the progress of these initiatives and the cessation of hostilities.

[Adopted at the 2,218th meeting by twelve votes to none, with three abstentions (German Democratic Republic, the Union of Soviet Socialist Republics and the United States).]

APPENDIX 2
RESOLUTIONS OF THE SECURITY COUNCIL: SOMALIA

Resolution 794 (1992) of 3 December 1992

The Security Council,

Reaffirming its resolutions 733 (1992) of 23 January 1992, 746 (1992) of 17 March 1992,751 (1992) of 24 April 1992, 767 (1992) of 27 July 1992 and 775 (1992) of 28 August 1992,

Recognizing the unique character of the present situation in Somalia and mindful of its deteriorating, complex and extraordinary nature, requiring an immediate and exceptional response,

Determining that the magnitude of the human tragedy caused by the conflict in Somalia, further exacerbated by the obstacles being created to the distribution of humanitarian assistance, constitutes a threat to international peace and security,

Gravely alarmed by the deterioration of the humanitarian situation in Somalia and underlining the urgent need for the quick delivery of humanitarian assistance in the whole country,

Noting the efforts of the League of Arab States, the Organization of African Unity, and in particular the proposal made by its Chairman of the Assembly of Heads of State and Government of the Organization of African Unity, at the forty-seventh regular session of the General Assembly for the organization of an international conference on Somalia, and the Organization of the Islamic Conference and other regional agencies and arrangements to promote reconciliation and political settlement in Somalia and to address the humanitarian needs of the people of that country,

Commending the ongoing efforts of the United Nations, its specialized agencies and humanitarian organizations and of non-governmental organizations and of States to ensure delivery of humanitarian assistance in Somalia,

Responding to the urgent calls from Somalia for the international community to take measures to ensure the delivery of humanitarian assistance in Somalia,

Expressing grave alarm at continuing reports of widespread violations of international humanitarian law occurring in Somalia, including reports of violence and threats of violence against personnel participating lawfully in impartial humanitarian relief activities; deliberate attacks on non-combatants, relief consignments and vehicles, and medical and relief facilities; and impeding the delivery of food and medical supplies essential for the survival of the civilian population,

Dismayed by the continuation of conditions that impede the delivery of humanitarian supplies to destinations within Somalia, and in particular reports of looting of relief supplies destined for starving people, attacks on aircraft and ships bringing in humanitarian relief supplies, and attacks on the Pakistani UNOSOM contingent in Mogadishu of the United Nations Operation in Somalia,

Taking note with appreciation of the letters of the Secretary-General of 21 November 1992 (5/24859) and of 29 November 1992 (5/24868),

Sharing the Secretary-General's assessment that the situation in Somalia is intolerable and that it has become necessary to review the basic premises and principles of the United Nations effort in Somalia and that UNOSOM's existing course would not in present circumstances be an adequate response to the tragedy in Somalia,

Determined to establish as soon as possible the necessary conditions for the delivery of humanitarian assistance wherever needed in Somalia, in conformity with resolutions 751 (1992) and 767 (1992),

Noting the offer by Member States aimed at establishing a secure environment for humanitarian relief operations in Somalia as soon as possible,

Determined also to restore peace, stability and law and order with a view to facilitating the process of a political settlement under the auspices of the United Nations, aimed at national reconciliation in Somalia, and encouraging the Secretary-General and his Special Representative to continue and intensify their work at the national and regional levels to promote these objectives,

Recognizing that the people of Somalia bear ultimate responsibility for national reconciliation and the reconstruction of their own country,

1. *Reaffirms* its demand that all parties, movements and factions in Somalia immediately cease hostilities, maintaining a cease-fire throughout the country, and cooperate with the Special Representative of the Secretary-General for Somalia as well as with the military forces to be established pursuant to the authorization given in paragraph 10 below in order to promote the process of relief distribution, reconciliation and political settlement in Somalia;
2. *Demands* that all parties, movements and factions in Somalia take all measures necessary to facilitate the efforts of the United Nations, its specialized agencies and humanitarian organizations to provide urgent humanitarian assistance to the affected population in Somalia;
3. *Also demands* that all parties, movements and factions in Somalia take all measures necessary to ensure the safety of United Nations and all other personnel engaged in the delivery of humanitarian assistance, including the military forces to be established pursuant to the authorization given in paragraph 10 below;
4. *Further demands* that all parties, movements and factions in Somalia immediately cease and desist from all breaches of international humanitarian law including from actions such as those described above;

5. *Strongly condemns* all violations of international humanitarian law occurring in Somalia, including in particular the deliberate impeding of the delivery of food and medical supplies essential for the survival of the civilian population, and affirms that those who commit or order the commission of such acts will be held individually responsible in respect of such acts;

6. *Decides* that the operations and the further deployment of the 3,500 personnel of the United Nations Operation in Somalia (UNOSOM) authorized by paragraph 3 of resolution 775 (1992) should proceed at the discretion of the Secretary-General in the light of his assessment of conditions on the ground; and requests him to keep the Council informed and to make such recommendations as may be appropriate for the fulfillment of its mandate where conditions permit;

7. *Endorses* the recommendation by the Secretary-General in his letter of 29 November 1992 (S/24868) that action under Chapter VII of the Charter of the United Nations should be taken in order to establish a secure environment for humanitarian relief operations in Somalia as soon as possible;

8. *Welcomes* the offer by a Member State described in the Secretary-General's letter to the Council of 29 November 1992 (5/24868) concerning the establishment of an operation to create such a secure environment;

9. *Welcomes also* offers by other Member States to participate in that operation;

10. *Acting* under Chapter VII of the Charter of the United Nations, *authorizes* the Secretary-General and Member States cooperating to implement the offer referred to in paragraph 8 above to use all necessary means to establish as soon as possible a secure environment for humanitarian relief operations in Somalia;

11. *Calls* on all Member States which are in a position to do so to provide military forces and to make additional contributions, in cash or in kind, in accordance with paragraph 10 above and requests the Secretary-General to establish a fund through which the contributions, where appropriate, could be channeled to the States or operations concerned;

12. *Also authorizes* the Secretary-General and the Member States concerned to make the necessary arrangements for the unified command and control of the forces involved, which will reflect the offer referred to in paragraph 8 above;

13. *Requests* the Secretary-General and the Member States acting under paragraph 10 above to establish appropriate mechanisms for coordination between the United Nations and their military forces;

14. *Decides* to appoint an *ad hoc* commission composed of members of the Security Council to report to the Council on the implementation of this resolution;

15. *Invites* the Secretary-General to attach a small UNOSOM liaison staff to the field headquarters of the unified command;

16. Acting under Chapters VII and VIII of the Charter, *calls upon* States, nationally or through regional agencies or arrangements, to use such measures as may be necessary to ensure strict implementation of paragraph 5 of resolution 733 (1992);

17. *Requests* all States, in particular those in the region, to provide appropriate support for the actions undertaken by States, nationally or through regional agencies or arrangements, pursuant to this and other relevant resolutions;

18. *Requests* the Secretary-General and, as appropriate, the States concerned to report to the Council on a regular basis, the first such report to be made no later than fifteen days after the adoption of this resolution on the implementation of the present resolution and the attainment of the objective of establishing a secure environment so as to enable the Council to make the necessary decision for a prompt transition to continued peace-keeping operations;

19. *Also requests* the Secretary-General to submit a plan to the Council initially within fifteen days after the adoption of the present resolution to ensure that UNOSOM will be able to fulfill its mandate upon the withdrawal of the unified command;

20. *Invites* the Secretary-General and his Special Representative to continue their efforts to achieve a political settlement in Somalia;

21. *Decides* to remain actively seized of the matter.

Resolution 814 (1993) of 26 March 1993

The Security Council,

Reaffirming its resolutions 733 (1992) of 23 January 1992, 746 (1992) of 17 March 1992, 751 (1992) of 24 April 1992, 767 (1992) of 27 July 1992, 775 (1992) of 28 August 1992 and 794 (1992) of 3 December 1992,

Bearing in mind General Assembly resolution 47/167 of 18 December 1992,

Commending the efforts of Member States acting pursuant to resolution 794 (1992) to establish a secure environment for humanitarian relief operations in Somalia,

Acknowledging the need for a prompt, smooth and phased transition from the Unified Task Force (UNITAF) to the expanded United Nations Operation in Somalia (UNOSOM II),

Regretting the continuing incidents of violence in Somalia and the threat they pose to the reconciliation process,

Deploring the acts of violence against persons engaging in humanitarian efforts on behalf of the United Nations, States, and non-governmental organizations,

Noting with deep regret and concern the continuing reports of wide-spread violations of international humanitarian law and the general absence of the rule of law in Somalia,

Recognizing that the people of Somalia bear the ultimate responsibility for national reconciliation and reconstruction of their own country,

Acknowledging the fundamental importance of a comprehensive and effective programme for disarming Somali parties, including movements and factions,

Noting the need for continued humanitarian relief assistance and for the rehabilitation of Somalia's political institutions and economy,

Concerned that the crippling famine and drought in Somalia, compounded by the civil strife, have caused massive destruction to the means of production and the natural and human resources of that country,

Expressing its appreciation to the Organization of African Unity, the League of Arab States, the Organization of the Islamic Conference and the Non-Aligned Countries for their cooperation with, and support of, the efforts of the United Nations in Somalia,

Also expressing its appreciation to all Member States which have made contributions to the Fund established pursuant to paragraph 11 of resolution 794 (1992) and to all those who have provided humanitarian assistance to Somalia,

Commending the efforts, in difficult circumstances, of the initial United Nations Operation in Somalia (UNOSOM) established pursuant to resolution 751 (1992),

Expressing its appreciation for the invaluable assistance the neighboring countries have been providing to the international community in its efforts to restore peace and security in Somalia and to host large numbers of refugees displaced by the conflict and noting the difficulties caused to them due to the presence of refugees in their territories,

Convinced that the restoration of law and order throughout Somalia would contribute to humanitarian relief operations, reconciliation and political settlement, as well as to the rehabilitation of Somalia's political institutions and economy,

Convinced also of the need for broad-based consultations and deliberations to achieve reconciliation, agreement on the setting up of transitional government institutions and consensus on basic principles and steps leading to the establishment of representative democratic institutions,

Recognizing that the re-establishment of local and regional administrative institutions is essential to the restoration of domestic tranquility,

Encouraging the Secretary-General and his Special Representative to continue and intensify their work at the national, regional and local levels, including and encouraging broad participation by all sectors of Somali society, to promote the process of political settlement and national reconciliation and to assist the people of Somalia in rehabilitating their political institutions and economy,

Expressing its readiness to assist the people of Somalia, as appropriate, on a local, regional or national level, to participate in free and fair elections, with a view towards achieving and implementing a political settlement,

Welcoming the progress made at the United Nations-sponsored Informal Preparatory Meeting on Somali Political Reconciliation in Addis Ababa from 4 to I5 January 1993, in particular the conclusion at that meeting of, three agreements by the Somali parties, including movements and factions, and welcoming also any progress made at the Conference on National Reconciliation which began in Addis Ababa on I5 March 1993,

Emphasizing the need for the Somali people, including movements and factions, to show the political will to achieve security, reconciliation and peace,

Taking note of the reports of States concerned of 17 December 1992 (5/24976) and 19 January 1993 (5/25126) and of the Secretary-General of 19 December 1992 (5/24992) and 26 January 1993 (5/25168) on the implementation of resolution 794 (1992),

Having examined the report of the Secretary-General of 3 March 1993 (5/25354 and Add.1 and 2),

Welcoming the intention of the Secretary-General to seek maximum economy and efficiency and to keep the size of the United Nations presence, both military and civilian, to the minimum necessary to fulfill its mandate,

Determining that the situation in Somalia continues to threaten peace and security in the region,

A

1. *Approves* the further reports of the Secretary-General of 3, 11 and 22 March 1993;
2. *Expresses* its appreciation to the Secretary-General for convening the Conference on National Reconciliation for Somalia in accordance with the agreements reached during the Informal Preparatory Meeting on Somali Political Reconciliation in Addis Ababa in January 1993 and for the progress achieved towards political reconciliation in Somalia, and also for his efforts to ensure that, as appropriate, all Somalis, including movements, factions, community leaders, women, professionals, intellectuals, elders and other representative groups are suitably represented at such conferences;
3. *Welcomes* the convening of the Third United Nations Coordination Meeting for Humanitarian Assistance for Somalia in Addis Ababa from 11 to 13 March 1993 and the willingness expressed by Governments through this process to contribute to relief and rehabilitation efforts in Somalia, where and when possible;
4. *Requests* the Secretary-General, through his Special Representative, and with assistance, as appropriate, from all relevant United Nations entities, offices and specialized agencies, to provide humanitarian and other assistance to the people of Somalia in rehabilitating their political institutions and economy and promoting political settlement and national reconciliation, in accordance

with the recommendations contained in his report of 3 March 1993, including in particular:

(a) Assistance in the provision of relief and in the economic rehabilitation of Somalia, based on an assessment of clear, prioritized needs, and taking into account, as appropriate, the 1993 Relief and Rehabilitation Programme for Somalia prepared by the United Nations Department of Humanitarian Affairs of the Secretariat;

(b) Assistance in the repatriation of refugees and displaced persons within Somalia;

(c) Assistance to help the people of Somalia to promote and advance political reconciliation, through broad participation by all sectors of Somali society, and the re-establishment of national and regional institutions and civil administration in the entire country;

(d) Assistance in the re-establishment of Somali police, as appropriate at the local, regional or national level to assist in the restoration and maintenance of peace, stability and law and order, including in the investigation and facilitating the prosecution of serious violations of international humanitarian law;

(e) Assistance to the people of Somalia in the development of a coherent and integrated programme for the removal of mines throughout Somalia;

(f) Development of appropriate public information activities in support of the United Nations activities in Somalia;

(g) Creation of conditions under which Somali civil society may have a role at every level in the process of political reconciliation and in the formulation and realization of rehabilitation and reconstruction programmes;

B

Acting under Chapter VII of the Charter of the United Nations,

5. *Decides* to expand the size of the UNOSOM force, and its mandate in accordance with the recommendations contained in paragraphs 56–88 of the report of the Secretary-General of 3 March 1993, and the provisions of this resolution;

6. *Authorizes* the mandate for the expanded UNOSOM (UNOSOM II) for an initial period through 31 October 1993, unless previously renewed by the Security Council;

7. *Emphasizes* the crucial importance of disarmament and the urgent need to build on the efforts of UNITAF in accordance with paragraphs 59–69 of the report of the Secretary-General of 3 March 1993;

8. *Demands* that all Somali parties, including movements and factions, comply fully with the commitments they have undertaken in the agreements they

concluded at the Informal Preparatory Meeting on Somali Political Reconciliation at Addis Ababa, and in particular with their agreement on implementing the cease-fire and on Modalities of Disarmament (S/25168, annex III);

9. *Also demands* that all Somali parties, including movements and factions, take all measures to ensure the safety of the personnel of the United Nations and its agencies as well as the staff of the International Committee of the Red Cross (ICRC), intergovernmental organizations and non-governmental organizations engaged in providing humanitarian and other assistance to the people of Somalia in rehabilitating their political institutions and economy and promoting political settlement and national reconciliation;

10. *Requests* the Secretary-General to support from within Somalia the implementation of the arms embargo established by resolution 733 (1992), utilizing as available and appropriate the UNOSOM II forces authorized by this resolution, and to report on this subject, with any recommendations regarding more effective measures if necessary, to the Security Council;

11. *Calls upon* all States, in particular neighboring States, to cooperate in the implementation of the arms embargo established by resolution 733 (1992);

12. *Also requests* the Secretary-General to provide security, as appropriate, to assist in the repatriation of refugees and the assisted resettlement of displaced persons, utilizing UNOSOM II forces, paying particular attention to those areas where major instability continues to threaten peace and security in the region;

13. *Reiterates its demand* that all Somali parties, including movements and factions, immediately cease and desist from all breaches of international humanitarian law and reaffirms that those responsible for such acts be held individually accountable;

14. *Further Requests* the Secretary-General, through his Special Representative to direct the Force Commander of UNOSOM II to assume responsibility for the consolidation, expansion and maintenance of a secure environment throughout Somalia, taking account of the particular circumstances in each locality, on an expedited basis in accordance with the recommendations contained in his report of 3 March 1993, and in this regard to organize a prompt, smooth and phased transition from UNITAF to UNOSOM 11;

C

15. *Requests* the Secretary-General to maintain the fund established pursuant to resolution 794 (1992) for the additional purpose of receiving contributions for maintenance of UNOSOM II forces following the departure of UNITAF forces and for the establishment of Somali police, and calls on Member States to make contributions to this fund, in addition to their assessed contributions;

16. *Expresses appreciation* to the United Nations agencies, intergovernmental and non-governmental organizations and the ICRC for their contributions and assistance and requests the Secretary-General to ask them to continue to extend financial material and technical support to the Somali people in all regions of the country;

17. *Also requests* the Secretary-General to seek as appropriate, pledges and contributions from States and others to assist in financing the rehabilitation, of the political institutions and economy of Somalia;

18. *Further requests* the Secretary-General to keep the Security Council fully informed on action taken to implement the present resolution, in particular to submit as soon as possible a report to the Council containing recommendations for establishment of Somali police forces and thereafter to report no later than every ninety days on the progress achieved in accomplishing the objectives set out in the present resolution;

19. *Decides* to conduct a formal review of the progress towards accomplishing the purposes of the present resolution no later than 31 October 1993;

20. *Decides* to remain actively seized of the matter.

Resolution 837 (1993) of 6 June 1993

The Security Council,

Reaffirming its resolutions 733 (1992) of 23 January 1992, 746 (1992) of 17 March 1992, 751 (1992) of 24 April 1992, 767 (1992) of 27 July 1992, 775 (1992) of 28 August 1992, 794 (1992) of 3 December 1992 and 814 (1993) of 26 March 1993,

Bearing in mind General Assembly resolution 47/167 of 18 December 1992,

Gravely alarmed at the premeditated armed attacks launched by forces apparently belonging to the United Somali Congress (USC/SNA) against the personnel of the United Nations Operation in Somalia (UNOSOM II) on 5 June 1993,

Strongly condemning such actions, which directly undermine international efforts aimed at the restoration of peace and normalcy in Somalia,

Expressing outrage at the loss of life as a result of these criminal attacks,

Reaffirming its commitment to assist the people of Somalia in reestablishing conditions of normal life,

Stressing that the international community is involved in Somalia in order to help the people of Somalia who have suffered untold miseries due to years of civil strife in that country,

Acknowledging the fundamental importance of completing the comprehensive and effective programme for disarming all Somali parties, including movements and factions,

Convinced that the restoration of law and order throughout Somalia would contribute to humanitarian relief operations, reconciliation and political settlement, as well as to the rehabilitation of Somalia's political institutions and economy,

Condemning strongly the use of radio broadcasts, in particular by the USC/ SNA, to incite attacks against United Nations personnel,

Recalling the statement made by its president on 31 March 1993 (5/25493) concerning the safety of United Nations forces and personnel deployed in conditions of strife and committed to consider promptly measures appropriate to the particular circumstances to ensure that persons responsible for attacks and other acts of violence against United Nations forces and personnel are held to account for their actions,

Noting of the information provided to the Council by the Secretary-General on 6 June 1993,

Determining that the situation in Somalia continues to threaten peace and security in the region,

Acting under Chapter VII of the Charter of the United Nations,

1. *Strongly condemns* the unprovoked armed attacks against the personnel of UNOSOM II on 5 June 1993, which appear to have been part of a calculated and premeditated series of cease-fire violations to prevent by intimidation UNOSOM II from carrying out its mandate as provided for in resolution 814 (1993);

2. *Expresses its condolences* to the Government and people of Pakistan and the families of the UNOSOM II personnel who have lost their lives;

3. *Re-emphasizes* the crucial importance of the early implementation of the disarmament of all Somali parties, including movements and factions, in accordance with paragraphs 56–69 of the report of the Secretary-General of 3 March 1993 (S/25354), and of neutralizing radio broadcasting systems that contribute to the violence and attacks directed against UNOSOM II;

4. *Demands once again* that all Somali parties, including movements and factions, comply fully with the commitments they have undertaken in the agreements they concluded at the Informal Preparatory Meeting on Somali Political Reconciliation in Addis Ababa, and in particular with their Agreement on Implementing the Cease-fire and on Modalities of Disarmament (S/25168, annex III);

5. *Reaffirms* that the Secretary-General is authorized under resolution 814 (1993) to take all necessary measures against all those responsible for the armed attacks referred to in paragraph 1 above, including against those responsible for publicly inciting such attacks, to establish the effective authority of UNOSOM II throughout Somalia, including to secure the investigation of their actions and their arrest and detention for prosecution, trial and punishment;

6. *Requests* the Secretary-General urgently to inquire into the incident, with particular emphasis on the role of those factional leaders involved;

7. *Encourages* the rapid and accelerated deployment of all UNOS0M II contingents to meet the full requirements of 28,000 men, all ranks, as well as equipment, as indicated in the Secretary-General's report of 3 March 1993 (5/25354);

8. *Urges* Member States to contribute, on an emergency basis, military support and transportation, including armored personnel carriers, tanks and attack helicopters, in order to provide UNOS0M II the capability appropriately to confront and deter armed attacks directed against it in the accomplishment of its mandate;

9. *Also requests* the Secretary-General to submit a report to the Council on the implementation of the present resolution, if possible within seven days from the date of its adoption;

10. *Decides* to remain actively seized of the matter.

APPENDIX 3
RESOLUTIONS OF THE SECURITY COUNCIL: KOSOVO

Resolution 1244 (1999) of 10 June 1999

The Security Council,

Bearing in mind the purposes and principles of the Charter of the United Nations, and the primary responsibility of the Security Council for the maintenance of international peace and security,

Recalling its resolutions 1160 (1998) of 31 March 1998, 1199 (1998) of 23 September 1998, 1203 (1998) of 24 October 1998 and 1239 (1999) of 14 May 1999,

Regretting that there has not been full compliance with the requirements of these resolutions,

Determined to resolve the grave humanitarian situation in Kosovo, Federal Republic of Yugoslavia, and to provide for the safe and free return of all refugees and displaced persons to their homes,

Condemning all acts of violence against the Kosovo population as well as all terrorist acts by any party,

Recalling the statement made by the Secretary-General on 9 April 1999, expressing concern at the humanitarian tragedy taking place in Kosovo,

Reaffirming the right of all refugees and displaced persons to return to their homes in safety,

Recalling the jurisdiction and the mandate of the International Tribunal for the Former Yugoslavia,

Welcoming the general principles on a political solution to the Kosovo crisis adopted on 6 May 1999 (S/1999/516, annex 1 to this resolution) and welcoming also the acceptance by the Federal Republic of Yugoslavia of the principles set forth in points 1 to 9 of the paper presented in Belgrade on 2 June 1999 (S/1999/649, annex 2 to this resolution), and the Federal Republic of Yugoslavia's agreement to that paper,

Reaffirming the commitment of all Member States to the sovereignty and territorial integrity of the Federal Republic of Yugoslavia and the other States of the region, as set out in the Helsinki Final Act and annex 2,

Reaffirming the call in previous resolutions for substantial autonomy and meaningful self-administration for Kosovo,

Determining that the situation in the region continues to constitute a threat to international peace and security,

Determined to ensure the safety and security of international personnel and the implementation by all concerned of their responsibilities under the present resolution, and acting for these purposes under Chapter VII of the Charter of the United Nations,

1. *Decides* that a political solution to the Kosovo crisis shall be based on the general principles in annex 1 and as further elaborated in the principles and other required elements in annex 2;

2. *Welcomes* the acceptance by the Federal Republic of Yugoslavia of the principles and other required elements referred to in paragraph 1 above, and demands the full cooperation of the Federal Republic of Yugoslavia in their rapid implementation;

3. *Demands* in particular that the Federal Republic of Yugoslavia put an immediate and verifiable end to violence and repression in Kosovo, and begin and complete verifiable phased withdrawal from Kosovo of all military, police and paramilitary forces according to a rapid timetable, with which the deployment of the international security presence in Kosovo will be synchronized;

4. *Confirms* that after the withdrawal an agreed number of Yugoslav and Serb military and police personnel will be permitted to return to Kosovo to perform the functions in accordance with annex 2;

5. *Decides* on the deployment in Kosovo, under United Nations auspices, of international civil and security presences, with appropriate equipment and personnel as required, and welcomes the agreement of the Federal Republic of Yugoslavia to such presences;

6. *Requests* the Secretary-General to appoint, in consultation with the Security Council, a Special Representative to control the implementation of the international civil presence, and further requests the Secretary-General to instruct his Special Representative to coordinate closely with the international security presence to ensure that both presences operate towards the same goals and in a mutually supportive manner;

7. *Authorizes* Member States and relevant international organizations to establish the international security presence in Kosovo as set out in point 4 of annex 2 with all necessary means to fulfil its responsibilities under paragraph 9 below;

8. *Affirms* the need for the rapid early deployment of effective international civil and security presences to Kosovo, and demands that the parties cooperate fully in their deployment;

9. *Decides* that the responsibilities of the international security presence to be deployed and acting in Kosovo will include:

   (a) Deterring renewed hostilities, maintaining and where necessary enforcing a ceasefire, and ensuring the withdrawal and preventing the return into Kosovo of Federal and Republic military, police and paramilitary forces, except as provided in point 6 of annex 2;

(b) Demilitarizing the Kosovo Liberation Army (KLA) and other armed Kosovo Albanian groups as required in paragraph 15 below;

(c) Establishing a secure environment in which refugees and displaced persons can return home in safety, the international civil presence can operate, a transitional administration can be established, and humanitarian aid can be delivered;

(d) Ensuring public safety and order until the international civil presence can take responsibility for this task;

(e) Supervising demining until the international civil presence can, as appropriate, take over responsibility for this task;

(f) Supporting, as appropriate, and coordinating closely with the work of the international civil presence;

(g) Conducting border monitoring duties as required;

(h) Ensuring the protection and freedom of movement of itself, the international civil presence, and other international organizations;

10. *Authorizes* the Secretary-General, with the assistance of relevant international organizations, to establish an international civil presence in Kosovo in order to provide an interim administration for Kosovo under which the people of Kosovo can enjoy substantial autonomy within the Federal Republic of Yugoslavia, and which will provide transitional administration while establishing and overseeing the development of provisional democratic self-governing institutions to ensure conditions for a peaceful and normal life for all inhabitants of Kosovo;

11. *Decides* that the main responsibilities of the international civil presence will include:

(a) Promoting the establishment, pending a final settlement, of substantial autonomy and self-government in Kosovo, taking full account of annex 2 and of the Rambouillet accords (S/1999/648);

(b) Performing basic civilian administrative functions where and as long as required;

(c) Organizing and overseeing the development of provisional institutions for democratic and autonomous self-government pending a political settlement, including the holding of elections;

(d) Transferring, as these institutions are established, its administrative responsibilities while overseeing and supporting the consolidation of Kosovo's local provisional institutions and other peacebuilding activities;

(e) Facilitating a political process designed to determine Kosovo's future status, taking into account the Rambouillet accords (S/1999/648);

(f) In a final stage, overseeing the transfer of authority from Kosovo's provisional institutions to institutions established under a political settlement;

(g) Supporting the reconstruction of key infrastructure and other economic reconstruction;

   (h) Supporting, in coordination with international humanitarian organizations, humanitarian and disaster relief aid;

   (i) Maintaining civil law and order, including establishing local police forces and meanwhile through the deployment of international police personnel to serve in Kosovo;

   (j) Protecting and promoting human rights;

   (k) Assuring the safe and unimpeded return of all refugees and displaced persons to their homes in Kosovo;

12. *Emphasizes* the need for coordinated humanitarian relief operations, and for the Federal Republic of Yugoslavia to allow unimpeded access to Kosovo by humanitarian aid organizations and to cooperate with such organizations so as to ensure the fast and effective delivery of international aid;

13. *Encourages* all Member States and international organizations to contribute to economic and social reconstruction as well as to the safe return of refugees and displaced persons, and emphasizes in this context the importance of convening an international donors' conference, particularly for the purposes set out in paragraph 11 (g) above, at the earliest possible date;

14. *Demands* full cooperation by all concerned, including the international security presence, with the International Tribunal for the Former Yugoslavia;

15. *Demands* that the KLA and other armed Kosovo Albanian groups end immediately all offensive actions and comply with the requirements for demilitarization as laid down by the head of the international security presence in consultation with the Special Representative of the Secretary-General;

16. *Decides* that the prohibitions imposed by paragraph 8 of resolution 1160 (1998) shall not apply to arms and related matériel for the use of the international civil and security presences;

17. *Welcomes* the work in hand in the European Union and other international organizations to develop a comprehensive approach to the economic development and stabilization of the region affected by the Kosovo crisis, including the implementation of a Stability Pact for South Eastern Europe with broad international participation in order to further the promotion of democracy, economic prosperity, stability and regional cooperation;

18. *Demands* that all States in the region cooperate fully in the implementation of all aspects of this resolution;

19. *Decides* that the international civil and security presences are established for an initial period of 12 months, to continue thereafter unless the Security Council decides otherwise;

20. *Requests* the Secretary-General to report to the Council at regular intervals on the implementation of this resolution, including reports from the leaderships of the international civil and security presences, the first reports to be submitted within 30 days of the adoption of this resolution;

21. *Decides* to remain actively seized of the matter.

Annex 1 Statement by the Chairman on the Conclusion of the Meeting of the G-8 Foreign Ministers held at the Petersberg Centre on 6 May 1999

The G-8 Foreign Ministers adopted the following general principles on the political solution to the Kosovo crisis:

1. Immediate and verifiable end of violence and repression in Kosovo;
2. Withdrawal from Kosovo of military, police and paramilitary forces;
3. Deployment in Kosovo of effective international civil and security presences, endorsed and adopted by the United Nations, capable of guaranteeing the achievement of the common objectives;
4. Establishment of an interim administration for Kosovo to be decided by the Security Council of the United Nations to ensure conditions for a peaceful and normal life for all inhabitants in Kosovo;
5. The safe and free return of all refugees and displaced persons and unimpeded access to Kosovo by humanitarian aid organizations;
6. A political process towards the establishment of an interim political framework agreement providing for a substantial self-government for Kosovo, taking full account of the Rambouillet accords and the principles of sovereignty and territorial integrity of the Federal Republic of Yugoslavia and the other countries of the region, and the demilitarization of the KLA;
7. Comprehensive approach to the economic development and stabilization of the crisis region.

Annex 2

Agreement should be reached on the following principles to move towards a resolution of the Kosovo crisis:

1. An immediate and verifiable end of violence and repression in Kosovo.
2. Verifiable withdrawal from Kosovo of all military, police and paramilitary forces according to a rapid timetable.
3. Deployment in Kosovo under United Nations auspices of effective international civil and security presences, acting as may be decided under Chapter VII of the Charter, capable of guaranteeing the achievement of common objectives.
4. The international security presence with substantial North Atlantic Treaty Organization participation must be deployed under unified command and control and authorized to establish a safe environment for all people in Kosovo and to facilitate the safe return to their homes of all displaced persons and refugees.
5. Establishment of an interim administration for Kosovo as a part of the international civil presence under which the people of Kosovo can enjoy substantial

autonomy within the Federal Republic of Yugoslavia, to be decided by the Security Council of the United Nations. The interim administration to provide transitional administration while establishing and overseeing the development of provisional democratic self-governing institutions to ensure conditions for a peaceful and normal life for all inhabitants in Kosovo.

6. After withdrawal, an agreed number of Yugoslav and Serbian personnel will be permitted to return to perform the following functions:

   (a) Liaison with the international civil mission and the international security presence;
   (b) Marking/clearing minefields;
   (c) Maintaining a presence at Serb patrimonial sites;
   (d) Maintaining a presence at key border crossings.

7. Safe and free return of all refugees and displaced persons under the supervision of the Office of the United Nations High Commissioner for Refugees and unimpeded access to Kosovo by humanitarian aid organizations.

8. A political process towards the establishment of an interim political framework agreement providing for substantial self-government for Kosovo, taking full account of the Rambouillet accords and the principles of sovereignty and territorial integrity of the Federal Republic of Yugoslavia and the other countries of the region, and the demilitarization of UCK. Negotiations between the parties for a settlement should not delay or disrupt the establishment of democratic self-governing institutions.

9. A comprehensive approach to the economic development and stabilization of the crisis region. This will include the implementation of a stability pact for South-Eastern Europe with broad international participation in order to further promotion of democracy, economic prosperity, stability and regional cooperation.

10. Suspension of military activity will require acceptance of the principles set forth above in addition to agreement to other, previously identified, required elements, which are specified in the footnote below.[1] A military-technical agreement will then be rapidly concluded that would, among other things, specify

---

[1] Other required elements:

1. A rapid and precise timetable for withdrawals, meaning, e.g., seven days to complete withdrawal and air defence weapons withdrawn outside a 25 kilometre mutual safety zone within 48 hours;

2. Return of personnel for the four functions specified above will be under the supervision of the international security presence and will be limited to a small agreed number (hundreds, not thousands);

3. Suspension of military activity will occur after the beginning of verifiable withdrawals;

4. The discussion and achievement of a military-technical agreement shall not extend the previously determined time for completion of withdrawals.

additional modalities, including the roles and functions of Yugoslav/Serb personnel in Kosovo:

(a) Withdrawal

    (1) Procedures for withdrawals, including the phased, detailed schedule and delineation of a buffer area in Serbia beyond which forces will be withdrawn;

(b) Returning personnel

    (1) Equipment associated with returning personnel;

    (2) Terms of reference for their functional responsibilities;

    (3) Timetable for their return;

    (4) Delineation of their geographical areas of operation;

    (5) Rules governing their relationship to the international security presence and the international civil mission.

BIBLIOGRAPHY

Books

Abi-Saab, G. (ed.), *Essays in Honour of F. Kalshoven*, Dordrecht: Martinus Nijhoff, 1991

Amerasinghe, C. F., *Principles of the Institutional Law of International Organization*, Cambridge: Cambridge University Press, 1996

Azar, E. E., Jureidini, P. A., McLaurin, R. D., Norton, A. R., Pranger, R. J., Shnayerson, K., Snider, L. W., and Starr, J. R., *The Emergence of a New Lebanon: Fantasy or Reality*, New York: Praeger, 1984

Bailey, S. D., *Prohibitions and Restraints on War*, Oxford: Oxford University Press, 1972

  The UN Security Council and Human Rights, London: Macmillan, 1994

Bailey, S. D., and Daws, S., *The Procedure of the United Nations Security Council*, 3rd edn, Oxford: Clarendon Press, 1998

Ball, G. W., *Error and Betrayal in Lebanon: An Analysis of Israel's Invasion of Lebanon and Implications for US–Israeli Relations*, Washington, DC: Ford Foundation for Middle East Peace, 1987

Barros, J. (ed.), *The United Nations: Past, Present and Future*, London: Collier Macmillan, 1972

Bassiouni, M. C., *The Statute of the International Criminal Court: A Documentary History*, New York: Transnational, 1998

Becker, J., *The PLO: The Rise and Fall of the Palestinian Liberation Organization*, New York: St Martin's Press, 1984

Benvenuti, P., 'The Implementation of International Humanitarian Law in the Framework of Peacekeeping Operations', in *Law in Humanitarian Crises*, Brussels: European Commission, 1995, vol. 1

Berdal, M. R., *Whither UN Peacekeeping*, Adelphi Paper No. 281, Oxford: Oxford University Press, October 1993

Berdal, M., and Caplan, R. (eds.), *The Politics of International Administration*, 10(1) Special Edition, *Global Governance*, 2004

Best, G., *War and Law since 1945*, Oxford: Oxford University Press, 1994

Biermann, W., and Vadset, M., *UN Peacekeeping in Trouble: Lessons Learned from the Former Yugoslavia*, Aldershot: Ashgate, 1998

Bland, D. L., *Chiefs of Defence: Government and the Unified Control of the Armed Forces*, Toronto: Brown Book Co., 1995

Blechman, B. M., and Vaccaro, J. M., *Training for Peacekeeping: The UN Role*, Report No. 12, Washington, DC: Henry L. Stimson Center, July 1994

Boisson de Chazournes, L., and Sands, P. (eds.), *International Law, the International Court of Justice and Nuclear Weapons*, Cambridge: Cambridge University Press, 1999

Boutros-Ghali, B., *Unvanquished: A US–UN Saga*, New York: Random House, 1999

Bowden, M., *Black Hawk Down*, New York: Penguin, 2000

Bowens, G., *Legal Guide to Peace Support Operations*, Carlisle, PA: US Army Peacekeeping Institute, 1998

Bowett, D. W., *United Nations Forces*, London: Stevens, 1964

Boyd, J. M., *UN Peacekeeping Operations: A Military and Political Appraisal*, New York: Praeger, 1971

Brodeur, J. P., *Violence and Racial Prejudice in the Context of Peacekeeping*, a study prepared for the Commission of Inquiry into the Deployment of Canadian Forces to Somalia, 1997

Brons, M. H., *Society, Security, Sovereignty and the State: From Statelessness to Statelessness?*, Utrecht: International Books, 2001

Brown, M. A., *United Nations Peacekeeping: Historical Overview and Current Issues*, Report for Congress, Washington, DC: Congressional Research Service, 1993

Brownlie, I., *International Law and Use of Force by States*, Oxford: Oxford University Press, 1963

Buckley, W. (ed.), *Kosovo – Contending Voices on Balkan Intervention*, Grand Rapids, MI, and Cambridge: Eerdmans, 2000

Carter, J., *Keeping Faith: Memoirs of a President*, New York and London: Bantam Books, 1982

   The Blood of Abraham, Boston: Houghton Mifflin, 1985

Casey, J., *Constitutional Law in Ireland*, 3rd edn, Dublin: Round Hall Sweet and Maxwell, 2000

Cassese, A. (ed.), *United Nations Peacekeeping: Legal Essays*, The Hague: Sijthoff and Noordhoff, 1978

Castermans, M., Van Hoof, F., and Smith, J. (eds.), *The Role of the Nation State in the 21st Century*, Dordrecht: Kluwer, 1998

Charters, D. A., *Peacekeeping and the Challenge of Civil Conflict Resolution*, Frederiction: University of New Brunswick, Centre for Conflict Resolution, 1994

Chesterman, S., *The Use of Force in UN Peace Operations*, New York: External Study for the Best Practices Unit, UN Department of Peacekeeping Operations, 2004

Childers, E. (ed.), *Challenges to the United Nations*, London: St Martin's Press, 1994

Churchill, W., *The Grand Alliance*, The Second World War Series, Vol. 5, London: Cassells, 1950

Clark Arend, A., and Beck, R. J., *International Law and the Use of Force*, London and New York: Routledge, 1993

Clarke, W., and Herbst, J., *Learning from Somalia*, Boulder: Westview Press, 1997

Claude, I. L., *Swords into Plowshares*, 3rd edn, London: University of London Press, 1964

Craig, P., *Administrative Law*, 3rd edn, London: Sweet and Maxwell, 1989

CruisO'Brien, C., *To Katanga and Back: A UN Case History*, New York: Grosset and Dunlap, 1962

  The Siege: The Saga of Israel and Zionism, London: Weidenfeld and Nicolson, 1986

Daniel, D., and Hayes, F. (eds.), *Beyond Traditional Peacekeeping*, London: Macmillan, 1995

Daniker, G., *The Guardian Soldier: On the Nature and Use of Future Armed Forces*, United Nations Institute for Disarmament Research, New York: United Nations, 1995

Delissen, A., and Tanja, G. (eds.), *Humanitarian Law of Armed Conflict*, Dordrecht: Martinus Nijhoff, 1991

Diehl, P., *International Peacekeeping*, Baltimore and London: Johns Hopkins University Press, 1993

Dinstein, Y. (ed.), *International Law at the Time of Perplexity*, Dordrecht: Kluwer, 1989

Dinstein, Y. and Tabory, M., *War Crimes in International Law*, The Hague: Martinus Nijhoff, 1996

Diriye Abdullahi, M., *Fiasco in Somalia: US–UN intervention*, Africa Institute of South Africa, Occasional Paper No. 61, Africa Institute of South Africa, 1995

Duggan, J. P., *A History of the Irish Army*, Dublin: Gill and Macmillan, 1991

Dunant, H., *A Memory of Solfoll*, Geneva: ICRC, 1986

Dupuy, René-Jean (ed.), *A Handbook on International Organizations*, The Hague: Martinus Nijhoff, 1998

Durch, W. J. (ed.), *The Evolution of Peacekeeping*, New York: St Martin's Press, 1993

  (ed.), *UN Peacekeeping, American Politics, and the Uncivil Wars of the 1990s*, London: Macmillan, 1997

Eccles, H., *Military Concepts and Philosophy*, Piscatway: NJ Rutgers University Press, 1965

Eknes, A., and McDermott, A. (eds.), *Sovereignty, Humanitarian Intervention and the Military*, Oslo: Norwegian Institute of International Affairs, 1996

Erskine, E., *Mission with UNIFIL*, London: Hurst and Co., 1989

Evans, G., *Cooperating for Peace: The Global Agenda for the 1990s and Beyond*, St Leonards, NSW: Australia: Allen and Unwin, 1993

Evelagh, R., *Peace Keeping in a Democratic Society: The Lessons of Northern Ireland*, London: Hurst and Co., 1978

Fabian, L., *Soldiers Without Enemies*, Washington, DC: Brookings Institution, 1977

Faite, A., and Grenier, J. L. (eds.), *Expert Meeting on Multinational Operations, Geneva 11–12 December 2003*, Geneva: International Committee of the Red Cross, 2004

Fassbender, B., *UN Security Council Reform and the Right of Veto: A Constitutional Perspective*, The Hague: Kluwer, 1998

Fetherston, A. B., *Towards a Theory of United Nations Peacekeeping*, London: St Martin's Press, 1994

Fisk, R., *Pity the Nation*, London: Andre Deutsch, 1990

Fleck, D. (ed.), *Handbook of Humanitarian Law in Armed Conflicts*, Oxford: Oxford University Press, 1995

(ed.), *The Handbook of the Law of Visiting Forces*, Oxford: Oxford University Press, 2001

Fontaine, A., *History of the Cold War*, New York: Vintage Books, 1970

Freedman, R. O., *Soviet Policy Toward the Middle East Since 1970*, 3rd edn, New York: Praeger, 1982

(ed.), *The Middle East After the Invasion of Lebanon*, Syiacuse, NY: Syracuse University Press, 1986

Friedland, M. L., *Controlling Misconduct in the Military*, a study prepared for the Commission of Inquiry into the Deployment of Canadian Forces to Somalia, 1997

Frydenberg, P. (ed.), *Peacekeeping: Experience and Evaluation – The Oslo Papers*, Oslo, NUPI, 1964

Gabriel, R., *To Serve with Honour*, Westport: Greenwood Press, 1982

Operation Peace for Galilee: The Israeli PLO War in Lebanon, Toronto: Collins, 1985

Gaffen, F., *In the Eye of the Storm: A History of Canadian Peacekeeping*, Toronto: Denlau and Wayne, 1987

Gallagher, T., and O'Connell, J. (eds.), *Contemporary Irish Studies*, Manchester: Manchester University Press, 1983

Gasser, H.-P., *International Humanitarian Law: An Introduction*, Geneva: Henri Dunant Institute, 1993

Gilmore, D., *Lebanon: The Fractured Country*, London: Sphere Books, 1984

Ginifer, J. (ed.), *Beyond Emergencies: Development Within Peacekeeping Missions*, Special Edition, *International Peacekeeping*, London: Frank Cass, 1996

Goodman, A. E. (ed.), *The Diplomatic Record, 1992–1993*, Boulder: Westview Press, 1994

Goodrich, L. M., *The United Nations*, London: Stevens, 1960

The United Nations in a Changing World, London: Columbia University Press, 1974

Goodrich, L. M., Hambro, E., and Simons, A. P., *Charter of the United Nations*, 3rd edn, New York: Columbia University Press, 1969

Gordenker, L., *The UN Secretary General and the Maintenance of Peace*, London: Columbia University Press, 1967

Green, L. C., *The Contemporary Law of Armed Conflict*, Manchester: Manchester University Press, 1993

Greenwood, C., *Command and the Laws of Conflict*, Shrivenham: Strategic and Combat Studies Institute, 1993

Gutman, R., and Reif, D. (eds.), *Crimes of War*, New York: Norton and Co., 1999

Gutteridge, J. A. C., *The United Nations in a Changing World*, Manchester: Manchester University Press, 1962

Gwynn Morgan, D., *Constitutional Law of Ireland*, 2nd edn, Dublin: Round Hall Press, 1990

Haig, A. M., *Caveat, Realism, Reagan and Foreign Policy*, New York: Macmillan, 1984

Hamill, D., *Pig in the Middle: The Army in Northern Ireland*, London: Methuen, 1985

Harbottle, M., *The Blue Helmets*, London: Leo Cooper, 1975

Harris, J. (ed.), *The Politics of Humanitarian Intervention*, London: Pinter, 1995

Henkin, L., *et al.*, *Right v. Might: International Law and the Use of Force*, New York and London: Council on Foreign Relations Press, 1988

Herzog, C., *The Arab-Israeli Wars*, London: Arms and Armour Press, 1982

Higgins, R., *The Development of International Law through the Political Organs of the Nations*, Oxford: Oxford University Press, 1963

   The United Nations Peacekeeping 1946–1967, Oxford: Oxford University Press, 1969

   The United Nations Operation in the Congo (ONUC) 1960–1962, London: Royal Institute of International Affairs, 1980

   Problems and Process: International Law and How We Use It, Oxford: Clarendon Press, 1994

Hilderbrand, R. C., *Dumbarton Oaks: The Origins of the UN and the Search for Post War Security*, Chapel Hill: University of North Carolina Press, 1990

Hirsch, J., and Oakley, R., *Somalia and Operation Restore Hope*, Washington, DC: US Institute of Peace, 1995

Hiscocks, R., *The Security Council*, London: Longmans, 1974

Hof, F. C., *Galilee Divided: The Israel Lebanon Frontier, 1916–1984*, Boulder, Westview Press, 1985

Hogan, G., and Morgan, D., *Administrative Law in Ireland*, 3rd edn, Dublin: Round Hall Sweet and Maxwell, 1998

Hogan, G., and Whyte, G., *J. M. Kelly: The Irish Constitution*, 4th edn, Dublin: Butterworths, 2003

Holbrooke, R., *To End a War*, New York: Random House, 1998

Holzgrefe J. L., and Keohane, R. O. (eds.), *Humanitarian Intervention*, Cambridge: Cambridge University Press, 2003

Howard, M. (ed.), *Restraints on War: Studies in the Limitation of Armed Conflict*, Oxford: Oxford University Press, 1979

Humphreys, G., and Craven, C., *Military Law in Ireland*, Dublin: Round Hall Sweet and Maxwell, 1997

Ignatieff, M. *Empire Lite: Nation-Building in Bosnia, Kosovo and Afghanistan*, London: Vintage, 2003

Independent International Commission on Kosovo, *Kosovo Report: Conflict – International Response – Lessons Learned*, Oxford: Oxford University Press, 2000

International Commission on Intervention and State Sovereignty, *The Responsibility to Protect: Report of the International Commission on Intervention and State Sovereignty*, Ottawa: International Development Research Centre, 2001

International Committee of the Red Cross, *Commentary on the Additional Protocols of 8 June 1977 to the Geneva Conventions of 12 August 1946*, Geneva: ICRC, 1987

  Symposium on Humanitarian Action and Peacekeeping Operations Report, Geneva: ICRC, 1994

  Model Manual of the Law of Armed Conflict for Armed Forces, Geneva: ICRC, 1999

International Peace Academy, *The Peacekeeping Handbook*, New York: International Peace Academy, 1984

Israel in Lebanon: Report of the International Commission to Enquire into Reported Violations of International Law by Israel During Its Invasion of the Lebanon, London: Ithaca Press, 1983

James, A., *The Politics of Peacekeeping*, London: Chatto and Windus, 1969

  The Role of Force in International Order and United Nations Peacekeeping, Report of a Conference at Ditchley Park, 16–19 May 1969, Ditchley Paper No. 20, Enstone, Oxford-shire: Ditchley Foundation, 1969

  Interminable Interim: The UN Force in Lebanon, London: Centre for Security and Conflict Studies, 1986

  Peacekeeping in International Politics, London: Macmillan, 1990

Janowitz, M., *The Professional Soldier*, New York: Free Press, 1960

Jansen, M., *The Battle of Beirut: Why Israel Invaded Lebanon*, London: Zed Press, 1982

Jones, S. G., Crane, K., Rathmell, A., Steele, B., Telschik, R., and Timilsina, A., *The UN's Role in Nation Building: From Congo to Iraq*, Santa Monica, CA: Rand Corporation, 2005

Jett, D. C., *Why Peacekeeping Fails*, New York: Palgrave, 2001

Johnstone, I., *Aftermath of the Gulf War: An Assessment of UN Action*, International Peace Academy, Occasional Paper Series, Boulder and London: Lynne Rienner, 1994

Jordan, H., *Crisis: The Last Year of the Carter Presidency*, New York: G. P. Putnam's Sons, 1982

Joulwan, A., and Shoemaker, C. C., *Civilian–Military Cooperation in the Prevention of Deadly Conflict*, a report to the Carnegie Commission on the Prevention of Deadly Conflict, New York, December 1998

Kalshoven, F., *Constraints on the Waging of War*, Geneva: ICRC, 1987

Kaslhoven, F., and Sandoz, Y. (eds.), *Implementation of International Humanitarian Law*, Dordrecht: Martinus Nijhoff, 1989

Katayanagi, M., *Human Rights Functions of Peacekeeping Operations*, The Hague: Kluwer, 2002

Kelly, M. J., *Restoring and Maintaining Order in Complex Peace Operations*, The Hague: Kluwer, 1999

Kennedy, M., and McMahon, D., *Obligations and Responsibilities: Ireland and the United Nations 1955–2005*, Dublin: Institute of Public Administration, 2005

Khalidi, W., *Conflict and Violence in the Lebanon: Confrontation in the Middle East*, Harvard Studies in International Affairs No. 39, Cambridge, MA: Harvard University Center for International Affairs, 1980

Kirgis, F. L., *International Organisations in their Legal Setting*, 2nd edn, Egan, MN: West Publishing Co., 1992

Kissinger, H., *Years of Upheaval*, London: Weidenfeld and Nicholson, 1982

Kuhne, W., Lenzi, G. A., and Vasconcelos, A., *WEU's Role in Crisis Management: Conflict Resolution in Sub-Saharan Africa*, Paris: Institute for Strategic Security Studies, Western European Union, 1995

LaRose-Edwards, P., Dangerfield, J., and Weeks, R., *Non-Traditional Military Training for Canadian Peacekeepers*, a study prepared for the Commission of Inquiry into the Deployment of Canadian Forces to Somalia

Last, D., *Theory, Doctrine and Practice of Conflict De-escalation in Peacekeeping Operations*, Clementsport, Nova Scotia: Canadian Peacekeeping Press, 1997

Lee, R. (ed.), *The International Criminal Court: The Making of the Rome Statute*, Dordrecht: Kluwer, 1999

Lefever, E., *Crisis in the Congo: A United Nations Force in Action*, Washington DC: Brookings Institution, 1965

Uncertain Mandate: Politics of the UN Congo Operation, Chicago: University of Chicago Press, 1967

Levie, H. S., *When Battle Rages: How Can Law Protect?*, Working Papers and Proceedings of the Fourteenth Hammarskjold Forum No. 6, John Carey (ed.), New York: Oceana Publications, 1971

Levite, A. E., *et al.* (eds.), *Foreign Military Intervention*, New York: Columbia University Press, 1992

Lewis, I. M., *A Modern History of Somalia: Nation and State in the Horn of Africa*, London: Longmans, 1980

Lie, T., *In the Cause of Peace*, New York: Macmillan, 1954

Liu, F. T., *United Nations Peacekeeping and the Non-Use of Force*, New York: International Peace Academy, 1992

Loomis, D., *The Somalia Affair: Reflections on Peacemaking and Peacekeeping*, Ottawa: DGL Publications, 1996

Lowe, A., and Fitzmaurice, M. (eds.), *Fifty Years of the International Court of Justice: Essays in Honour of Sir Robert Jennings.*, Cambridge: Cambridge University Press, 1996

Lui, F. T., *United Nations Peacekeeping and the Non-Use of Force*, New York: International Peace Academy, 1992

MacKenzie, L., *Peacekeeper: The Road to Sarajevo*, Toronto: Harper Collins, 1994

MacKinlay, J., *The Peacekeepers: An Assessment of Peacekeeping Operations at the Arab-Israeli Interface*, London: Unwin Hyman, 1989

MacKinnon, M., *US Peacekeeping Policy under Clinton*, London: Frank Cass, 1999

MacQueen, N. J. D., *Irish Neutrality: The United Nations and the Peacekeeping Experience, 1945–1969*, DPhil thesis, New University of Ulster, 1981

Maguire, J., *Defending Peace: For an Alternative to NATO/PfP and a Militarised Europe*, Dublin: Afri, 1999

Makinda, S., *Seeking Peace from Chaos: Humanitarian Intervention in Somalia*, Boulder and London: Lynne Rienner, 1993

Malan, M. (ed.), *Whither Peacekeeping in Africa?*, International Security Studies Monograph No. 36, Pretoria: Institute for Security Studies, April 1999

Malanczuk, P., *Humanitarian Intervention and the Legitimacy of the Use of Force*, The Hague: Martinus Nijhoff, 1993

Malone, D., *Decision Making in the UN Security Council: The Case of Haiti, 1990–1997*, Oxford: Clarendon Press, 1998

Marantz, P., and Stein, J. G. (eds.), *Peace Making in the Middle East: Problems and Prospects*, London: Croom Helm, 1985

Mayall, J. (ed.), *The New Interventionism 1991–1994: UN Experience in Cambodia, Former Yugoslavia, and Somalia*, Cambridge: Cambridge University Press, 1996

McCann, E., *War and an Irish Town*, 3rd edn, London: Pluto Press, 1993

McCoubrey, H., *International Humanitarian Law*, Aldershot: Dartmouth, 1990

McCaughran, T., *The Peacemakers at Niemba*, Dublin: Brown and Nolan, 1966

McCoubrey, H., and White, N., *International Organisations and Civil Wars*, Aldershot: Dartmouth, 1995

　　The Blue Helmets: Legal Regulation of United Nations Military Operations, Aldershot: Dartmouth, 1996

McDermott, T. (ed.), *Ethnic Conflict and International Security*, Oslo: Norsk Untenrikspolitisk Institute, 1995

McDonald, H., *IISHBATT: The Story of Ireland's Blue Berets in the Lebanon*, Dublin: Gill and Macmillan, 1993

McNair, Lord, and Watts, A. D., *The Legal Effects of War*, 4th edn, Cambridge: Cambridge University Press, 1966

Meron, T., *Human Rights in Internal Strife: Their International Protection*, Cambridge: Grotius, 1987

Meyer, M. A., and McCoubrey, H. (eds.), *Reflections on Law and Armed Conflicts*, The Hague: Kluwer Law International, 1998

Miller, R., *The Law of War*, Lexington MA: Lexington Books, 1975

Morgan, D. G., *Constitutional Law of Ireland*, 2nd edn, Dublin: Round Hall Press, 1990

Morris, B., *Righteous Victims: A History of the Zionist–Arab Conflict, 1881–2000*, New York: Vintage, 2001

Morrison, A., Fraser, D., and Kiras, J., *Peacekeeping with Muscle: The Use of Force in International Conflict Resolution*, Cornwallis: Canadian Peacekeeping Press, 1997

Morrison Skelly, J., *Irish Diplomacy at the United Nations, 1945–65*, Dublin: Irish Academic Press, 1997

Mulinen, F. de, *The Law of War and the Armed Forces*, Series Ius in Bello, No. 1, Geneva: Henry Dunant Institute, 1992

Mullins, C., *The Leipzig Trials: An Account of the War Criminals Trials and a Study of the German Mentality*, London: H. F. and G. Witherby, 1921

Murphy, D., *Humanitarian Intervention*, Philadelphia: University of Pennsylvania press, 1996

Murphy, J. F., *The United Nations and the Control of International Violence: A Legal and Political Analysis*, Manchester: Manchester University Press, 1983

Murphy, R., *Ireland, Peacekeeping and Policing the 'New World Order'*, Belfast: Centre for Research and Documentation, 1997

Nakleh, K., and Wright, C. A., *After the Palestine Israel War, Limits to US and Israeli Policy*, Belmont, MA: Institute of Arab Studies, 1983

Ní Aolain, F., *The Politics of Force*, Belfast: Blackstaff, 2000

Nordquist, M., *What Color Helmet?: Reforming Security Council Peacekeeping Mandates*, Newport, RI: Naval War College, Center for Naval Warfare Studies, 1997

O'Halpin, E., *Defending Ireland*, Oxford: Oxford University Press, 1999

O'Neill, J. T., and Rees, N., *United Nations Peacekeeping in the Post-Cold War Era*, London: Routledge, 2005

O'Neill, W., *Kosovo: An Unfinished Peace*, Colorado and London: Lynne Rienner Publishers, 2002

O'Reilly, J. W., and Healy, P., *Independence in the Prosecution of Offences in the Canadian Forces: Military Policing and Prosecutorial Discretion*, a study prepared for the Commission of Inquiry into the Deployment of Canadian Forces to Somalia, 1997

Operation Iron Fist: Israeli Policy in Lebanon, London: League of Arab States, May 1985

Operational Law Handbook 2002, Charlottesville, VA: International and Operational Law Department, Judge Advocates General's School, US Army, 2002

Padelford, N. J., and Goodrich, L. (eds.), *The United Nations in the Balance*, London: Praeger, 1965

Palin, N., *Multinational Military Forces: Problems and Prospects*, Adelphi Paper No.294, International Institute for Strategic Studies, Oxford: Oxford University Press, 1995

Pearson, R., *National Minorities in Eastern Europe 1849–1945*, London: Macmillan, 1983

Pelcovits, N. A., *Peacekeeping on Arab-Israeli Fronts*, Boulder and London: Westview Press and Foreign Policy Institute, School of Advanced International Studies, 1984

Pictet, J. S., *et al.*, *Commentary: Geneva Convention for the Amelioration of the Condition of the Wounded and Sick in Armed Forces in the Field*, Geneva: International Committee of the Red Cross, 1952

    Commentary: Geneva Convention IV Relative to the Protection of Civilian Persons in Time of War, Geneva: International Committee of the Red Cross, 1958

Playfair, E. (ed.), *International Law and the Administration of Occupied Territories*, Oxford: Oxford University Press, 1992

Pugh, M., *The UN, Peace and Force*, London: Frank Cass, 1996

Pugh, M., and Sidhu, W. P. S. (eds.), *The United Nations and Regional Security*, Boulder: Lynne Rienner, 2003

Ratner, S. R., *The New UN Peacekeeping*, London: Macmillan, 1995

Right v. Might – International Law and the Use of Force, New York and London: Council on Foreign Relations Press, 1989

Rikhye, I. J., *The Theory and Practice of Peacekeeping*, London: Hurst and Co., 1984

    Military Advisor to the Secretary-General: UN Peacekeeping and the Congo Crisis, London: Hurst and Co., 1993

    The Politics and Practice of United Nations Peacekeeping: Past, Present and Future, Clementsport, Nova Scotia: Canadian Peacekeeping Press, 2000

Rikhye, I. J., and Skjelsbaek, K. (eds.), *The UN and Peacekeeping*, New York: St Martin's Press, 1991

Roberts, A., and Guelff, R. (eds.), *Documents on Laws of War*, Oxford: Clarendon Press, 1982

Roberts, A., *Humanitarian Action in War*, Adelphi Paper No.305, Oxford: Oxford University Press, 1996

Roberts, A., and Kingsbury, B., *United Nations, Divided World: The UN's Role in International Relations*, Oxford: Clarendon Press, 1988

Rodal, B., *The Somalia Experience in Strategic Perspective: Implications for the Military in a Free and Democratic Society*, a study prepared for the Commission of Inquiry into the Deployment of Canadian Forces to Somalia, 1997

Roper, J., Nishihara, M., Otunnu, O., and Schoettle, E., *Keeping the Peace in the Post-Cold War Era: Strengthening Multilateral Peacekeeping*, New York: Trilateral Commission, 1993

Rotberg, R. I. (ed.), *Namibia: Political and Economic Prospects*, Lexington, MA: Lexington, Books, 1983

Rowe, P., *Defence: The Legal Implications, Military Law and the Law of War*, London: Brassey's Defence Publishers, 1987

Rules of Engagement (ROE) for Judge Advocates, Charlottesville, VA: Centre for Law and Military Operations (CLAMO), 2000

Sahnoun, M., *Somalia: The Missed Opportunities*, Washington, DC: United States Institute of Peace, 1994

Sarooshi, D., *The United Nations and the Development of Collective Security*, Oxford: Clarendon Press, 1999

Sassoli, M., and Bouvier, A., *How Does Law Protect in War*, 2nd edn, Geneva: ICRC, 2006

Schabas, W. A., *Genocide in International Law*, Cambridge: Cambridge University Press, 2000

  An Introduction to the International Criminal Court, 2nd edn, Cambridge: Cambridge University Press, 2004

Schafer, A., *The Buck Stops Here: Reflections on Moral Responsibility, Democratic Accountability and Military Values*, a study prepared for the *Commission of Inquiry into the Deployment of Canadian Forces to Somalia*, 1997

Schermers, H. G., and Blokker, N. M., *International Institutional Law*, 3rd edn, The Hague: Martinus Nijhoff, 1995

Schiff, Z., and Ya'ari, E., *Israel's Lebanon War*, London: George Allen and Unwin, 1985

Schiffer, R. (ed.), *Building the Future Order*, London: Collier Macmillan, 1980

Schindler, D., and Toman, J., *The Laws of Armed Conflicts: A Collection of Conventions, Resolutions and Other Documents*, 4th edn, Leiden: Martinus Nijhoff, 2004

Schlisinger, A., *The Imperial Presidency*, Boston: Houghton Mifflin, 1973

Schmidl, E., *Peace Operations Between War and Peace*, London: Frank Cass, 2000

Schnabel, A., and Thakur, R. (eds.), *Kosovo and the Challenge of Humanitarian Intervention*, Tokyo and New York: United Nations University Press, 2000

Schwarzenberger, G., *International Law The Law of Armed Conflict*, London: Stevens, 1968

Segal, David R., and Segal, Mandy Wechsler, *Peacekeepers and their Wives*, London: Greenwood Press, 1993

Sens, A. G., *Somalia and the Changing Nature of Peacekeeping: The Implications for Canada*, a study prepared for the Commission of Inquiry into the Deployment of Canadian Forces to Somalia, 1997

Shaw, M. N., *International Law*, 5th edn, Cambridge: Cambridge University Press, 2003

Shawcross, W., *Deliver Us from Evil*, London: Bloomsbury, 2000

Siekmann, R., *Basic Documents on United Nations and Related Peace-Keeping Forces*, 2nd edn, Dordrecht: Martinus Nijhoff, 1989

National Contingents in United Nations Peacekeeping, Dordrecht: Martinus Nijhoff, 1991

Simma, B. (ed.), *The Charter of the United Nations: A Commentary*, 2nd edn, Oxford: Oxford University Press, 2002

Simpson, J., *Law Applicable to Canadian Forces in Somalia 1992/93*, a study prepared for the Commission of Inquiry into the Deployment of Canadian Forces to Somalia, 1997

Skogmo, B., *International Peacekeeping in Lebanon, 1978–1988*, Boulder and London: Lynne Rienner, 1989

Smith, H. (ed.), *The Force of Law: International Law and the Land Commander*, Canberra: Australian Defence Studies Centre/Australian Defence Forces Academy, 1994

Smith, D., *The State of War and Peace Atlas*, International Peace Research Institute, Oslo, London: Penguin, 1997

Smith, R., *Under the Blue Flag*, Dublin: Aherlow, 1980

Stone, J., *Legal Controls of International Conflict: A Treatise on the Dynamics of Disputes and War Law*, Sydney: Maitland Publications, 1958

Storch, K., *Peacekeeping: The Role of UNIFIL 1978–1984*, Thesis, American University of Beirut, 1984

Suter, K., *An International Law of Guerilla Warfare*, London: Pinter, 1984

Tamir, A., *A Soldier in Search of Peace*, London: Weidenfeld and Nicolson, 1988

Thakur, R., *International Peacekeeping in Lebanon*, Boulder: Westview Press, 1987
(ed.), *International Conflict Resolution*, Boulder: Westview Press, 1988

Thornberry, P., *International Law and the Rights of Minorities*, Oxford: Oxford University Press, 1991

Triffterer, O. (ed.), *Commentary on the Rome Statute of the International Criminal Court*, Baden-Baden: Nomos, 1999

Tueni, G., *Une Guerre pour les Autres*, Paris: Jean Claude Lattes, 1985

Twitchett, K. (ed.), *International Security: Reflections on Security and Survival*, London: Oxford University Press, 1971

United Kingdom Army Field Manual, vol. 5, *Wider Peacekeeping*, 5th Draft Revision, London: HMSO, 1995

United Nations, *Managing Arms in Peace Processes: Somalia*, New York: United Nations Institute for Disarmament Research, 1995
The Blue Helmets: A Review of United Nations Peacekeeping, 3rd edn, New York: United Nations, 1996

United Nations, *The United Nations and Somalia 1992–1996*, United Nations Blue Book Series, Vol. VIII, New York: United Nations, 1996

Urquhart, B., *Hammarskjöld*, New York: Alfred Knopf, 1972
A Life in Peace and War, London: Weidenfeld and Nicolson, 1987

Van Doorn, J. (ed.), *Armed Forces and Society*, Sociological Essays, The Hague: Mouton, 1968

Van Hoof, C., and Smith, H. (eds.), *The Role of the Nation State in the 21st Century*, Dordrecht: Kluwer, 1998

Venkata Raman, K., *The Ways of the Peacemaker*, New York: United Nations Institute for Training and Research, 1975

Verrier, A., *International Peacekeeping*, Harmondsworth: Penguin, 1981

Vocke, H., *The Lebanese War, Its Origins and Political Dimensions*, London: Hurst and Co., 1978

Wade, H., and Forsyth, C., *Administrative Law*, 7th edn, Oxford: Clarendon Press, 1994

Wainhouse, D., *International Peacekeeping at the Crossroads*, Baltimore: Johns Hopkins University Press, 1973

Waldheim, K., *Building the Future Order*, Schiffer, R. C. (ed.), London: Collier Macmillan, 1980

Weiss, T. G. (ed.), *Beyond UN Subcontracting*, London: Macmillan, 1998

Weiss, T. G., Forsythe, D. P., and Coate, R. A., *The United Nations and Changing World Politics*, Boulder: Westview Press, 1994

White, N. D., *Keeping the Peace: The United Nations and the Maintenance of International Peace and Security*, 2nd edn, Manchester: Manchester University Press, 1997

White, N. D., and Klassen, D. (eds.), *The UN, Human Rights and Post-Conflict Situations*, Manchester: Manchester University Press, 2005

Wilson, A. J., *Some Principles for Peacekeeping Operations: A Guide for Senior Officers*, Monograph No. 2, Paris: International Information Centre on Peacekeeping Operations, 1967

Winslow, D., *The Canadian Airborne Regiment in Somalia: A Socio-Cultural Inquiry*, a study prepared for the Commission of Inquiry into the Deployment of Canadian Forces to Somalia, 1997

Wiseman, H. (ed.), *Peacekeeping: Appraisals and Proposals*, Oxford: Pergamon Press, 1983

Wright, R., *Sacred Rage: The Crusade of Islam*, London and New York: Linden Press and Simon and Schuster, 1985

Wurmser, D., and Berg Dyke, N., *The Professionalism of Peacekeeping: A Study Group Report*, Washington, DC: United States Institute of Peace, 1994

Yermiya, D., *My War Diary: Israel in Lebanon*, London and Sydney: Pluto Press, 1983

Articles and essays

Abi-Saab, G., 'Humanitarian Law and Internal Conflicts: The Evolution of Legal Concern', in Abi-Saab, R. (ed.), *Essays in Honour of F. Kalshoven*, Dordrecht: Martinus Nijhoff, 1991

'The United Nations and International Humanitarian Law – Conclusions', *Actes du Colloque International de l'Universite de Geneve*, 1996

Adams, M. P., 'Peace Enforcement versus American Strategic Culture', 23(1) *Strategic Review*, 1995

Ajami, F., 'The Mark of Bosnia: Boutros-Ghali's Reign of Indifference', 75(3) *Foreign Affairs*, 1996

Akashi, Y., 'The Use of Force in a United Nations Peacekeeping Operation: Lessons Learnt from the Safe Areas Mandate', 19 *Fordham International Law Journal*, 1995

　　'The Use of Force in a United Nations Peacekeeping Operation', 28(3) *Akron Law Review*, 1995

　　'The Use of Force in a United Nations Peacekeeping Operation: Lessons Learnt from the Safe Areas Mandate', 19 *Fordham International Law Journal*, 1999

Alden, C., 'The Issue of the Military: UN Demobilization, Disarmament and Reintegration in Southern Africa', *International Peacekeeping*, 1996

Aldrich, G., 'Human Rights in Armed Conflict: Conflicting Views', 67 *American Society of International Law*, 1973

　　'The Laws of War on Land', 94 *American Journal of International Law*, 2000

Alger, C., 'Thinking About the Future of the UN System', 2(3) *Global Governance*, 1996

Ambos, K., 'NATO, the UN and the Use of Force: Legal Aspects: A Comment on Simma and Cassese', 2 *Humanitares Volkerrecht* (Deutsches Rotes Kreuz), 1999

Amerasinghe, C. F., 'The Use of Armed Force by the United Nations in the Charter Travaux Preparatoires', 5 *Indian Journal of International Law*, 1965

Andassy, J., 'Uniting for Peace', 50 *American Journal of International Law*, 1956

Annan, K., 'UN Peacekeeping Operations and Cooperation with NATO', No. 5 *NATO Review*, 1993

　　'Peacekeeping in Situations of Civil War', 26 *New York University Journal of International Law and Politics*, 1994

Archibugi, D., 'The Reform of the UN and Cosmopolitan Democracy: A Cultural Review', 30 *Journal of Peace Research*, 1993

Arnold, Maj. Gen. L. S., 'Somalia: An Operation Other Than War', 73(1) *Military Review*, December 1993

Arsanjani, M., 'The Rome Statute of the International Criminal Court', 93 *American Journal of International Law*, 1999

'At-Tiri Remembered – 6 April to 13 April 1980', *An Cosantoir*, April 1990

Azar, E. E., and Shnayerson, K., 'United States–Lebanese Relations: A Pocketful of Paradoxes', in Azar, E. E. *et al.*, *The Emergence of a New Lebanon: Fantasy or Reality*. New York: Praeger, 1984

Baxter, R., 'Some Existing Problems of Humanitarian Law', in *The Concept of International Armed Conflict: Further Outlook*, Proceedings of the International Symposium on Humanitarian Law, Brussels, 1974

Benvenuti, P., 'The Implementation of International Humanitarian law in the Framework of Peacekeeping Operations', in *Law in Humanitarian Crises*, European Commission, 1995, Vol. 1

Bloom, E., 'Protecting Peacekeepers: The Convention on the Safety of UN and Associated Personnel', 89 *American Journal of International Law*, 1995

Boerma, M., 'The United Nations Interim Force in the Lebanon: Peacekeeping in a Domestic Conflict', 8(1) *Millennium Journal of International Studies*, 1979

Bongiorno, C., 'A Culture of Impunity: Applying International Human Rights Law to the United Nations in East Timor', 33 *Columbia Human Rights Law Review*, 2002

Bothe, M., 'Peacekeeping and International Humanitarian Law: Friends or Foes?', 3 *International Peacekeeping*, 1996

Bourloyannis, M.C., 'The Security Council of the United Nations and the Implementation of International Humanitarian Law', 20(2) *Denver Journal of International Law and Policy*, 1993

Bourloyannis-Vrailis, C., 'The Convention on the Safety of UN and Associated Personnel', 44 *International and Comparative Law Quarterly*, July 1995

Boustany, K., 'Brocklebank: A Questionable Decision of the Court Martial Appeal Court of Canada', 1 *Yearbook of International Humanitarian Law*, 1998

Bouvier, A., 'Convention on the Safety of UN and Associated Personnel', No. 309, *International Review of the Red Cross*, 1995

Boutros-Ghali, B., 'Empowering the United Nations', 71 *Foreign Affairs*, 1992/3

Boyle, K., 'Comments on "Human Rights and Intervention: A Case for Caution"', 6 *Irish Studies in International Affairs*, 1994

Brady, C., and Daws, S., 'UN Operations: The Political-Military Interface', 1 *International Peacekeeping* (Frank Cass), 1994

Bratt, D., 'Assessing the Success of UN Peacekeeping Operations', 3(4) *International Peacekeeping* (Frank Cass), 1996

Brownlie, I., 'Decisions of British Courts During 1968 Involving Questions of International Law', 42 *British Yearbook of International Law*, 1968–9

Bruning, C., 'The United Nations Military Staff Committee: Future or Failure', *Revue de Droit Penal Militaire et de Droit de la Guerre/The Military Law and the Law of War Review*, 1974

Bush, G., 'Humanitarian Mission to Somalia: Address to the Nation, Washington DC, December 4, 1992', 3(49) *US Department of State Dispatch*

Byron, C., 'Armed Conflicts: International or Non-International?', 6(1) *Journal of Conflict and Security Law*, 2001

Caflisch, L., 'Toward the Establishment of a Permanent International Criminal Jurisdiction', 4(5) *International Peacekeeping* (Kluwer), 1998

Campbell, C., and Murphy, R., 'Geneva Conventions (Amendment) Act, 1998', *Irish Current Statutes Annotated 1998*, Dublin: Round Hall/Sweet and Maxwell, 1998

Carlowitz, L. von, 'Crossing the Boundary from the International to the Domestic Legal Realm: UNMIK Lawmaking and Property Rights in Kosovo', 10(3) *Global Governance*, 2004

Carr, C., 'The Consequences of Somalia', 10 *World Policy Journal*, 1993

Carter, Lt-Col. K., 'The Legal Basis of Canada's Participation in United Nations Operations', 1(4) *International Peacekeeping* (Kluwer), 1994

Cassese, A., 'Recent Trends in the Attitude of the Superpowers Towards Peacekeeping', in Cassese, A. (ed.), *United Nations Peacekeeping: Legal Essays*, The Hague: Sijthoff and Noordhoff, 1978

'Ex Iniuria Ius Oritur: Are We Moving Towards International Legitimation of Forcible Humanitarian Countermeasures in the World Community?', 10 *European Journal of International Law*, 1999

'The Martens Clause: Half a Loaf or Simply Pie in the Sky?', 11(1) *European Journal of International Law*, 2000

Chalmers, M., and Greene, O., 'The Development of the United Nations Register of Conventional Arms: Prospects and Proposals', paper presented to the International Studies Association, Washington DC, 29 March 1994

Chopra, J., Eknes, A., and Nordbo, T., 'Fighting for Hope in Somalia', *Peacekeeping and Multinational Operations*, No. 6, Norwegian Institute of International Affairs, 1995

Ciechanski, J., 'Enforcement Measures under Chapter VII of the UN Charter: UN Practice after the Cold War', 3(4) *International Peacekeeping* (Frank Cass), 1996

Ciombanu, D., 'The Power of the Security Council to Organise Peacekeeping Operations', in Cassese, A. (ed.), *United Nations Peacekeeping: Legal Essays*, The Hague: Sijthoff and Noordhoff, 1978

Clarke, W., and Herbst, J., 'Somalia and the Future of Humanitarian Intervention', 75(2) *Foreign Affairs*, 1996

Claude, I., 'Peace and Security: Prospective Roles for the Two United Nations', 2(3) *Global Governance*, 1996

Cockayne, J., and Malone, D. M., 'The Ralph Bunche Centennial: Peace Operations Then and Now', 11(3) *Global Governance*, 2005

Cockell, J. G., 'Civil–Military Responses to Security Challenges in Peace Operations: Ten Lessons from Kosovo', 8(4) *Global Governance*, 2002

Conroy, R., 'Peacekeeping and Peace Enforcement in Somalia', paper delivered to the International Studies Association Conference, Washington, DC, March/April 1994

Cotton, J., 'Financing Peacekeeping: Trouble Again', 11 *Cornell International Law Journal*, 1978

Couton, M., 'The Development of UN Peacekeeping Concepts since 1945: The UN Perspective', 20(79) *The Irish Sword*, Summer 1996

Crocker, C. A., 'The Lessons of Somalia: Not Everything Went Wrong', 74(3) *Foreign Affairs*, 1995

Dai, P., 'Canada and the Review of United Nations Peacekeeping Operations', 12 *Canadian Yearbook of International Law*, 1974

'The United Nations Interim Force in Lebanon and Canadian Participation', 17 *Canadian Yearbook of International Law*, 1979

Daniel, D., and Hayes, B., 'Securing Observance of UN Mandates through the Employment of Military Force', 3(4) *International Peacekeeping* (Frank Cass), 1996

De Lange, J. O., 'Peacekeeping Operations of the UN and Public International Law: Some Legal Aspects in the Netherlands', 23 *Netherlands International Law Review*, 1981

De Schutter, B., and Van De Wyngaert, C., 'Coping with Non-International Armed Conflicts: The Borderline Between National and International Law', 13 *Georgia Journal of International and Comparative Law*, 1983

De Waal, A., and Omaar, R., 'Can Military Intervention Be "Humanitarian"?', 24(2–3) *Middle East Report*, March–June 1994

Di Blase, A., 'The Role of Host State's Consent with Regard to Non Coercive Actions by the United Nations', in Cassese, A. (ed.), *United Nations Peacekeeping: Legal Essays*, The Hague: Sijthoff and Noordhoff, 1978

Diehl, P., 'With the Best of Intentions: Lessons from UNOSOM I and UNOSOM II', 19 *Studies in Conflict and Terrorism*, 1996

Dobbie, C., 'A Concept for Post Cold War Peacekeeping', 36(3) *Survival*, 1994

Doherty, R., 'Partnership for Peace: The *Sine Qua Non* for Irish Participation in Regional Peacekeeping', 7(2) *International Peacekeeping* (Frank Cass), 2000

Donnelly, J., 'Human Rights, Humanitarian Crisis, and Humanitarian Intervention', 48 *International Journal*, Autumn 1993

Dorr, N., 'The Development of UN Peacekeeping Concepts over the Past Fifty Years: An Irish Perspective', 20 *The Irish Sword*, Summer 1976

Doswald-Beck, L., 'International Humanitarian Law and the Advisory Opinion of the International Court of Justice on the Legality of the Threat or Use of Nuclear Weapons', No. 316 *International Review of the Red Cross*, 1997

Doswald-Beck, L., and Vite, S., 'International Humanitarian Law and Human Rights Law', No. 293 *International Review of the Red Cross*, 1993

Doyle, C., 'UN Observer Missions in the Middle East and Central America', 20(79) *The Irish Sword*, Summer 1976

Dragon, S., 'Permanent Neutrality and Peacekeeping', 5(1–2) *International Peacekeeping* (Kluwer), 1999

Draper, G. I. A. D., 'The Legal Limitations upon the Employment of Weapons by the United Nations Force in the Congo', 12 *International Comparative Law Quarterly*, 1963

'The United Nations Force in Cyprus', 6 *Revue de Droit Penal Militaire et de Droit de la Guerre/The Military Law and the Law of War Review*, 1967

Driscoll, D., 'Is Ireland Really "Neutral"?', 1(3) *Irish Studies in International Affairs*, 1980

Duke, S., 'The United Nations and Intra-State Conflict', 1(4) *International Peacekeeping* (Frank Cass), 1994

Dunlap, Col. C., 'US Legal Issues in Coalition Operations', *Peacekeeping and International Relations*, September/October 1996

Dworken, J. T., 'Rules of Engagements: Lessons from Restore Hope', 74(9) *Military Review*, September 1994

Eide, A., Rosas, A., and Meron, T., 'Combating Lawlessness in Gray Zone Conflicts Through Minimum Humanitarian Standards', 89 *American Journal of International Law*, 1995

Erskine, Maj. Gen. E. A., 'UNIFIL and UNDOF', paper presented at the International Peace Academy Seminar, Lagos, April 1979

Fairlie, M., 'Affirming Brahimi: East Timor Makes the Case for a Model Criminal Code', 18 *American University International Law Review*, 2003

Falk, R., 'Reflections on the Kosovo War', 1(2) *Global Dialogue*, 1999

Farrell, T., 'Sliding into War: The Somalia Imbroglio and US Army Peace Operations Doctrine', 2(2) *International Peacekeeping* (Frank Cass), 1995

Fink, J. E., 'From Peacekeeping to Peace Enforcement: The Blurring of the Mandate for the Use of Force in Maintaining International Peace and Security', 19(1) *Maryland Journal of International Law and Trade*, 1995

Fleck, D., and Saalfeld, M., 'Combining Efforts to Improve the Legal Status of UN Peacekeeping Forces and their Effective Protection', 1(3) *International Peacekeeping* (Kluwer), 1994

Fomerand, J., 'UN Conferences: Media Events or Genuine Diplomacy?', 2(3) *Global Governance*, 1996

Forsythe, D., 'Human Rights and International Security: United Nations Field Operations Redux', in Castermans, M., van Hoof, F., and Smith, J. (eds.), *The Role of the Nation State in the 21st Century*, Dordrecht: Kluwer, 1998

Franck, T. M., and Patel, F., 'Agora: The Gulf Crisis in International and Foreign Relations Law: UN Police Action in Lieu of War: "The Old Order Changeth"', 85 *American Journal of International Law*, 1991

Freeman, W. D., '"Operation Restore Hope": A US Centcom Perspective', 73(1) *Military Review*, September 1993

Ganzglass, M., 'The Restoration of the Somali Justice System', 3(1) *International Peacekeeping*, Spring 1996

Garcia-Sayan, D., 'Human Rights and Peace-Keeping Operations', 29 *University of Richmond Law Review*, 1995

Gasser, H. P., 'A Measure of Humanity in Internal Disturbances and Tensions: Proposals for a Code of Conduct', No. 38 *International Review of the Red Cross*, 1988

Gehring, R., 'Loss of Civilian Protections under the Fourth Geneva Convention and Protocol I,' 19(1–2) *Revue de Droit Militaire et de Droit de la Guerre/The Military Law and the Law of War Review*, 1980

Gemayel, A., 'The Price and the Promise', 63(4) *Foreign Affairs*, 1985

Ghali, B. B., 'Empowering the United Nations', 71(5) *Foreign Affairs*, 1992/3
'Global Leadership after the Cold War', 75(2) *Foreign Affairs*, 1996

Gibbs, D. N., 'Dag Hammarskjold, the United Nations, and the Congo Crisis of 1960–61: A Reinterpretation', 31(1) *Journal of Modern African Studies*, 1993

Gill, M. N., 'Development of the Military Jurisdiction of the Irish Defence Forces', 18 *Revue de Droit Penal Militaire et de Droit de la Guerre/The Military Law and the Law of War Review*, 1980

Ginifer, J., 'Development and the UN Peace Mission: A New Interface Required?', 3(2) *International Peacekeeping* (Frank Cass), 1996

Glennon, M., 'The Constitution and Chapter VII of the United Nations Charter', 85 *American Journal of International Law*, 1991

Glick, R. D., 'Lip Service to the Laws of War: Humanitarian Law and UN Armed Forces', 17 *Michigan Journal of International Law*, 1995

Goodman, H., 'Placing Blame for PLO Raid', *Jerusalem Post*, 17 January 1979

Gordenker, L., 'The UN Secretary-General: Intellectual Leadership and Maintaining Peace', 28 *International Spectator*, 1993

Goulding, M., 'The Evolution of UN Peacekeeping', 69(3) *International Affairs*, 1993
'The Use of Force by the United Nations', 3(1) *International Peacekeeping* (Frank Cass), 1996

Green, L. C., 'Superior Orders and the Reasonable Man', 8 *Canadian Yearbook of International Law*, 1970
'Humanitarian Law and the Man in the Field', 14 *Revue de Droit Penal Militaire et de Droit de la Guerre/The Military Law and the Law of War Review*, 1976
'Superior Orders and Command Responsibility', 27 *Canadian Yearbook of International Law*, 1989
'Iraq, the UN and the Law', 29 *Alberta Law Review*, 1991
'Peacekeeping and War Crimes', 34 *Revue de Droit Militaire et de Droit de la Guerre/The Military Law and Law of War Review*, 1995

Greenwood, C., 'The Relationship of Ius ad Bellum and Ius in Bello', 9 *Review of International Studies*, 1983
'The Concept of War in Modern International Law', 36 *International and Comparative Law Quarterly*, 1987
'Self-Defence and the Conduct of International Armed Conflict', in Dinstein, Y. (ed.), *International Law at a Time of Perplexity*, Dordrecht: Kluwer, 1989

'Terrorism and Protocol I', 19 *Israel Yearbook of Human Rights*, 1989

'Is Britain at War in the Gulf?', 135 *Solicitors Journal*, 1991

'Is There a Right of Humanitarian Intervention?', 49(2) *World Today*, 1993

'The International Tribunal for the Former Yugoslavia', 69 *International Affairs*, 1993

'Historical Development and Legal Basis', in Fleck, D. (ed.), *The Handbook of Humanitarian Law in Armed Conflict*, Oxford: Oxford University Press, 1995

'Scope of Application of Humanitarian Law', in Fleck, D. (ed.), *The Handbook of Humanitarian Law in Armed Conflict*, Oxford: Oxford University Press, 1995

'International Humanitarian Law and the Tadic Case', 7 *European Journal of International Law*, 1996

'Protection of Peacekeepers: The Legal Regime', 7 *Duke Journal of International and Comparative Law*, 1996

'The International Court and the Use of Force', in Lowe, A., and Fitzmaurice, M. (eds.), *Fifty Years of the International Court of Justice*, 1996

'The Advisory Opinion on Nuclear Weapons and the Contribution of the International Court of Justice to International Humanitarian Law', No. 316 *International Review of the Red Cross*, 1997

'International Humanitarian Law and United Nations Military Operations', 1 *Yearbook of International Humanitarian Law*, 1998

International Humanitarian Law and the Laws of War: Preliminary Report for the Centennial Commemoration of the First Hague Peace Conference 1899, May 1999

Grey, R. T., 'Strengthening the United Nations to Implement the Agenda for Peace', 21 *Strategic Review*, 1993

Griffin, M., 'Blue Helmet Blues: Assessing the Trend Towards "Subcontracting" UN Peace Operations', 30(1) *Security Dialogue*, 1999

Guicherd, C., 'International Law and the War in Kosovo', 41(2) *Survival*, 1999

Halberstam, M., 'The Copenhagen Document: Intervention in Support of Democracy', 34 *Harvard International Law Journal*, 1993

Halderman, J. W., 'Legal Basis for United Nations Armed Forces', 56 *American Journal of International Law*, 1962

Halim, O., 'A Peacekeeper's Perspective of Peacebuilding in Somalia', 3(2) *International Peacekeeping* (Frank Cass), 1996

Handler Chayes, A., 'Beyond Reform: Restructuring for More Effective Conflict Intervention', 3(2) *Global Governance*, 1997

Harrington Gagnon, M., 'Peace Forces and the Veto: The Relevance of Consent', 21(4) *International Organization*, 1967

Hass, R., 'The Middle East: No More Treaties', 75(5) *Foreign Affairs*, 1996

Heathcote, N., 'Ireland and the United Nations Operation in the Congo', 3 *International Relations*, 1971

Heffernan, L., and Whelan, A., 'Ireland, the United Nations and the Gulf Conflict: Legal Aspects', 3(3) *Irish Studies in International Affairs*, 1991

Heiberg, M., 'Observations on UN Peacekeeping in Lebanon', Norwegian Institute of International Affairs, Working Paper No. 305, September 1984

'Norway and Keeping the Peace in Lebanon', Norwegian Institute of International Affairs, Working Paper No. 317, February 1985

Heiberg, M., and Holst, J. J., 'Keeping the Peace in Lebanon: Assessing International and Multinational Peacekeeping', Norwegian Institute of International Affairs, Working Paper No. 357, June 1986

'Peacekeeping in Lebanon: Comparing UNIFIL and the MNF', 28(5) *Survival*, 1986

Helms, J., 'Saving the UN: A Challenge to the Next Secretary General', 75(5) *Foreign Affairs*, 1996

Herbst, J., 'The Everyday Lives of Peacemakers in Somalia', 3(1) *International Peacekeeping*, 1996

Higgins, R., 'The Advisory Opinion on Namibia: Which UN Resolutions Are Binding under Article 25 of the Charter?', 21 *International and Comparative Law Quarterly*, 1972

'A General Assessment of Peacekeeping', in Cassese, A. (ed.), *United Nations Peacekeeping: Legal Essays*, The Hague: Sijthoff and Noordhoff, 1978

'The United Nations' Role in Maintaining International Peace: The Lessons of the First Fifty Years', 16 *New York Law School Journal of International and Comparative Law*, 1996

Hirsch, J., Oakley, R., and Natsios, A. S., 'Humanitarian Relief Interventions in Somalia: The Economics of Chaos', 3(1), *International Peacekeeping*, 1996

Holland, J., 'Canadian Court Martial Resulting from Participation in the UNITAF Mission in Somalia', 1(4) *International Peacekeeping* (Kluwer), 1994

Holmes, K. R., 'New World Disorder: A Critique of the United Nations', 46(2) *Journal of International Affairs*, 1993

Homan, C., 'Regional and Multinational Peacekeeping Forces', 47 *International Spectator*, 1993

Houck, J. W., 'The Command and Control of UN Forces in the Era of "Peace Enforcement" ', 4(1) *Duke Journal of Comparative and International Law*, 1993

Hutchinson, M. R., 'Restoring Hope: UN Security Council Resolutions for Somalia and an Expanded Doctrine of Humanitarian Intervention', 34 *Harvard International Law Journal*, 1993

International Committee of the Red Cross, 'Action by the International Committee of the Red Cross in the Event of Breaches of International Humanitarian Law', *International Review of the Red Cross*, March–April 1981

'Armed Conflicts Linked to the Disintegration of State Structures', preparatory document for the first periodical meeting on international humanitarian law, ICRC, Geneva, 19–23 January 1998

'The Kosovo Crisis and International Humanitarian Law', No. 837 *International Review of the Red Cross*, 2000

'International Workshop: "Towards a Future for Peacekeeping: Perspectives of a New Italian/German Co-operation", Pisa, 17–18 November 1995', 2(6) *International Peacekeeping* (Kluwer), 1995

Jabbra, J. W., and Jabbra, N. W., 'Lebanon, Gateway to Peace?', 38 *International Journal*, 1983

Jackson, J. A., 'The Irish Army and the Development of the Constabulary Concept', in Van Doorn, J. (ed.), *Armed Forces and Society: Sociological Essays*, The Hague: Mouton, 1968

James, A., *The Role of Force in International Order and United Nations Peacekeeping*, Report of a Conference at Ditchley Park, 16–19 May 1969, Ditchley Paper No. 20, Enstone, Oxfordshire: Ditchley Foundation

'The Security Functions of the United Nations', in Twichett, K. (ed.), *International Security: Reflection on Security and Survival*, London: Oxford University Press, 1971

'Problems of Internal Peacekeeping', 5 *Diplomacy and Statecraft*, 1994

'A Review of UN Peacekeeping', *International Spectator*, 1993

'Internal Peacekeeping: A Dead End for the UN?', 24(4) *Security Dialogue*, 1993

'Internal Peacekeeping', in Charters, D. A. (ed.), *Peacekeeping and the Challenge of Civil Conflict Resolution*, Fredericton: Centre for Conflict Studies, University of New Brunswick, 1994

'Painful Peacekeeping: The United Nations in Lebanon, 1978–1982', 38(4) *International Journal*, 1983

'The Congo Controversies', 1 *International Peacekeeping* (Frank Cass), 1994

Johansen, R., 'UN Peacekeeping: How Should We Measure Success?', 38(2) *Mershon International Studies Review*, 1994

'The Future of United Nations Peacekeeping and Enforcement: A Framework for Policymaking', 2(3) *Global Governance*, 1996

Jonah, J. O. C., 'Peacekeeping in the Middle East', 31 *International Journal*, 1976

Junod, S., 'Additional Protocol II: History and Scope', 33 *American University Law Review*, 1983

Kalshoven, F., 'The Undertaking to Respect and Ensure Respect in All Circumstances: From Tiny Seed to Ripening Fruit', 2 *Yearbook of International Humanitarian Law*, 1999

Kassan, N. T., 'The Legal Limits to the Use of Force Through the United Nations Practice', 35 *Revue Egyptienne de Droit International*, 1979

Kennedy, K. M., 'The Relationship between the Military and Humanitarian Organizations in Operation Restore Hope', 3(1) *International Peacekeeping*, 1996

Kinloch, S., 'Utopian or Pragmatic? A UN Permanent Military Volunteer Force', 3(4) *International Peacekeeping* (Frank Cass), 1996

Kirsch, P., 'The Convention on the Safety of UN and Associated Personnel', 2(5) *International Peacekeeping* (Kluwer), 1995

Knight, W. A., 'Success and Failures of United Nations Adaptations and Reforms', paper presented to International Studies Association, Washington, DC, March/April 1994

Knudsen, T., 'Humanitarian Intervention Revisited: Post-Cold War Responses to Classical Problems', 3(4) *International Peacekeeping* (Frank Cass), 1996

Kriendler, J., 'NATO's Changing Role: Opportunities and Constraints for Peacekeeping', 41(3) *NATO Review*, 1993

Kritsiotis, D., 'Security Council Resolution 1101 (1997) and the Multi-national Protection Force of Operation Alba in Albania', 12 *Leiden Journal of International Law*, 1999

Laursen, F., 'The Common Foreign and Security Policy (CFSP): Words or Deeds?', paper delivered to the International Studies Association, Washington, DC, 1994

Lepper, S. J., 'War Crimes and the Protection of Peacekeeping Forces', 28(3) *Akron Law Review*, 1995

Leurdijk, D. A., and Siekmann, R. C. R., 'The Legal Basis for Military Action Against Iraq', 4(3–4) *International Peacekeeping* (Kluwer), 1988

Levran, A., 'UN Forces and Israel's Security', 37 *Jerusalem Quarterly*, 1986

Lillich, R. B., 'Humanitarian Interventions through the United Nations: Towards the Development of Criteria', 53(2) *Heidelberg Journal of International Law*, 1993

Lloyd Roberts, D., 'Training the Armed Forces to Respect International Humanitarian Law: The Perspective of the ICRC Delegate to the Armed and Security Forces of South Asia', No. 319 *International Review of the Red Cross*, 1997

Lipniczki, I., ' "Endangered Communities": The Situation of Minorities in Kosovo, De Jure versus De Facto Treatment', unpublished paper, Irish Centre for Human Rights, National University of Ireland, Galway, 2004

Lubin, W., 'Towards the International Responsibility of the UN in Human Rights Violations During "Peacekeeping" Operations: The Case of Somalia', 52 *The Review, International Commission of Jurists*, June 1994

Lunn, J., 'The Need for Regional Security Commissions Within the UN System', 24(4) *Security Dialogue*, 1993

Lupi, N., 'Report by the Enquiry Commission on the Behaviour of Italian Peacekeeping Troops in Somalia', 1 *Yearbook of International Humanitarian Law*, 1998

MacDougall, M. H., 'UN Operations: Who Should Be in Charge?', 33 *La Guerre*, 1994

MacEinri, P., 'Receding from Lebanon!', 62 *Focus* (Dublin: Comhlámh), 2000
    'Why We Still Need the United Nations', 62 *Focus* (Dublin: Comhlámh) 2000

MacInnis, J., 'Peacekeeping and International Law', 3(3) *International Peacekeeping* (Frank Cass), 1996

MacKinlay, J., 'Successful Intervention', 28 *International Spectator*, 1993

MacKinlay, J., and Chopra, J., 'Second Generation Multinational operations', 15 *Washington Quarterly*, 1992

MacKinlay, J., and Kent, R., 'A New Approach to Complex Emergencies', 4(4) *International Peacekeeping*, 1997

MacKinnnon, C., 'Rape, Genocide, and Women's Human Rights', 17 *Harvard Women's Law Journal*, 1994

MacQueen, N., 'National Politics and the Peacekeeping Role: Ireland and the United Nations Operations in the Congo', 6(1) *War and Society*, 1988

MacSweeney, B., 'Irish Defence in the Context of Irish Foreign Policy', 51 *Irish Studies*, 1998

Makinda, S., 'Sovereignty and Security: Challenges for the United Nations', 2(2) *Global Governance*, 1996

Malaquias, A., 'The UN in Mozambique and Angola: Lessons Learned', 3(2) *International Peacekeeping* (Frank Cass), 1996

Maloney, S. M., 'Insights into Canadian Peacekeeping Doctrine', 76(2) *Military Review*, 1996

Mani, R., 'Conflict Resolution, Justice and the Law: Rebuilding the Rule of Law in the Aftermath of Complex Political Emergencies', 5(3) *International Peacekeeping* (Frank Cass), 1998

Marshall, D., and Inglis, S., 'The Disempowerment of Human Rights-Based Justice in the United Nations Mission in Kosovo', 16 *Harvard Human Rights Journal*, 2003

Marx, R., 'A Non-Governmental Human Rights Strategy for Peacekeeping', 14(2) *Netherlands Quarterly of Human Rights*, 1996

Matheson, M. J., 'United Nations Governance of Post Conflict Societies', 95 *American Journal of International Law*, 2001

McCoubrey, H., 'International Humanitarian Law and United Nations Military Action in the "New World Order" ', 1 *International Law and Armed Conflict: Commentary*, 1994

　'International Law and National Contingents in UN Forces', 12(3) *International Relations*, 1994

McDonald, Lt-Col. O., 'Peacekeeping Lessons Learned: An Irish Perspective', 4 *International Peacekeeping* (Kluwer), 1997

McMahon, G., 'The Defence Forces and the United Nations', 20(79) *The Irish Sword*, Summer 1996

Meijer, M., 'Notes on the Conference on "The UN and International Humanitarian Law", Geneva, 19–20 October 1995', 2(6) *International Peacekeeping* (Kluwer), 1995

Menkhaus, K., 'International Peacebuilding and the Dynamics of Local and National Reconciliation in Somalia', 3(1) *International Peacekeeping* (Frank Cass), 1996

Meron, T., 'On the Inadequate Reach of Humanitarian and Human Rights Law and the Need for a New Instrument', 77 *American Journal of International Law*, 1983

'Draft Model Declaration on Internal Strife', *International Review of the Red Cross*, 1988

'The Protection of the Human Person under Human Rights and Humanitarian Law', *UN Bulletin of Human Rights 91/1*, UN, 1992, 33–45

'War Crimes in Yugoslavia and the Development of International Law', 88 *American Journal of International Law*, 1994

'The Humanization of Humanitarian Law', 94 *American Journal of International Law*, 2000

'The Martens Clause, Principles of Humanity, and Dietates of Public Conscience', 94 *American Journal of International Law*, 2000

Meron, T., and Rosas, A., 'A Declaration of Minimum Humanitarian Standards', 85 *American Journal of International Law*, 1991

Miller, G. E., 'Public Law and the Military Commander: Responsibility and Authority', 4 *Naval War College Review*, 1971

Moreillon, J., 'Actions by the International Committee of the Red Cross and the Protection of Political Detainees', *International Review of the Red Cross*, November 1974 and April 1975

Morillion, P., 'UN Operations in Bosnia: Lessons and Reality', 138 *RUSI Journal*, 1993

Mortimer, E., 'International Administration of War-Torn Societies', 10 *Global Governance*, 2004

Mrazek, J., 'Prohibition of the Use and Threat of Force: Self-Defence and Self-Help in International Law', 17 *Canadian Yearbook of International Law*, 1989

Murray, J., 'Who Will Police the Peace-Builders? The Failure to Establish Accountability for the Participation of United Nations Civilian Police in the Trafficking of Women in Post-Conflict Bosnia and Herzegovina', 34(2) *Columbia Human Rights Law Review*, 2003

Murphy, R., 'Background to the 1980 "Battle of At-Tiri": A Personal Assessment', *An Cosantoir*, October 1988

'Ireland: Legal Issues Arising from Participation in United Nations Operations', 1(2) *International Peacekeeping* (Kluwer), 1994

'Ireland, the United Nations and Peacekeeping Operations', 5(1) *International Peacekeeping* (Frank Cass), 1998

'A Comparative Analysis of the Municipal Legal Basis for Canadian and Irish Participation in United Nations Forces', 38 *Revue de Droit Militaire et de Droit de la Guerre/The Military Law and the Law of War Review*, 1999

'The Legal Framework of UN Forces and Issues of Command and Control of Canadian and Irish Forces', 4 *Journal of Armed Conflict Law*, 1999

'UN Peacekeeping in Lebanon and the Use of Force', 6(2) *International Peacekeeping* (Frank Cass), 1999

'International Humanitarian Law and Training for Multinational Peace Support Operations', No. 840 *International Review of the Red Cross*, 2000

'Kosovo: Reflections on the Legal Aspects of the Conflict and Its Outcome', 11 *Irish Studies in International Affairs*, 2000

Murphy, T., 'Sanction and Enforcement of the Humanitarian Law of the Four Geneva Conventions of 1949 and Geneva Protocol I of 1977', 103 *Military Review*, 1984

Nahlik, S., 'A Brief Outline of International Humanitarian Law', *International Review of the Red Cross*, July–August 1984

Natsios, A. S., 'Food Through Force: Humanitarian Intervention and US Policy', 17(1) *Washington Quarterly*, 1994

'Humanitarian Relief Interventions in Somalia: The Economics of Chaos', 3(1) *International Peacekeeping*, 1996

Nelson, R. W., 'Multinational Peacekeeping in the Middle East and the United Nations Model', 61(1) *International Affairs*, 1985

Nier, C., 'The Yugoslavian Civil War: An Analysis of the Applicability of the Laws of War Governing Non-International Armed Conflicts in the Modern World', 10 *Dickley Journal of International Law*, 1992

Normak, S., 'Building Local Political Institutions: District and Regional Councils', paper to the Comprehensive Seminar on Lessons Learned from the UN Operation in Somalia, Lessons Learned Unit, Department of Peacekeeping Operations, Plainsboro, NJ, 13–15 September 1995

Norton, A. W., 'UNIFIL and the Shiite Community', paper presented at the International Workshop on UNIFIL, Oslo, Norway, 1–4 July 1986

Nweke, A., 'Behind the Compound Wall: Volunteerism under Challenge in Somalia', in United Nations Volunteers, *Volunteers Against Conflict*, Tokyo: United Nations University Press, 1996

Nye, J. S., and Owens, W. A., 'America's Information Edge', 75(2) *Foreign Affairs*. 1996

Okimoto, K., 'Violations of International Humanitarian Law by United Nations Forces and Their Legal Consequences', 6 *Yearbook of International Humanitarian Law*, 2003

O Murchú, Capt. A., 'Learning from Somalia', *An Cosantoir*, September 1997

O'Neill, B., Russett, B., and Sutterlin, J., 'Restructuring Options for the UN Security Council', paper delivered to the International Studies Association Conference, Washington, DC, March/April 1994

'Operation Iron Fist', pamphlet published by the League of Arab States, London, May 1985

Padelford, N. J., 'Financing Peacekeeping: Politics and Crises', in Padelford, N. J., and Goodrich, L. (eds.), *The United Nations in the Balance*, London: Praeger, 1965

Palwankar, U., 'Applicability of International Humanitarian Law to UN Peacekeeping Forces', No. 80 *International Review of the Red Cross*, 1993

Pease, K., and Forsythe, D., 'Humanitarian Intervention and International Law', 45 *Austrian Journal of Public and International Law*, 1993

Peck, J., 'The UN and the Laws of War: How Can the World's Peacekeepers Be Held Accountable?', 21 *Syracuse Journal of International Law and Commerce*, 1995

Puchala, D. J., 'American Interests and the United Nations', 97(4) *Political Science Quarterly*, 1982/3

Pugh, M., 'Peacekeeping and Critical Theory', 11(1) *International Peacekeeping*, 2004

Ramsbotham, D., 'UN Operations: The Art of the Possible', 138(6) *The RUSI Journal*, 1993

Randel, J., 'Aid, the Military, and Humanitarian Assistance: An Attempt to Identify Recent Trends', 6(3) *Journal of International Development*, 1994

Rees, N., 'The Kosovo Crisis, the International Response and Ireland', 11 *Irish Studies in International Affairs*, 2000

Reich, B., and Hollis, R., 'Peacekeeping in the Reagan Administration', in Maranatz, P., and Stein, J. G. (eds.), *Peacemaking in the Middle East: Problems and Prospects*, London: Croom Helm, 1985

Reisman, M., 'Peacemaking', 18 *Yale Journal of International Law*, 1993
'The Constitutional Crises in the United Nations', 87(1) *American Journal of International Law*, 1993

Reumiller, Lt-Col. E., 'Peacemaking/Peacekeeping: The Irish and Canadian Experiences', Dublin: Association of Canadian Studies in Ireland, 1997
'Canadian Perspectives and Experiences with Peacekeeping: General Policy Considerations', in P. O Gormaile and R. Murphy (eds.), *Conflict Resolution and Peacemaking/Peacekeeping: The Irish and Canadian Experience*, Dublin: Association for Canadian Studies in Ireland, 1997
'Security in a New World Order: A Canadian Perspective', in P. O Gormaile and R. Murphy (eds.), *Conflict Resolution and Peacemaking/Peacekeeping: The Irish and Canadian Experience*, Dublin: Association for Canadian Studies in Ireland, 1997

Rieff, D., 'The Illusion of Peacekeping', 20(3) *World Policy Journal*, 1994

Risse-Kappen, T., 'Faint Hearted Multilateralism: The Re-emergence of the United Nations in World Politics', paper presented to International Studies Association, Washington, DC, March/April 1994

Roberts, A., 'From San Francisco to Sarajevo: The UN and the Use of Force', 37(4) *Survival*, 1995–6
'The So-Called "Right" of Humanitarian Intervention', 3 *Yearbook of International Humanitarian Law*, 2001

Roberts, L. D., 'Training the Armed Forces to Respect International Humanitarian Law: The Perspective of the ICRC Delegate to the Armed and Security Forces of South Asia', No. 319 *International Review of the Red Cross*, 1997

Robinson, D., and von Hebel, H., 'War Crimes in Internal Conflicts: Article 8 of the ICC Statute', in 2 *Yearbook of International Humanitarian Law*, 2000

Rosenfeld, S. S., 'Testing the Hard Line', 61(3) *Foreign Affairs*, 1982

Roth, B., 'Whatever Happened to Sovereignty? Reflections on International Law Methodology', in Ku, C., and Weiss, T. (eds.), *Toward Understanding Global Governance*, ACUNS Reports and Papers 1998, No. 2, 1998

Rowe, P., 'Maintaining Discipline in UN Peace Support Operations: The Legal Quagmire for Military Contingents', 5(1) *Journal of Conflict and Security Law*, 2000

Rowe, P., and Meyer, M., 'Ratification by the United Kingdom of the 1977 Protocols Additional to the Geneva Conventions of 1949: Selected Problems in Implementation', 45(4) *Northern Ireland Legal Quarterly*, 1994

Rudd, M., 'The Term Combatant: An Analysis', 24 *Revue de Droit Militaire et de Droit de la Guerre/The Military Law and the Law of War Review*, 1985

Ruggie, J. G., 'Wandering in the Void: Charting the UN's New Strategic Role', 72(5) *Foreign Affairs*, 1993

'The United Nations and the Collective Use of Force: Whither or Whether?', 3(4) *International Peacekeeping* (Frank Cass), 1996

Sahnoun, M. M., 'Prevention in Conflict Resolution: The Case of Somalia', 5 *Irish Studies in International Affairs*, 1994

'Managing Conflict after the Cold War', 8(4) *Peace Review*, 1996

Sandoz, Y., 'Respect for the Law of Armed Conflict: The ICRC's Observations and Experiences', paper presented at the International Seminar on International Humanitarian Law in a New Strategic Environment: Training of Armed Forces, Stockholm, 17–18 June 1996

Schachter, O., 'United Nations in the Gulf Conflict', 85 *American Journal of International Law*, 1994

Schiff, Z., 'Green Light Lebanon', 50 *Foreign Policy*, Spring 1983

Schindler, D., 'The Different Types of Armed Conflicts According to the Geneva Conventions and Protocols, 163 *Recueil de Cours*, 1979

'Significance of the Geneva Conventions for the Contemporary World', No. 836 *International Review of the Red Cross*, 1999

Schwartzberg, J., 'A New Perspective on Peacekeeping: Lessons from Bosnia and Elsewhere', 3(1) *Global Governance*, 1997

Schwarzenberger, G., 'Beirut 1982: An Interdisciplinary Test Case', 38 *Yearbook of World Affairs*, 1984

Sears, C., 'Somalia: Faith, Hope and Charity', *In Dublin*, 11–24 May 1994

Segal, A., 'Peacemaking Versus Peacekeeping', paper presented to the International Studies Association, Washington, DC, 30 March–2 April 1994

Sepulveda, C., 'Interrelationships in the Implementation and Enforcement of International Humanitarian Law', 33 *American University Law Review*, 1983

Seyersted, F., 'United Nations Forces: Some Legal Problems', 37 *British Yearbook of International Law*, 1961

Shannon, M., 'Thirty Years of Peacekeeping: A Perspective on Staff Appointments', *An Cosantoir*, April 1989

Sharp, J., 'Intervention in Bosnia: The Case for', 29(2) *World Today*, 1999

Sharp, W. G., 'Protecting the Avatars of International Peace and Security', 7 *Duke Journal of International and Comparative Law*, 1996

Shaw, T., 'Beyond Post-Conflict Peacebuilding: What Links to Sustainable Development and Human Security?', 3(2) *International Peacekeeping* (Frank Cass), 1996

Sheikh, A., 'UN Peacekeeping Forces: A Reappraisal of Relevant Charter Provisions', 7 *Belgian Review of International Law*, 1971

Sherry, G. L., 'The United Nations, International Conflict and American Security', 101(5) *Political Science Quarterly*, 1986

Shraga, D., and Zacklin, R., 'The Applicability of International Humanitarian Law to United Nations Peacekeeping Operation: Conceptual. Legal and Practical Issues', in Palwankar, U. (ed.), *Report on a Symposium on Humanitarian Action and Peacekeeping Operations: June 22–24 Geneva*, Geneva: ICRC, 1994

Siekmann, R., 'The Financing of Peacekeeping Operations', 47(2) *International Spectator*, 1993

'The Legal Position of Dutchbat vis-à-vis Srebrenica', 1 *Yearbook of International Humanitrian Law*, 1998

Simma, B., 'NATO, the UN and the Use of Force: Legal Aspects', 10 *European Journal of International Law*, 1999

Skjelbaek, K., and Hess, H. M., 'The Predicament of UNIFIL', Norwegian Institute of International Affairs (NUPI) Working Paper No. 343, 1990

Slim, H., 'The Stretcher and the Drum: Civil–Military Relations in the Peace Support Operations', 3(2) *International Peacekeeping*, 1996

Sonnenfeld, R., 'The Obligation of the UN Member States "To Accept and Carry Out the Decisions of the Security Council"', 8 *Polish Yearbook of International Law*, 1976

Sorensen, T., 'United States Policy on United Nations Peacekeeping Operations', 18 *Yale Journal of International Law*, 1993

Spring, D., 'New Forms of Intervention in World Politics: Opening Address', 5 *Irish Studies in International Affairs*, 1994

Stavros, S., 'The Right to a Fair Trial in Emergency Situations', 41 *International and Comparative Law Quarterly*, 1992

Stiles, K., and MacDonald, M., 'After Consensus, What? Performance Criteria for the UN in the Post Cold War Era', 29 *Journal of Peace Research*, 1992

Storch, K., 'Peacekeeping: The Role of UNIFIL 1978–1984', thesis, American University of Beirut, 1984

Subedi, S. P., 'The Concept of Safe Havens, Safe Areas, Enclaves and No-Fly Zones in International Law', paper delivered to the International Studies Association, Washington, DC, March/April 1994

Sullivan, D., 'The Failure of US Foreign Aid: An Examination of Causes and a Call for Reform', 2(3) *Global Governance*, 1996

Szayna, T., Niblack, P., and O'Malley, W., 'Assessing Armed Forces' Deficiencies for Peace Operations: A Methodology', 3(3) *International Peacekeeping* (Frank Cass), 1996

Takai, S., 'Japan: A Hesitant But Interested Partner', paper presented to the 35th Annual Convention of the International Studies Association, Washington, DC, 28 March–1 April 1994

Tanner, F., 'Weapons Control in Semi-Permissive Environments: A Case for Compellence', 3(4) *International Peacekeeping* (Frank Cass), 1996

Thakur, R., 'Non-Intervention in International Relations: A Case Study', 42(1) *Political Science*, 1990

   'From Peacekeeping to Peace Enforcement: The UN Operation in Somalia', 39(3) *Journal of Modern African Studies*, 1994

   'Human Rights: Amnesty International and the United Nations', 31(2) *Journal of Peace Research*, 1994

Theodorides, J., 'The United Nations Interim Force in Lebanon', 20(3–4) *Revue de Droit Penal Militaire et de Droit de la Guerre/The Military Law and the Law of War Review*, 1981

Thomas, C., 'Human Rights and Intervention: A Case for Caution', 5 *Irish Studies in International Affairs*, 1994

Tittemore, B. D., 'Belligerents in Blue Helmets: Applying International Humanitarian Law to United Nations Peace Operations', 33 *Stanford Journal of International Law*, 1997

Torelli, M., 'From Humanitarian Assistance to Intervention on Humanitarian Grounds?', *International Review of the Red Cross*, May–June 1992

Tueni, G., 'Lebanon: A New Republic', 61(1) *Foreign Affairs*, 1982

   'After the Lebanon Israeli Agreement', 3(1) *Middle East Insight*, 1983

Turley, S. L., 'Keeping the Peace: Do the Laws of War Apply?', 73 *Texas Law Review*, 1994

Turns, D., 'Some Reflections on the Conflict in Southern Lebanon: The "Quana Incident" and International Humanitarian Law', 5 *Journal of Conflict and Security Law*, 2000

Tzartzouras, M. E., 'The Law of Humanitarian Intervention After Somalia', 46 *Revue Hellenique de Droit International*, 1993

Ulich, O., 'Peacekeeping and Human Rights: Is There a Duty to Protect?', *International Human Rights Advocacy*, 1996

Urquhart, B., 'United Nations Peacekeeping in the Middle East', *World Today*, March 1980

  'Peacekeeping: A View from the Operational Centre', in Wiseman, H. (ed.), *Peacekeeping: Appraisal and Proposals*, New York and Oxford: Pergamon Press, 1983

  'The United Nations in 1992: Problems and Opportunities', 68(2) *International Affairs*, 1992

  'The United Nations: Post Cold War Challenges', 47(11) *International Spectator*, 1993

US Military, 'Somalia: Hopeful Handbook', 34(8) *Africa Confidential*, 16 April 1993

Uvin, P., and Biagiotti, I., 'Global Governance and the "New" Political Conditionality', 2(3) *Global Governance*, 1996

Van Hegelsom, G., 'The Law of Armed Conflict and UN Peace-Keeping and Peace-Enforcement Operations', 6 *Hague Yearbook of International Law*, 1993

Vatikiotis, P. J., 'The Crisis in Lebanon: A Local Historical Perspective', 40 *World Today*, 1984

Vayrynen, R., 'Preventive Action: Failure in Yugoslavia', 3(4) *International Peacekeeping* (Frank Cass), 1996

Vogt, Lt-Col. M., 'Experiences of a German Legal Adviser to the UNOSOM II Mission', 35(1–4) *Revue de Droit Penal Militaire et de Droit de la Guerre/The Military Law and the Law of War Review*, 1996

Wedgwood, R., 'United Nations Peacekeeping Operations and the Use of Force', 5 *Journal of Law and Policy*, 2001

Weinberger, N. J., 'Peacekeeping Options in Lebanon', 37(3) *Middle East Journal*, 1983

  'The Palestinian National Security Debate', 34(3) *Journal of Palestine Studies*, 1995

Weiner, R. O., and Ni Aolain, F., 'Beyond the Laws of War: Peacekeeping in Search of a Legal Framework', 27 *Columbia Human Rights Law Review*, 1996

Weiss, T., 'New Challenges for UN Military Operations: Implementing An Agenda for Peace', 16 *Washington Quarterly*, 1993

  'Intervention: Whither the United Nations?', 17(1) *Washington Quarterly*, 1994

  'Military–Civilian Humanitarianism: The "Age" of Innocence Is Over', 2(2) *International Peacekeeping*, 1995

Westhusing, T., 'Taking Terrorism and ROE Seriously', 2(1) *Journal of Military Ethics*, 2001

Whaley, J. D., 'Improving UN Development Coordination within Peace Missions, 3(2) *International Peacekeeping* (Frank Cass), 1996

White, N. D., 'The UN Charter and Peacekeeping Forces: Constitutional Issues', 3(4) *International Peacekeeping* (Frank Cass), 1996

White, N. D., and Ulgen, O., 'The Security Council and the Decentralised Military Option: Constitutionality and Function', 44(3) *Netherlands International Law Review*, 1997

Whitman, J., and Bartholomew, I., 'Collective Control of UN Peace Support Operations: A Policy Proposal', 25(1) *Security Dialogue*, 1994

Wilkinson, P., 'Sharpening the Weapons of Peace: The Development of a Common Military Doctrine for Peace Support Operations', International Security Information Service (ISIS), Briefing Paper No. 18, April 1998

Wills, S., 'Military Interventions on Behalf of Vulnerable Populations: The Legal Responsibilities of States and International Organizations Engaged in Peace Support Operations', 9 *Journal of Conflict and Security Law*, 2004

Wiseman, H., 'United Nations Peacekeeping: An Historical Overview', in Wiseman, H. (ed.), *Peacekeeping Appraisals and Proposals*, New York and Oxford: Pergamon Press, 1983

Woerlee, M. G., 'A Standing Peacekeeping Force', 28 *Netherlands International Law Review*, 1981

Womack, Lt-Col. S. M., 'Rules of Engagement in Multinational Operations', *Marine Corps Gazette*, February 1996

Yannis, A., 'The UN Government in Kosovo', 10(1) *Global Governance*, 2004

Yonekawa, M., 'Part of the System: Varieties of Volunteer Support Roles', in Minear, L., and Weiss, T. G. (eds.), *Volunteers Against Conflict*, Tokyo: United Nations University Press, 1996

Yorke, V., 'Retaliation and International Peacekeeping in Lebanon', 30(5) *Survival*, 1978

Zengel, P., 'Assassination and the Law of Armed Conflict', 43 *Mercer Law Review*, 1992

Zhang, Y., 'China and UN Peacekeeping: From Condemnation to Participation', 3(3) *International Peacekeeping* (Frank Cass), 1996

Zwanenburg, M., 'The Secretary-General's Bulletin on Observance by United Nations Forces of International Humanitarian Law: Some Preliminary Observations', 5(4–5) *International Peacekeeping* (Kluwer), 1999

'The Statute for an International Criminal Court and the United States: Peacekeepers under Fire?', 10(1) *Journal of International Law*, 1999

Reports and documents

Afri, *Towards Real Security: A Contribution to the Debate on Irish Defence and Security Planning*, Afri Position Paper No. 2, Dublin: Afri 1999

African Rights, *Operation Restore Hope: A Preliminary Assessment*, London: African Rights, May 1993

Somalia – Human Rights Abuses by the United Nations Forces, African Rights Report, London: African Rights, July 1993

Allied Joint Publication (AJP) 3.4.1, *Peace Support Operations*, Brussels: NATO, July 2001

Amnesty International, *Bosnia-Hertzgovinia: Rape and Sexual Abuse by Armed Forces*, AI Index EUR 63/01/93 January 1993

　Amnesty International Concerns in Europe: January–June 1997, AI Index EUR 01/06/97, 1997

　Italy: A Briefing for the UN Committee Against Torture, AI Index EUR 30/02/99, 1999

　Prisoners in Our Homes: Amnesty International's Concerns for the Human Rights of Minorities in Kosovo/Kosova, AI Index EUR 70/010/2003, 2003

Canadian Government, *Dishonoured Legacy: Report of the Commission of Inquiry into the Deployment of Canadian Forces to Somalia*, Ottawa: Canadian Government Publishing, 1997

Department of National Defence (Canada), *Joint Doctrine for the Canadian Forces' Joint and Combined Operations*, undated

Eide, E. B., Kasperen, A. T., Kent, R., and von Heppel, K., *Report on Integrated Missions*, Independent Study for the Expanded UN Executive Committee on Humanitation Assistance Core Group, May 2005

European Commission for Democracy Through Law (Venice Commission), *Opinion on Human Rights in Kosovo: Possible Establishment of Review Mechanisms*, Opinion No. 280/2004, Strasbourg: Council of Europe, 11 October 2004

European Stability Initiative, *The Lausanne Principle: Multiethnicity, Territory and the Future of Kosovo's Serbs*, Berlin and Pristina: European Stability Initiative, June 2004

Foreign and Commonwealth Office, *Somali Clans and Their Political Role*, Research and Analysis Department Note, London: Foreign and Commonwealth Office, April 1992

Gil-Roberts, A., *Kosovo: The Human Rights Situation and the Fate of Persons Displaced from Their Homes*, Strasbourg: Council of Europe, 2003

Human Rights Watch, 'Beyond the Warlords: The Need for a Verdict on Human Rights Abuses', 5(2) *Human Rights Watch*, 1993

　Civilian Pawns: Laws of War Violations and the Use of Weapons on the Israeli–Lebanon Border, New York: Human Rights Watch, 1996

　Democratic Republic of Congo: War Crimes in Bukavu, Briefing Paper, New York: Human Rights Watch, June 2004

　Failure to Protect: Anti-Minority Violence in Kosovo, New York: Human Rights Watch, March 2004

　'Somalia Faces the Future: Human Rights in a Fragmented Society', 7(2) *Human Rights Watch*, 1995

Human Security Centre, *Human Security Report*, Vancouver: Human Security Centre, University of British Columbia, October 2005, available at www.humansecurityreport.info

Independent International Commission on Kosovo, *Kosovo Report: Conflict – International Response – Lessons Learned*, Oxford: Oxford University Press, 2000

Institute of International Law, *The Application of International Humanitarian Law and Fundamental Human Rights, in Armed Conflicts in Which Non-State Entities Are Parties*, Fourteenth Commission, Berlin Session, 25 August 1999

International Commission on Intervention and State Sovereignty, *The Responsibility to Protect: Report of the International Commission on Intervention and State Sovereignty*, Ottawa: International Development Research Centre, 2001

International Criminal Tribunal for the Former Yugoslavia, *Final Report to the Prosecutor by the Committee Established to Review the NATO Bombing Campaign Against the Federal Republic of Yugoslavia*, 8 June 2000

International Crisis Group, *Who's Killing Whom in Kosovo?*, Balkans Report No. 78, Brussels: International Crisis Group, 2 November 1999

Kosovo's Linchpin: Overcoming Division in Mitrovica, Balkans Report No. 96, Brussels: International Crisis Group, 31 May 2000

What Happened to the KLA, Balkans Report No. 88, Brussels: International Crisis Group, 3 March 2000

Collapse in Kosovo, Europe Report No. 155, Brussels: International Crisis Group, 22 April 2004

Counter-Terrorism in Somalia: Losing Hearts and Minds?, Africa Report No. 95, Brussels: International Crisis Group, 11 July 2005

Jones, S. G., Crane, K., Rathmell, A., Steele, B., Telschik, R., and Timilsina, A., *The UN's Role in Nation Building: From Congo to Iraq*, Santa Monica, CA: Rand Corporation, 2005

Malan, M., (ed.), *Whither Peacekeeping in Africa?*, ISS Monograph 36, Pretoria: Institute for Security Studies, April 1999

Message from the President of the United States: A Report on the Military Operation in Somalia, October 13, 1993, US Government Printing Office, 1993

Ocaya-Lakidi, D., *Africa's Internal Conflicts: The Search for Response*, Report of the OAU/IPA high-level consultation, Arusha, Tanzania, March 1992

Organization for Security and Co-operation in Europe (OSCE) Mission in Kosovo, *Parallel Structures in Kosovo*, Kosovo: Department of Human Rights and Rule of Law, October 2003

Palwankar, U. (ed.), *Report on a Symposium on Humanitarian Action and Peacekeeping Operations, June 22–24 1994, Geneva*, Geneva: ICRC, 1994

'*Peace Support Operations: A Working Draft Manual for African Military Practitioners*' DWM 1-2000, Preforia: Institute for Security Studies, February 2000

Report of the Constitution Review Group, Dublin: Government Publications, May 1996

'Report on the International Workshop: "Towards a Future for Peacekeeping: Perspectives of a New Italian/German Co-operation", Pisa, 17–18 November 1995', 2(6) *International Peacekeeping*, 1995

Towards a European Vision for Use of Land Forces? Multinationality and Interoperability within the Framework of Operational Missions Ranging from High to Low Intensity (from Combat to Peace Support), France: Commandement de la Doctrine et de l'Enseignement Militaire Supérieur de l'Armée de Terre, 2001

United Kingdon House of Commons Foreign Affairs Committee, Fourth Report, Session 1999–2000

United Kingdom Ministry of Defence, *The Military Contribution to Peace Support Operations*, Joint Warfare Publication (JWP) 3-50 2nd edn, Shrivenham: Joint Doctrine and Concepts Centre, 2004

United Nations, *Report of the Military Staff Committee: General Principles Governing the Organisation of the Armed Forces Made Available to the Security Council by Member Nations of the UN*, UN Security Council Official Records Supp. (No. 1), UN Doc. S/336, 1947

Summary Study of the Experience Derived from the Establishment and Operation of the Force: Report of the Secretary-General, General Assembly Official Records, 13 Session, Annex 1: Document A/3943, 9 October 1958

An Agenda for Peace, Preventative Diplomacy, Peacemaking and Peacekeeping: Report of the Secretary-General Pursuant to the Statement Adopted by the Summit Meeting of the Security Council on 31 January 1992, UN Doc. A/47/277-S/24111, 17 June 1992, 1992

Report of the Commission of Inquiry Established Pursuant to Resolution 885 (1993) to Investigate Armed Attacks on UNOSOM II Personnel Which Led to Casualties Among Them, UN Doc. S/1994/653, 1 June 1994

Supplement to An Agenda for Peace: Position Paper of the Secretary-General on the Occasion of the 50th Anniversary of the United Nations, UN Doc. S/1995/1-A/50/60, 25 January 1995, 1995

Report of the Secretary-General on Administrative and Budgetry Aspects of the Financing of United Nations Peacekeeping Operations, UN Doc. A/51/389, 20 September 1996

Operation Artemis: The Lessons of the Interim Emergency Multinational Force, Department of Peacekeeping Operations, Peacekeeping Best Practices Unit, Military Division, New York: United Nations, October 2004

Report of the Secretary-General on the Implementations of the Recommendations of the Special Committee on Peacekeeping Operations, UN Doc. A/AC.121/43, 23 February 1999

Secretary-General's Bulletin on Observance by UN Forces of International Humanitarian Law, UN Doc. ST/SGB/1993/3, 6 August 1999

Secretary-General's Report on the Protection of Civilians in Armed Conflict, UN Doc. S/1999/957, 8 September 1999

Report of the Secretary-General Pursuant to General Assembly Resolution 53/35: The Fall of Srebrenica, UN Doc. A/54/549, 15 November 1999

Report of the Independent Inquiry into the Actions of the United Nations during the 1994 Genocide in Rwanda, UN Doc. S/99/1257, 15 December 1999

Handbook on UN Multinational Peacekeeping Operations, New York: United Nations, 2003

Comprehensive Review of the Whole Question of Peacekeeping Operations in All Their Aspects: Report of the Special Committee on Peacekeeping Operations, UN Doc. A/57/767, 28 March 2003

Report of the Panel on UN Peacekeeping Operations (Brahimi Report), UN Doc. A/55/305-S/2000/809, 21 August 2000

International Law Commission: Special Report on Responsibility of International Organizations, UN Doc. A/CN.4/541, 2 April 2004

Minimum Humanitarian Standards: Analytical Report of the Secretary-General Submitted Pursuant to Human Rights Commission Resolution 1997/21, UN Doc. E/CN.4/1998/87, 5 January 1998

A More Secure World: Our Shared Responsibility: Report of the High-Level Panel on Threats, Challenges and Change, UN Doc. A/59/565, 2 December 2004

In Larger Freedom: Towards Development, Security and Human Rights for All: Report of the Secretary-General, UN Doc. A/59/2005, 21 March 2005

Human Rights Committee: Report Submitted by the United Nations Interim Administration Mission in Kosovo to the Human Rights Committee on the Human Rights Situation in Kosovo Since June 1999, UN Doc. CCPR/C/UNK/1, 13 March 2006

United Nations Association of the USA (UNA-USA), *The Preparedness Gap: Making Peace Operations Work in the 21st Century*, Policy Report, New York: UNA-USA, 2001

United Nations High Commissioner for Refugees/Organization for Security and Co-operation in Europe Report, *Preliminary Assessment of the Situation of Ethnic Minorities in Kosovo*, 26 July 1999

United States, 'Military Operations in Somalia', *Report to the Congress on US Policy in Somalia*, October 13,1993, and 'Message from the President of the United States', Washington, DC: US Government Printing Office, 1993

United States, *Report of the Department of Defense Commission on Beirut International Airport Terrorist Attack Act, October 23, 1983*, Department of Defense, 20 December 1983

Wurmser, D., and Dyke, N., 'The Professionalization of Peacekeeping', A Study Group Report, Washington, DC: United States Institute of Peace, 1994

INDEX

CPSIA information can be obtained at www.ICGtesting.com
Printed in the USA
LVOW13s2007130514

385613LV00005B/1056/P